*Transnationalism in Contemporary
German-Language Literature*

Studies in German Literature, Linguistics, and Culture

Transnationalism in Contemporary German-Language Literature

Edited by
Elisabeth Herrmann,
Carrie Smith-Prei, and
Stuart Taberner

 CAMDEN HOUSE
Rochester, New York

First published 2015
by Camden House

Camden House is an imprint of Boydell & Brewer Inc.
668 Mt. Hope Avenue, Rochester, NY 14620, USA
www.camden-house.com
and of Boydell & Brewer Limited
PO Box 9, Woodbridge, Suffolk IP12 3DF, UK
www.boydellandbrewer.com

ISBN-13: 978-1-57113-925-2
ISBN-10: 1-57113-925-7

Library of Congress Cataloging-in-Publication Data

CIP data applied for.

This publication is printed on acid-free paper.
Printed in Great Britain by CPI Group (UK) Ltd, Croydon, CR0 4YY

Contents

Acknowledgments

THE FOUNDATION FOR THIS VOLUME was laid at a three-day-long seminar workshop entitled "Transnationalisms: Sexualities, Fantasies, and the World Beyond" that took place at the Thirty-Seventh Annual Conference of the German Studies Association in Denver, Colorado, October 3–6, 2013. Scholars from the United States, Canada, and Europe working in different fields and disciplines came together to debate fundamental questions regarding the form, concerns, and impact of German-language transnational literature today.

This volume expands the shared readings, inspiring discussions, and intellectual exchange that developed in the course of the seminar. The editors of this volume would like to thank all our participants. This exchange happened because the German Studies Association offered, for the first time at its 2013 conference, extended seminars series as a forum for bringing together scholars working on the same topic. We are grateful to the GSA for this innovative initiative.

A very special thank-you is owed to German-Bulgarian author Ilija Trojanow, who participated in the seminar in Denver as a special guest and active contributor. Ilija Trojanow was prevented from traveling to the United States in person—the authorities' refusal to grant him permission to enter caused controversy in both the United States and Europe—but he was able to participate via Skype. This form of participation, and the reasons for it, in itself demonstrates both the possibilities and limitations of transnationalism.

An impression of Ilija Trojanow's contribution to the seminar may be gained from the transcription of an interview conducted by the editors a few weeks after the GSA conference in Denver that appears at the end of the volume.

We were able to invite Ilija Trojanow to participate in our discussions thanks to the generous financial support of the German Academic Exchange Service (DAAD) and the GSA. We are grateful to Sebastian Fohrbeck, at that time director of the DAAD, DAAD Senior Program Officer Michael Thomanek, the executive director of the GSA David Barclay, Suzanne Marchand, at that time president of the GSA, and Irene Kacandes, at that time vice-president of the GSA.

Finally, our most sincere thanks go to Camden House, and Jim Walker in particular, who supported this volume from its inception. We are grateful to the anonymous readers whose critical feedback greatly improved the book. We thank Ryan Peterson for seeing the volume through the production stages, as well as the copyeditor, and we also wish to acknowledge our research assistants Corinne Painter and Brendan Cavanagh for their work on the volume.

Elisabeth Herrmann
Carrie Smith-Prei
Stuart Taberner

Introduction: Contemporary German-Language Literature and Transnationalism

Elisabeth Herrmann, Carrie Smith-Prei, and Stuart Taberner

TRANSNATIONALISM IS "not new and has been around since ancient times," Michael Howard reminds us.[1] Yet in the contemporary era the "ties, interactions, exchange and mobility" that connect across and between nations, Steven Vertovec argues, "function intensively and in real time while being spread throughout the world."[2] Economic globalization, instantaneous electronic media, and the movement of millions around the globe today appear to be rendering national borders—and the cultures, polities, and frameworks of understanding that they are imagined to contain—more porous than ever before.

Transnationalism—understood in this volume as a plurality of intersecting, and crosscutting flows of products, ideas, and people back and forth over borders—presents a number of challenges to scholars working in the humanities and social sciences. How are they to conceptualize transnationalism beyond the conventional focus on the experience of those "minority" individuals or groups who span two or more cultures as migrants, refugees, or exiles? That is, how can they move beyond a focus on diasporic formations, hybridity, or notions of center and periphery in order to theorize how contemporary transnationalism's characteristic multidirectionality and saturation of all aspects of everyday life, from consumption to culture, impacts *everyone*, whether "settled" residents of a given national space or transient "guests"? How can they best conceptualize the nation's continued salience—the persistence of the nation in trans*nation*alism—for its citizens, and for those it refuses to accept as such? And how are they to rethink the nation's continued centrality to persistent global imbalances in economic, geopolitical, and military power, even as transnationalism appears to weaken that nation's claim to be *sovereign*?

For literary scholars, specifically, the reality of contemporary transnationalism prompts us to think more closely about the ways fiction written in a particular time and in a particular place—in the context of this volume, in the German-speaking countries—connects to, circulates through, and is rechanneled by *global* patternings and *global* debates on identity, mobility, hospitality, universalism, self-forming, and cosmopolitanism. It is only by holding nation and world in tension with one another, we—the editors of this volume—would argue, that we can avoid the "method-ological nationalism" (to adopt Ulrich Beck's term)[3] that for too long plagued literary studies, while also avoiding the opposite trap of idealizing (or demonizing) the global as abstracted from the very real borders that still define and divide us as much as they may suggest new opportuni-ties and experiences, refuge or protection, or at least the expectation of a warm welcome. Transnationalism as a system of plurality and encounter with the other rather than one of homogeneity and standardization may be best described in its connection and contrast to globalization.

Globalization and Transnationalism

It is no coincidence that the *transnational turn* in literary studies—as in the social sciences and humanities more generally—has taken place against the backdrop of globalization. In 1999, John Tomlinson described glo-balization as being characterized by a "rapidly developing and ever-dens-ening network of interconnections and interdependencies."[4] It certainly appears to be at the very least a necessary precondition for the intensive cross-border flows of people, goods, and ideas that the term transnation-alism, on the face of it, would seem to connote. As David Harvey notes, "There has undoubtedly been a deepening as well as a widening of these transnational connections during the phase of neoliberal globalization, and it is vital that these connectivities be acknowledged."[5] Yet transna-tionalism is not simply a subcategory of—or a synonym for—globaliza-tion, just as neither are wholly novel or even entirely recent phenomena. There are important distinctions between what is denoted by the terms *globalization* and *transnationalism*, with important consequences.

To begin with, globalization was most often understood in the 1990s as a *homogenizing* tendency. In an essay of 1998, Fredric Jameson described globalization as a "most ambiguous ideological concept," but in the wake of the apparent triumph of neoliberalism after the end of the Cold War, it is likely that most of his readers would have understood it to be the "worldwide Americanization or standardization of culture, the destruction of local differences, the massification of all the peoples on the planet" rather than the "multiple heterogeneities" of a postmod-ern culture.[6] On those occasions that the word "transnational"—not yet "transnationalism"—appears in the work of globalization theorists, it most often simply describes globalization's *reach* rather than having any particular conceptual force of its own. In his seminal work, *Modernity at Large: Cultural Dimensions of Globalization* (1996), Arjun Appadurai argues that "these sodalities are often transnational, even postnational, and they frequently operate beyond the boundaries of the nation."[7]

The recent shift from the adjective *transnational* to the noun *transnationalism* usefully complicates theories of globalization in ways that reflect actual developments in planetary power relations, economics, and culture in the twenty-first century. The term *transnational* de-emphasizes the center-periphery model that was generally at least implicit in most theorizations of globalization in the 1990s. With transnationalism, by contrast, scholars can begin to conceptualize the emerging multipolarity of the twenty-first century—the United States and the West more generally will not dictate global fashions—*and* the multidirectionality of cross-border flows of people, goods, and ideas. Today, in short, global interactions and intersections are more distributed, diffuse, and diverse than they ever were before. Power, people, and finance now flow intra- and interregionally, cutting across and partially superseding imperial and postimperial circulations. This flow is not only between the wealthy nations of the northern hemisphere, as it has been for many centuries, but also east to west, south to north, and south to south, even as the "first world," as it was once was known, still enjoys, in absolute terms, the highest standard of living. Paul Jay hints at this multipolarity and multidirectionality—the "complex back-and-forth flows of people and cultural forms"[8]—but in absorbing them back into his redefinition of globalization, he relativizes the novelty of his focus on *transnationalism* as well as the consequences and the significance of transnationalism's more diffuse patterns of circulation. Appadurai's suggestion in his 1996 book that "the United States is no longer the puppeteer of a world system of images but is only one node of a complex transnational construction of imaginary landscapes" is more prescient, although even here his presumption of a "globalized, deterritorialized world"[9] may nowadays appear to overstate the case for some kind of really existing, if chaotic, "world imperium."

Literary scholars working with concepts of globalization and transnationalism have been most influenced by postcolonial studies—for instance, Appadurai, Homi Bhabha, and James Clifford—and they tend to be most interested in what have typically been described as minority, exogenous, or diasporic authors. Indeed, *minority writer* and *transnational writer* are often used interchangeably to describe, say, German-language authors of Turkish provenance or Chicano and Chicana authors. Just as globalization has been equated with neocolonialism, so has transnationalism, at least in the literary context, generally been associated with those writers who are most obviously "marked" by colonial and neocolonial histories and relations. In their book *Minor Transnationalism*, for example, Françoise Lionnet and Shu-mei Shih argue for a "transnationalism from below" and make the case for "an awareness and recognition of the creative interventions that networks of minoritized cultures produce within and across national boundaries."[10] Similar arguments are advanced by postcolonial thinkers, such as Pheng Cheah,[11] and by scholars interested in the recent growth of transnational networks of social activism, for example Donatella Della Porta and Sidney Tarrow.[12] This interest in the formerly colonized and in minorities and migrants, of course, mirrors the conventional association in the social sciences in recent years of the words *transnational* and *transnationalism* with diasporic networks, that is, with what Kachig Tölölyan has called the "exemplary communities of the transnational moment."[13]

The contention of this volume, however, is that using transnationalism as an analytical tool prompts us to shift our focus away from the movement of *some*—migrants, refugees, exiles, or trafficked people—across borders toward the implication of *all*. Indeed, the intensity and multidirectionality of transnationalism imply that *all* are impacted by the flows of people, products, and ideas across borders, including those who do not themselves move. The residents of so-called developed nations, for example, are not simply the privileged consumers of goods and services produced elsewhere—in the colonies and postcolonies—or the passive consumers of globalized culture. Rather, the daily experience of all kinds of otherness, difference, and plurality makes evident the urgency of issues of belonging, inclusion and exclusion, citizenship, forced and unforced movement, status and privilege.

Integral to this argument is the matter of positionality. The fact that *all* are implicated in transnationalism does not mean that all experience it in the same way. Refugees, undocumented persons, sex workers and trafficked women, legal migrants, naturalized citizens, and citizens "by birth" all experience differing degrees of precarity in relation to the rules and regulations that govern residence and mobility. As Regina Römhild argues, transnationalism means that "the ideal of fixed territories of culture turns into a fiction, and mobility becomes the common ground for the proliferation of diasporic life-worlds, cultures and identities."[14] But the fact that more people than ever before are mobile does not mean that all are impacted in the same way, or *equally*. The editors and contributors to this volume, for example, are scholars working in Europe, Canada, and the United States—traveling easily between those two continents—whose experience of transnationalism is, self-evidently, quite different from the experience of those who lack the "right" papers.

Using the term *transnationalism* in order to further specify the impact that globalization has on daily life draws attention to the perhaps surprising prominence of the nation in the present day, though it is probably the case that the nation never stopped mattering to countries that only gained their independence in the twentieth century, where the nation has been the primary means of social consolidation, self-projection, education, and welfare. At the same time it might be safe to assume that people in the West have once again become concerned with the nation only because the "integrity" of their own nations now appears to be less secure. Financial crisis, changing demography, and geopolitical shifts have created a sense of vulnerability at the level of the nation that to a certain extent at least may have closed the gap between "the West and the rest."[15]

The term *transnationalism* makes it possible to conceptualize the continued importance of the nation as the organizing unit of global affairs *and* the continued significance—indeed increased significance— of borders in a world in which the ease, or difficulty, of border crossing defines not only products but also people. In his 1994 book *The Location of Culture*, Homi Bhabha spoke of the imminent death of the nation,[16] just as Appadurai argued that globalization meant that "states throughout the world are under siege."[17] Other scholars, such as Michael Kearney, were perhaps prescient in emphasizing even in the mid-1990s—during the heyday of globalization theory—the distinction between global processes that are somewhat independent of nation-states and transnational processes that, by definition, take place in relation to particular national places and pasts.[18] Nowadays—that is post-9/11 and post-economic-crisis of 2008—scholars are, in fact, more likely to point to the role nations play in controlling whether and how people travel, who may settle where, whether rights are to be extended, denied or revoked, and when and in what ways citizens may be surveilled, and by whom, and what kind of data are circulated within and beyond national borders.[19] Eric Cazdyn and Imre Szeman, for example, argue in *After Globalization* (2011) that the 2008 financial crisis has exposed globalization as an ideological fiction that only "naturalizes" (US, or neoliberal) capitalism as an irresistible and irreversible new world order.[20] The real change, as Grace Darlene Skogstad suggests, is not that nations have diminished in significance— even if they are no longer as sovereign as they once were—but that the reality of transnationalism now saturates domestic discourses, for example, on the subject of citizenship as well as personal data and privacy, that were once thought to be relatively insulated.[21]

Germany as Exemplary Transnational Space

Germany makes an interesting example when exploring transnational spaces in our current time. The country is today a dynamic export-driven economy that boasts a significant balance of payments surplus with its trading partners. Germany is present around the world. It is China's number one trading partner in the EU, and China is the top foreign investment destination for German companies.[22] Germany is far more important to India than its erstwhile colonial master, Great Britain, much to the chagrin of Prime Minister David Cameron.[23] Germany is also increasingly visible in the regulation of global affairs. Its refusal to become involved in the Western intervention in Libya's civil war in 2011 was a throwback to a previous era of military self-restraint that continues to be regretted by large sections of its foreign policy elite. Modern-day Germany is certainly not gung ho for military action, but engagements in Kosovo, Afghanistan, off the Horn of Africa, Lebanon, the two Sudans, Uganda, Congo, and elsewhere, suggest that Helmut Kohl's salami tactics, continued by the SPD, have succeeded in accustoming Germans to at least a limited projection of German military power.[24] Just as striking, in the wake of the near collapse of the financial markets in 2008 and during the ensuing Eurozone crisis, has been—notwithstanding its vital role in keeping the Eurozone and indeed the EU together[25]—the Federal Republic's more assertive insistence upon its national self-interest, suggesting that its traditional postwar commitment to multilateralism and values-led foreign policy is now buttressed by a more pragmatic stance.[26]

However, Germany's intensified postmillennial international and foreign policy engagement is only part of the story. Transnationalism, and its significance today as constitutive of individuals' daily experience, prompts us to consider not just how the Federal Republic is more present in the world than it once was in the days of its preunification semisovereignty,[27] but also how the world is now more present in Germany. Here, changing demography is key. In the 2011 census, just over 12% of residents in the Federal Republic were residents without German citizenship,[28] but, as important, there were 2.3 million families with a child under 18 where at least one parent had a migration background. That means around 29% of the total of 8.1 million such families.[29] Overall, 20% of people with German citizenship have a familial connection to another country, rising to 25% of those under 25.[30] Moreover, the number of new arrivals has exceeded the number of departures of other nationals, sometimes by a factor of two, in every year since 1991, with very large inflows particularly in the early to mid-1990s—the time of the Balkans wars—of asylum seekers,[31] but also of Jews from the former Soviet Union. In the same period, and indeed until the early 2000s, very large numbers of ethnic Germans—just under a quarter of a million a year from 1991 to 1995—from across the formerly communist states of Eastern Europe were "repatriated" to Germany, a country that the overwhelming majority of them had never before seen.[32] Many Germans seem to be quite unaware of these numbers, reflecting their strong reluctance to accept the fact that they live in an immigration country.

Today's Germany is demographically—and not just politically or culturally—a very different place from the preunification Federal Republic, and certainly from the former German Democratic Republic (GDR). It is not simply that the number of people with a migration background has increased. Germany's new residents are far more diverse than ever before. They are not just Turkish, but come from other EU countries, as well as Russia, Bosnia, Serbia, North Africa, the Middle East, South East Asia, and many others besides. Indeed, certain cities are experiencing the emergence of what Steven Vertovec recently called "super-diversity,"[33] or what Azade Seyhan has called "paranational communities."[34] These new residents are younger, on average, than "settled" Germans, whose low birthrate[35] also means that large-scale immigration is essential if the country's population is not to fall dramatically—perhaps by as much as a fifth by 2060[36]—and the economy is to continue to maintain a high standard of living.

This volume argues that the developments described above make Germany today what might be termed an "exemplary transnational space." Certainly, the reality of transnationalism permeates domestic debates to an extent that would have been unthinkable in the rather enclosed provinciality of the preunification Federal Republic (and East Germany).[37] The ferocity of the *Historikerstreit*—a decidedly high-brow debate of the mid-1980s on the significance of the Nazi past for German identity[38]—might thus appear rather parochial, as indeed do many of the "memory contests"[39] even of the 1990s. As can easily be observed, the Nazi past is now more likely to be reworked in a rather stylized and fictionalized form in film and literature to appeal to a transnational interest in this aspect of German history, which is often utilized to demonstrate the inconceivability of evil.[40]

More pressing in today's Federal Republic are recent controversies relating to the supposed *Überfremdung* ("swamping") of German society, German *Leitkultur* (the preeminence of German culture), Frank Schirrmacher's *Das Methusalem-Komplott* (The Methusalem Conspiracy, 2004) and Thilo Sarrazin's *Deutschland schafft sich ab* (Germany Is Doing Away with Itself, 2010), both of which warned of the aging of "native" Germans and an islamification of Germany through immigration. Or, Germany's incipient euroskepticism in the wake of the Eurozone crisis might be cited: the emergence of the euro-critical political party *Alternative for Germany*; the country's recent wavering between "principled" (post-Holocaust) and "realist" (self-interested) positions on domestic and external affairs (e.g., political asylum, or relations with China), or, more generally, its struggle to reconcile its traditional, postwar reflexive multilateralism with its sense of increased vulnerability within what Ulrich Beck has termed the "world risk society."[41]

German-Language Literature and Transnationalism

As implied in the discussion above of the way transnationalism impacts on *all*, German-language writers engaging with the theme emerge from "minority" *and* "majority" backgrounds. They work with, through, and against Christian, Muslim, Jewish, and many other backgrounds and heritages, and bring many and various histories of settlement and migration to bear. Although the writer's background is important and does impact the writing, the adjective "transnational" may be better applied to *texts* dealing with a contemporary phenomenon rather than solely to *authors* who happen to have a migration background.[42]

In contemporary German-language fiction, there are a large number of grittily realist works that deal with transnationalism's impact on the lives of the undocumented, the trafficked, and the exploited. Here, the Hungarian-German writer Terézia Mora's *Alle Tage* (*Day in, Day Out*, 2004) is perhaps the best known. Mora's novel also stands out for its inclusion of elements of magical realism that punctuate its depiction of everyday violence.[43] Other authors from a variety of backgrounds depict the lack of hospitality that "unwanted" border crossers encounter. Alongside these avowedly socially-engaged texts, there is a plethora of more fanciful, diverting, or experimental works in which transnationalism is linked to mobility and self-realization, for example in Feridun Zaimoglu's *Hinterland* (2009), or the reconfiguration of personal and national identity (e.g., Felicitas Hoppe's self-naming novel *Hoppe* from 2012), or of sexual identity, such as in Antje Rávic Strubel's 2001 *Offene Blende* (Open Shutter) and 2002 *Fremd Gehen* (Going Strange). Indeed, conventionally *trans*gressive sexual identities are frequently associated with the *trans* in "transnationalism," for example in Sibylle Berg's *Vielen Dank für das Leben* (Thanks for Life, 2012), which features a globe-trotting hermaphrodite (as does Ulrike Draesner's 2002 *Mitgift* [Dowry]),[44] and in many of the texts discussed in this volume. To appropriate Jack Halberstam's striking phrase,[45] it seems that transnationals often exist "in *a queer time and place*" characterized by their "unnatural" sexuality, "promiscuous" multilingualism, or refusal to be fixed and defined. Finally, there are a surprising number of more or less historical novels that "rediscover" the age of Enlightenment, the age of European exploration, or the age of European empire as previous instances of transnationalism, which allow authors to reflect on present-day developments. It is in this context that several chapters in this volume focus on Daniel Kehlmann's *Die Vermessung der Welt* (Measuring the World, 2005), Ilija Trojanow's *Der Weltensammler* (The Collector of Worlds, 2006), and Christian Kracht's *Imperium* (Empire, 2012). In each of these novels too, *trans*gressive sexuality is related to the apparent threat posed by "queer transnationals."

It perhaps goes without saying that a key concern running through contemporary German-language literary works focused on transnationalism is the (productive or disruptive) tension between the particular and the universal. Whether postimperial, realist, fanciful or fantastical, socially engaged or gender oriented, almost all such texts implicitly or explicitly thematize their authors' awareness that—in our transnational era especially—fiction too is a product that circulates back and forth across borders, absorbing or rejecting other cultural influences and constantly restating, challenging, or reconfiguring nation *and* world. This self-awareness of their own mobility—their own transnationalism—may even frame some contemporary German-language works as *world litera-ture*, if world literature is conceived of as a theoretical concept that con-nects *worldliness* to mobility and cosmopolitan ideals, rather than simply as an expression for literature translated into other languages or for works that are considered the most outstanding examples of each national cul-ture (*the classics* and *the masterpieces*). This discussion of recent German-language literature as world literature is adumbrated in the chapters in this volume by Elisabeth Herrmann, Stuart Taberner, and Claudia Breger insofar as it clearly connects to transnationalism, but it is a theme that urgently requires further research in its own right.[46]

The book opens with three wide-ranging, theoretically focused essays that map the *contexts* of the discussion of contemporary German-language literature in relation to transnationalism. Using fictional works as well as theoretical reflections by authors of different national and transnational backgrounds as examples—Ilija Trojanow's *Der Weltensammler*, Daniel Kehlmann's *Die Vermessung der Welt*, Christian Kracht's *Imperium*, Felicitas Hoppe's *Hoppe*, and Dan Vyleta's mystery series *Pavel & I* (2008), *The Quiet Twin* (2008), and *The Crooked Maid* (2013)—Elisabeth Herrmann drafts concepts of literary mobility, transnationalism, and world literature that enable us to analyze the changing conditions and features of literature in times of globalization, as well as to redefine the term *contemporary German literature* for the twenty-first century against the backdrop of transnationalism. In Stuart Taberner's contribu-tion, transnationalism is considered in relation to the renewed interest in cosmopolitanism in recent years on the part of both scholars and writers—Taberner examines a number of contemporary German-language texts as part of a broader societal and indeed global conversation on the question of how, in an age defined by transnational contact, we can live ethically and harmoniously with "others." Closing part 1, Carrie Smith-Prei exam-ines how the affective turn, as it has been theorized across the humani-ties and social sciences, opens up a manner of engaging with the literary appearance of sexuality and corporeality when thought transnationally. In chapter 3, she pursues affect in terms of emotional aesthetics, biopower, and technology to highlight the importance of the political in theorizing transnational literature. Finally, this chapter suggests that affect allows for a categorization of transnational contemporary literature as a literature of the present. Together, the chapters in part 1 provide a detailed overview of and intervention into some of the key debates on transnationalism and literature, both in the German context and globally.

The chapters in part 2 illuminate, complicate, and expand on these theoretical considerations through extended analyses of individual *texts*. They thus provide detailed discussions of the debates outlined in the introduction and particularly in the three opening essays in part 1. More specifically, these chapters circle around a number of key themes: the place of literature written in German within the global circulation of cultures and within "world literature"; the "fascination" of transnational experience by writers from both "majority" and "minority" backgrounds; and challenges to Western ideologies of gender and queerness as a normalizing factor in relation to nation, culture, race, ethnicity, and class.

The first three chapters of part 2 engage specifically with transnationalism's theoretical basis through a critical engagement with mobility, national mythologies, and cosmopolitanism as well as a reconsideration of transnationalism and the contemporary. Katharina Gerstenberger examines Thomas von Steinaecker's 2012 novel *Das Jahr, in dem ich aufhörte, mir Sorgen zu machen, und anfing zu träumen* (The Year in Which I Stopped Worrying and Began Dreaming) and Kathrin Röggla's 2010 short story "das recherchegespenst" (The Research Ghost) for their engagement with the lived realities of transnationalism and interaction with national and individual identity in a global world. She does so through the issue of mobility in particular. She argues that these texts are particularly appropriate for engaging with the contemporary moment for the manner in which transnationalism is a marker of the present, an aspect that she urges us to engage with critically; transnationalism, so the texts propose, is not an easy alternative to national narratives of the recent past. Claudia Breger also engages critically with transnationalism through an examination of Christian Kracht's *Imperium* and Teju Cole's *Open City* (2012). Through a development of her understanding of transnationalism as a methodological approach that highlights a critique of nationalism and its mythologies, Breger discusses how the transnational dimensions of Kracht's novel fall short due to the production of what she calls a colonial loop. She places Cole's novel in stark contrast for its reference to cosmopolitanism, a term the novel complicates in transnational terms through a reference to national histories. An approach to transnationalism through critical cosmopolitanism, Breger argues, lends historical and national legacies of violence and colonialism to the humanistic and connective ethos. Christina Kraenzle also engages with the interchange between transnationalism and cosmopolitanism through an examination of Ilija Trojanow's travel writing. In chapter 6, she illuminates the fraught relationship between the two concepts in that a desire for more openness, exchange, and ethical accountability found in cosmopolitan thought often collides with national boundaries and myths that shape notions of self and other. Through an analysis of *Nomade auf vier Kontinenten* (Nomad on Four Continents, 2008) and *An den inneren Ufern Indiens* (Along the Inner Banks of India, 2003), Kraenzle draws on the long tradition of European travel writing to explore how Trojanow engages in a subversion of the genre through an experimental narrative portrayal of power relations, authority, and difference as well as through the use of non-European understandings of transnationalism and cosmopolitanism.

The next three chapters turn more specifically to issues of gender, sexuality, and corporality as they intervene, appear, or construct the transnational in German-language literature. Maria Mayr examines *Die Erdfresserin* (The Woman Who Eats Dirt, 2012) by Julya Rabinowich for its engagement with transnational spaces as marked by neoliberal global capitalism. Focusing on the depiction of the precarious life of the illegal sex worker, Mayr shows how concepts of identity often central to cultural transnationalism become irrelevant when the material realities of transnational bodies are taken into account. Here also the critical perspective on transnationalism suggests that it is not a positive and hybrid reality open to all. Building on this discussion, Hester Baer also identifies a distinct relationship between the concepts of neoliberalism and transnationalism, particularly in the rise of the precariat. In chapter 8, Baer engages in the transnational and global dimensions of precarity, examining how as a concept it both subverts neoliberal dynamics as well as leverages its paradoxes toward new structural formations. By focusing on precarious sexuality in two pop-feminist novels—*Feuchtgebiete* (Wetlands, 2008) by Charlotte Roche and *Axolotl Roadkill* (2010) by Helene Hegemann—she shows how they intervene politically into contemporary transnational literature at the level of global capitalism and sexual subjectivity, thereby making visible what she calls the "imperceptible present." Faye Stewart's discussion of Antje Rávic Strubel's *Vom Dorf: Abenteuergeschichten zum Fest* (From the Village: Adventure Stories for the Holiday, 2007) and *Kältere Schichten der Luft* (Colder Layers of Air, 2007) also foregrounds sexuality, this time queerness, while also returning more specifically to theoretical conceptions of transnationalism in the form of German–German border crossings. In chapter 9, Stewart proposes the term *posttransnational* to apply to postwall East German literature. Specifically, she looks at Strubel's engagement with *trans* in *transnationalism* to apply also to "transgressions, transformations, and transgenderedness," in its confrontation with the persistence of inner-German national boundaries. Posttransnationalism, therefore, offers a different view of global citizenship that also emphasizes a revising of national narratives and belonging.

The next two chapters of the volume return in very different ways to notions of nationhood and cultural specificity embedded with transnationalism, whereas the final chapter opens this specificity up to concerns of politics and conflict. Anke Biendarra returns to transnationalism in its specific utility within German-language literature. Speaking to the term's transformation in recent years, which is also the primary claim of this volume, she claims that transnationalism in all of its forms over the past decades has disrupted national literatures in line with world literature, and is further open to more and more hybrid texts. Biendarra proposes the term "lived transnationalism" to account for the everyday appearance of transnational features in autobiographically inspired texts. She does so through a discussion of the negotiation of Russian minority and German mainstream society in lived reality as depicted in Lena Gorelik's *Meine weißen Nächte* (My White Nights, 2004), Alina Bronsky's *Scherbenpark* (Broken Glass Park, 2008), and Olga Grjasnowa's *Der Russe ist einer, der Birken liebt* (All Russians Love Birch Trees, 2012). Chapter 11 turns to Juli Zeh's work and sets it in the context of transnationalism. Here, Lars Richter looks at what he calls "the situatedness" of Zeh's texts, and her public engagement, to illuminate transnational discourses. He approaches the dialectical relationship between deterritorialization and reterritorialization, the increased mobility and flows of migration under globalism, the simultaneous shoring up of geographical borders as a means of control, and the increase in national rhetoric. He does so in an examination of *Adler und Engel* (Eagles and Angels, 2001), *Die Stille ist ein Geräusch* (Silence is a Sound, 2002), the stage and novel version of *Corpus Delicti* (*The Method*, 2007/2009), and *Nullzeit* (*Decompression*, 2012). Through an examination of these spaces, Richter's analysis shows how nation continues to prove a forceful concept despite porous borders. In the final chapter of the volume, chapter 12, Tanja Nusser compares Wolfgang Herrndorf's novel *Sand* (2011) with Friedrich Dürrenmatt's 1986 work *Der Auftrag oder Vom Beobachten des Beobachters der Beobachter: Novelle in 24 Sätzen* (The Assignment, or On the Observing of the Observer of the Observers, 1986) for their depictions of global transnational relations, in particular between the West and North Africa and the Middle East. Here, the political, which while having a role throughout the chapters in this volume has remained perhaps diffuse, is specifically delineated in the conflict zone and under the transnational reach of terrorism. Furthermore, while the texts are set in the specific historical decade of the 1970s and early 1980s, Nusser's contention that they point to the contemporary political era highlights the urgency of politics in present discussions of transnationalism.

This volume is designed to document that literature, in the contemporary period, both reflects on the transnational reality described above and participates in it. The individual chapters provide evidence that a great deal of contemporary literature maps—and also critiques—the opportunities and fears, the inequalities and inequities of as well as the fantasies around contemporary transnationalism, but also itself circulates between national contexts, along axes of translation, transmission, and reception, and perhaps even aspires to become something that might be imagined as world literature. Literature, as David Damrosch and other theorists of world literature have amply demonstrated, has always been and has even more become a "moving medium" that creates a transnational space both by discussing the topic as well as by circulating around the world through adoption, intertextuality, and translation. Finally, this volume seeks to refine—and indeed define—an understanding of transnationalism, not only as a contemporary reality but also as a concept and an analytical tool. Our goal is to advance the discussion of transnationalism emerging across disciplines while at the same time to engage specifically with the potential that transnationalism, as a literary theme and concept, has to reshape German literary studies. This will be achieved by building on and at the same time further developing and critically exceeding the work that has been done in recent years on "minority" writers, German-language literature and globalization, gender and sexuality in relation to the "nation," and German-language fiction and "world literature."

The volume closes with an interview with author Ilija Trojanow, which engages with some of the key concepts coming out of the preceding twelve chapters from the perspective of a literary practitioner. In this interview, Trojanow—whose work is discussed throughout this volume—debates with two of its three editors transnationalism as a literary concept, cosmopolitanism and confluence, world literature, the political and engaged positions of the cosmopolitan author, and transnational concerns for German-language contemporary literature today.

Notes

[1] Michael C. Howard, *Transnationalism and Society* (Jefferson, NC: McFarland, 2011), 3. See also Roland Robertson, *Globalization* (London: Sage, 1992). Robertson argues that there have been successive waves of globalization over the centuries.

[2] Steven Vertovec, *Transnationalism* (New York: Routledge, 2009), 3.

[3] Ulrich Beck, *Power in the Global Age: A New Global Political Economy*, trans. Kathleen Cross (Malden, MA: Polity, 2005), esp. 43–50.

[4] John Tomlinson, *Globalization and Culture* (Cambridge: Polity, 1999), 2.

[5] David Harvey, *A Brief History of Neoliberalism* (Oxford: Oxford University Press, 2005), 35.

[6] Fredric Jameson, "Notes on Globalisation as a Philosophical Issue," in *The Cultures of Globalization*, ed. Fredric Jameson and Masao Miyoshi (Durham, NC: Duke University Press, 1998), 56–57.

[7] Arjun Appadurai, *Modernity at Large: Cultural Dimensions of Globalization* (Minneapolis: University of Minnesota Press, 1996), 8.

[8] Paul Jay, *Global Matters: The Transnational Turn in Literary Studies* (Ithaca, NY: Cornell University Press, 2010), 3.

[9] Appadurai, *Modernity at Large*, 31, 52.

[10] Françoise Lionnet and Shu-mei Shih, "Introduction: Thinking through the Minor, Transnationally," in *Minor Transnationalism*, ed. Françoise Lionnet and Shu-mei Shih (Durham, NC: Duke University Press, 2005), 5–6.

[11] See, for example, Pheng Cheah, "Given Culture: Rethinking Cosmopolitical Freedom in Transnationalism," *boundary* 24, no. 2 (1997): 157–97.

[12] See Donatella Della Porta and Sidney Trarrow, eds., *Transnational Protest and Global Activism* (Lanham, MD: Rowman & Littlefield, 2004).

[13] Kachig Tölölyan, "The Nation-State and Its Others: In Lieu of a Preface," *Diaspora* 1 (1991): 3. See also Alejandro Portes, "Introduction: The Debates and Significance of Immigrant Transnationalism," *Global Networks* 1, no. 3 (2001): 181–93.

[14] Regina Römhild, "Global Heimat Germany: Migration and the Transnationalization of the Nation State," *Transit* 1, no. 1 (2005), http://escholarship.org/uc/item/57z2470p.

[15] Kishore Mahbubani, "The Dangers of Decadence: What the Rest Can Teach the West," *Foreign Affairs* 72, no. 4 (1993): 10–14.

[16] Homi K. Bhabha, *The Location of Culture* (New York: Routledge, 1994).

[17] Arjun Appadurai, "Disjuncture and Difference in the Global Cultural Economy," *Public Culture* 2, no. 2 (1990): 1–11.

[18] See Michael Kearney, "The Local and the Global: The Anthropology of Globalization and Transnationalism," *Annual Review of Anthropology* 24 (1995): 547–65.

[19] See the very useful introduction to Brenda S. A. Yeoh and Katie Willis, eds., *State Nation / Transnation: Perspectives on Transnationalism in the Asia-Pacific* (London: Routledge, 2004). For a fascinating analysis of the interplay between transnationalism, citizenship, migration, and national sovereignty, see Seyla Benhabib, *The Rights of Others: Aliens, Residents, and Citizens* (Cambridge: Cambridge University Press, 2004).

[20] Eric Cazdyn and Imre Szeman, *After Globalization* (Malden, MA: Blackwell, 2011).

[21] Grace Darlene Skogstad, *Policy Paradigms, Transnationalism, and Domestic Politics* (Toronto: University of Toronto Press, 2011).

[22] See Jonas Parello-Plesner and Hans Kundnani, "China and Germany: A New Special Relationship?" *European Council on Foreign Relations*, accessed April 6, 2015, http://www.ecfr.eu/publications/summary/china_and_germany_a_new_special_relationship.

[23] George Parker, "Cameron Bats for British Trade with India," *Financial Times*, February 13, 2013.

[24] See Tom Dyson, *The Politics of German Defence and Security: Policy Leadership and Military Reform in the Post-Cold War Era* (Oxford: Berghahn Books, 2007).

[25] See Ulrich Beck, *German Europe* (Cambridge: Polity, 2013).

[26] Simon Bulmer and William E. Patterson, "Germany and the European Union: From 'Tamed Power' to Normalized Power?" *International Affairs* 86, no. 5 (2010): 1051–73.

[27] Peter J. Katzenstein, *Policy and Politics in West Germany: The Growth of a Semi-Sovereign State* (Philadelphia: Temple University Press, 1987).

[28] Statistisches Bundesamt (Federal Statistics Bureau), "Population based on the 2011 Census," accessed February 12, 2014, https://www.destatis.de/EN/FactsFigures/SocietyState/Population/CurrentPopulation/Tables/Census_SexAnd Citizenship.html;jsessionid=B58C5E5FE3388117E1D73F42A1A84D82.cae2.

[29] Statistisches Bundesamt (Federal Statistics Bureau), "Migration. Integration," accessed February 12, 2014, https://www.destatis.de/EN/FactsFigures/Society State/Population/MigrationIntegration/MigrationIntegration.html.

[30] Francesca Dziadek, "Germany Grapples with Diversity," Inter Press Service, December 7, 2012, accessed February 12, 2014, http://www.ipsnews.net/2012/12/germany-grapples-with-diversity/.

[31] Statistisches Bundesamt (Federal Statistics Bureau), "Migration of Foreign Citizens between Germany and Foreign Countries," accessed February 12, 2014, https://www.destatis.de/EN/FactsFigures/SocietyState/Population/Migration/Tables/MigrationForeignCitizensBetweenGermanyForeignCountries.html.

[32] Statistisches Bundesamt (Federal Statistics Bureau), "Migration of German Citizens."

[33] For Steven Vertovec's analysis of superdiversity in Frankfurt am Main, see "Super-Diversity in Frankfurt," accessed February 12, 2014, http://www.mmg.mpg.de/fileadmin/user_upload/powerpoint/Super-diversity_in_Frankfurt/Super-diversity_in_Frankfurt.pdf.

[34] Azade Seyhan, *Writing Outside the Nation* (Princeton: Princeton University Press, 2001), 10.

[35] Jürgen Dorbritz, "Germany: Family Diversity with Low Actual and Desired Fertility," *Demographic Research* 19 (2008), 557–98, http://www.demographic-research.org/volumes/vol19/17/19-17.pdf.

[36] Statistisches Bundesamt (Federal Statistics Bureau), "Germany's Population by 2060," accessed February 12, 2014, https://www.destatis.de/EN/Publications/Specialized/Population/GermanyPopulation2060.pdf?__blob=publicationFile.

[37] After unification, many West German writers in particular looked back nostalgically at the relatively predictable, insulated, secure—boring—provinciality of the "old" Federal Republic before Germany, after the end of the Cold War, was exposed to the altogether more challenging pressures of globalization. See Andrew Plowman, "'Was will ich denn als Westdeutscher erzählen?': The 'Old' West and Globalisation in Recent German Prose," *German Literature in The Age of Globalization*, ed. Stuart Taberner (Birmingham, AL: Birmingham University Press, 2004), 47–66. See also Andrew Plowman, "'Westalgie'? Nostalgia for the 'Old' Federal Republic in Recent German Prose," *Seminar* 40, no. 3 (2004), 249–61. The phenomenon of *Ostalgie*, of nostalgia for the now defunct German Democratic Republic (East Germany), was not dissimilar, though it typically had a stronger anticapitalist inflection. See Paul Cooke, *Representing East Germany since Unification: From Colonization to Nostalgia* (Oxford: Berg, 2005).

[38] See Charles Maier, *The Unmasterable Past* (Cambridge, MA: Harvard University Press, 1988).

[39] See Anne Fuchs, Mary Cosgrove, and Georg Grote, eds., *Germany Memory Contests: The Quest for Identity in Literature, Film, and Discourse since 1990* (Rochester, NY: Camden House, 2006).

[40] See chapters 3 and 4 ("Heritage Cinema, Authenticity and Dealing with Germany's Past" and "Transnational Cinema, Globalisation and Multicultural Germany") in Paul Cooke, *Contemporary German Cinema* (Manchester, Manchester University Press, 2012).

[41] Ulrich Beck, *World Risk Society* (Oxford: Wiley-Blackwell, 1999).

[42] See Stuart Taberner, "Transnationalism in Contemporary German-Language Fiction by Nonminority Writers," *Seminar* 47, no. 5 (2011), 624–45, and Elisabeth Herrmann, "Transnationale Literatur und europäischer Kulturtransfer im Fokus germanistischer Literaturwissenschaft," in *Begegnungen: Das VIII. Nordisch-Baltische Germanistentreffen in Sigtuna vom 11. bis zum 13.6.2009*, ed. Elisabeth Wåghäll Nivre et al. (Stockholm: Acta Universitas Stockholmiensis, 2011), 371–85.

[43] Brigid Haines devotes several pages of her chapter on "Writing from Eastern and Central Europe," in *Contemporary German Fiction: Writing in the Berlin Republic*, ed. Stuart Taberner (Cambridge: Cambridge University Press, 2007), 214–27, especially 225–27. See also Anke Biendarra, "Terézia Mora, *Alle Tage*: Transnational Traumas," in *Emerging German-Language Novelists of the Twenty-First Century*, ed. Lyn Marven and Stuart Taberner (Rochester, NY: Camden House, 2011), 46–61, and Lyn Marven, "Crossing Borders: Migration, Gender, and Language in Novels by Yadé Kara, Jeannette Lander and Terézia Mora," *Gegenwartsliteratur*, 8 (2009): 148–69.

[44] See Lyn Marven, "German Literature in the Berlin Republic: Writing by Women," in *Contemporary German Fiction: Writing in the Berlin Republic*, ed. Stuart Taberner (Cambridge: Cambridge University Press, 2007), 159–76.

[45] See Jack Halberstam, *In a Queer Time and Place: Transgender Bodies, Subcultural Lives* (New York: New York University Press, 2005).

[46] A worthy attempt to begin this debate is presented by Thomas Beebee, ed., *German Literature as World Literature from 1800 to the Present* (London: Bloomsbury, 2014).

Part I. Contexts

1: How Does Transnationalism Redefine Contemporary Literature?

Elisabeth Herrmann

WHEN EXPLORING THE EFFECTS that transnationalism has on contemporary societies, cultures, and economies, on different lifestyles and individual biographies, and more specifically—as is the objective of this volume—when exploring the ramifications of transnationalism within contemporary literature, it is necessary to not only look at each of those areas separately but also inspect their interdependency and reciprocal impact. Accordingly, this chapter is devoted to a definition of contemporary German literature in the twenty-first century that links an investigation of transnationalism to the question of how daily life experience and literature actively shape each other. Transnationalism in this context is understood as the local, national, cultural, and economic, but also biographical manifestations of globalization in everyday life.[1] It will be investigated particularly with regard to the fact that writing in Germany has increasingly become transnational over the last two decades.[2]

As a first step, this chapter will refine the often used but not precisely defined term "contemporary literature" in order to identify specific features and the changing conditions of literature in times of globalization. The chapter further establishes a theoretical basis that identifies transnationalism not solely as a theme but as a literary concept that can fruitfully be connected with a reconceptualization of *world literature* as a phenomenon of literary mobility. Fictional works by German authors of different national and transnational backgrounds will be used as examples to demonstrate that transnationalism builds a significant pillar in contemporary German literature and redefines it in various ways. The textual examples examined in this context are Ilija Trojanow's *Der Weltensammler* (The Collector of Worlds, 2006), Daniel Kehlmann's *Die Vermessung der Welt* (Measuring the World, 2005), Christian Kracht's *Imperium* (Empire, 2012), Felicitas Hoppe's *Hoppe* (2012), and Dan Vyleta's crime fiction *Pavel & I* (2008), *The Quiet Twin* (2011), and *The Crooked Maid* (2013). Within the examination of these texts special attention will be paid to the correlation between language and national identity or affiliation, physical and intellectual mobility, and the conditions under which literature travels the world. This will eventually lead us to ask how national, transnational, and world literature are connected with each other and how literature mirrors those changes that are currently happening in our society.

How Literature and Reality Shape Each Other

Through literary fiction, different and alternate worlds are created. These correspond to the readers' experiences in lived reality, but are not identical with them, or, to refer back to Aristotle: literature produces and puts experiences at our disposal that are probable, but not real.[3] Thus literature proves to be both a mirror and a reflective space, but also an experimental field for human existence—it has a direct reference and dual relationship to the world. On the one hand, literary fiction is informed by real-life experience, while real life in return is also informed by fiction, as literary—and all sorts of other—texts assist in circulating *Lebenswissen* (knowledge on life).[4] Aleida Assmann has made a convincing case that every culture discusses, reflects upon, and documents those experiences, historical events, and collective memories that are pivotal for its self-conception in the present.[5] Germanists, such as Doris Bachmann-Medick,[6] Hartmut Böhme[7] and Wilhelm Vosskamp,[8] speak about literature as a medium of self-reflection and self-presentation for societies and cultures, while James Young has pointed out that the world and its representation never operate independently of one another.[9]

An analysis of the most recent contemporary German literature as pursued in this volume and chapter will allow us to trace the mutual influence of literature and life directly as we can verify it with our own experience. As a sociopolitical reality of the contemporary period, globalism—and transnationalism as one of its seminal manifestations in the literary text—denotes contemporaneousness. This chapter is designed to investigate what contemporaneousness is as well as to establish definitions of the terms *contemporary German* and *contemporary German-language literature* that can be used as a reference frame for this volume, which investigates transnationalism not as a new phenomenon[10] but as one that impacts our lives in a more pervasive and global way than it has ever done before.

Defining Contemporary German Literature

The journal *Gegenwartsliteratur: Ein germanistisches Jahrbuch* (Contemporary Literature: A German Studies Yearbook), founded by Paul Michael Lützeler in 2002, offers a starting point for a definition of the term *contemporary literature*. In the preface to the first issue, the editors state, "Das neue Jahrbuch 'Gegenwartsliteratur' beschäftigt sich mit der Literatur der letzten drei Jahrzehnte der Bundesrepublik Deutschland,

Österreich und der deutschsprachigen Schweiz."[11] (The new German Studies Yearbook *Gegenwartsliteratur* focuses on the literature that was produced in the Federal Republic of Germany, Austria, and the German-speaking part of Switzerland during the three most recent decades.)

Here the emphasis is placed on a temporal, national-geographic and linguistic determination of contemporary literature. However, looking at most current developments in German-language literature and its literary classification, it becomes obvious that identifying temporal, spatial, and linguistic parameters is not sufficient to define contemporary literature.[12] While literature is always bound to a specific language of origin or source language, which over centuries, and even in Goethe's plea for a new emerging "Weltliteratur (world literature),"[13] has often been equated with the language of a nation, the relationship between literature, language, culture, and nation is much more complex. Thus, the term *national literature* proves to be no longer valid, or more likely, has never been so,[14] as languages transcend national containment and are not anchored within geographic or national borders. German literature is transnational as the language is used in different national and cultural contexts. This would be an argument for the use of the term *German-language literature* instead of *German literature* when the focus of investigation is on either a comparative or a universal approach. In addition, the transnational circulation of literary texts through translation as well as the increasing phenomenon of *exophonic literature*, that is, literature written in a language that has been adopted by the author,[15] as well as the increased publication of multilingual texts, such as Emine Sevgi Özdamar's *Das Leben ist eine Karawanserei: Hat zwei Türen—aus einer kam ich rein aus der anderen ging ich raus* (*Life Is a Caravanserai. Has Two Doors. I Came In One. I Went Out the Other*, 1992) or Yoko Tawada's *Talisman* (1996), furthermore support the thesis that there is literature that is, contrary to what Azade Seyhan has stated,[16] not located "outside the nation," but that operates with a perception of the world that actively challenges the acceptance of national borders and boundaries.[17]

While there is no doubt that the formation of literature both as an individual act of creation and as a phenomenon of cultural expression depends on the biography, heritage, and socialization of individuals and at the same time is bound to specific historical, cultural, and linguistic contexts and traditions, literature proves to be mobile and changes over time. The role that history, culture, and national affiliation play in the context of literary classification requires a more detailed consideration when aiming to establish a concept of transnational literature.

Up until 1990, German contemporary literature in many chronicles and scholarly works was classified as *Literatur nach 1945* (literature after 1945), using the political caesura of the end of the Second World War as the demarcation line. With the fall of the Berlin Wall in 1989 and

Germany's unification in 1990, however, it became clear that a new era had begun, marking another significant historical and political, but also literary, turning point. The political era of the forty-year-long postwar period and the separation of Germany had come to an end, and it was not only the two German states that had been reunited and were struggling with the political, social, and economic consequences of unification. Their literatures (the former GDR and FRG literatures) too were challenged to reflect and participate in this process.[18]

Today the classification period for contemporary German literature that is most often used begins in the year 1989 and is denoted accordingly as *Literatur nach 1989* (Literature after 1989) or, more specifically, *post-Wende* or *postunification literature*.[19] Both the time after 1945 and the time after 1989 constituted a shift and a turning point in the collective German self-understanding and collective identity, which were not only reflected but also actively negotiated in the respective bodies of each contemporary literature. This raises the issue of German—rather than German-language—literature's distinctiveness, which turns out to be directly linked to the nation's history. Literary periodization based on historical timelines has rightly been challenged by scholars over the last decades because such a categorical framework imposes standardizing features with regard to content and form as well as analog patterns for development and change that by no means apply to all texts or authors of the same time period. There is in fact, however, a correlation between literary writing and the reception of the historical, political, and social world we live in, which cannot be ignored when labeling literature as contemporary.

My suggestion and intervention in this field therefore is to redefine contemporary literature by extending the parameters of time, space, and language and identifying contemporary literature as based on a common ground and joint horizon of experience. Determining factors for this common denominator are first of all a common history and historical context, or more specifically, a collectively recognized benchmark in history to which the current self-definition of a nation or culture refers in its collective memory. Furthermore it is the current political, societal, and cultural developments, changes, and turnarounds that influence and shape our present. Closely related to the memories, experiences, and self-awareness of a specific time is a common horizon of understanding based on generational experience, which comprises the 25–30 year time span to which Paul Michael Lützeler refers when he speaks of the "three decades."[20] Members of a peer group share a specific atmosphere, key experiences and values, hopes and obsessions, which can be denoted as "der gemeinsame Erfahrungshorizont einer Generation" (the lived experience of a generation).[21] Against the backdrop of a common historic, societal, and generation-specific horizon, contemporary literature proves to be the product of a community or collective—which can, but does not necessarily, refer to a nation—articulating itself and the topics of its time in multiple and various ways. In this respect, contemporary literature comes to serve as a means of identity formation that refers to a specific time and collective center of reference, the latter of which can be located within or across nations.

This nature of contemporary literature has further implications. As a medium of individual and collective self-reflection and self-presentation, and also as a medium of identity formation, contemporary literature is a moving term and refers to a "gleitende Zeit" (gliding time)[22] that has "einen wandelbaren Anfang und ein unabsehbares Ende" (a changeable beginning and an incalculable end).[23] The time "after 1945" is no longer to be considered our "contemporary time" but has moved into history. Our present time, "the time after 1989," will in turn be the past of tomorrow and will constitute the next generation's history.

When considering the joint horizon of experience and the creation of a common collective (and national) identity that build the ground for contemporary literature, it is important to note that in post-1989 Germany, it is not only the fall of the Berlin Wall and the unification of the two German states that have had a crucial impact on the country's society and culture, but also that Germany is becoming more and more a transnational space. This again has caused a change in the nation's collective identity.

Whereas for many decades German national identity was first and foremost defined by its history during the twentieth century, we now have to consider that a part of the German population does not share in that collective identity, which was and often still is undermined by an either explicit or underlying resistance to national affiliation: Germans do not want to be identified as Germans. There are Germans whose national identity is no longer defined by the Nazi past, the Second World War, and the Holocaust, and consequently the question of who does or does not relate to an ethnically inherited Nazi past has become a subject of discussion in German society. Not only Germans with an immigration or intercultural or transcultural background[24] but also the younger generation of adult Germans may not identify themselves with their grandparents' and great-grandparents' generation of Nazi perpetrators, bystanders, or victims.[25]

At the same time, the experiences and memories of the GDR are moving further into the distance, and the second and third generations of "East Germans" no longer correlate their place of belonging or heritage with a particular political past, but rather primarily with a cultural-geographical space. This may suggest that we have moved beyond the 1989 demarcation line; a new phase of contemporary literature is about to arise.

Transnationalism Shapes Contemporary German Society and Redefines Contemporary Literature

Since the beginning of the twenty-first century, Germany has been challenged to finally accept the reality of having been an "immigration nation" for more than half a century. This new national self-conception, in turn, has ignited and extended a set of debates as, for example, on the need to reform German immigration policy,[26] the role of Islam in German society,[27] and the possibility of receiving dual citizenship.[28] The multiculturalism that is the German nation's present reality is in fact equally part of its twentieth-century history and builds as common a ground of experience as the Holocaust and German unification, although this remains hardly acknowledged.

Transnationalism, however, is not limited to the question of immigration and physical mobility, but is to be identified as both a practice and a mindset in terms of societal and economic interests, politics, and marketing on a global scale.[29] As Stuart Taberner has stated, with the end of the Cold War, Germany became a global player and, as such, is increasingly exposed to the transformation of global relationships.[30] As a result, Germany has played a part in global conflict interventions, such as receiving refugees from Bosnia in the 1980s and 1990s, and engaging in military involvement in Afghanistan, Somalia, and other places. In international relations, Germany has assumed a leading role within Europe. The country's economy has become increasingly open and oriented to a global market, and, last but not least, Germans have "gone global," as Anke Biendarra put it,[31] by investing, consuming, traveling, thinking, and writing transnationally.

Considering the many effects globalization has on our lives, *transnationalism* has recently become a key term in debates across the social sciences and humanities. Prominent scholars, such as Azade Seyhan, Paul Jay, Leslie Adelson, Tom Cheesman, Deniz Göktürk, B. Venkat Mani, and Elke Segelcke, among others,[32] laid the foundation for a deeper understanding of *transnational literature* within the field of literary and, as to the latter scholars, more specifically, of German studies. Imbedded in discourses of postcolonial and migration studies, the term as used by these scholars is based upon and directly connected with existing concepts or versant terms, such as migration, minority, diaspora, and hybrid literatures.[33] Other literary scholars use the term simply as a descriptor and speak about "transnational literature" as literature written by a "transnational writer," which means not much more than an author with a migration, bi- or multicultural background.[34] The goal of this chapter, like the goal of the entire volume, however, is to prove that the limited definition and existing concept of transnationalism is no longer sufficient to describe new developments in German literature in the twenty-first century.

It is also worth noting that the term *transnational literature*—while well established in the anglophone context within and outside German studies—has barely made its way into the German-speaking academic discourse. Instead, "inter*cultural*" and "trans*cultural* literature" continue to be the predominant terms used in this context.[35] This rejection of the term "trans-*national*" may be due to the inexplicit resistance to national affiliation that has defined German collective identity as a reflection of its national history and a self-imposed "ethical imperative."[36] The reluctance towards national identification, in turn, could build a causal connection to the new desire for a German "*trans*-national" or "*non*-national identity" that has appeared increasingly as a main theme in German literature over the last two decades and which will also be discussed in the following.

While authors of different nationalities and transnational heritage belong today to the predominant authors in Germany, and have long opposed the designation "minority authors,"[37] it has also become evident that topics like migration and mobility, globalization and transnationalism are no longer exclusively the domain of specifically that group of authors who, on the basis of their biographies, understand themselves as cultural intermediaries and border crossers, and who are at home in multiple languages. In contemporary literature, it can be determined, authors of both German and transnational backgrounds engage in transnationalism by choosing themes or topics that reflect on an individually or collectively experienced historical or contemporary transnational reality, while at the same time using transnationalism as an aesthetic device.[38]

Taking five authors as examples, the following section will illustrate how Germany's transnational present has impacted contemporary literature and how it challenges existing concepts of not only national but also transnational literature, literary mobility, and world literature.

Ilija Trojanow's *Der Weltensammler*

Ilija Trojanow may be considered as one of the classic representatives of transnational literature in the established sense. He is a writer, a journalist, a publisher, and an important intellectual voice in Germany. He was born in Bulgaria and fled with his parents to Germany as a child. Soon after the immigration to Germany, the family moved to Kenya, where his father worked as an engineer. Trojanow lived in Nairobi from 1972 to 1984 with a three-year stay in Germany. He studied law and ethnology in Munich, and in 1989, he founded the Marino Publishing House, which specialized in African literature. In 1998, he moved to Mumbai, where he stayed for five years. He also lived in Cape Town before returning to Germany. In 2001, he undertook a three-month-long journey on foot through Tanzania, which became an inspiring source for his 2006 historical novel *Der Weltensammler*. In his travelogue *An den inneren*

Ufern Indiens (*Along the Ganges*, 2003), he traces a second trip through India and Bangladesh. In 2003, Ilija Trojanow traveled from Mumbai to Mecca. The travelogue *Zu den heiligen Quellen des Islams* (To the Sacred Sources of Islam, 2004) describes this. When not traveling, Ilija Trojanow lives in Vienna or Stuttgart.

The symbiosis between author and work, in which a lived transnationalism is reflected not through a fictionalization of the author's own life, but rather in a specific conception of literature and writing style, is illustrated by Trojanow's five-hundred-page bestselling novel *Der Weltensammler*. The novel marks—as Dirk Göttsche has stated—nothing less than "a new departure in the history of writing cross-cultural experience and representing the 'Other.'"[39]

The historical novel, set in the nineteenth century, portrays the life of British officer and explorer Sir Richard Francis Burton in his travels across three continents to India, Arabia, and East Africa. The novel undertakes a subversion of the postcolonial perspective insofar as the protagonist is not portrayed as a typical representative of British colonialism, but rather becomes the figuration of an emphatic merger of various foreign cultures. In Burton's case, this cultural fusion can best be described as camouflage. He obsessively learns the languages of each respective country through which he travels, immerses himself in several religions, converts, and masquerades as a local.

Extreme cultural assimilation and disguise lead, in Burton's case, to transformation and to multiple identities, or in fact to a change of personality and a lack of identity. With this, the author assumes a position critical to cultural assimilation, which he considers to be the ability to "acquire one's own identity in reflection of the identity expectations that the social environment supposes on us," as Matthias Rath stated.[40] In this regard the novel implicitly confirms the view expressed by Karl Pellens, Susanne Popp, and others that, even in an age of globalization, transnationalism can only be lived and conceived under the premise of existing cultural diversity and difference, as well as national demarcations.[41]

In addition, the cultural inclusion Burton pursues throughout the novel is thwarted both structurally and stylistically by a polyphonic narrative style unique to this novel: In all three sections of the text, both Richard Burton's cultural experiences and his narrative perspective are complemented by a counterplot and narrative voice, "which represent indigenous perspectives and the experience of the colonized."[42] In the first section, "British India," it is Burton's servant Naukuram who provides the opposing voice. In the second section of the novel, "Arabia," it is the report of a governor, who interrogates Burton's travel companions because the authorities suspect the pilgrimage to Mecca to be an act of espionage. In the third section, "East Africa," it is Burton's by now elderly guide, the also historical figure Sidi Mubarak Bombay, who regales his neighbors with evening tales of his travels with Burton. Trojanow himself described these thoroughly "unreliable" and, just like Burton, only partially informed narrators as "counter-narrators."[43] They serve to relocate the British officer back in the world from which he originally came.

Der Weltensammler is not a novel about the dissolution of borders or the fusion of cultures, but rather a novel about different cultures, languages, horizons, and conceptions of the world. The actual "collector" of worlds is the author, who conveys to the reader his own extensive knowledge about the cultures described, as well as his personal perspective on the same. In this respect, Trojanow's implementation of a poetology of making accessible various worlds and modes of perception in this work corresponds with the definition David Damrosch has formulated with respect to *world literature*—that literature translated from other languages and cultures offers the reader a "set of windows on the world."[44]

The peculiarity of Trojanow's text is that it provides the reader with insight into other worlds without presenting these from a domesticated—that is, from a European (be it German or British)—perspective. With this specific technique of "foreignizing"—which is well known from the theory of translation and can be productively deployed in literary studies too—in which the cultures are presented without adjusting them to the reader's expectation, *Der Weltensammler* proves itself to be part of a new and expanded form of "world literature."[45] One could even go as far as to call Trojanow's novel not a "German novel," but rather a transcultural, transnational, and even transcontinental novel written in German. The book has received great recognition both in Germany and internationally, and has been translated into twenty-five different languages.

Transnationalism with respect to a historical past figures prominently as a theme in the two following examples as well. Here, however, it is not British but German history that is at the forefront.

Daniel Kehlmann's *Die Vermessung der Welt*

At the heart of Daniel Kehlmann's immensely successful novel *Die Vermessung der Welt*[46] are two very German personalities: the mathematical genius and astronomer Carl Friedrich Gauß and the naturalist and explorer Alexander von Humboldt. In sixteen alternating chapters and less than three hundred pages, the author presents the biographies of these two men, whose discoveries changed our perception of the world. The title of this work—*Measuring the World*—refers back to the time in which it is set, that is, the beginning of the nineteenth century and the beginning of the modern age. Both scientists, Gauß and Humboldt, took part in the process of measuring the world, which constitutes nothing less than the source and early beginnings of globalization. While Humboldt traveled the Occident and Americas, empirically exploring and mapping the uncharted world, mathematician Gauß stayed in his provincial hometown of Göttingen, challenging euclidean mathematics by discovering that space must be conceived of as curved, and that therefore all parallel lines must finally meet.

The novel follows exactly this concept of parallelization in its systematic contrasting of the two dissimilar personalities. Though Kehlmann bases his novel on historical facts, he does not shy away from fictionalizing them. The distinctiveness and comedic effect of this novel lie in the portrayal of both protagonists as geniuses, but also as humans with clearly notable flaws. Both scientists mutate into caricatures of themselves within this novel.

What makes this novel a transnational novel in the manner described above is first and foremost the theme. A measuring of the world can, by definition, only take place on a global and transnational scale. Both Humboldt and Gauß actively contributed to developing internationally viable methods of measuring spaces and transcending them in even shorter time. However, the novel also reveals a further dimension of transnationalism. Both Karina von Tippelskirch[47] and Katharina Gerstenberger[48] have pointed out that the metaphor of measurement, in addition to temporal and spatial dimensions, has an important additional significance for the novel: the author uses his text to chart a new approach to contemporary German literature. He leaves behind the style of writing common in German literature after 1945, and still after 1989, namely the style "of German-German self-reflection, self-referential introspectiveness and roller-coasters of political activism," as Alexander Honold describes it in his article "Ankunft in der Weltliteratur" (Arrival in World Literature).[49]

Kehlmann's *Die Vermessung der Welt* is a literary experiment. What is new is not the fictionalization of historical facts; this we know from historical novels and fictional biographies already. What is new is the author's consciously breaking with the expectation of a historically accurate recreation of the lives and characters of the two historical figures. This is accomplished, above all, through humor and irony. Through the portrayal of the two German geniuses in their all-too-human nature, typical German characteristics are caricatured in a way that is easily accessible to both a German and an international audience.

The formula for success, with which *Die Vermessung der Welt* conquered the world literary market, is to write a light and entertaining novel that simultaneously attains great depth through a deliberate and targeted amalgamation of various national styles, as well as cross-references spanning world literature. In his poetic lecture at the University of Göttingen in the fall of 2006, Kehlmann characterized literature as a net of motives, images, repetitions, references, and styles.[50] It is precisely this net that he implements on a transnational level in his novel *Die Vermessung der*

Welt. Kehlmann, an author who locates himself both in Austria and Germany, has developed new literary territory by injecting contemporary German literature (and in this context again, I am deliberately not speaking of German-language literature) with South American magic realism and American postmodernism. He has created a stylistic mix in order to achieve a genetic revitalization of German literature that deals with Germanness. This is what makes this text a piece of world literature.

Christian Kracht's *Imperium*

Christian Kracht's novel *Imperium*, published in 2012, exhibits a number of parallels to Kehlmann's text. Like *Die Vermessung der Welt*, this novel is also written by an author who is not considered a migration author in the classical sense, but can rather be identified—as the Swiss magazine *Schweizer Monat* (Swiss Month) states—as one who lives the life of a "Bildungsnomade,"[51] someone who travels in pursuit of education, learning, and entertainment. This form of transnationalism can be understood as a privileged globe-trotting that stands in opposition to migration forced by financial needs, displacement, or exile, which most often is connected with the intention to become a citizen of the country of immigration. In the case of Kracht no one ever knows "wo er gerade lebt, woran er gerade schreibt und aus welcher Richtung er angereist kommt"[52] (where he currently lives, what he's currently writing about, or from which direction he will arrive). According to his own statements during several readings, Kracht sees himself as a cosmopolitan.

Imperium also tells, in a humorous, ironic, and highly provocative manner, the story of a piece of Germany's transnational history.[53] The novel fictionalizes the biography of health fanatic and visionary August Engelhardt, who bought a coconut plantation on the small island of Kabakon in the colony of German New Guinea at the end of the nineteenth century. His goal was to start there and eventually change the world. The self-proclaimed sectarian offered his few followers (in total, perhaps a dozen) naked hiking, vegetarianism, and sun worship as remedies for the unhealthy aspects of the civilization he rejected. Until his fictional revival through Kracht's novel, this whimsical representative of the turn-of-the-century *Lebensreformbewegung* (life reformation movement) had fallen into almost total obscurity.

Here, as with Trojanow's and Kehlmann's novels, the question is raised—what function does the fictionalization of historical examples of German or European transnationalism have, and how does it establish a reference, or connection, to the present? In fact it is not Engelhardt's relocation to the colonies that is to be considered a transnational act (and here Kracht might deliberately send the reader down the wrong track), but it is the novel itself that acts as a transnational transmitter.

In his essay on transnationalism in contemporary German-language fiction by nonminority writers, Stuart Taberner describes the desire "to discover universal principles across cultures while also endeavouring to emphasize what is uniquely German"[54] as a form of "ideal transnationalism"[55] that is applied by German authors with no migration background. Taberner associates this new transnationalism with the (conscious or unconscious) attempt to search for a German identity that can be defined outside of the frame of reference of the German national-socialist past. This hypothesis, however, does not seem to be confirmed by Christian Kracht's *Imperium*, as the novel contains not only direct references to anti-Semitism and the Holocaust, but the protagonist Engelhardt is linked and equated with Hitler in the novel. "Dieser Bericht spielt ganz am Anfang des zwanzigsten Jahrhunderts" (This account takes place at the very beginning of the twentieth century), the author states only a few pages after the novel's beginning,

> welches ja bis zur knappen Hälfte seiner Laufzeit so aussah, als würde es das Jahrhundert der Deutschen werden; das Jahrhundert, in dem Deutschland seinen rechtmäßigen Ehren- und Vorsitzplatz an der Weltentischrunde einnehmen würde. . . . So wird nun stellvertretend die Geschichte nur eines Deutschen erzählt werden, eines Romantikers, der wie so viele dieser Spezies verhinderter Künstler war, und wenn dabei manchmal Parallelen zu einem späteren deutschen Romantiker und Vegetarier ins Bewußtsein dringen, der vielleicht lieber bei seiner Staffelei geblieben wäre, so ist dies durchaus beabsichtigt und sinniger Weise, Verzeihung, in nuce auch kohärent.[56]

> [which, until close to halfway through, looked as though it was to become the century of the Germans, the century in which Germany would take its legitimate place of honor and chairmanship at the world table. . . . Now representatively, the story of only one German will be told, a romantic, who, like so many of this species, was a would-be artist, and if, in this process, at times parallels to a later German romantic and vegetarian come to mind, who perhaps would have been better to stick with the brush and easel, well then this is thoroughly intentional and aptly—forgive me—, *in nuce*, also coherent.]

This and further linkages are presented in a similarly banal style with which Kracht's narrator describes both the hero of his story, as well as Hitler, as romantics caught up in a delusion of salvation, and equates them both—literally—with other "crazies," who grew out of the same German "romantic"—that is, nationalistic—spirit. This connection has unleashed enormous controversy in the German press.[57] In the context outlined here, however, it is not the detailed content of the debate, or the arguments presented for or against the integrity and political correctness of the novel that are of particular interest. Of much greater significance is the fact that the author, Kracht, has used a deliberately provocative style of writing in his novel *Imperium*[58] (and here, if not earlier, the title of the novel confirms the double reference to German fantasies of colonial power and the Third Reich) to break a taboo: one is not—and especially as a German—supposed to write ironically about Hitler, anti-Semitism, and the Holocaust.[59] In his novel, however, Kracht transgresses two unspoken commandments and links them through the figure of Engel-hardt and the telling of his story: He uses an ironic treatment for the Holocaust theme, and he gives the novel's narrator as well as major and minor characters a postcolonial (including racist and sexist) perspective and rhetoric.[60] By confronting German readers with a style of writing that consciously contradicts or locates itself beyond the ethnic imperative of inherited guilt for Nazi crimes and at the same time ludicrously plays with a colonial past and postcolonial history, Kracht has transnationalized contemporary German literature and maybe even intentionally blurred the line (or category) that designates "literature after 1989." While Kracht in his novel does not seem to negate the ethnic association of the Holocaust with German identity, he declines to follow the applicable (national) rules of how to speak about it. The reconstruction of individual fantasies about German superpower is bluntly mixed with allusions to the reality of genocide. This appears all the more flagrant when the novel openly presents inherited guilt as a theme by making a personal connection: namely when the narrator recounts how his grandparents would pretend not to have noticed the Jews collected at the Hamburg train station Dammtor for deportation.[61] At this point, the novel outs itself as a specifically "German novel" after all.

This is even more interesting when considering the fact that Kracht has referred to himself as a Swiss writer for some time now. He was born in Switzerland to German parents and spent the first years of his childhood there. Switzerland itself regards him with utmost skepticism and confirms for him that he is an unwanted child. The aforementioned *Schweizer Monat* article says, "'Christian Kracht ist Schweizer', so steht es in neueren Publikationen des Autors. Reicht aber dafür sein Schweizer Pass, auf den er sich gern beruft? Und: ist der Schweizer Pass das letzte wahre Statussymbol?"[62] ("Christian Kracht is Swiss," at least that is what the author's recent publications state. But is his Swiss passport, to which he so readily refers, sufficient though? And: is a Swiss passport the last true status symbol?) Even in the age of globalization and transnationalism, the question of an author's national affiliation seems not to have lost its significance—a topic to be investigated further in the last two examples.

Felicitas Hoppe's *Hoppe*

Felicitas Hoppe's novel *Hoppe* appeared in 2012, the same year as Christian Kracht's *Imperium*. It was distinguished with Germany's prestigious literary honor, the *Georg-Büchner-Preis*. The novel is an invented autobiography in which the author Felicitas Hoppe conjures up a transnational biography for her fictitious alter ego of the same name.

The first-person narrator grows up with an unsettled father, a German patent lawyer, who kidnapped his daughter and took her overseas after his divorce from his Polish wife. Felicitas spends a restless but "dream-come-true" childhood in Canada. Not only does she play hockey and is trained by Walter Gretzky, best known as the father of Wayne Gretzky, but she also finds a place in the Gretzky family as a quasi-foster child and stepsister to Canadian hockey superstar-to-be Wayne Gretzky. As a teenager she moves with her father to Australia and plays the piano, but is unable to pursue the career she envisions as a composer. The last third of her life she lives in the USA, where she experiences Las Vegas as "die schönste und prächtigste Stadt der Welt"[63] (the most beautiful and magnificent city in the world), until she finally disappears from this world at an unknown location.

A direct tie to the author's real biography is established in the novel in that the rootless and globe-trotting protagonist and first-person narrator is also an author who writes in German and whose literary productions have exactly the same titles as the author's real publications with just one exception: The fictitious protagonist creates a parallel identity for herself through writing a fictional autobiography. This fake autobiography, recounted in the novel by the first-person narrator, tells the life story of a similarly fictional character who—just as the real author Felicitas Hoppe—grew up as the third of five children in the city of Hameln.

The novel *Hoppe* begins with the entry: "Felicitas Hoppe, geboren am 22. Dezember 1960 in Hameln, ist eine deutsche Schriftstellerin." (Felicitas Hoppe, born on December 22, 1960 in Hameln, is a German author). This corresponds directly to the first sentence of the German Wikipedia entry for Felicitas Hoppe.[64] The deliberate connection can be interpreted as a sign that Felicitas Hoppe's doubled autobiography is not only a masterpiece of language and a highly artificial construct of a novel that seeks its counterpart in contemporary German literature, but that the novel is, above all, the author's attempt to position herself within the contemporary literary landscape.

Sonja Klocke has convincingly pointed out that Felicitas Hoppe's "dream biography" (as it reads on the dust cover) creates "a transnational space that only surfaces as the precondition for the invention"[65] of the fictional biography. In fact, the creation of this transnational biography confirms a specific literary identity—that is, the author's self-stylization as an intellectual and avant-garde author, who gains her inspiration not from a transnational or specifically national biography, but rather much more from the richness of her own creative abilities.

This is confirmed in the novel itself, where the narrator states:

> Talent und Erkenntnis sind nicht an Orte, Zeiten und Biographien gebunden. Die vermeintliche Idyllenautorin Felicitas Hoppe wäre zweifellos weder eine bessere noch eine schlechtere Autorin, wenn sie ein anderes Schicksal hätte. Würden wir sie tatsächlich lieber lesen, wenn sie keine Hamelner, sondern, sagen wir, eine sibirische Kindheit hätte? Gut möglich—nur dass Mängel und Qualität ihres Werkes davon vollkommen unberührt blieben.[66]

> [Talent and insight are not tied to places, times, and biographies. The presumably idyllic author Felicitas Hoppe would doubtlessly be neither a better nor a worse author, if she had a different life story. Would we actually rather read her books, if she were not from Hameln, but rather had had, say, a Siberian childhood? It's very possible—only that the deficiencies and quality of her work would remain completely unaffected by this].

More simply formulated, this means: Those who—like the real author—have no extraordinary or transnational, but rather simply a "normal" biography, can also write good literature. This last statement almost reads like an anticipated counterattack on Maxim Biller's provocatively posed and self-answered question printed recently in the weekly newspaper *Die Zeit*: "Warum ist die deutsche Gegenwartsliteratur so unglaublich langweilig? Weil die Enkel der Nazi-Generation noch immer bestimmen, was gelesen wird. Was hier fehlt, sind lebendige literarische Stimmen von Migranten."[67] (Why is contemporary German literature so unbelievably boring? Because the grandchildren of the Nazi generation continue to dictate what is read. What is missing here are the lively literary voices of migrants.) It can be assumed, however, that Maxim Biller, a literary critic in Germany and himself a transnational German author, would hardly recognize the novel *Hoppe* as a great hope for the renewal of contemporary German literature nor as an example of a literary text that has the potential to circulate the world, despite its transnational theme, the critical acclaim it has received, and the prestigious literary prize it has won. An important criterion for a novel to be distinguished as *world literature* is, for Biller, that it is "universal verständlich"[68] (universally comprehensible).

Hoppe's *Hoppe* by no means fulfills this requirement. The average German reader probably feels lost in the novel's vast network of both real and fictional transnational references. (Wayne Gretzky is most likely familiar to German readers; but who in Germany knows where Brantford or Edmonton are located, or understands the reference to a Canadian backpack?) And, how would in return a potentially international readership find its way through this difficult-to-disentangle literary thought experiment, in which the city of Hameln forms the fictional center of the world and the father of the children in the story builds a "Kasperletheater" (Punch and Judy show)? A book like Hoppe's *Hoppe* proves to be immobile and less interesting for an international market, because the author does not succeed in portraying transnationalism as a constituent part of present reality. Instead, she fantasizes herself into the phenomenon of transnationalism in order to position herself as a writer in a universal space outside of the context of any national literature.

Dan Vyleta's Crime Fiction Series

Author Dan Vyleta has followed the opposite path: instead of inventing a transnational biography, he has pursued an actual literary emigration and lived transnationally. His three novels *Pavel & I* (2008), *The Quiet Twin* (2011), and *The Crooked Maid* (2013), which are written in English and deal extensively with the time of National Socialism and the postwar period in Germany and Austria, bring up once more the question of language, national affiliation, and identity and whether this author should be included in the lineup of *German* authors discussed in the context of transnational literature.

His debut novel *Pavel & I*, published in 2008, is set in Berlin in the aftermath of the Second World War and concentrates on a number of days in the harsh winter of 1946–47. The spy thriller charts a picture of the mood and mentality of the German capital, ripped asunder by war. The novel is based on meticulously researched facts, and enriched by a wealth of literary allusions from Heinrich Böll to Günter Grass.

Vyleta's second novel, *The Quiet Twin*, published in 2012, takes place over the course of a few weeks in 1939 Vienna in a multistory apartment building, where everyone is creepily observant of the neighborhood's goings-on. The core plot involves a series of murders in the area, but the book is not so much a mystery story as "a mood piece about the oppressive atmosphere and escalating paranoia"[69] that intensify as the totalitarian regime comes to power.

Vyleta's 2013 *The Crooked Maid* is almost set up as a follow-up novel to the previous work, both in character development and timeline. Once again, the murder mystery is a depiction of the suspicion and fear of the postwar period, while the initial phase of denazification is winding down and the citizens of Vienna struggle to rebuild their lives and a new society from the rubble. This novel is an elliptical parable of guilt, repression, and reconciliation.

The question that has already been raised in discussing the novels by Trojanow, Kehlmann, Kracht, and Hoppe—namely, what connection exists between the transnational setting and plot, and the national identity, the biography, and the physical mobility of the authors—proves to be, in the case of Dan Vyleta and his works, even more clearly a question of the national or transnational affiliation of the texts, as well as of the author.

Dan Vyleta is the son of Czech refugees, who in the late 1960s emigrated to Germany, where he spent his childhood and youth. He studied history in the United Kingdom and holds a PhD from the University of Cambridge. He spent several years in the United States, lived in Berlin and Vienna, came to Canada in 2008, lived in Edmonton, Alberta, and Sackville, New Brunswick, and moved back to the United Kingdom in 2012, where he holds a position as senior lecturer in the Department of Film and Creative Writing at the University of Birmingham. While he himself avoids any kind of labeling, he usually is addressed in the press and media as a German-Canadian author, as Canada is the country in which he started his writing career.

What makes Dan Vyleta interesting in the context of the discussion of a redefinition of transnational literature and its influence on contemporary literature is the fact that this author, who grew up in Germany and holds a German passport, positions himself through his writing outside the national (German) frame of reference. He not only dedicates his work to a transnational topic (the Second World War) but "translates" the German past to a contemporary international audience without domesticating the foreignness of the source culture nor of the unique historical frame of reference.[70] By writing in English, the author adopts a "third party position"[71] and assumes an outside perspective while focusing specifically on that section of German history that has largely determined German identity since 1945. At the same time Vyleta's novels prove to be particularly accessible to both an international and a German audience because the author avails himself of the traditional and internationally well-established genre of the mystery story, or thriller. Indeed, all three novels appeared in German translation almost simultaneously with their release in English. Thus this author does in fact become a "nonstate actor" in Steven Vertovec's sense and a facilitator of German history on an international level.

Conclusion

Looking back at the definition of contemporary literature established at the beginning of this chapter—that it is based on a common ground and joint horizon of experience—it has become obvious that it is the historical, cultural, and societal conditions that shape the context of literary production, as well as the reception of it in its own time. This, however, does not mean that within each nation there is only one joint or unified horizon of experience to which its literature refers. One of the major challenges of German "literature after 1989" or *post-Wende* and *postunification literature*, for example, has been to reflect upon, and at the same time, to assist in overcoming the split between the two divergent collective and cultural identities that were established after the war. The investigations of the five textual examples, however, have demonstrated that transnationalism builds a new significant "pillar" within contemporary German literature[72] and redefines it in the following ways—and in this context German literature can be seen both as representative of contemporary literature and as exemplary.

Authors of German and transnational heritage make transnationalism a theme in their literary works and practice it in that they refer to an individually or collectively experienced transnational reality, choose a historical theme outside of their own national context, or establish the setting of their text overseas. Thus their novels map a collective experiential horizon, which has for many of us become a key factor in determining our identity in the age of globalization. Because transnationalism is, by definition, a global phenomenon, this experience constitutes a common denominator for a new contemporary literature, which may be tied to one or more specific languages, but which otherwise largely rejects categorization within a particular national literature. Correspondingly, I have designated Trojanow's *Der Weltensammler* as a transnational novel written in German, and I understand Dan Vyleta's works to be thrillers, written in English, which deal with the German history of the Nazi era from a transnational perspective. Both authors have produced transnational literature by making an "ethical choice"— as Lawrence Venuti would call it—that is flagging or signaling rather than assimilating or domesticating the foreignness of the cultures and historical periods they write about in their texts.[73]

Taking Daniel Kehlmann's *Die Vermessung der Welt*, Christian Kracht's *Imperium*, and Felicitas Hoppe's *Hoppe* as examples, we can see that transnationalism in contemporary German literature is also used, however, to redefine German identity—whether collectively or individually. In all three of these works, German personalities or individuals (two famous scientists, a historically authentic "weirdo" and a doubly fictitious and thus "almost real again" author) take center stage. Transnational biographies are attributed to all of them. These are used by the authors to formulate not so much a transnational but rather a nonnational or universal German identity, which distinguishes itself through being located outside the frame of reference of National Socialism, the Second World War, and the Holocaust. Through imagining a "different" and "universal" German identity or "Germanness," however, these works locate themselves clearly within a German national context and literature (and in this respect both Kehlmann's and Kracht's works can be identified as German literature, not Austrian or Swiss).

A transnationalism simultaneously experienced and imagined by the authors, or a global nomadism, as well as a desired universalism in one's own writing, are not reflected solely in the choice of topics in these works but rather influence the texts stylistically as well. Through intertextual references and allusions to world literature; style and genre mixing; and alienation as well as humorous and ironic distancing from one's own identity, collective mentality, or national particularities—through all these, transnationalism is applied as an aesthetic device with which new literary possibilities can be sought out, and through which German literature is finally brought into sync with international currents. In these ways, German literature is renewed and revitalized.

This transnationalization of German and (as is shown in other chapters of this volume) also of German-language literature, challenges us to embrace anew the interdependency between national, transnational, and world literature. Among literary scholars the term *national literature* has been largely regarded as obsolete. I would agree that this proves true with reference to "national language" and the ethnic affiliation of authors. But still, national affiliation *is* relevant insofar as nation describes a community whose identity is based on a common history and horizon of experience. "Transnational literature" transcends this experiential, mental, cultural, and intellectual horizon by describing and reflecting a new collective life experience, namely the manifestation of globalization through the phenomenon of transnationalism that has started to create a new identity not outside the nation but across nations.

"World literature" at the same time can be defined as literature that travels the world and, speaking with Steven Vertovec, becomes a nonstate actor itself insofar as it reaches beyond the horizon of the culture and language in which it is written.[74] The textual examples presented in this chapter have shown that works of contemporary literature only attain literary mobility and become transnational actors when they translate into other cultures, that is, when they can awaken international interest through "worldliness"[75] and are universally understandable. Literary texts travel according to their information and entertainment value; some travel because they carry a universal and identifying message, others invoke a unique fascination through exoticism or a specific situation of a nation or culture—be it in history or in the present.

Notes

[1] For a definition of transnationalism in this direction see Victor Roudometof, "Transnationalism, Cosmopolitanism and Glocalization," *Current Sociology* 53 (2005): 118; Steven Vertovec, *Transnationalism* (London: Routledge, 2009), 2; and Venkat B. Mani and Elke Segelcke, "Cosmopolitical and Transnational Interventions in German Studies," *Transit* 7, no. 1 (2011): 1–27.

[2] In the introduction to his book *Transnational Canadas: Anglo-Canadian Literature and Globalization* (Waterloo: Wilfried Laurier Press, 2009), xvii, Kit Dobson makes a critical claim about transnational Canadian literature that largely coincides with what this volume intends to prove for German-language fiction too: "Writing in Canada is concerned with crossing national borders thematically, just as it is concerned with marketing on a global scale. This transnational mindset can be seen in the writing, in Canada's cultural industries and cultural institutions, and in our methods of reading."

[3] Aristotles, *Poetik*, transl. by Arbogast Schmitt (Darmstadt: Wissenschaftliche Buchgesellschaft, 2008). In the ninth chapter of his work *Ars Poetica*, Aristotle states that action depicted in literature is not actually true but corresponds to plausibility and thus approximates general human experiences.

[4] Ottmar Ette, *ÜberLebenswissen: Die Aufgabe der Philologie* (Berlin: Kulturverlag Kadmos, 2004).

[5] Aleida Assmann, *Der lange Schatten der Vergangenheit: Erinnerungskultur und Gedächtnispolitik* (München: C. H. Beck 2006).

[6] Doris Bachmann-Medick, ed., *Kultur als Text: Die anthropologische Wende in der Literaturwissenschaft* (Tübingen: Francke, 2004).

[7] Hartmut Böhme, "Zur Gegenstandfrage der Germanistik und Kulturwissenschaft," *Jahrbuch der deutschen Schillergesellschaft* 42 (1998): 476–85.

[8] Wilhelm Vosskamp, "Die Gegenstände der Literaturwissenschaft und ihre Einbindung in die Kulturwissenschaften," *Jahrbuch der deutschen Schillergesellschaft* 42 (1998): 503–10.

[9] James E. Young, "Writing the Holocaust," in *The Holocaust: Theoretical Readings*, ed. Neil Levi and Michael Rothberg (New Brunswick, NJ: Rutgers University Press, 2003), 337.

[10] See the "Interview with Ilija Trojanow" in this volume.

[11] Paul Michael Lützeler and Stephen K. Schindler, *Gegenwartsliteratur: Ein germanistisches Jahrbuch*, ed. Paul Michael Lützeler and Stephan K. Schindler (Tübingen: Stauffenburg, 2002), XVII.

[12] The following discussion further develops the approach to contemporary literature that Carsten Gansel and I have outlined in the introduction to our coedited volume on the topic: Carsten Gansel and Elisabeth Herrmann, "'Gegenwart' bedeutet die Zeitspanne einer Generation: Anmerkungen zum Versuch, Gegenwartsliteratur zu bestimmen," in *Entwicklungen in der deutschsprachigen Gegenwartsliteratur nach 1989*, ed. Carsten Gansel and Elisabeth Herrmann (Göttingen: V&R unipress, 2013), 7–21.

[13] Johann Peter Eckermann, *Gespräche mit Goethe in den letzten Jahren seines Lebens*, ed. Heinz Schlaffer (München: Hanser, 1986), 207.

[14] For an overview on the discussion of the validity of the term *national literature* in contrasting juxtaposition to the term *world literature*, see Elisabeth Herrmann, "Transnationale Literatur und europäischer Kulturtransfer im Fokus germanistischer Literaturwissenschaft," in *Begegnungen: Das VIII. Nordisch-Baltische Germanistentreffen in Sigtuna vom 11. bis zum 13. 6. 2009*, ed. Elisabeth Wåghäll Nivre et al. (Stockholm: Acta Universitas Stockholmiensis, 2011), 371–85.

[15] Chantal Wright, "Writing in the 'Grey Zone': Exophonic Literature in Contemporary Germany," *GFL—German as a Foreign Language* 3 (2008): 26–42.

[16] Azade Seyhan, *Writing Outside the Nation* (Princeton: Princeton University Press, 2000), 10.

[17] See Wright, "Writing," 32; similarly, Ilija Trojanow in his interview at the end of this volume.

[18] In this regard German unification can be considered a process of transnationalization—an aspect Faye Stewart focuses on in her chapter "Dislocation, Multiplicity, and Transformation" in this book.

[19] See Gansel and Herrmann, "Gegenwart," 7–21; also Barbara Beßlich, Kathtarina Grätz, and Olaf Hildebrand, eds., *Wende des Erinnerns? Geschichtskonstruktionen in der deutschen Literatur nach 1989* (Berlin: Erich Schmidt, 2006); Clemens Kammler, Jost Keller, and Reinhard Wilczek, *Deutschsprachige Gegenwartsliteratur seit 1989: Gattungen, Themen, Autoren. Eine Auswahlbibliographie* (Heidelberg: Synchron, 2003); and Gerhard Fischer and David Roberts, eds., *Schreiben nach der Wende: Ein Jahrzehnt deutscher Literatur 1989–1999* (Tübingen: Stauffenburg, 2001).

[20] Lützeler and Schindler, *Gegenwartsliteratur*, XVII.

[21] Gansel and Herrmann, "Gegenwart," 16.

[22] Lützeler and Schindler, *Gegenwartsliteratur*, XVII.

[23] Michael Braun, *Die deutsche Gegenwartsliteratur: Eine Einführung* (Stuttgart: UTB, 2010), 21.

[24] According to the online statistic portal *Statista: Statistiken und Studien zu Einwanderern und Einwanderung in Deutschland*, in today's Germany approximately 20% of the population and about a quarter of people under twenty-five have foreign roots, accessed June 15, 2014, http://de.statista.com/themen/46/einwanderung/.

[25] One illustration of this would be the Yahoo blog "Gibt es eine (vererbte) Kollektivschuld am Holocaust für Deutsche, die nach dem Kriegsende geboren wurden?" (Is there an (inherited) collective guilt for Germans who were born after the end of the Second World War?)

[26] With reference to prototypical immigration countries such as the United States, Canada, and Australia, Holger Stelzner called in his *Frankfurter Allgemeine Zeitung* article of May 20, 2014 entitled "Migration. Einwanderungsland Deutschland" (Germany—Nation of Immigration) for a more selective immigration policy in Germany.

[27] In his "Rede zum 20. Jahrestag der Deutschen Einheit" (speech on the occasion of the twentieth anniversary of German unification), Federal President Christian Wulff said on October 3, 2010, "Der Islam gehört zu Deutschland" (Islam is part of Germany).

[28] On February 10, 2014, Federal Minister of the Interior Thomas De Maizière took a turn in a new direction with regard to the continued discussion on dual citizenship by proposing graduation from a German high or middle school as a possible prerequisite for applying for dual citizenship. "Innenminister de Maizière

stellt deutschen Schulabschluss in den Mittelpunkt einer neuen Doppelpass-Regelung," *Der Tagesspiegel*, February 8, 2014.

[29] Dobson, *Transnational Canadas*, xviii.

[30] Stuart Taberner, "The Meaning of the Nazi Past in the Post-Postwar: Recent Fiction by Günter Grass, Christa Wolf and Martin Walser," *Seminar: A Journal of Germanic Studies* 50 (2014): 161–64.

[31] Anke Biendarra, *Germans Going Global: Contemporary Literature and Cultural Globalization* (Boston: De Gruyter, 2012).

[32] Seyhan, *Writing Outside the Nation*; Paul Jay, *Global Matters: The Transnational Turn in Literary Studies* (Ithaca, NY: Cornell University Press, 2010); Leslie Adelson, *The Turkish Turn in Contemporary German Literature: Toward a New Critical Grammar of Migration* (New York: Palgrave Macmillan, 2005); Tom Cheesman and Deniz Göktürk, "German Titles, Turkish Names: The Cosmopolitan Will," accessed April 14, 2014, http://www.new-books-in-german. com/featur03.htm; Venkat B. Mani and Elke Segelcke, "Cosmopolitical and Transnational Interventions in German Studies," *Transit* 7, no. 1 (2011): 1–27.

[33] In their contributions to this volume, Katharina Gerstenberger, Anke Biendarra, and Maria Mayr will be following up on a critical discussion of existing scholarship on "transnational literature."

[34] See for example Eva Hausbacher, *Poetik der Migration: Transnationale Schreibweisen in der russischen zeitgenössischen Literatur* (Tübingen: Stauffenburg, 2009).

[35] In the introduction to her book *Die neue Weltliteratur und ihre großen Erzähler* (München: C. H. Beck, 2013), in which Sigrid Löffler introduces an "nichtwestliche Literatur, die von Migranten und Sprachenwechslern aus ehemaligen Kolonien und Krisenregionen geschrieben ist" (non-Western literature written by migrants and language switchers from former colonies and crisis regions, 8), the author significantly uses the word "transnational" only once (17) and continues to describe this type of literature elsewhere as "Migrationsliteratur."

[36] Karina Berger and Stuart Taberner, introduction to *Germans as Victims in the Literary Fiction of the Berlin Republic*, ed. Karina Berger and Stuart Taberner (Rochester, NY: Camden House, 2009), 1–14.

[37] Interview with Navid Kermani "Die Macht der Sprache: Der Schriftsteller und Publizist im Gespräch mit Klaus Hübner über sprachliche Heimat, Mehrsprachigkeit und 'literarische Patchwork-Identität,'" accessed May 4, 2014, http://www. goethe.de/lhr/prj/mac/msp/de2391179.htm.

[38] Herrmann, "Transnationale Literatur," 380–82.

[39] Dirk Göttsche, "Hans Christoph Buch's *Sansibar Blues* and the Fascination of Cross-Cultural Experience in Contemporary German Historical Novels about Colonialism," *German Life & Letters* 65, no. 1 (2012): 127.

[40] Matthias Rath, "On the Impossibility of Settling into the Foreign Arcadia," *International Journal for Literary Studies* 45, no. 2 (2010): 457.

[41] Karl Pellens et al., eds., *Historical Consciousness and History Teaching in a Globalizing Society* (Frankfurt am Main: Lang, 2001).

[42] Göttsche, "Hans Christoph Buch's," 134.

[43] Ilija Trojanow, *Komplot(t): Wie plant der Autor den perfekten Plot*, 10, http://www.ilija-trojanow.de/downloads/Komplott.pdf.

[44] David Damrosch, *Teaching World Literature* (New York: Modern Language Association, 2009), 5.

[45] For more on the term *foreignization* as a characteristic of a new type of world literature, see Elisabeth Herrmann and Chantal Wright. "Reconceptualising World Literature: A Platonic Dialogue between Literary and Translation Studies," in *Translation and Translating in German Studies: A Festschrift for Raleigh Whitinger*, ed. John L. Plews and Diana Spokiene (Waterloo: Wilfrid Laurier University Press, 2015). For a fruitful connection between literary and translation studies also Doris Bachmann-Medick, ed., *The Trans/National Study of Culture: A Translational Perspective* (Berlin: de Gruyter, 2014).

[46] In 2006, according to the *New York Times*, it was the second most frequently sold literary work in the world. Tom LeClair, "Geniuses at Work," *New York Times*, November 5, 2006. http://www.nytimes.com/2006/11/05/books/review/LeClair.t.html?_r=0.

[47] Karina von Tippelskirch, "Paradigms and Poetics in Daniel Kehlmann's *Measuring the World*," *Symposium: A Quarterly Journal in Modern Literatures* 63, no. 3 (2009): 194.

[48] Katharina Gerstenberger, "Historical Space: Daniel Kehlmann's *Die Vermessung der Welt* [Measuring the World, 2005]," in *Spatial Turns: Space, Place, and Mobility in German Literary and Visual Culture*, ed. Jaimey Fisher and Barbara Mennel (Amsterdam: Rodopi, 2010), 103.

[49] Alexander Honold, "Ankunft in der Weltliteratur: Abenteuerliche Geschichtsreisen mit Ilija Trojanow und Daniel Kehlmann," *Neue Rundschau* 1 (2007): 98.

[50] "Je dichter das so entstehende Netz, insbesondere im Roman, desto gelungener das Werk." Daniel Kehlmann, *Diese sehr ernsten Scherze: Poetikvorlesungen* (Göttingen: Wallstein, 2009), 19.

[51] Christian Döring, "Der schweizer Schriftsteller Christian Kracht?" *Schweizer Monat: Die Autorenzeitschrift für Politik, Wissenschaft und Kultur*, September 8 (2012), http://www.schweizermonat.ch/artikel/der-schweizer-schriftsteller-christian-kracht.

[52] Döring, "Der schweizer Schriftsteller."

[53] Claudia Breger, who also engages with Kracht's controversially received novel in her contribution to this volume, will offer a different reading of the text that strives to expose the alleged humor and postcolonial rhetoric that is used by the narrator as an expression of his mental attitude.

[54] Stuart Taberner, "Contemporary German-Language Fiction by Non-Minority Writers," *Seminar* 47, no. 5 (2011): 634.

[55] Taberner, "Contemporary German-Language Fiction," 634.

[56] Christian Kracht, *Imperium* (Köln: Kiepenheuer & Witsch, 2012), 18–19.

[57] See Breger's examination of Kracht's novel in this volume.

[58] As mentioned above, in this aspect my reading of Kracht's *Imperium* diverges from Claudia Breger's.

[59] The only legitimate exception would be authors with a Jewish background or descendants of a Holocaust victim, such as Edgar Hilsenrath, Henryk Broder, and Maxim Biller.

[60] For more details on this see Claudia Breger's chapter in this volume.

[61] Kracht, *Imperium*, 331.

[62] Döring, "Der schweizer Schriftsteller."

[63] Felicitas Hoppe, *Hoppe* (Frankfurt am Main: Fischer Taschenbuch, 2012), 266.

[64] Wikipedia contributors,"Felicitas Hoppe," in *Wikipedia, Die freie Enzyklopädie*, Bearbeitungsstand: November 2, 2014, 15:03 UTC, accessed April 2, 2014, http://de.wikipedia.org/wiki/Felicitas_Hoppe.

[65] Sonja Klocke, "Inventing a Transnational Biography," unpublished paper presented within the seminar "Transnationalism: Sexualities, Fantasies, and the World Beyond" at the Thirty-Seventh Annual Conference of the German Studies Association in Denver, October 2013.

[66] Hoppe, *Hoppe*, 36.

[67] Maxim Biller, "Letzte Ausfahrt Uckermark," *Die Zeit Online*, February 10, 2014, http://www.zeit.de/2014/09/deutsche-gegenwartsliteratur-maxim-biller.

[68] Biller, "Letzte Ausfahrt Uckermark."

[69] Ron Terpening, Review of *Pavel & I*, by Dan Vyleta, *Library Journal* 132, no. 20 (December 15, 2007): 1.

[70] For a detailed interpretation of *The Quiet Twin*, see Florentine Strzelczyk's article "Translating the Third Reich: *The Quiet Twin*" in *Festschrift for Raleigh Translation and Translating in German Studies: A Festschrift for Raleigh Whitinger*, ed. John L. Plews and Diana Spokiene (Waterloo: Wilfrid Laurier University Press, 2015).

[71] Strzelczyk, "Translating the Third Reich," 3.

[72] Here a reference can be made to Canadian author Joseph Boyden who has foregrounded the significance of various partial identities for the delineation of Canadian literature: "Native culture is what I'd call the first pillar of Canadian culture. My own theory is that four pillars exist in our country's foundation: the English, the French, the Contemporary Immigrant, and the First Nation." *Through Black Spruce* (Toronto: Penguin Canada, 2009), 415. This statement also confirms that language does not make a dependable identifier for national literature.

[73] Strzelczyk, "Translating the Third Reich," 3.

[74] See "Interview with Ilija Trojanow" in the appendix to this volume.

[75] Stuart Taberner will elaborate on this in the following chapter.

2: Transnationalism and Cosmopolitanism: Literary World-Building in the Twenty-First Century

Stuart Taberner

IT IS NO COINCIDENCE that the terms *transnationalism* and *cosmopolitanism* have become central to debates across the humanities and social sciences in recent years. Broadly speaking, transnationalism has typically been employed by social scientists exploring the intensification of migratory flows across borders that has characterized the era of globalization—and by literary and cultural-studies scholars interested in postcolonial and minority writing, hybridity, and deterritorialized identities—whereas cosmopolitanism has been favored by political scientists interested in the apparent weakening of the state system, and in global instability and insecurity, particularly after 9/11.[1] More recently, however, researchers from across all these fields have begun more explicitly to link the two terms.[2] Which challenges—and opportunities—does today's vastly intensified mobility of goods, people, and ideas across borders create in relation to the ideal of a unified humankind living in peace? In short, scholars have been searching for answers to the question of whether, as Victor Roudometof puts it, "transnationalism [may] lead to greater levels of cosmopolitanism?"[3]

In this chapter, I offer an overview of the way much of today's German-language literary fiction likewise links transnationalism and cosmopolitanism—of course in a less explicit, less programmatic, more allusive manner. In essence, my focus is on what might come *after* transnationalism, that is, on the utopian potential that is at least implicit in the erasure of boundaries that both contain and separate people. (If we accept that this is what is taking place. Many would argue that transnationalism simply means the unregulated flow of capital rather than progress toward a Kantian *Weltgemeinschaft*, or world society.) To this extent, transnationalism moves to the background of this chapter. Many German-language authors, I argue, are currently reflecting not only on how transnationalism has rendered borders both more and less significant—nations are more permeable and yet still regulate who and what may circulate—but also on the equally pressing question of *how* we can inhabit proximate but also worldly spaces simultaneously. As Maria Mayr, Anke Biendarra, Claudia Breger, Katharina Gerstenberger, and Christina Kraenzle will explore in subsequent chapters, with more detailed reference to individual texts than is possible in an overview chapter such as this, these writers are asking: How can we live with "others," both at home *and* globally?

Types of Cosmopolitanism

Pauline Kleingeld identifies six variants of eighteenth-century German thinking about cosmopolitanism that build on the ancient Cynics and Stoics and continue to inform debates today. These are cosmopolitan law, international federative cosmopolitanism, market cosmopolitanism, moral cosmopolitanism, cultural cosmopolitanism, and romantic cosmopolitanism.[4] Cosmopolitan law and international federative cosmopolitanism are primarily associated with Kant and his thinking about the relationship between states, the need for a league of peoples (Fichte and Schlegel are also referenced in this discussion), as well as *Weltbürgerrecht* (cosmopolitan right) and the duty to offer hospitality to strangers. Today, Jürgen Habermas's concept of "communicative reason" owes much to this tradition. Market cosmopolitanism, on the other hand, is concerned with the free movement of goods and trade around the globe. Here, Kleingeld mentions the long-forgotten German historian Dietrich Hermann Hegewisch. Moral cosmopolitanism is associated with the ancient Cynics and the Stoics, and it sets out that all human beings belong to a single moral community, regardless of race, nationality, or creed. Writing in the late seventeenth and early eighteenth century, the German Enlightenment thinker Christoph Martin Wieland is a proponent of this, and of the notion that we are all citizens of the world and duty-bound to eschew chauvinism. Today, the American philosopher Martha Nussbaum might be mentioned in this context, as might Kwame Anthony Appiah, although they also allow for the benefits of patriotism and "rootedness," respectively. Cultural cosmopolitanism, alternatively, is concerned less with the duty we owe to fellow humans beings as individuals than with respect for the diversity *and* particularity of cultures—key names are Georg Forster and Johann Gottfried von Herder. Finally, romantic cosmopolitanism— with Novalis an important eighteenth-century representative—emphasizes the spiritual connectedness of humans to one another, which can only be rediscovered and fostered through acts of the poetic imagination.

Political scientists tend to focus on the relevance of Kant for present-day debates on the possibility of a cosmopolitan global order in an era defined by connectivity, multipolarity, ethnic, religious, and ideological conflict, and sociologists typically reference cultural cosmopolitanism when discussing multiculturalism, assimilation, and integration. In contrast, writers—certainly in the German language—engage with all of the variants of cosmopolitan thinking outlined above, albeit in ways that are generally oblique rather than concrete, often blurred, and always aesthetic rather than analytical. In literary fiction, therefore—perhaps particularly in the German-speaking world, where "the nation" has always been fraught—the bewildering, brutal, or banal reality of present-day transnationalism may be pushing writers, two hundred years after the last flourishing of German cosmopolitan thinking when Europe and the world stood at the threshold of the first age of globalization,[5] to imagine what it might mean not only to cross borders but to transcend them.

Already in the early 1990s—in the midst of the wars in the ex-Yugoslavia, the genocide in Rwanda, and the upsurge in ethnic and religious conflict across the world—a significant strand of German-language writing was concerned (mostly in essay form) with rethinking Kantian notions of cosmopolitan law, universal reason, and the duty of hospitality. Hans Magnus Enzensberger's *Die Große Wanderung* (The Great Migration, 1992) and *Aussichten auf den Bürgerkrieg* (Prospects for Civil War, 1993), for example, focuses on the wars in the ex-Yugoslavia.[6] In *Ein hinreissender Schrotthändler* (An Enticing Scrap-Merchant, 1999), alternatively, the conservative author Arnold Stadler satirizes the way that the—to his mind—politically correct modern-day Federal Republic construes hospitality as a legalistic obligation to welcome all comers. In this novel, the narrator's wife answers the door to an asylum seeker fleeing the wars in the ex-Yugoslavia whereupon she "ließ sich am Tag der deutschen Einheit mehrfach von ihm durchficken" (allowed herself to be fucked by him, multiple times, on the Day of German Unity).[7] Stadler and other conservative writers defend a particularist attachment to a local or national *culture* against the anemic rationality of cosmopolitan law. Cosmopolitanism, for these authors, is located in the global spiritual communities we form with others through, for example, religious belief. After 9/11, which for many in the West announced the rise of "Islamicist fundamentalism," the Kantian vision of a global humanity united in a common capacity for reason has been much debated. Enzensberger's 2006 *Schreckens Männer: Versuch über den radikalen Verlierer* (Bogey Men: An Essay on the Radical Loser) turns to the causes of terrorist acts carried out by Muslims and may repeat the West's self-congratulatory mantra that the islamic world missed out on the Enlightenment,[8] whereas Navid Kermani's *Wer ist wir* (Who Is We?, 2010) argues that Muslims are entirely capable of enlightened tolerance, as do Zafer Senoçak's *Das Land hinter den Buchstaben: Deutschland und der Islam im Umbruch* (The Country behind the Letters: Germany and Islam in Transition, 2006) and his volume of essays *Deutschsein: Eine Aufklärungsschrift* (Being German: An Enlightenment Manifesto, 2011). Indeed, after 9/11 even Feridun Zaimoglu—once a fierce critic of the majority population's hypocrisy toward German-Turks—aligns himself with the "abendländisch inspirierten Humanisten"[9] (humanists inspired by Western values) that, in his early work, he had often derided. These words appear in his contribution to a 2011 volume of essays edited by Hilal Sezgin with the programmatic title *Manifest der Vielen: Deutschland erfindet sich neu* (Manifest of the Many: Germany Invents Itself Anew), alongside pieces by Ilija Trojanow, Navid Kermani, and a number of mainly Turkish-German academics, writers, journalists, and activists.

Recent "novels of lost? empire"[10]—Trojanow's *Der Weltensammler* (The Collector of Worlds, 2006), and Christian Kracht's *Ich werde hier sein im Sonnenschein und im Schatten* (I'll Be Here in Sunshine and in Shadow, 2008), and *Imperium* (Empire, 2011)—recall Kant's concern with the possibility of a federative cosmopolitanism and chime with our contemporary interest in the Age of Empire as an antecedent of today's multipolar world. As I will discuss toward the end of this chapter, this is not the only variety of cosmopolitan thought that these texts connect to, but a concern with states in the global system is a key theme here and in similar works.

A third strand of recent German-language writing sets itself against the market's radicalization in neoliberalism and against the reduction of cosmopolitanism to a borderless opportunity for profit-taking. Here, we might think of Christian Kracht's *Faserland* (Frayed-Land, 1995), which—among a plethora of other themes—takes aim at the reduction of human exchange to commerce. Or we might think of Sybille Berg's *Die Fahrt* (The Journey, 2007), whose German (and other) characters fail to find happiness anywhere in the globalized consumer society, or Katharina Hacker's *Die Habenichtse* (The Have-Nots, 2007), which juxtaposes the precarity of the post-9/11 world with the existential soullessness of its German protagonists' uprooted lives in London. In Stadler's *Eines Tages, vielleicht auch nachts* (One Day, or Perhaps Also at Nighttime, 2003), similarly, Cuba seems to present Franz, the novel's Austrian protagonist, with an opportunity to satisfy his "Sehnsucht nach einer anderen Welt als seiner" (desire for a world other than his), until it becomes clear that his interactions with the locals are only ever transactional and—even in communist Cuba—always predetermined by the inequalities of global-ized capitalism.[11] Finally, we might refer to Juli Zeh's *Adler und Engel* (Eagles and Angels, 2001; which is briefly discussed by Lars Richter later in this volume), or to "realist" engagements with transnationalism such as Julya Rabinowich's *Die Erdfresserin* (The Woman Who Eats Dirt, 2012; discussed by Maria Mayr in a subsequent chapter), which deal with cross-border prostitution and the trafficking of women. In these, and other similar texts, transnationalism *as* cosmopolitanism now simply means the homogenization of commodities, culture, and experiences within global-ized consumer capitalism.

In what remains of this chapter, I focus on echoes of moral, cul-tural, and romantic varieties of cosmopolitan thinking in four key literary works: Terézia Mora's *Alle Tage* (Day in, Day Out, 2004), Christa Wolf's *Stadt der Engel* (City of Angels, 2010), Feridun Zaimoglu's *Hinterland* (2009), and Ilija Trojanow's *Der Weltensammler* (The Collector of Worlds, 2006). These novels touch upon key themes—sexuality and contemporaneousness—that are introduced in my coeditors' overview chapters and explored further with detailed reference to particular texts in many of the contributions that follow. But they also, I hope, allow me to show the value of thinking transnationalism and cosmopolitanism *together* in exploring literary responses to what may be the key question of our age. To paraphrase Kwame Anthony Appiah: How can we live ethically "in a world of strangers?"

Moral Cosmopolitanism: Terézia Mora's *Alle Tage*

Moral cosmopolitanism begins from the simple premise that all of us, regardless of origins, ethnicity, or creed, form part of one human community, and that as such ill-treatment of one constitutes an ill-treatment of all. This premise is easily grasped, and moral cosmopolitanism is thus probably the most commonsensical, or intuitively "right," form of cosmopolitan thinking—this "rightness" (or even righteousness) may motivate texts by a number of contemporary German-language writers, including Norbert Gstrein, Lukas Bärfuss, Hans Christoph Buch, and Jeannette Lander, who have thematized human rights abuses around the world.[12] Indeed, moral cosmopolitanism may be emotionally satisfying, even as one of the effects of globalization has been the apparently greater demand of seeing repeated affronts to humankind's moral unity across multiple media platforms. At the same time, moral cosmopolitanism can also easily become purely rhetorical—outrage at injustices that take place far away—or it may disintegrate as we experience more intimate contact with those "others" who have crossed our borders as refugees, asylum seekers, or migrants.

In Terézia Mora's *Alle Tage*, Abel Nema arrives in B., a city in western Europe, as a refugee from S., a town in Eastern Europe. In B., Nema contacts his countryman Professor Tibor, who arranges for him to be given a stipend to study at university. A short time after his arrival, Nema is injured in a gas explosion, and once he regains consciousness he finds that he is able to learn new languages with a remarkable, even supernatural facility. He swiftly becomes proficient in ten different tongues and is subjected to experiments conducted by academics who wish to understand the structure of his brain. Subsequently, he marries Mercedes in order to regularize his residence in B., and is then divorced from her. In addition, he is befriended and later rejected by Konstantin, a fellow immigrant; mothered and sexually harassed by Kinga, who offers him space in a block inhabited by the undocumented masses nicknamed the Bastille;

and beaten up by a gang of youths led by the allusively and ironically named Cosma. (*Cosmos*, as readers might recognize, is the ancient Greek word for "of the world" and also the root of the word "cosmopolitan"). Toward the end of the novel, Nema awakens from a loss of consciousness induced by the beating and—having lost his amazing linguistic skills—settles down to live a "normal" life with Mercedes and his stepson Omar.

Abel Nema is the embodiment of the *conditionality* of hospitality. He is no longer secure at home—he flees in order to avoid military service in the wars about to erupt between his newly independent state and its neighbors—but neither is he allowed to settle elsewhere on his own terms. One of the novel's key motifs is the railway station and railway tracks—Nema never circulates far beyond the means of his arrival and the most likely manner of his deportation. Indeed, he is marginalized and assaulted, and he is only permitted to establish a "*bürgerliches* Leben" in the *polis* of B. (*bourgeois* existence;[13] implying the rights of citizenship but also a mundane conformity) when, as a consequence of his beating, a form of aphasia causes his language to become entirely functional (*AT*, 427–28). Nema is only acceptable to his hosts as the guest whose impoverished—"migrant"—language allows them to feel secure in their stereotyping of him as ignorant or gratifyingly deferential.

Nema's "otherness" and his sexuality are linked in complicated ways. The other characters' efforts to define him as homosexual—as a "Schwuler" (*AT*, 301; homo), "Arschkrampe" (*AT*, 186; cocksucker), "Arschficker!" (*AT*, 217; assfucker)—most likely demonstrate a need to denigrate but also *fix* him. The focus on his sexuality is one way of making him knowable, and thus of controlling him. Yet while it seems that Nema most likely *is* gay, the other characters' urge to categorize him cannot be fully satisfied by this simplistic definition. Nema exerts an attraction that *neither* sex can resist. After he signs the papers for his divorce, both Mercedes and her female lawyer fall into step with him on leaving the courthouse (*AT*, 79). Kinga regularly fondles him. And violence inflicted upon him by Erik, the gang led by Cosma—including Danko, with whom he has an unconsummated sexual relationship—and other male characters, most likely points not only to jealousy or homophobic disgust but also to the detested and repressed desire they feel for him.

Abel Nema is therefore not only *fremd* (strange)—he is "queer."[14] He is "ein seltsamer Zwitter" (a strange hermaphrodite), Mercedes suggests, who appears "kein bestimmtes Geschlecht mehr zu haben" (*AT*, 328; no longer to have a specific sex). Certainly, insofar as Nema seems to manifest what Joseph Vogl calls the "sex without place,"[15] his hermaphroditism might connote his status as an exemplary *trans*national subject. His *unnatural* grasp of languages not only facilitates his (unregulated) intercourse with natives and (all manner of) foreigners alike, it is also a marker of his own lack of place and his undermining of the conventional association of culture with rootedness: "Deswegen ist alles, was er sagt, so, wie soll ich sagen, ohne *Ort*, so klar, wie man es noch nie gehört hat, kein Akzent, kein Dialekt, nichts—er spricht wie einer, der nirgends herkommt" (*AT*, 13; that's why everything he says is so, how shall I put it, *placeless*, so uniquely clear—no accent, no dialect, nothing: he speaks like a person who comes from nowhere). Nema not only cuts across normative categories of sexuality but also of nation—what Carrie Smith-Prei, following Puar, specifies in her chapter in the present volume as homonationalism.[16] This is surely the reason that the "natives" *and* his fellow refugees punish him. He fails to observe the conventions of inclusion and exclusion by which both groups define themselves.

In the last pages of *Alle Tage*, Nema's stepson Omar—born of a European mother and an African father—emerges as a potential new transnational subject. His name, like Nema's, is allusive and multivalent. (Abel's first name recalls the biblical Abel who was killed by his older brother Cain; his second name not only connotes Nemo, or "nobody," but also echoes the Slav words for "mute foreigners" and "barbarians" [*AT*, 14]). In Arabic, Omar's name means "Lösung, Mittel, Ausweg" (*AT*, 166; solution, means, exit); and its first syllable (Om) recalls the "heilige Silbe" (*AT*, 167–68; sacred syllable) of Hinduism, mystically embodying in its incantation the essence of the entire universe.[17] And, as significant, the text concludes with a description of how he is coming to exert the same ambivalent fascination for natives and migrants in equal measure:

> Die Schönheit, die aus seinem perfekten Gesicht und seinem gesamten Körper, auch aus den unsichtbaren, von Kleidung verdeckten Teilen strahlt, ist so überwältigend, dass geschlossene Räume, Metrowagen, kleine Geschäfte vollständig verstummen können, wenn er in ihnen anwesend ist, aber auch unter freiem Himmel verdrehen Frauen und empfängliche Männer schmerzhaft die Augen, um ihn verstohlen zu mustern. (*AT*, 429–30)

> [The beauty streaming from his perfect face and entire body, even the invisible parts hidden by clothing, is so overpowering that closed rooms, metro trains, and small shops can fall silent when he enters, and, even outdoors, women and sensitive men will twist their eyes painfully to take furtive glances at him.]

Like Nema, Omar promises a transcendence of borders and boundaries. Yet the *moral* ideal of a unified humanity—or Om—that his perfect beauty appears to embody may also, again like Nema, be just a little too "queer." Cosmopolitanism, Mora's *Alle Tage* seems to suggest, is certainly a compelling abstraction. But it may also be too "exotic" for the majority of citizens—and even for those excluded from citizenship—to tolerate in *reality*.

Cultural Cosmopolitanism:
Christa Wolf's *Stadt der Engel*

Cultural cosmopolitanism may be most closely associated with the vigorous recent debates on multiculturalism across Western societies, especially post-9/11—including in Germany, where in 2010, Angela Merkel famously declared that that "Multikulti" (multiculturalism) was "gescheitert, absolut gescheitert" (failed, absolutely failed). Cultural cosmopolitanism, then, emphasizes the diversity of different cultures and the right of each to be equally respected. And it is here that the terms transnationalism and cosmopolitanism most often coincide within literary studies. Gerard Delanty speaks of the "cosmopolitan turn in postcolonial studies" in particular, where scholars such as James Clifford, Sheldon Pollock, Homi Bhabha, Carol Breckenridge, Dipesh Chakrabarty, and Pheng Cheah have explored "discrepant" (Clifford) or "vernacular" cosmopolitanism (Bhabha), that is, the "worldliness" or "Weltbewanderheit" of minority, migrant, or once colonized cultures as they travel from place to place.[18]

In contemporary German-language literature, cultural cosmopolitanism is invoked across a range of texts thematizing a range of issues. On the one hand, we have texts such as Maxim Biller's *Esra* (2003), Vladimir Vertlib's *Am Morgen des zwölften Tages* (On the Morning of the Twelfth Day, 2009), and Navid Kermani's *Die Kurzmitteilung* (The Memo, 2007), which—post-9/11—examine how Christians and Muslims (and Jews) might learn to respect each other's cultures. Already in 1999, Martin Mosebach's *Die Türkin* (The Turkish Woman) takes its protagonist to Anatolia to retrace the ancient encounter of Greek and Oriental, then Christian and Muslim cultures. Fellow conservative writer Arnold Stadler's 2002 volume *Tohuwabohu: Heiliges und Profanes gelesen und wiedergelesen von Arnold Stadler nach dem 11. September 2001 und darüber hinaus* (Chaos: Sacred and Profane Read and Re-Read by Arnold Stadler after September 11, 2001) juxtaposes extracts by writers of Jewish, Christian, and Muslim origins. On the other hand, we have a variety of works featuring global travel. These include "pop" works such as Judith Hermann's collection of short stories *Nichts als Gespenster* (Nothing but Ghosts, 2003), whose young German protagonists struggle to feel "at home" in the global destinations to which they travel,[19] and Yadé Kara's *Café Cyprus* (2008), which sends its Turkish-German protagonist to London to experience what sociologist Steven Vertovec calls superdiversity and a kind of supermulticulturalism. They also include docufictions and travelogues exploring conflicts around the world. Here, we might think of Hans Christoph Buch's Haiti trilogy or his "African" books (e.g., *Sansibar Blues*, 2009), Urs Widmer's *Im Kongo* (In the Congo, 1996), and Bodo Kirchhoff's book on Somalia *Herrenmenschlichkeit* (Master

Humanity, 1994), which build on a well-established tradition of German writers globe-trotting in solidarity with the "Third World."[20] Likewise, Navid Kermani's travel reports *Ausnahmezustand* (State of Emergency, 2013) reveal a "Welt im Aufruhr" (world in revolt; from the cover of the hardback edition) across the Middle East, the Indian subcontinent, and Afghanistan, whereas Trojanow's *Nomade auf vier Kontinenten* (Nomad on Four Continents, 2008) and *An den inneren Ufern Indiens* (Along the Inner Banks of India, 2003) sets cultural clashes in global hot spots in a historical perspective. (Christina Kraenzle examines Trojanow's travel-logues elsewhere in this volume.)

Other writers are concerned not only with the way *people* travel but also—calling to mind scholarly debates on the transnational circulation of cultures and on "world literature"—with the way *cultures* travel. Daniel Kehlmann's *Die Vermessung der Welt* (Measuring the World, 2005; discussed by my coeditor Elisabeth Herrmann in this volume), for example, self-consciously styles itself as a paradox within the global circulation of cultures. The novel positions itself to travel transnationally by adopting an "international" aesthetic that erases its German origins while also, covertly, expressing nostalgia for this loss of cultural particularity and despair at the way its German subject matter has to be "bent" to conform to "cosmopolitan norms." "Queer" is again a key topos, here related to the marketing of "otherness." Speaking with Graham Huggan, we might even describe German culture in this context as a "postcolonial exotic."[21] Similarly, Felicitas Hoppe's *Hoppe* (2012, also examined in detail by Herrmann) undercuts both the cosmopolitan and the transnational ideal that its protagonist seems to achieve. Hoppe's fictional alter ego—who invents an alternative biography for the author—travels freely around the world, making friends wherever she goes, but must accept the reduction of German culture to a marketing label, a folk festival, or a fairy tale.[22]

Sociologist Ulf Hannerz asserts that cultural cosmopolitanism generally entails "an orientation, a willingness to engage with the other . . . intellectual and aesthetic openness towards divergent cultural experiences, a search for contrasts rather than uniformity."[23] And this is certainly true of Christa Wolf's *Stadt der Engel* (City of Angels, 2010), which relates the author's period of residence as a visiting scholar at the Getty Research Institute in Los Angeles (the City of Angels) from September 1992 to May 1993. Not only does the (explicitly autobiographical) text depict Wolf's receptiveness toward the variety of other cultures that she encounters in Los Angeles, including the young Europeans and Americans who are her peers at the institute; Peter Gutman, the son of Jewish refugees from Germany who becomes her close friend; Jewish survivors and the children of survivors; the Hopis and Navajos she meets on the reservations of the Great American Desert; and, last but certainly not least, Angelina, the African-American woman who becomes, somewhat whimsically, her "black angel."[24] The novel's narrative technique also embodies and displays what we might think of as a "cosmopolitan aesthetic." *Stadt der Engel* is highly discursive, personal and even intimate, and more often than not conversational in its implied address to the reader as confidant, all within an "open" narrative framework that, to cite Michael Minden, is defined by a "loosely plotted, if not plotless, prose manner."[25]

Cultural cosmopolitanism—revealing its debt to Herder—requires respect not only for the diversity of all cultures but also for the particularity of individual cultures. (As Richard White points out, Herder can be seen as a champion of both nationalism and multiculturalism.)[26] Certainly, Wolf's embrace of the "otherness" that she encounters in Los Angeles simultaneously implies the right of German culture to be acknowledged within the diversity of world cultures. But—as in Kehlmann's *Die Vermessung der Welt*, Kracht's *Imperium*, Hoppe's *Hoppe*, and other texts too—the question arises as to which German culture.[27] Wolf's personal implication in the disasters of twentieth-century German history and their consequences thus determines the novel's primary storyline. We read, then, of the author's adolescence in National Socialism, the Holocaust, her family's expulsion by the Red Army, youthful political idealism, uneasy compromises with the communist authorities in East Germany, and post-1989 revelations of her brief involvement with the Stasi and subsequent persecution in the media. But narrated in parallel to, and also intertwined with her own biography is the story of the Germany that could have been: the Weimar modernism that was uprooted by the Nazis and relocated on the West Coast of the United States.[28] In Los Angeles, Wolf retraces the steps—and recreates the aesthetic—of the German and especially German-Jewish exiles who, for her, embody the "better Germany": Brecht, Döblin, Marcuse, Zuckmayer, Feuchtwanger, Remarque, Eisler, Schönberg, Werfel, Leonard Frank, Heinrich and Thomas Mann, Adorno, and especially the much less well known Salka Viertel, the woman writer, who created a latter-day "Jewish salon"[29] in Los Angeles, consciously or unconsciously modeled on the Berlin salons hosted by women such as Rahel Levin Varnhagen and Henriette Herz in the romantic period. In particular, Wolf's inclusion of the stories of Jewish émigrés, of their children and grandchildren, some of whom Wolf befriended in California, and of friendships between non-Jews and Jews—including Wolf's own attachment to the East German writer Anna Seghers and the pioneering Jewish lesbian feminist psychotherapist Charlotte Wolff—suggest the possibility of a truly cosmopolitan German tradition that can be counted as an equal among world cultures.

At the same time, the particular form of cultural cosmopolitanism that Wolf imagines in *Stadt der Engel*—and specifically its rehabilitation of a German culture that is ultimately rooted in ethnicity—may reinscribe the very same myopia that marks the Federal Republic today. It is true that Wolf's close friendship with Peter Gutman reimagines the famed (but always fragile) German-Jewish symbiosis, but her invention of this character—among her peers at the institute, he alone is not based on a real-life character—may also imply the exclusion of other "others" (notably Muslims) from Germany's self-understanding. As Elisabeth Herrmann discusses in her chapter in this volume, the horrors of the German past—including the Holocaust—may paradoxically restate the ethnic basis of presumptions about who does, and does not, belong. Even as other cultures merit respect, they may also become irretrievably "other." They may become as exotic as the Hopis and Navajos, whose "simple," "premodern" lives fascinate Wolf, or as outlandish as Angelina, the black angel whose laconic serenity both reassures and elevates the anxiously "European" author.

Romantic Cosmopolitanism: Feridun Zaimoglu's *Hinterland*

In her essay on Novalis's controversial treatise "Christianity or Europe" (1799), Pauline Kleingeld usefully reminds us that German romanticism, typically seen as the antithesis of the Enlightenment, in fact endorses many of its ideals, namely "individuality, freedom, anti-authoritarianism, and equality." Romanticism's critique of the Enlightenment, Kleingeld goes on to argue, lies not in its rejection of these fundamental principles, but in its assertion that Enlightenment thinking has "degraded these very ideals to atomistic individualism, rootlessness, self-interestedness, and abstract legalism." For the romantics, in summary, the Enlightenment failed to appreciate "the most essential components of truly human life: love, emotional bonds, beauty, shared faith, and mutual trust."[30]

Although commonly associated with nationalism—the rejection of a Kantian emphasis on universal reason and an emphasis on the individual's emotional attachment to particularity—romanticism, Kleingeld argues, may nonetheless also propagate its own version of cosmopolitanism. Romantic cosmopolitanism, in essence, suggests the *emotional* connectedness of all humankind, and our common capacity for spirituality, aesthetic creativity and appreciation, and love. Even within our particularities, therefore, we are bonded together by our emotional and spiritual vulnerability as human beings.

Kleingeld's rethinking of romanticism's relationship to the Enlightenment and to cosmopolitan ideals offers a useful way of considering the resurgence in romantic motifs in German-language literature since at least the early 1990s, particularly among conservative authors, such as Martin Walser, Arnold Stadler, and Martin Mosebach. While it is true that these writers focus on *German* culture to an extent that is certainly unusual—and, for many commentators, highly provocative—in postwar German-language literature, it has been less well appreciated that they frequently root this celebration of particularity within an emphasis on *cosmopolitan* attachments and loyalties. Mosebach's novels, for example, stress the universality of the Catholic liturgy and the attachment it fosters between believers. Stadler, similarly—if more playfully—recalls Christianity's reiteration of a single humanity joined together in the hope of redemption, for example in *Komm, wir gehen* (Come, Let's Go, 2008) and *Salvatore* (2008), both of which allude to Matthew's gospel of mercy.[31] (Stadler also identifies universal values of love and mercy in Judaism and Islam, as mentioned above.) And, in his strikingly idiosyncratic old-age work *Muttersohn* (Mother's Boy, 2011), Walser imagines an Augustinian "City of God" that is held together not by an attachment to nation or national culture but by a shared religiosity and a cosmopolitan commitment to the acknowledgment of others' pain, existential inadequacy, and psychic vulnerability.[32]

A romantic cosmopolitanism also features in a series of novels by a quite different set of authors, namely so-called minority writers. In Maxim Biller's *Esra*, for instance, cultural cosmopolitanism blurs into romantic cosmopolitanism as a celebration of the material *diversity* of cultures coexists with a neoromantic belief in their spiritual oneness, or at least underlying complementarity. In this novel, Germans (Christians), Jews, and Muslims are bound together by history, travel, tradition, and love.[33] And in Zafer Şenocak's work, especially *Gefährliche Verwandtschaft* (Dangerous Relations, 1998) and *Der Erottomane* (The Erot[t]omaniac, 1999), the romantic motif of "affinities" connects protagonists across time, place, and nation.[34] (Wolf's *Stadt der Engel* may also blur into a romantic cosmopolitanism. At the close of the novel, the protagonist soars to the skies, accompanied by her black angel, and reconnects with nature, humanity, and her own idealism.)

Feridun Zaimoglu's recent novels engage particularly insistently with German romanticism.[35] Thus *Rom intensiv* (Rome Intensively, 2007) recalls a tradition of German artistic fascination with that city that reaches back to Goethe's *Italienische Reise* (Italian Journey, 1816–17) and *Römische Elegien* (Roman Elegies, 1788–90).[36] The epistolary form of *Liebesmale, scharlachrot* (Love Bites, Scarlet, 2000), and what Michael Hoffmann calls its "sublimated Romanticism,"[37] alludes to Goethe's *Die Leiden des Jungen Werther* (The Sorrows of Young Werther, 1774) and Hölderlin's *Hyperion* (1797–99), just as *Liebesbrand* (Blazing Love, 2008), *Hinterland* (2009), and *Ruß* (Soot, 2011) contain a series of recognizably Romantic motifs: unpredictable passions, folk mythology; forests, mountains, and islands; and rebellion against rationalism and conformity.[38] In *German Amok* (2002), similarly, a neoromantic Turkish-German "poéte maudit"[39] vacillates between a liberating aesthetic amorality and a lingering sense of his responsibility to expose social injustice.

Zaimoglu's *Hinterland* (2009) may be the most interesting of these works in the present context, to the extent that it was written following the author's receipt of a grant in 2008 from the Robert Bosch Foundation under its *Grenzgänger* (border crossers) program.[40] This funding is designed to assist writers to travel transnationally, that is across national frontiers, particularly in Central and Eastern Europe, and to prepare publications that "inspire discussion and promote dialog and mutual understanding."[41] Zaimoglu spent time in Prague, Poland (Poznan, Warsaw, and Krakow), Budapest, and Lake Balaton, but endeavored *not* to give up his "status as a tourist"—he styles himself as an anthropologist of sorts tangled up in "strange stories" and "small wonders." In each of these places, he discovered "German-speaking locals" ready to welcome him in his own language. Traveling abroad, the Turkish-German author—to his hosts as to himself—now appears to be simply a "German."[42]

Something of the genesis of the novel as a commissioned work written in fulfilment of its author's remit to "cross borders" may be evident in its highly contrived, often convoluted, "transnational" plot. Indeed, few of the novel's characters are fixed to one place only. Ferda, the novel's protagonist and its author's alter ego, travels restlessly between Berlin, Prague, Budapest, and Istanbul, meeting a variety of (to him) eccentric strangers and experiencing "strange stories" and "small wonders" while pining for Aneschka, his Czech girlfriend, who moves back and forth between the German capital, where she lives, and Prague. Indeed, the story of their yearning for one another across borders, and of the affective power of love, both drives the plot—to the extent that we can speak of a plot in this disconnected, largely formless work—and recapitulates, as it were, the longing and sense of displacement that motivate the peregrinations of the novel's many other characters.

A significant aspect of the novel's formal and narrative complexity is the way transnationalism is "written into" the (far) longer history of empire, conquest, colonization, and collapse. The historical traumas that have shaped Central and Eastern Europe—ethnic conflict, warfare, and expulsion, the Soviet and Nazi empires—as much as the Ottoman, and post-Ottoman domain of South-East Europe and Asia Minor, thus define the characters, frequently refugees, expellees, or migrants, who are dispersed across the novel's locations. At the same time, the (seemingly) universal experience of trauma appears to open up the possibility of a reanimated emotional connection between individuals. Certainly, Ferda—"der Fremde" (the stranger)[43]—is afforded hospitality more or less everywhere he travels, and almost all of the novel's extensive cast of minor characters similarly offer and receive from one another the most spontaneous welcomes, the most unexpected affinities, and the most improbable love affairs.

In Zaimoglu's *Hinterland*, romantic cosmopolitanism—a web of felt affinities also invoked by the novel's references to the moss damsels, elves, and pixies that populate the mythologies spanning Europe and Asia Minor—is reinvented as what postcolonialist theorist James Clifford defines as a *discrepant* cosmopolitanism,[44] Bonaventura de Sousa Santos as "subaltern cosmopolitanism,"[45] or Stuart Hall as "vernacular cosmopolitanism."[46] Minor characters, marginalized by history or colonized by the empires aspiring toward world domination (and, more recently, neoliberalism), connect with one another across the borders that divide them and fashion from their narratives a vision of a *transnational* solidarity. Indeed, the novel's title invokes something of this postcolonial, transnational shared affinity. Germany is the "Land hinter den Sieben Bergen" (land behind the seven mountains, as suggested by the novel's title *Hinterland*), always a provincial hinterland even as it has traditionally dominated its nearest neighbors.

Kleingeld's efforts to move beyond the common association of German romanticism with nationalism to define a romantic version of cosmopolitanism are welcome. Nonetheless, it remains the case that, in romantically tinged texts both past and present, nationalism and cosmopolitanism generally coexist awkwardly with one another. This is also true of *Hinterland*. As the novel progresses, Ferda becomes increasingly (content to be) defined as "Der Deutsche" (*H*, 98–99, 111, 112, 120, 125, 133, 168, 329, 350, 429–30; The German), and he decisively rebuffs the "queerness" that, here as in other contemporary novels, often functions as a metaphor for border crossing and the destabilization of national entities. For example, he can hardly resist his urge to strike the "Fraumann" (woman-man) Tööö: "Ich bin keiner von deiner Sorte" (*H*, 253; I am not one of your kind). And, although he can just about *tolerate* Tunk, a mythical "Zwitterwesen" (*H*, 47; hermaphrodite), he has no desire to himself be so "unplaceable." Insofar as it exoticizes the *particular* in both what "belongs" to me and what belongs to "otherness," even a cosmopolitanally inclined romanticism may simply reinscribe boundaries.

A "Kynical" Cosmopolitanism?: Ilija Trojanow's *Der Weltensammler*

In the interview that appears in the appendix to this volume, Bulgarian-German author Ilija Trojanow states that he prefers the term *cosmopolitanism* to *transnationalism*. And it is certainly true, as Trojanow points out, that *transnationalism* has "a very formal ring," being suggestive of "the state" and of the bureaucracy of border crossing and settlement, whereas *cosmopolitanism* "includes also an ideal."[47] Yet it may be that, under present-day global conditions, the one term cannot be thought without the other. Intensified mobility and intensified encounter with the other create both the aspiration toward cosmopolitanism and the anxieties that cause individuals to fear a world without borders. In each of the texts I have examined, therefore, transnationalism not only opens up the possibility of inhabiting proximate and worldly spaces simultaneously. It also amplifies the tension between particularity and universality that resides within—and disturbs—cosmopolitan thinking, of whatever kind. Whether we are speaking of moral cosmopolitanism and Mora's *Alle Tage*, cultural cosmopolitanism and Wolf's *Stadt der Engel*, or romantic cosmopolitanism and Zaimoglu's *Hinterland*—the distinctions between variants of cosmopolitan thinking in any case blur in these novels, as elsewhere—the *nation* reasserts itself time and again to interrupt, or even block, the transnational flows, encounters, and affinities the texts depict.

Christian Kracht's *Imperium*, which is discussed in detail in this volume by Elisabeth Herrmann and Claudia Breger, may offer a melancholically resigned reflection on this tension between the continued, even amplified significance of the nation in the context of contemporary trans*nationalism* and the ideal of cosmopolitanism. In Kracht's novel, August Engelhardt's initially idealistic, late-romantic cosmopolitanism, which is inspired by the *Lebensreformbewegung* (life reform movement) of the late nineteenth and early twentieth centuries, ultimately and seemingly inexorably collapses back into particularism and, in Kracht's version of history, into Hitler's anti-Semitic reactionary nationalism.

The ancient Cynics—if we recall Diogenes's assertion: "I am a citizen of the world (*cosmopolites*)"—defined cosmopolitanism as precisely the most radical repudiation of the *polis*, that is, the city, the state, or (in modern terms), the nation. Imagining a truly global coexistence, therefore, may require a different—but perhaps also more original—kind of cosmopolitan thinking. This would be a *Cynical* cosmopolitanism (named by Gilbert Leung as a *Kynical* cosmopolitanism)[48] that sustains an ironic distance from *all* particularist claims and a posture that, following Rosi Braidotti, may best be described as a kind of *nomadic ethics*, that is, a noncolonizing openness to otherness that grasps that, for the other, I too am also always other.[49] As postcolonial theorist Costas Douzinas puts it, the fact that "the other is never fully present to me"[50] is a starting point of cosmopolitan engagement rather than its end, just as for Gayatri Spivak "alterity contains us as much as it flings us away."[51]

In *Der Weltensammler*, Trojanow recounts the story of the nineteenth-century British military officer and explorer Sir Richard Francis Burton as he travels between India, the Arabian peninsula, and East Africa, absorbing—occasionally colonizing—and reproducing local customs and cultures within a narrative framework which itself brings different traditions, and voices, into a kind of transnational dialogue—or rather multilogue—with one another. Julian Preece argues that the novel presents an "account of intercultural failure,"[52] and sly allusions to our contemporary "clash of civilizations," "the war on terror," "extraordinary rendition," and state-sanctioned torture might imply a rather pessimistic assessment of the actual operations of transnationalism in the present day too. Indeed, Trojanow is neither unaware of, nor disengaged from the debate on the way nation-states have drained the cosmopolitan promise inherent within today's transnational flows. In 2013, the author was barred from the United States, quite possibly as a consequence of his outspoken views on the National Security Agency's electronic surveillance operations.[53]

Yet the point of *Der Weltensammler* may be precisely that the attempt to *know* the other is—at best—always doomed to fail, and, at worst, to replicate a form of colonialism that masks itself as enlightened but which always remains exploitative. As the British explorer, professional soldier, and servant of the empire Sir Richard Francis Burton moves from India to Arabia to East Africa, his no doubt genuine curiosity drives him first to attempt to "pass" as a "native," then to try to "become" one—he undertakes the Hajj as a Muslim[54]—and, following the failure of these efforts to morph into a different body, simply to dominate the otherness that he cannot physically assimilate. Ultimately, Burton's lack of irony—in relation to his quest to know the other, and his sense of cultural superiority—means that he cannot step outside of his prejudices in order to share a common world with others.

In *Der Weltensammler*, a more genuine cultural exchange is fostered by the novel's ostensibly secondary characters who relate, from their subaltern perspectives, Burton's in the end quite clumsy attempts to dissolve their unknowability and, often to great comic effect, the misunderstandings, missteps, and missed opportunities that complicate our efforts to engage the "other." This is not to say that the novel sets up a simplistic dichotomy between "good" colonials and "bad" colonizers. Burton's Indian servant Naukaram, for example, desires to "know" Kundalini, Burton's unknowable mistress, and to penetrate her womanly otherness as much as the British officer does. It simply means that these "minor" figures on the world stage understand—much better than Burton—that history is not made only by one side or the other; and that the world is a discursive construction emerging from the narratives that circulate between us. Naukaram's account of Burton, as much as the chronicle developed by the Ottoman rulers of the Arabian peninsula in part 2 of the novel, or by Sidi Mubarak Bombay in part 3, tell of the conversations between cultures, and of the world that these (multiple, multilogic) conversations construct precisely through the dialectic of sameness and difference. Irony is the lubrication for this negotiation of familiarity and unknowability, universality and particularity. As Sidi Mubarak Bombay, formerly a slave of the Arabian traders marauding through the African interior and now Burton's factotum in East Africa, puts it, "die Wazungu wollen für jedes Ding nur einen Namen gelten lassen, sie sind verstockt wie Esel, sie wollen nicht die vielen verschiedenen Namen akzeptieren, die ein Ort haben kann" (the wazungu [foreigners] would only accept one name for everything: they are stubborn as mules, and won't tolerate the different names a place can have).[55] Bombay, unlike Burton and his Arab and Ottoman colonizer counterparts, knows that "the world of things"[56] that exists between nations, societies, and communities is created in common, in conflict and in cooperation, and can thus belong to no one *in particular*.

World-Building: Transnationalism and the Future of German-Language Literature

Trojanow's *Der Weltensammler* is self-evidently about nations. Set in the age of empire, it portrays Britain's aspiration toward hegemony over "the Orient," but it also anticipates the emergence of new nations across the Indian subcontinent, the Arabian peninsula, and East Africa in our postcolonial present. And it is also self-evidently about *trans*nationalism. People and cultures circulate back and forth across the borders imposed by colonial (and subsequent) dispensations, disrupting attempts to categorize and regulate them.

At the same time, in its insistence upon a degree of ironic detachment from both the self and the other, Trojanow's novel may elaborate a variant of cosmopolitanism that is strikingly absent in the other texts examined in this chapter, and indeed noticeably rare in contemporary German-language literature as a whole. This *kynical* cosmopolitanism acknowledges origins, particularities, and specificities. But it does see these as givens that are to be reconciled with the duty of hospitality (moral cosmopolitanism), or defined—and defended—within the diversity of other cultures (cultural cosmopolitanism), or restated within the affinities and attachments that arise spontaneously between individuals (romantic cosmopolitanism). Nor does it presume that living together would become unproblematic if only we *knew* each other fully. Rather, it views particularity as the source of the productive *unknowability* that, counterintuitively, may make possible a genuine cosmopolitanism. The encounter with others alienates me from myself—if I choose to embrace rather than resist this—and positions me as a stranger (to myself too) among strangers. In a similar spirit, cultural theorist Paul Gilroy speaks of "a carefully cultivated degree of estrangement."[57] Such ironic self-detachment on all sides may open up a space for conversations shaped by a (shared) self-relativizing understanding that a world is only ever made in common with others whose customs and practices are as unfamiliar to me as mine are to them.

Hannah Arendt calls this *world-building*—a recognition that the world is a shared endeavor (a "fabrication of human hands"), and that this shared endeavor requires not the elimination of difference but a willingness to engage others in the "in-between that relates and separates men at the same time."[58] For Arendt, in fact, men (and women) "make their appearance in the human world" through "acting and speaking."[59] (William Smith notes Arendt's emphasis on *theatricality* or *performance*).[60] Motivated by our shared passion for the world—our "*amor mundi*," to use Arendt's alternative title for her *Human Condition* (1958)—we present ourselves in ways that stylize our distance, from ourselves and others, precisely so that we can approach one another as equal partners in world-building.

Trojanow's *Der Weltensammler*, we might argue, stands out precisely for its investment in world-building. In contrast to the large majority of other recent German-language novels thematizing transnationalism, the novel is not simply concerned with redefining the relationship between the (German or any other) nation and the world. Instead, it imagines a cosmopolitanism to be realized *through* the everyday reality of transnationalism but existing *beyond* the nation. This is a kind of *worldliness* that may have been missing in modern German-language writing, certainly during the long decades of its postwar introspection, and perhaps still even today. It remains to be seen whether, in the near future, we will see more novels in German in the style of Trojanow's *Der Weltensammler*—novels with a truly global compass, and a truly global ambition.

Notes

[1] As just one of many examples, see David Held, "Cosmopolitanism after 9/11," *International Politics* 47, no. 1 (2010): 52–61.

[2] In literary studies, see for example Sheldon Pollock et al., "Cosmopolitanisms," special issue, *Public Culture* 12, no. 3 (2000).

[3] Victor Roudometof, "Transnationalism, Cosmopolitanism and Glocalization," *Current Sociology* 53, no. 1 (2005): 113–35.

[4] Pauline Kleingeld, "Six Varieties of Cosmopolitanism in Late Eighteenth-Century Germany," *Journal of the History of Ideas* 60 (1999): 505–24.

[5] For a lucid and engaging account of nineteenth-century globalization as a precursor to globalization today, see Jürgen Osterhammel, *The Transformation of the World: A Global History of the Nineteenth Century* (Princeton, NJ: Princeton University Press, 2014).

[6] For a comprehensive account of German writers' postunification engagement with the outbreak of ethnic conflict across the globe, see Paul Michael Lützeler, *Bürgerkrieg Global* (München: Wilhelm Fink, 2009).

[7] Arnold Stadler, *Ein hinreissender Schrotthändler* (Köln: DuMont, 1999), 228.

[8] Monika Shafi, "The Lure of the Loser: On Hans Magnus Enzensberger's *Schreckens Männer* and Ian Buruma's *Murder in Amsterdam*," in *Encounters with Islam in German Literature and Culture*, ed. James Hodkinson and Jeffrey Morrison (Rochester, NY: Camden House, 2009), 247–58.

[9] Feridun Zaimoglu, "Es tobt in Deutschland ein Kulturkampf," in *Manifest der Vielen: Deutschland erfindet sich neu*, ed. Hilal Sezgin (Berlin: Blumenbar, 2011), 11.

[10] As Jörn Leonard and Rolf Renner put it, "Empires are in." Jörn Leonard and Rolf G. Renner, "Koloniale, Vergangenheiten (post-)imperiale Gegenwart: Prozesse und Repräsentationen im Umriss," in *Koloniale, Vergangenheiten—(post-)imperiale Gegenwart*, ed. Jörn Leonard and Rolf G. Renner (Berlin: Berliner Wissenschafts-Verlag, 2010), 7. Cited in Dirk Göttsche, *Remembering Africa: The Rediscovery of Colonialism in Contemporary German Literature* (Rochester, NY: Camden House, 2013), 1.

[11] Arnold Stadler, *Eines Tages, vielleicht auch nachts* (Salzburg, Jung und Jung, 2003), 27.

[12] See Paul Michael Lützeler, *Bürgerkrieg global: Menschenrechtsethos und deutschsprachiger Gegenwartsroman* (Munich: Wilhelm Fink Verlag, 2010).

[13] Terézia Mora, *Alle Tage* (Munich: Luchterhand, 2004), 24. Hereafter *AT* in parentheses after quotations in the main body of the text.

[14] The word "queer," of course, derives from the Germanic root *quer*, meaning "across" or athwart."

[15] Joseph Vogl, "Geschlecht ohne Ort," in *Autorschaft: Genus und Genie in der Zeit um 1800*, ed. Ina Schabert and Barbara Schaff (Berlin: Erich Schmidt Verlag, 1994), 41–54.

[16] Jasbir Puar, *Terrorist Assemblages: Homonationalism in Queer Times* (Durham, NC: Duke University Press, 2007).

[17] See the *Encyclopædia Britannica* online, http://www.britannica.com/EBchecked/topic/428173/Om.

[18] Gerard Delanty, *The Cosmopolitan Imagination: The Renewal of Social Theory* (Cambridge: Cambridge University Press, 2009), 60.

[19] See Anke Biendarra, *Germans Going Global* (Berlin: De Gruyeter, 2012), especially 153–57.

[20] See Paul Michael Lützeler, ed., *Schriftsteller und "Dritte Welt": Studien zum postkolonialen Blick* (Tübingen: Stauffenburg, 1998).

[21] Graham Huggan, *The Postcolonial Exotic: Marketing the Margins* (London: Routledge, 2001).

[22] Hoppe's novel exemplifies the "banal cosmopolitanism" described by Bronislaw Szerszynski and John Urry, "Cultures of Cosmopolitanism," *Sociological Review* 50 (2002): 461–81.

[23] Ulf Hannerz, "Cosmopolitans and Locals in World Culture," *Theory Culture Society* 7 (1990): 239.

[24] See my *Aging and Old-Age Style in Günter Grass, Ruth Klüger, Christa Wolf, and Martin Walser: The Mannerism of a Late Period* (Rochester: Camden House, 2013).

[25] Michael Minden, "Social Hope and the Nightmare of History: Christa Wolf's *Kindheitsmuster* and *Stadt der Engel*," *Publications of the English Goethe Society* 80, no. 2/3 (2011): 199.

[26] Richard White, "Herder: On the Ethics of Nationalism," *Humanitas* 18, no. 1/2 (2005): 166–81.

[27] Kehlmann's *Die Vermessung der Welt* focuses on the competition between late eighteenth- and early nineteenth-century German Enlightenment thought and the emerging pernicious nationalism of the post-Napoleonic period. Kracht's *Imperium* focuses on the way emancipatory elements of German modernism—including some with a strongly cosmopolitan outlook—degenerate into a reactionary nationalism in the early twentieth century. Hoppe's *Hoppe* suggests that German myths, which are often associated with romantic nationalism, can also circulate globally as flag-bearers of an open, responsive German culture.

[28] See Ehrhard Bahrs, *Weimar on the Pacific* (Berkeley: University of California Press, 2007).

[29] See Emily D. Bilski and Emily Braun, *Jewish Women and Their Salons: The Power of Conversation* (New York: Yale University Press, 2005).

[30] Pauline Kleingeld, "Romantic Cosmopolitanism: Novalis's "Christianity or Europe," *Journal of the History of Philosophy* 46, no. 2 (2008): 269.

[31] See my "Arnold Stadler: Eine Poetik des Glaubens," in *Poetologisch-poetische Interventionen: Gegenwartsliteratur schreiben*, ed. Alo Allkemper, Norbert Otto Eke, and Hartmut Steineke (Munich: Wilhelm Fink Verlag, 2012), 273–86.

[32] See my *Aging and Old-Age Style*.

[33] See Stuart Taberner, "Germans, Jews and Turks in Maxim Biller's Novel *Esra*," *The German Quarterly* 79, no. 2 (2006): 234–48.

[34] Şenocak suggests that his attachment to Turkish, a "language which confronts feelings directly," allowed him to reintroduce the emotional expressivity of romanticism to postwar Germans who had repressed it in their postwar overreaction to its association with the irrationality of National Socialism. (Zafer Şenocak, "Dichter ohne Lieder," in *Deutschsein: Eine Aufklärungsschrift*, ed. Zafer Şenocak [Hamburg: Körber-Stiftung, 2011], 79).

[35] It is worth noting that Zaimoglu prefers his name to be spelled without the Turkish diacritic ğ: "Den Querbalken . . . habe ich abgeschafft" (I abolished the crossbeam [over the *g* in my surname]). Cited in Tom Cheesman and Katrin E. Yeşilada, Preface to *Feridun Zaimoglu*, ed. Tom Cheesman and Karin E. Yeşilada (Bern: Peter Lang, 2012), 3.

[36] See Petra Fachinger, "Rome Seen through the Eyes of a Muslim German Latter-Day Flâneuer," in Cheesman and Yeşilada, *Feridun Zaimoglu*, 183–200.

[37] Michael Hoffmann, "Romantic Rebellion: Feridun Zaimoglu and Anti-Bourgeois Tradition," in Cheesman and Yeşilada, *Feridun Zaimoglu*, 247.

[38] Taberner, "Romantic Rebellion," 253. On Romantic motifs in *Liebesbrand* in particular, see Margaret Littler, "Between Romantic Love and War Machine: *Liebesbrand*," in Cheesman and Yeşilada, *Feridun Zaimoglu*, 219–38.

[39] Cheesman and Yeşilada, preface to Cheesman and Yeşilada, *Feridun Zaimoglu*, 5.

[40] "Feridun Zaimoglu: Hinterland," Robert Bosch Stiftung, accessed July 24, 2014, http://www.bosch-stiftung.de/content/language1/html/29705.asp.

[41] "Border Crossers Europe and Its Neighbors," Robert Bosch Stiftung, accessed July 20, 2014, http://www.bosch-stiftung.de/content/language2/html/1100.asp.

[42] These quotations from "Feridun Zaimoglu: Hinterland," Robert Bosch Stiftung, accessed July 20, 2014, http://www.bosch-stiftung.de/content/language1/html/29705.asp.

[43] Feridun Zaimoglu, *Hinterland* (Cologne: Kiepenheuer und Witsch Verlag, 2009), 96–97, and repeated throughout the text. Hereafter *H* in parentheses after quotations in the main body of the text.

[44] James Clifford, "Traveling Cultures," in *Cultural Studies*, ed. Lawrence Grossberg, Cary Nelson, and Paula Treichler (New York: Routledge, 1992), 96–116.

[45] Bonaventura de Sousa Santos, *Toward a New Legal Common Sense: Law, Globalization, and Emancipation* (London: Butterworths, 2002).

[46] Stuart Hall, "Cosmopolitanism, Globalisation and Diaspora: Stuart Hall in Conversation with Pnina Werbner," in *Anthropology and the New Cosmopolitanism: Rooted, Feminist and Vernacular Perspectives*, ed. Pnina Werbner (Oxford: Berg, 2008), 233–60.

[47] See page 266 in this volume.

[48] Gilbert Leung, "A Critical History of Cosmopolitanism," *Law, Culture and the Humanities* 5 (2009): 370–90.

[49] Rosi Braidotti, *Transpositions: On Nomadic Ethics* (London: Polity, 2006).

[50] Costas Douzinas, *Human Rights and Empire: The Political Philosophy of Cosmopolitanism* (London: Routledge, 2007), 293.

[51] Gayatri Spivak, *Death of a Discipline* (New York: Columbia University Press, 2003), 73.

[52] Julian Preece, "*Der Weltensammler:* Separate Bodies, or An Account of Intercultural Failure," in *Emerging German-Language Novelists of the Twenty-First Century*, ed. Lyn Marven and Stuart Taberner (Rochester, NY: Camden House, 2011), 119. Preece draws particular attention to Ingo Arend's review in the weekly magazine *Freitag*, "Einer von ihnen: Ilija Trojanows Roman *Der Weltensammler* ist ein Plädoyer für die Aneignung des Fremden," *Freitag*, May 5, 2006.

[53] See the interview with Trojanow following the United States' refusal to allow him entry in late 2013: "NSA-Kritiker Ilija Trojanow: 'Die Regierung verteidigt unsere Rechte nicht," by Stefan Kuzmany, Spiegel Online, October 02, 2013, http://www.spiegel.de/kultur/literatur/

interview-mit-ilija-trojanow-ueber-sein-usa-einreiseverbot-a-925643.html.   Trojanow was to be as one of the guest speakers at the Thirty-Seventh Annual Conference of the German Studies Association in Denver in October 2013 and had
been invited to participate in a panel organized by the coeditors of this volume.

[54] See Ernest Schonfield, "On the Road to Mecca with Trojanow and Burton,"
in *Ilija Trojanow*, ed. Julian Preece (Oxford: Peter Lang, 2013), 81–97. See also
Julian Preece, "Faking the Hadj in Ilija Trojanow's *Der Weltensammler*," in *Religion and Identity in Contemporary German Literature and Film: Seekers, Believers,
Doubters*, ed. Julian Preece, Frank Finlay, and Sinead Crowe (Berne: Lang, 2010),
211–25.

[55] Ilija Trojanow, *Der Weltensammler* (München: Carl Hanser Verlag, 2006),
435. Translation: William Hobson *The Collector of Worlds* (London: Faber and
Faber, 2008), 414–15.

[56] Hannah Arendt, *The Human Condition* (London: University of Chicago Press,
1958), 52.

[57] Paul Gilroy, *Postcolonial Melancholia* (New York: Columbia University Press,
2005), 70.

[58] Arendt, *Human Condition*, 52.

[59] Arendt, *Human Condition*, 79.

[60] William Smith, "Cosmopolitan Citizenship: Virtue, Irony and Worldliness,"
European Journal of Social Theory 10, no. 1 (2007): 45.

3: Affect, Aesthetics, Biopower, and Technology: Political Interventions into Transnationalism

Carrie Smith-Prei

FEMINIST AND QUEER THEORETICAL SCHOLARSHIP from a broad range of humanities and social science disciplines (including emotional geography, sociology, political science, critical race studies, postcolonial studies, and psychology, to name a few) have increasingly addressed the affective experience of transnationalism on both individuals and communities.[1] Taking as their starting point an intersectional understanding of difference developed in feminist work since the 1980s, these studies examine how race, class, sexuality, and gender together become useful categories in the "making and theorizing of transnational domains."[2] Literature is one such transnational domain. Since German unification, German-language writing by minority and nonminority authors alike has become increasingly "globalized and transnational,"[3] which includes the subject matter, setting, languages, translations, distribution, and reception, ranging from the media promotion of texts and their authors to the awarding of prizes. These literary texts are populated with circulating bodies, both literally and figuratively, and therefore also contain the emotional and physical resonances of the border-crossing experience, such as destabilized feelings of belonging, reconfiguration of identity in travel, the impact of space and place on familial or sexual intimacy, the trauma of exile, or the corporeal results of economic precarity and racially motivated violence. More recent trends in affect studies move away from concerns of identity or subjecthood, and instead ask after the political frameworks, undercurrents, and aftershocks of these contents.

Building on the engagement with and definitions of transnationalism, cosmopolitanism, world literature, and contemporary literature offered by Elisabeth Herrmann and Stuart Taberner in the preceding chapters, the following will trace the affective features in and of the transnational in order to mine for the politically engaged moments in contemporary literature. I suggest that a reconsideration of the affective turn that has taken hold in feminist and queer research since the new millennium is essential for understanding transnationalism in its function as a category, feature, or "pillar" (Herrmann) of literature, for it acts as a conduit through which literature is connected to the broader reach of politicized feminist studies; affect illuminates not only the connective charges between bodies as they move across or straddle borders, but it also captures the impact of transnational flows on individuals and social collectives working within power structures. Finally, the turn to affect allows for a process-based understanding of the contemporary or emergent moment in research, literature, and culture, an understanding that highlights the immediacy of the present. Affect "consolidates and extends some of the most productive existing trends in research" while it at the same time "opens new avenues for study, casts previous work in a fresh light, and indicates novel possibilities for politics."[4] Drawing on readings from affect and sexuality studies published since the 1990s, I begin with a brief assessment of the affective turn across disciplines, out of which three general areas for this reconsideration emerge: aesthetics, biopower, and technologies. I then utilize these areas to chart a path through a selection of German-language literary texts published since the new millennium. By understanding literature as a transnational domain both made and theorized by affect, we can access the interplay between the impact of literature on the public sphere and, conversely, engage with the contextual framework within which poetic or narrative structure is developed, thereby divulging how the temporal present unfolds as a political impulse in the category of contemporary literature.

The Affective Turn and the Transnational

Since the mid-1990s, and increasingly since the new millennium, the humanities and social sciences have been marked by an "affective turn," driven by work on the body and emotions coming out of feminist and queer studies in the decades prior, but also by examinations of subjectivity, identity, and culture by critical theory on the heels of deconstructionism and poststructuralism.[5] As with all turns, the affective turn marks a reconsideration of individual fields from within, but also an interconnection between fields as well as their methodologies and objects of study.[6] And as with all turns, affect is differently defined across disciplines, although common to all is an understanding of affect as politically charged.

Michael Hardt defines affect (reading Baruch Spinoza) as the simultaneous correspondence of the "mind's power to think" and the "body's power to act," and along with this, the relationship between the "power to act and the power to be affected."[7] Hardt's definition suggests an openness, receptivity, and passion in the manner in which we think through and feel encounters with the other, our abilities to act and react to these encounters, and our ability to turn that receptivity into ethical, social, or political action. Thus, approaching anything—an object, a person, a situation—through affect is simultaneously an intellectual and corporeal project. Eve Kosofsky Sedgwick (indebted to Silvan Tomkins) also sees affect to be thoroughly embodied and connected: "Affects can be, and are, attached to things, people, ideas, sensations, relations, activities, ambitions, institutions, and any number of other things, including other affects."[8] This high range of connectivity suggests also the reconfiguration of multiple domains of experience and capacity. Patricia Ticineto Clough (drawing on the work of Brian Massumi and Gilles Deleuze, as well as Félix Guattari) sees in the affective turn an expression of a "new configuration of bodies, technology, and matter" in a manner that suggests a movement toward open systems "in the domain of biopolitical control."[9] Technology becomes important in her reading because it not only reconfigures bodily capacities, it also demands we rethink representation of these capacities. Ann Pellegrini and Jasbir Puar (in reaction to Fredric Jameson) also define affect in terms of the corporeal and technological; affect is a concept that "allows the body to become an open system, always in concert with its virtuality, the potential of becoming."[10] This is the case because affect taps into aspects of the body that cannot be addressed in linguistic terms; affect is "both a 'precognitive' attribute . . . of the body as well as emotion's trace effect."[11]

In her writings on affect, Clough makes a distinction between the work done on affect in literary studies on the one hand, and in cultural studies and critical theory on the other. She sees the former to return repeatedly to the emotional foundation of affect and its application to defining subjectivities in text, whereas the latter emphasizes "pre-individual bodily forces" and the technologies engaged in these forces, that is, a movement away from "subjectively felt emotional states" and toward what Clough calls the biomediated body.[12] I would like to suggest that the category of the transnational, in its focus on movement and connectivity, renders this disciplinary boundary porous. In many ways akin to forms of cosmopolitanism discussed by Taberner, studies undertaken on the basis of affect ask us to enter what Hardt calls the "realm of causality": "They illuminate, in other words, both our power to affect the world around us and our power to be affected by it, along with the relationship between these two powers."[13] This causality extends also to the study of affect itself. Affect allows for the examination of causal connections in a multipronged manner; affect charts a messy and diffuse set of interconnected relations, relations that collide in the transnational literary text.

What comes out of this brief sketch is the manner in which affect is utilized to address connectivity, action and reaction (both potential and real), resonances between people or things (such as objects, events, or spaces), emotional and precognitive physical responses, and the powers and technologies working on and in these responses. Affect, as well as its attendant features, including emotion, feeling, corporeality, and sexuality, allows us access to the connection between subjectivity, materiality, and social or political action in the neoliberal economy, which "has reduced possibilities for collective political praxis."[14] Affect offers us a vision of collectivity, made up of individual corporeal experiences across geopolitical systems. Affect, therefore, is specifically suited to engage with transnationalism. Clough identifies a relationship between the increased interest in affect and the period in which critical theory was faced with the challenges that the realities of terrorism, torture, international imprisonment, and human rights abuses presented following 9/11. Judith Butler's *Precarious Life*, written in the wake of 9/11, shows particularly well these interconnections; the text is a response to what she sees a failure on the part of the United States to "redefine itself as part of a global community," in favor of closing off in security, nationalism, and fear.[15] Clough explains: "If these world events can be said to be symptomatic of ongoing political, economic, and cultural transformations, the turn to affect may be registering a change in the cofunctioning of the political, economic, and cultural."[16] The turn to affect, thought such, is "necessary to theorizing the social" in a global community.[17] While this makes clear affect's utility in capturing the collective, bodily, and nonconscious residue of transnationalism, it underscores how affect is also engaged in enacting or spurring on transnational flows, for, as Clough continues to explain, examinations of affect must be done in tandem with the recognition of the "ongoing transformations of relations of power across international organizations, regions, nations, states, economies, and private and public spheres."[18] The affective turn sheds light on the consequences of bodies and materials as they are buffeted across borders, both now and as this might be shaped in the future, but it also spurs these bodies and materials into motion.

Much of the research on affect and transnational mobility is concerned with the lived experiences of diaspora, exile, and migration. Affect, in this sense, is deemed a key aspect of the real and possible encounter between bodies in or across spaces; affect is the "consequence of the interactions that occur between the bodies, objects and materials that comprise particular ecologies of place."[19] In this sense, the body, in its encounter with other bodies on the street, creates configurations and alliances. Affect is a tool for the analysis of the impact of such alliances, as seen for example in Arjun Appadurai's discussion of fear and rage in minority communities under globalization, Sara Ahmed's engagement with how hate structures national communities, or Thomas Solomon's approach to community belonging across multiple geopolitically bound nations in Turkish hip-hop collectives. In each of these readings, affect not only describes the transnational experience, it also creates it in that it engenders movement and connections within and across boundaries.

If affect is a useful concept for capturing the sociopolitical and contextual resonances of transnationalism in lived experiences and how their traces are embedded in bodies or, in turn, how bodies might create transnational landscapes, then this relationship between affect and the transnational also has implications for literature. As a category, transnational literature often describes a crossing of borders in the form of cultures, nations, histories, languages, and memories embedded in fictional stories. Thought not merely as a category but instead as an impulse, it also describes the intersection of poetics with intimacies of place or genealogies of belonging, including also the reader's own experiences of these with and beyond text. When thought affectively, both category and impulse are socially or politically charged. In what follows, I examine three aspects of the affective turn as they have emerged from my readings above—aesthetics, biopower, and technology—as three different routes to the transnational in German-language literature. These three areas cut across and conjoin the many disciplinary approaches to affect and, as will become apparent below, specifically point to circulation, connectivity, border crossings, and open systems that are also central to transnationalism. In light of Clough's assessment of the increased interest in affect together with a global critical assessment of transnational structures since 9/11, I focus on German-language literature published since the new millennium, for it is around this time that critics often ascertain a caesura in the form of a discernable call for engaged or political texts.[20]

Emotional and Social Aesthetics: Narrativizing Affect

Ilija Trojanow, whose work is addressed by Christina Kraenzle in this volume as well as in the preceding chapters by Herrmann and Taberner, writes in an introductory essay to *Der entfesselte Globus* (The Unbound Globe, 2009) emotionally of the memory of traveling across borders as a young boy in exile: "Auf dieser Flucht waren wir gewissermaßen nackt. Es ist ein Zustand, bei dem die Welt einen Abdruck auf dem eigenen Körper hinterläßt." (During our flight we were essentially naked. It is a state of being in which the world leaves an imprint on one's body.)[21] The corporeal dimension of movement speaks to the affective, embodied, and collective nature of the transnational in Trojanow's writings. The young boy's body is imprinted as it attempts to understand the other ("einen Reim darauf zu machen," to make sense of it all) in its move across borders.[22] This corporeal dimension of movement away from home and through a foreign place is not only emotional, but also geopolitical. He writes in a separate essay in the same volume:

> Wenn wir uns für die Zukunft wappnen wollen, sollten wir unsere Grenzen als Zusammenflüsse begreifen, die uns in der Vergangenheit befruchtet haben, als Spielwiesen von Mischkulturen, die für die

Entwicklung des Kontinents von entscheidender Bedeutung waren und sind.[23]

[If we wish to prepare ourselves for the future, we must understand our borders as confluences that have fecundated us in the past, as playgrounds for mixed cultures, which have had and continue to have critical meaning for the development of the continent.]

His embodied experience of traveling across borders as a child is here transferred to the porous national boundaries of an expanding European Union. The "discursive capacity of places to affect emotional experiences" goes beyond social configurations of community, as is the focus of emotional geography, to include the movement through place, which is crisscrossed with affective charges.[24] Thought transversally, affect of place allows for an interconnected engagement with the multiple vectors associated with the transnational as a category and impulse.[25] This decenters the preference for terms such as local and global as binary replacements for home and abroad or national and international, and instead places the emphasis on "confluence," the term used by Trojanow in the interview contained at the end of this volume.

This coming together of confluence is created also through affective charges. As Ahmed claims, emotions "*do things*" to align "individuals with collectives" and "bodily space with social space" in a manner that is highly public.[26] They "secure collectives through the way in which they read bodies of others," these being apparent in the "emotionality of texts."[27] This would suggest that texts must be understood in terms of their "emotional aesthetics," to use Sianne Ngai's term. Ngai writes how, in her case negative, emotions become the "mediation between the aesthetic and the political in a nontrivial way."[28] Considering the emotional aesthetics of a text, therefore, allows for simultaneous access to how affect develops the narrative architecture of a literary text and, further, how the related emotions offer us windows on contextual configurations, be these social or political. In his approach to the aesthetics of the everyday, Ben Highmore deploys the term aesthetics in its historical meaning that "gestured thought towards the great left-over: the bodily creature; the paths of often unruly emotions; the whole sensual world in all its baseness and brilliance."[29] Aesthetics understood thus is intimately bound up with emotions and affects and is bodily and collective. Because of this, the social aesthetics of everyday life deeply connect the emotional and embodied lived experience to the contextual social and political world; this aesthetic experience Highmore calls "public intimacy": "Aesthetics, at its best, attends to public feelings that are experienced intimately: it posits our most subjective experiences as social."[30] This social is for Highmore global, for an inquiry into aesthetics must attempt to make sense of how the "opaque and oblique machinations of global politics (economic, environmental and culture) punctuate and syncopate the rhythms of ordinary life."[31] The social dimension of literary aesthetics therefore has transnational implications.

This understanding of texts and their aesthetics as emotional and sensual but also as an instrument able to forge collectives allows for an examination of the affective traces of the transnational in literary texts as a structuring force for border crossings found at the level of text-internal narrative-poetics, but also among the text-context-reader triad. In Yoko Tawada's *Das nackte Auge* (The Naked Eye, 2004), the transnational appears both as a plot device and as narrative composition. The novel tells of a young Vietnamese girl who travels to East Berlin to give a talk, knowing no German and instead communicating with her hosts in Russian. After her abduction by Jörg, a student from Bochum, she escapes on a train that takes her west to Paris where she spends her days at the cinema. It is here that she not only learns French, but also the embrace of home. "Die Straße sagte mir nicht, wo ich hingehen sollte. Mir fiel nur das Wort 'cinéma' ein. In diesem Wort trafen 'China' und 'Ma' zusammen. Der Eingang des Kinos empfing mich wie die Arme einer 'Ma.'" (The street did not tell me where I should go. I only thought of the word "cinéma." "China" and "Ma" came together in this word. The entrance to the movie theater embraced me like the arms of a "Ma.")[32] When at the end of the text Jörg finds her in Paris and demands she return with him to Bochum, she wishes not to leave her cinematic home in Paris, for it has replaced the home to which she can no longer return: "'Die sowjetische Regierung wird mich nach Hause bringen.' 'Es gibt sie nicht mehr. Du weißt das doch, oder?' 'Ja, ich weiß es. Aber durch welches Land soll ich fahren, um nach Hause zu kommen?' . . . Ich sprach nicht mehr, ich bellte." ("The Soviet government will bring me home." "It doesn't exist anymore. You know that, right?" "Yes, I know that. But which land should I travel through to get home?" . . . I no longer spoke, I barked.)[33] Historical, not national, borders determine her exile. The affective experience of homelessness comes through in the tenor of her response—"I barked"—the entrapment producing an animal sound.

The films she sees structure the novel. These films range from national French cinema to international productions, all of which star Catherine Deneuve. It is Deneuve's figure that determines the protagonist's movement between cities (appearing on the tracks of the Paris-bound train, for example), her navigation of foreign language replicated as text (French and English), and her embodied experience of home and displacement. Each film forms a chapter title and determines the figures, poetic voice, tone, and structure of the chapters. For example, the first chapter, "Repulsion," named after Roman Polanski's 1965 horror film of psychological distress and sexual violence experienced by Deneuve's figure who is entrapped in a London apartment, is characterized by passages depicting violence and bloodshed in the Bochum apartment. In these passages, which have an unclear relationship to reality, the protagonist inflicts violence on Jörg, assumedly as a result of his demands for sex.[34] The tone of these passages is markedly flat and the sentence structure simple, producing an aesthetic tension between the violence and the sober quality of the emotional description. The 1992 French film about colonial Indochina by director Régis Wargnier, "Indochine," is the title of chapter 5. In contrast, this chapter has a dream-like quality to its narrative structure. Taking on the role of the young Vietnamese girl adopted by Deneuve's character in the film, the protagonist's language, emotions, and sensual experience transform to match what she sees on screen:

> Gib mir auch ein bisschen Mango! Gib mir! Mir, mir, mir! Meine Sprache wird kindlich, wenn ich Sie anspreche. Die Wörter irren vereinzelt und ohne Zielpunkt umher, die Stimme steigt in die Höhe eines zwitschernden Vogels, und auf einmal sehe ich Sie vor mir stehen. . . . Stück für Stück eine Mango auf meine Zunge legen. Die saftige Frucht füllt meine Mundhöhle, und ich rede nur noch französisch, ohne den Sinn zu verstehen.[35]

> [Give me a little Mango, too! Give me! Me, me, me! My language becomes childish when I address you. The words wander about alone and directionless, my voice rises up to heights of a twittering bird, and suddenly I see you standing in front of me. . . . Placing a mango piece by piece on my tongue. The juicy fruit fills the cavity of my mouth and I only speak French, without understanding the meaning.]

The mango pieces replace the Vietnamese language and are then transformed into French. In these examples, the films are not merely thematically overlaid onto the novel, but instead become integral to the narrator's development, her voice, and the text's affective structure. The intimacy forged between the protagonist and Deneuve throughout the chapters, moreover, spans times and media, but also transnational spaces, histories, and languages.

By the end, this intimacy develops what might be called a community of care. This care is displayed in the final chapter of the novel, "Dancer in the Dark," which mirrors the 2000 film by Lars von Trier starring Deneuve and Björk. In it, our protagonist—now blind and living in Berlin—tells a Czech immigrant named Selma (the character played by Björk in the film) of her friend Kathy (filmic counterpart played by Deneuve), who appears next to her in the Berlin movie theaters and draws on her hand. "Meine Hand ist meine Leinwand, und die Finger von Kathy sind die Autoren, den ich bin mir sicher, dass sie die Geschichte umschreibt, wenn sie ihr nicht gefällt" (My hand is my screen, and Kathy's fingers are the authors, for I am sure that she rewrites the story if she does not like it).[36] Here, the body has become the text and visuality replaced by touch. The shift in the narrative voice from the first person to third person suggests further that the intimacy forged throughout the text with Deneuve is public. That this public intimacy is tied to transnational flows of media in the form of film points not only to an international industry, but hints at the nonsingular nature of the precarity experienced by the protagonist. Ultimately a victim of sexual trafficking at the outset of the novel, she remains in a situation of economic, linguistic, and corporeal vulnerability throughout. (See Maria Mayr's chapter in this volume for the link between migration and sex work; see also Hester Baer's chapter for an in-depth discussion of precarity and sexuality.) In a 2011 virtual roundtable with a number of scholars, including Jasbir Puar and Judith Butler, Lauren Berlant notes that precarity itself is an affect and a "rallying cry for a thriving new world of interdependency and care that's not just private"; it has become an "idiom of care as ground for what needs to change to better suture the social."[37] Berlant notes her own ambivalence around this idiom, an ambivalence that comes through also in the tone of Tawada's novel, a tone which formulates a marked contrast to Trojanow's belief in care as forging confluence. However, the ambivalence in Tawada's tonality may also be read as socially engaged. The third person shift in the final chapter paired with both the understanding of aesthetics and affect as forging communities as well as with the transnational implications of film asks us to engage with the vast transnational flow of precarious existence.

Biopower and Queer Border Crossings: Affect's Political Spaces

In this same conversation on precarity, Butler speaks of the power mechanisms at work on human lives as diffuse and without object.[38] These power mechanisms might roughly be defined as biopower, a further aspect of the affective turn. The term appears at the end of the first volume of *The History of Sexuality*, where Foucault writes of the deployment of sexuality as one of the great technologies of power in the nineteenth century leading to the development of capitalism.[39] He goes on to write, "One would have to speak of *bio-power* to designate what brought life and its mechanisms into the realm of explicit calculations and made knowledge-power an agent of transformation of human life."[40] It is this biopower, moreover, that allows for the implementation of normativity as the arbiter of law, for it acts at the level of life itself.[41] Beverley Best summarizes biopower as the "affective modality of power" that "works directly on and through bodies" in an unmediated and nonnarrative manner, for "affect 'permeates' subjects, incorporating them within an economy of nonsymbolic intensities."[42] Ben Anderson, on the other hand, makes the distinction between affect, as concerned with the dynamics of "lived experience," and biopower, which displays how life has become the object for "techniques and technologies of power."[43] Biopower thus joins the causality and connectivity of affect with a political investment in life forces, most often expressed by the body; when the connections are found between bodies in movement within or across borders, this investment has transnational implications. Indeed, it might be said that the transnational gives biopower a narrative framework within which to be read.

Two literary texts, both appearing in 2001, illustrate such transnational implications of biopower. Juli Zeh's *Adler und Engel* (Eagles and Angels, 2001), discussed also by Lars Richter in this volume, depicts trafficking and human rights abuses in an expanding European Union through the body of Max, a lawyer specializing in international human rights legislation. Set in the late 1990s, Max narrates his experience of trauma, depression, and increasing physical and emotional numbness spurred on by drug use. His Viennese law firm sends him to the Leipzig office after he discovers the firm's role in illegal drug trafficking through the former Yugoslavia—drugs that financed the Serbian side of the Balkan war. The firm's central function in the forging of UN agreements with states emerging from the instability of the postcommunist era is merely a front for the easier passage of drugs, the drug trade deemed by his boss Rufus a "nebensächliches Problem" (ancillary problem) in the European political landscape.[44] As the novel begins, we find Max distraught after Jessie, a child-like woman he has loved since boarding school, has committed suicide while on the phone with him. As he attempts to piece together her suicide, it becomes clear that Jessie was a pawn in the drug-trafficking scheme; Jessie became collateral damage of human rights law that made possible the drug trade that led to her death. Max's body is intimately connected to Jessie's death and therefore to those international power structures causing her death: not only does he work on the legislation in question, but he also receives a burst eardrum as a result of the gunshot. Furthermore, the cocaine he consumes throughout the novel, obtained through the above mentioned traffic ring, leaves him unable to have an erection. Through his body, the EU, international human rights legislation, and the UN are seen to be instable and impotent.

A similar embodiment of international instability is at work in Christian Kracht's *1979* (2001). The novel follows the abject and melancholic queer body as it travels haphazardly through Tehran on the eve of the Islamic revolution, travels around a mountain in Tibet, and lands in a Chinese gulag. Like Zeh's Max, Kracht's protagonist oscillates between drug-and-alcohol-induced numbness and nausea, spending the first half of the novel disengaged from his body. Furthermore, the protagonist is "ganz ohne eine Vergangenheit" (completely without a past), as ex-lover

Christopher says to him, and therefore consistently locates himself in the present.[45] After Christopher dies as a result of excessive drug use (as well as an unnamed sickness that creates pustules on his body) and following the protagonist's detention for questioning as a supposed CIA spy, he heads to Tibet where he joins in a prostrating ritual around a mountain. Just as he wonders whether he should increase the pain of the experience by removing the rubber kneepads, he is captured (again as a presumed CIA agent) and taken to a gulag in China.

His experiences in the gulag are thoroughly corporeal. He undergoes what is called in the language of his captors "*Selbstkritik*" (self-criticism), during which he is beaten until he learns the "correct" answers to the questions posed: that he is a parasite, that he is one of the capitalist exploiters, and that he himself is also being exploited and can, therefore, be saved.[46] His body is also wracked by diarrhea due to eating porridge made of maggots cultivated from the waste of the latrines. Despite the joy expressed at "seriously" (the original emphasis in English) losing weight as a result (at the end he weighs 38 kilos) and his near-obsessive desire to do as he is told, he remains emotionally disengaged throughout; indeed, the novel's primary affective mode is distance. Exemplary of this, the book ends with the following: "Alle zwei Wochen gab es eine freiwillige Selbstkritik. Ich ging immer hin. Ich war ein guter Gefangener. Ich habe immer versucht, mich an die Regeln zu halten. Ich habe mich gebessert. Ich habe nie Menschenfleisch gegessen." (Every two weeks there was a voluntary self-critique. I always attended. I was a good prisoner. I always tried to hold myself to the rules. I bettered myself. I never ate human flesh.)[47] Through short sentences that utilize the same repeated construction, the strange appearance of the negative statement at the end is drained of emotional charge. This final sentence mirrors the affective stumbling block presented to readers at the outset of the novel: "Auf dem Weg nach Teheran, sah ich aus dem Autofenster, mir wurde etwas übel, und ich hielt mich an Christophers Knie fest. Sein Hosenbein war von den aufgeplatzten Blasen ganz naß." (On the way to Teheran I looked out of the car window, felt somewhat sick, and held tight to Christopher's knee. His pant-leg was completely wet from the pustules that had burst open.)[48] The nausea and pustules set the tone for the text's abject and embodied physicality. This tone remains in the final sentence: because there is no reason given for the sudden disavowal of cannibalism, the assumption must be cannibalism is rampant.

The two literary examples very differently illuminate how biopower and affect come together under the literary depiction of transnational power structures. In Zeh's novel, the body of the protagonist displays the impossibilities of UN human rights legislation to counter the international drug trade, and therefore suggests a destabilizing of the EU powers as it expands. Kracht's novel, on the other hand, offers a highly ambivalent critique of the decadence of the West, ambivalent because the counterpraise for dictatorship is also dripping with an almost decadent, tongue-in-cheek satire. However, the protagonist's queer body tips the critique of the West away from dandyism and toward the biopolitical. In queer transnational analysis, the border-crossing queer subject is often understood as an outlaw, a slippery figure that places the heteronormative national framework found also in the transnational into question. (See in this context also Taberner's discussion of Terézia Mora's *Alle Tage* in the preceding chapter.) As a counterweight, Puar utilizes the term *homona-tionalism*, which she defines as the "use of 'acceptance' and 'tolerance' for gay and lesbian subjects as the barometer by which the legitimacy of, and capacity for national sovereignty is evaluated."[49] Homonationalism is a way of getting at "geopolitical and historical forces, neoliberal interests in capitalist accumulation both cultural and material, biopolitical state practices of population control, and affective investments in discourses of freedom, liberation, and rights."[50] It therefore suggests a "reorientation of the relationship between the state, capitalism, and sexuality" and as such is an "analytics of power" that must be engaged with as an option for transnational, and national, politics.[51] It is a way of thinking about how economies and states frame their discourse around progress (their own) and failure (that of others). Thinking of Kracht's text in these terms, we see the body of the protagonist not as a queer transnational outlaw, but rather as a homonational body neoliberally coded by the West to disturb forces of dictatorship in the East. Kracht's text becomes political in the failure of this disturbance; the neoliberal subject happily adapts and reorganizes his body to comply with the new power structure.

Feminist and queer scholars in a range of social sciences and humanities disciplines have engaged since the early 1990s in theorizations of "queer diasporas, racialized sexualities, and transnationalism; nationalisms and the policing of borders; global capitalism and gay subjectivities; and the heteronormative foundations of development ideologies and imperialism."[52] What these studies have shown is the manner in which identity and place come together very differently in discussions of transnationalism when it comes to sexuality and intimacy. "Spaces are sexualized as an active and often contentious process of place-making."[53] This applies to those zones that are obviously sexually charged, such as red-light districts or gay quarters, but also everyday spaces. In their 1998 essay "Sex in Public," Lauren Berlant and Michael Warner speak of multiple publics, including queer counterpublics, that are marked by sex, whether through the act itself, through discourses of regulation, or even by its enforced absence from the public sphere altogether.[54] Because "nonnormative sexuality is often tantamount to spatial displacement," occurring in or across a bordered community, when this place-making through sexuality is enacted transnationally, notions of familiar and foreign become tangled up in national and international frameworks, all of these libidinally charged.[55]

Kathrin Schmidt's *Du stirbst nicht* (You Will Not Die, 2009), for example, is a text that asks after the inter-national effects of just such place-making. The novel tells of Helene Wesendahl, a woman who experiences massive paralysis and memory loss—including language—after suffering an aneurism; she must relearn the workings of her body, her memories, history, and language. Part of this relearning takes the form of the memory of a love relationship with the transsexual woman Viola (formerly Viktor). This memory, furthermore, is intertwined with the remembered history of the German Democratic Republic and unification. The Russian language, an essential component of GDR culture, resurfaces as part of Viola's transidentity in Helene's memory:

> Irgendetwas steht ihr im Wege, als sie sich Viola bei sich vorstellt. Da fällt ihr ein: Sie spricht hervorragend Russisch. . . . *Malysch?* Das bezeichnet im Russischen den kleinen Jungen, den Knirps, man sagt es auch unter Männern, vielleicht ein bisschen abwertend? . . . Viola hieß "kleiner Junge" mit Zunamen und wollte doch lieber *Maljutka* sein, die Kleine, das Mädchen. Maljussenkaja gar, Kleinchen, aber solch zärtliches Wort findet sich im Deutschen gar nicht, das russische auch nur annähernd wiederzugeben. Helene hatte es schließlich bei *Maljutka Malysch* belassen, zweideutig war's, eben so, wie Viola ihr wirklich erschien, stückweis Mann, stückweis Frau.[56]

> [Something stands in her way as she imagines Viola with her. Then she remembers: She speaks excellent Russian. . . . *Malysch?* That denotes a little boy in Russian, the tyke, said also between men, maybe a little insultingly? . . . Viola's surname meant "little boy" and she would rather have had *Maljutka*, the lass, the girl. Maljussenkaja, even, little one, but German does not have such a tender word that could even begin to get close to the Russian. Helene finally left it at *Maljutka Malysch*, ambiguous, exactly like Viola really seemed to her, part man, part woman.]

The Russian language melds with the unclear gender of the remembered person and the tangled forgotten desires of the protagonist. Further, the return of her memories of love for Viola in the form of a kiss are embedded in her memories of returning "home" to East Berlin after having moved to western Germany following unification. The remembered transformation of the urban space—Warschauer Strasse, Ostkreuz—allows for a physical reaction in the present—"Gleichzeitig zieht es im Bauch. Sie hat Viola geliebt." (At the same time, she feels her stomach lurch. She loved Viola.)[57]—a moment that proves a further awakening and thus healing of her broken body. The unfolding of love for the transwoman occurs simultaneous to the resurfacing of the remembered transition of the East.

The transnational implications of this novel are embedded in the memory of the ghost nation still residing in the new nation through which Helene travels, just as the ghost of Viktor still resides in Viola. As is also seen in Antje Rávic Strubel's work discussed by Faye Stewart in this volume, the political is both identity-political and national-political, as public and private spheres are intertwined with Viktor's past experience of transitioning to Viola in the GDR, and that of Viola who, like many citizens of the former GDR, struggles to find her place in the unified Germany and forever shows her origins (as easterner and man), even in her last name (that it is Russian and in terms of its literal meaning). Here, the queer body stands in for national discussions of neocolonization and carves out a counterpublic within the public discourse of unification. The body of the transwoman is left incomplete, not having fully incorporated the biological man.

Each of the books discussed in this section ultimately illuminates how transnationalism also becomes a failure of connectivity and confluence. *Adler und Engel* points to the failure of the EU and the UN as transnational power structures to combat the drug trade, and *1979* offers an abject image of the continuing failure of the West to uphold its definition of freedom. The third example, Kathrin Schmidt's *Du stirbst nicht*, offers a reading of the nation as a failed transnation; Viola's figure suggests the failure of nation (the GDR and unified Germany) in the transnational in that neither nation can adequately deal with the transbody as it crosses borders. Her body is a field of power and process at the national and transnational levels. The affective experience of the trans in transnationalism is expressed in the body, not only its desires, but also and more importantly in the complex mediation of sexuality and its dispersal across spaces.[58]

Technologies as Bodily Capacities: Dislocating Transnational Affects

In the above readings, affect and its embodiment functioned to establish connections resonating between people, places, and material, to engineer the aesthetic architecture of text, and to expose powers at work in national and transnational contexts. If, to reiterate Clough, the affective turn is to be understood as an expression of a "new configuration of bodies, technology, and matter," for it offers us a way of accessing bodily capacity and affect working under "biopolitical control," and if, moreover, bodily capacity and affect not only are the result of but also create the transnational domain as contested above, then technology is essential to that domain.[59] Technology not only reconfigures bodily capacities but also demands we rethink the representation of these capacities. To refer to Teresa de Lauretis when she writes in her now seminal *Technologies of Gender* (1987) that gender is the product of "various social technologies," affect allows us access to the moment of interaction between gender as a bodily capacity and that technology.[60] Thinking of affect in response to the increasing technological dimension of transnationalism opens us to expansive, unlimited, and self-reproducing relations in the collision of the digital with the corporeal. In her discussion of homonationalism cited above, Puar uses the concept of virality to address the term's transmission to multiple contexts, a concept that further links digital circulation to the biological workings of the body. Virality simultaneously suggests "speed and reach of information transit" as well as "bodily contamination, uncontainability, unwelcome transgression of border and boundaries while pointing more positively to the porosity, indeed the conviviality, of what has been treated as opposed."[61] Virality reproduces affective tendencies that themselves virally reproduce; as Brian Massumi claims, affect becomes autonomous through its becoming virtual.[62] The flows of technology across borders are embodied and affective, but they are also process-based and future oriented, for they show, in the form of the biomediated body, what the body is becoming and can become.[63]

This relationship among the embodied openness of the digital, virtuality, and virality is essential to literary production in and of the present. Such novels as Helene Hegemann's *Axolotl Roadkill* (2010), discussed at length by Baer in this volume, show how technology is found at the level of content, poetics, and narrative construction, but also in reception, marketing, and critical debate.[64] The book, which follows sixteen-year-old Mifti as she takes drugs, hits the club scene, and stumbles through sexual encounters, is constructed out of snippets of quotations from mass media, including television, music—many of which are in English—email exchanges, and text messages. But technology in the text is not reserved solely for recognizable media forms. Bodies and language also act as technologies. The text begins with the body as a disorganized technology turned language: "O.k., die Nacht, wieder mal so ein Ringen mit dem Tod. . . . Nur die Klaviatur der absoluten Dunkelheit, das Kreischen im Kopf, dieses unrhythmische Trommeln, scheiße. Früher war das alles so schön pubertär hingerotzt und jetzt ist es angestrengte Literatur." (OK, nighttime, grappling again with death. . . . Only the claviature of absolute darkness, the screeching in my head, this unrhythmic drumming, shit. That all used to be beautifully pubescent vomit, and now it is laborious literature.)[65] The sounds (screeching, drumming), both engineered and primal, coming from the postpubescent body create the literature at hand. Later, in response to the contestation that she has destroyed language, Mifti says, "Irgendwann, wenn das Blut so technoplastizitätsmäßig durch die Gegend zirkuliert, ist alles wieder super." (Later, when the blood just circulates around technoplasticitally, everything will be super again).[66] The term *technoplasticity*, linked here to language and blood, suggests a technological basis to life forces and thus a nonspecific locality to the textual construction. However, it also references the Berghain techno scene, anchoring this broken language firmly in Berlin. Further, the word nods toward the virality of literature: *technoplasticity* is one of those phrases Hegemann copy-pasted from the blogger Airen.[67] The word thus directly points outward to the ensuing media circus of Hegemann's plagiarism. The circuit between textual bodies, virtuality, and virality here opens a literary space to transnational digital culture that takes on political qualities, particularly when thought of in line with the moralizing intellectual property discussions spurred on by the open access movement, such as Creative Commons or the Public Knowledge Project.[68] Puar claims that virality works as a potential disturbance of transnationalism, for "virality might also be a way of differently thinking geopolitical transversality that is not insistently routed through or against the nation-state, providing an alternative to notions of transnationalism."[69] This viral moment disengages transnationalism from conceptions of nationhood, but also from the distinction between local and global, linking it instead to digital embodiment.

Conclusion: Affective Transnationalism as Literature of the Present

The considerations offered in this chapter form by no means an exhaustive study of affect in transnational German-language literature, but rather are meant to tease out the manner in which the much-cited affective turn offers access to the political in contemporary literary transnationalism.[70] The political importance of affect in transnationalism was illustrated through the reach of social impulses resulting from the appearance of affect in the text's aesthetic architecture, in the depiction of embodied affect (including also the effect of affect) to uncover or destabilize power structures, or in the cofunctioning of affect, embodiment, and technology in open systems of digital circulation. In her chapter in this volume, Herrmann writes that the key factor for contemporary literature is common experience, much of which is determined by divergent experiences under the global reach of transnationalism. Further, in his chapter Taberner speaks of the possibilities of a globalism to take hold in transnational literary world-building, a globalism that points to a cosmopolitanism of the everyday. In the above, I have examined how the textual depiction of or narrative-poetic engagement with emotional labor, corporeality, intimate publics and counterpublics, libidinal desire, and embodied technologies as transnational common experiences that find their way into literary world-building form a bridge to their political context. Together, our readings confirm that transnational, in keeping with the prefix *trans*, is a much more fluid category than often apparent in German-language literary criticism: "What is particularly striking is the way the 'trans' contained within transnationalism, invoking both potential liberation and anxiety, frequently extends to other kinds of 'crossing.'"[71] These crossings, seen transversally, include those of the body, emotions, desires, love, sexual practices, and libidinal and digital spaces as well as the crossing of these experiences from the literary to the contextual.

It is this interaction with context in an engaged and political manner that I see to be the definitive marker of the contemporary or present moment in literature. Anderson writes that "affects are an inescapable element within an expanded definition of the political," and, for this reason, "attention to affect in cultural theory is not only necessary but contemporaneous," for it "provides a way of understanding and engaging with a set of broader changes in societal (re)production in the context of mutations in capitalism."[72] He lists these changes as new forms of labor, biopolitical networks of discipline, and digital developments, the appearance of which link the contemporary or present period to the transnational. Further, in *Cruel Optimism*, Berlant speaks of the present as "perceived affectively: the present is what makes itself present to us before it becomes anything else," and, further, as "a thing that is sensed and under constant revision," emerging from how we individually and collectively "filter" situations and events.[73] Affect is key to grasping the immediacy of the present or the now in that common experience. The present is, like transnationalism, in constant flow. Therefore the affective reach of transnational literature as a literature of the present is one of process and futurity.

Notes

[1] These effects include the impact of international events on the sex work trade, the medical demands of the outsider–insider experience, or concerns related to race or class in minority and majority positions. See also Maria Mayr's chapter in this collection.

[2] Sara Ahmed et al, "Introduction: Uprootings/Regroundings: Questions of Home and Migration," in *Uprootings/Regroundings: Questions of Home and Migration*, ed. Sara Ahmed et al. (Oxford: Berg, 2003), 3.

[3] See Stuart Taberner, "Transnationalism in Contemporary German-Language Fiction by Nonminority Writers," *Seminar* 47, no. 5 (2011): 624–45; Lyn Marven, "Introduction: New German-Language Writing since the Turn of the Millennium," in *Emerging German-Language Novelists of the Twenty-First Century*, ed. Lyn Marven and Stuart Taberner (Rochester, NY: Camden House, 2011), 1–2.

[4] Michael Hardt, "Foreword: What Affects Are Good For," in *The Affective Turn: Theorizing the Social*, ed. Patricia Ticineto Clough (Durham, NC: Duke University Press, 2007), ix.

[5] Hardt, "Foreword," ix. Patricia Ticineto Clough uses the term "affective turn" in the title of her essay contained in the volume *The Affect Studies Reader* as well as for the title of a collection of essays edited by her in 2007.

[6] See Doris Bachmann-Medick, *Cultural Turns: Neuorientierungen in den Kulturwissenschaften* (Reinbek: Rowohlt, 2006).

[7] Hardt, "Foreword," x. As becomes apparent in this paragraph, each contemporary take on affect theory draws on a long and differentiated history of thinking about affect. For a discussion of the important tensions found in this legacy, see Ann Pelligrini and Jasbir Puar, "Affect," *Social Text 100* 27, no. 3 (2009): 35–38.

[8] Eve Kosofsky Sedgewick, *Touching Feeling: Affect, Pedagogy, Performativity* (Durham, NC: Duke University Press, 2003), 19.

[9] Patricia Ticineto Clough, introduction to *The Affective Turn: Theorizing the Social*, ed. Patricia Ticineto Clough (Durham, NC: Duke University Press, 2007), 2.

[10] Pelligrini and Puar, "Affect," 37.

[11] Pelligrini and Puar, "Affect," 37.

[12] Patricia Ticineto Clough "The Affective Turn: Political Economy, Biomedia, and Bodies," in *The Affect Theory Reader*, ed. Melissa Gregg and Gregory J. Seigworth (Durham, NC: Duke University Press, 2010), 207.

[13] Hardt, "Forword," ix.

[14] Pelligrini and Puar, "Affect," 37.

[15] Judith Butler, *Precarious Life: The Powers of Mourning and Violence* (London: Verso, 2004), xi.

[16] Clough, introduction, 1.

[17] Clough, introduction, 2.

[18] Clough, introduction, 3.

[19] David Conradson and Alan Latham, "The Affective Possibilities of London: Antipodean Transnationals and the Overseas Experience," *Mobilities* 2, no. 2 (2007): 235.

[20] See for example Katharina Gerstenberger and Patricia Herminghouse, introduction to *German Literature in a New Century: Trends, Traditions, Transitions, Transformations* (New York: Berghahn, 2008), 1–12. An assessment of the new political reality of German-language literature contemporaneous to 9/11 is offered by editor Martin Hielscher. See Martin Hielscher, Thomas Hettche, and Wieland Freund, "Zurück in die Wirklichkeit: Ein Schriftsteller und ein Lektor diskutieren über die neue deutsche Literatur," *Die Welt*, November 24, 2001, http://www.welt.de/print-welt/article489029/Zurueck_in_die_Wirklichkeit.html.

[21] Ilija Trojanow, *Der entfesselte Globus: Reportagen* (München: Carl Hanser Verlag, 2008), 8. All translations are my own unless otherwise noted.

[22] Trojanow, *Der entfesselte Globus*, 7. This is indicative of what Julian Preece calls the "empathy for the other" that finds its place in Trojanow's writing. Julian Preece, *Ilija Trojanow*, ed. Julian Preece (Bern: Peter Lang, 2013), 131.

[23] Trojanow, *Der entfesselte Globus*, 185.

[24] Audrey Kobayashi, Valerie Preseton, and Ann Marie Murnaghan, "Place, Affect, and Transnationalism through the Voices of Hong Kong Immigrants to Canada," *Social & Cultural Geography* 12, no. 8 (2011): 873.

[25] See Jasbir Puar, "Transversal Circuits: Transnational Sexualities and Trinidad," in *A Companion to Feminist Geography*, ed. Lise Nelson and Joni Seager (Oxford: Blackwell, 2005), 398–413.

[26] Sara Ahmed, "Collective Feelings, or The Impressions Left by Others," *Theory Culture Society* 21, no. 2 (2004): 26.

[27] Ahmed, "Collective Feelings," 25, 27.

[28] Sianne Ngai, *Ugly Feelings* (Cambridge: Harvard University Press, 2005), 3.

[29] Ben Highmore, *Ordinary Lives: Studies in the Everyday* (New York: Routledge, 2011), x.

[30] Highmore, *Ugly Feelings*, 16, 17.

[31] Highmore, *Ugly Feelings*, 20.

[32] Yoko Tawada, *Das nackte Auge* (Tübigen: konkursbuch Verlag Claudia Gerkhe, 2004), 91.

[33] Tawada, *Das nackte Auge*, 166.

[34] Tawada, *Das nackte Auge*, 25.

[35] Tawada, *Das nackte Auge*, 86–87.

[36] Tawada, *Das nackte Auge*, 184.

[37] Jasbir Puar, ed, "Precarity Talk: A Virtual Roundtable with Lauren Berlant, Judith Butler, Bojana Cvejić, Isabell Lorey, Jasbir Puar, and Ana Vujanović," *Drama Review* 56, no. 4 (2012): 166.

[38] Puar, "Precarity Talk," 173.

[39] Michel Foucault, *The History of Sexuality: An Introduction*, vol. 1, trans. Robert Hurley (New York: Vintage Books, 1990), 140–41.

[40] Foucault, *History of Sexuality*, 142–43.

[41] See David Macey, "Rethinking Biopolitics, Race and Power in the Wake of Foucault," *Theory Culture Society* 26, no. 6 (2009): 186–205.

[42] Beverley Best, "'Fredric Jameson Notwithstanding': The Dialectic of Affect," *Rethinking Marxism* 23, no. 1 (2011): 61.

[43] Ben Anderson, "Affect and Biopower: Towards a Politics of Life," *Transactions of the Institute of British Geographers* 37 (2012): 30.

[44] Juli Zeh, *Adler und Engel* (Frankfurt am Main: Schöffling, 2001), 308.

[45] Christian Kracht, *1979* (Köln: Kiepenheuer & Witsch, 2001), 34.

[46] Kracht, *1979*, 158.

[47] Kracht, *1979*, 183.

[48] Kracht, *1979*, 17.

[49] Jasbir Puar, "Homonationalism as Assemblage: Viral Travels, Affective Sexualities," *Jindal Global Law Review* 4, no. 2 (2013): 24.

[50] Jasbir Puar, "Rethinking Homonationalism," *International Journal of Middle East Studies* 45 (2013): 337. This of course references her book, *Terrorist Assemblages: Homonationalism in Queer Times* (Durham, NC: Duke University Press, 2007), in which she outlines how sexuality has become a firm part in articulating a nation's self-understanding in opposition to other nations. She shows in particular how homonationalism supports a nation's work abroad, including also its justifications for foreign intervention. It should be said in this context that the concept of homonationalism and in particular Puar's discussions around Israel and pinkwashing caused great backlash in German intellectual circles.

[51] Puar, "Rethinking Homonationalism," 337.

[52] Jasbir Puar, Dereka Rushbrook, and Louisa Schein, "Guest Editorial," *Environment and Planning D: Society and Space* 21 (2003): 384. Already in 2001, the Sexuality and Space Specialty Group of the Association of American Geographers put on a conference entitled "Sexuality and Space: Queering Geographies of Globalization." See Puar, Rushbrook, and Schein. See also Puar, "Transversal Circuits," in which she lists a variety of scholars foundational for the queering of transnational studies.

[53] Puar, Rushbrook, and Schein, "Guest Editorial," 385–86.

[54] See Lauren Berlant and Michael Warner, "Sex in Public" *Critical Inquiry* 25 (1998): 547–66.

[55] Puar, Rushbrook, and Schein, "Guest Editorial," 386.

[56] Kathrin Schmidt, *Du stirbst nicht* (Köln: Kiepenheuer & Witsch, 2009), 148.

[57] Schmidt, *Du stirbst nicht*, 138.

[58] Puar, "Homonationalism as Assemblage," 39–40.

[59] Clough, introduction, 2.

[60] Teresa de Lauretis, *Technologies of Gender: Essays on Theory, Film, and Fiction* (Bloomington: Indiana University Press, 1987), ix.

[61] Puar, "Homonationalism as Assemblage," 42.

[62] See Brian Massumi, *Parables for the Virtual: Movement, Affect, Sensation* (Durham, NC: Duke University Press, 2002).

[63] Clough, "Affective Turn," 211.

[64] See also Anke S. Biendarra, *Germans Going Global: Contemporary Literature and Cultural Globalization* (Berlin: Walter de Gruyter, 2012).

[65] Helene Hegemann, *Axolotl Roadkill* (Berlin: Ullstein Verlag, 2010), 9.

[66] Hegemann, *Axolotl Roadkill*, 52.

[67] See the February 5, 2010, post on the blog *Gefühlskonserve.de* by Deef Pirmasens, http://www.gefuehlskonserve.de/axolotl-roadkill-alles-nur-geklaut-05022010.html#more-4775.

[68] On their website, the Public Knowledge Project, for example, claims to wish to "improve both the scholarly quality and public accessibility and coherence of this body of knowledge in a sustainable and globally accessible form" (accessed August 18, 2014, http://pkp.sfu.ca/about). Creative Commons, on the other hand, notes their vision as "universal access to research, education, full participation in culture, and driving a new era of development, growth, and productivity" (accessed August 18, 2014, http://creativecommons.org).

[69] Puar, "Homonationalism as Assemblage" 43.

[70] It is further worthwhile analyzing feminism in this context. See Gabriele Grifen, "More Trans than National?: Re-Thinking Transnational Feminism through Affective Orders" *Women: A Cultural Review* 23, no. 1 (2012): 24. Sara Ahmed, Claudia Castañeda, Anne-Marie Fortier, and Mimi Sheller bring this notion of affect together with the manner in which concepts of place are coded. Their intersectional investigation suggests that we cannot think these diverse notions attached to the "field of investigation around transnationalism" without "reconsidering long-standing categories of difference addressed in feminism through the framework of uprootings and regroundings" (introduction, 3).

[71] Stuart Taberner, "Introduction: The Novel in German since 1990," in *The Novel in German Since 1990*, ed. Stuart Taberner (Cambridge: Cambridge University Press, 2011), 14.

[72] Ben Anderson, "Modulating the Excess of Affect: Morale in a State of 'Total War,'" in *The Affect Theory Reader*, ed. Melissa Gregg and Gregory J. Seigworth (Durham, NC: Duke University Press, 2010), 164–65.

[73] Lauren Berlant, *Cruel Optimism* (Durham, NC: Duke University Press: 2011), 4.

Part II. Texts

4: "On the Plane to Bishkek or in the Airport of Tashkent": Transnationalism and Notions of Home in Recent German Literature

Katharina Gerstenberger

THE CONCEPT OF TRANSNATIONALISM, a term that has been well established among social scientists since the late 1990s,[1] has recently become popular among scholars of literature and culture as well. The MLA bibliography lists 185 entries with some combination of "transnational" and "German" since 2000, the majority of them journal articles. Definitions and, more importantly, applications vary across fields. Sociologist Steven Vertovec, in his recent book-length introduction to the topic that focuses on migrant communities and their economic and communication practices, stresses the importance of "non-state actors" and their "sustained linkages and on-going exchanges" (3) across national boundaries as central to any definition of transnationalism. Paul Jay, in his 2010 study *Global Matters: The Transnational Turn in Literary Studies*, takes economic globalization together with postcolonialism as his conceptual points of departure for his examination of the effects these developments have on contemporary literature, arguing that contemporary literature has become transnational as a result of its engagement with globalization.[2] Invoking oppositional pairings, such as global and local, economic and cultural, East and West, Jay insists that "mobility is the key process here" (12). Within the field of German studies, the term *transnationalism* has most often been used in the context of migrant communities and their depiction in literature and films typically produced by artists presumed to be representatives of these groups. The characterization of Turkish-German filmmaker Fatih Akın as a "preeminent transnational director" is just one example.[3] In the case of Germany, perhaps more so than in other national contexts, economic and particularly cultural transnationalism remain closely linked to the national and to definitions of German identity. Claudia Breger, though not explicitly referring to Germany, writes in her study *An Aesthetics of Narrative Performance* (2012) that the "national and the transnational are not to be positioned in opposition to one another. Rather," she continues, "the constitution of national imaginaries, identities, and institutions has always been an effect of transcultural flows."[4] Anke Biendarra makes a similar argument when she proposes that we "read contemporary German-language literature as *glocal*," referring to the fusion of the local and the global.[5] Taking these arguments further into the realm of cultural practice, Maria Stehle, who has published extensively on questions of transnationalism in German literature and film, has identified the "desire to transcend cultural, local, and national identifications" as an important motivation for the creation of transnational cultures.[6] This desire for broadening the meanings and implications of "German," I would add, also inspires the scholarly examination of cultural productions deemed transnational. Transnationalism and its analysis in the texts of nonminority Germans, a topic to which Stuart Taberner has drawn attention in a recent essay, is thus yet another way of rethinking and rewriting German national identity.[7]

A sociopolitical reality of the contemporary period, transnationalism in the literary text denotes contemporaneousness. Notoriously difficult to define, the parameters of contemporary literature shift over time and with the arrival of new generations of writers and readers. Michael Braun's suggestion that the literature of the contemporary period follows a "kulturelles Modell von Zeitgenossenschaft" (cultural model of contemporaneity) is useful here as it underscores contemporary literature's fundamental commitment to the debates and issues of the present.[8] Contemporary literature is thus not so much a question of literary style or form but reflective of the realities experienced by a particular group, an argument put forward by Carsten Gansel and Elisabeth Herrmann in their recent volume on developments in German literature since 1989.[9] The resulting proliferation of subject matters as well as the increasing internationalization of the writers' profession, Paul Michael Lützeler noted in the 2002 introduction to his newly inaugurated yearbook *Gegenwartsliteratur* (Contemporary Literature), is itself a transnational phenomenon, an observation that in turn raises the issue of German literature's distinctiveness.[10] For the literature of the 1990s, contemporaneity largely meant to reflect on the changes in German society after the fall of the wall. In the second decade of the twenty-first century, the impacts of globalization significantly shape German society and the debates about it. This is in part a response to the realization that Germany at this point is an immigrant nation.[11] The composition of the workforce or the student body at schools and universities increasingly includes people of different national backgrounds, turning Germany into a transnational setting also for those who do not claim a migrant background.

Yet this does not mean that notions of home and the connection to the local have disappeared as sociopolitical themes or concerns in the literary text. On the contrary, the tensions between transnationalism as a contemporary, highly mobile, postnational lifestyle and the continuing pull of home as the traditional location of German culture, history, and identity now also include the voices of those who have migrated to Germany.[12] What is more, the meanings of home and its connection to history are changing under the influence of transnationalism. No longer tainted by the association with Nazi ideology and beyond nostalgia for presumably simpler times, home itself becomes a concept that somehow must respond to transnationalism and the challenges it presents to ideas of rootedness and stable identities grounded in place.

In this chapter, I will look at two recent texts by nonminority writers, Thomas von Steinaecker's 2012 novel *Das Jahr, in dem ich aufhörte, mir Sorgen zu machen, und anfing zu träumen* (The Year in Which I Stopped Worrying and Began Dreaming) and Kathrin Röggla's 2010 short story "das recherchegespenst" (The Research Ghost), and argue that these two works respond to the current interest in the concept as well as the lived realities of transnationalism and their influence on notions of national or collective identity but also on the self-definition of the individual as participant in a global world. Stuart Taberner's suggestion that the concept of transnationalism allows us to think through constellations in which "identities and cultures do not relate exclusively to fixed territories but are increasingly mobile" (624) is a useful one in this context. The narratives under consideration here, I wish to show, seek to capture contemporary realities and mind-sets that result from the increased mobility demanded by economics as well as culture "gone global," to rephrase the title of Anke Biendarra's 2012 book on contemporary literature and cultural globalization. Focusing on aspects of economic and cultural globalization, both narratives feature nonminority German protagonists who seek to position themselves in response to these developments and in the process experience the disorientation that often accompanies the emergence of transnational cultures. Vulnerabilities result from the expectation of being able to process information and rapidly adapt to change in settings across national borders and from the cultural differences that do, of course, persist. Neither text contains the violence or harshness of the culture clashes depicted in transnational pieces like, for instance, the films of Fatih Akın and his portrayals of conflicts that arise from competing cultural values; nor are the protagonists capable of the sophisticated reflections about the confluences of cultures we find in the writings of, say, Yoko Tawada with their nuanced reflections on travel and creative adaptations across cultures. Instead, von Steinaecker and Röggla draw on irony and narrative distancing to explore the possibilities and the limits of transnationalism through literary figures who struggle, if not fail, to find their way in a much expanded but also increasingly difficult to grasp world. What is more, both writers train a critical light on the preoccupation with transnationalism as a way of reconfiguring what it means to be

German at a time when the territorial, cultural, and historical connection to Germany becomes integrated into larger concepts such as European identity or a global economy. Moving beyond Germany's borders, the texts suggest, does not necessarily turn the protagonists into successful members of a transnational community.

Set during the 2008 economic downturn, Thomas von Steinaecker's novel chronicles a three-month period in the life of forty-two-year-old insurance agent Renate Meißner just after Walter, a married man and senior partner in her company, ended their relationship and instigated her transfer away from the Frankfurt headquarters to a Munich branch office. After no more than ten weeks on the new job, Renate Meißner is among those let go, presumably in response to the global financial crisis but possibly also at Walter's request. The news of her layoff reaches her in the city of Samara in south-west Russia, where she had traveled to secure an insurance contract for a large amusement park a Russian company, owned by an elderly lady of German origin, is planning to build in Munich. In response to the news of her dismissal, Renate Meißner extends her stay in the regional Russian capital and does what the novel's descriptive title suggests, that is, she abandons her obsessively competitive lifestyle and quits her various anxiety medications and dream-suppressing sleeping pills. Interspersed throughout the novel are the protagonist's reminiscences about her own family, in particular her recently deceased mother, a remarkably cosmopolitan woman who gave up international travel for her husband, and the grandmother who presumably staged her own death in a car accident and subsequently began a new life away from her relatives. Contemporary reality in von Steinaecker's novel is characterized by uncertainty, insecurity and change, challenges the protagonist tries to combat with copious research, reliance on statistics, and an uncompromising regime of self-discipline. The fusion of locations and cultures, especially in the passages about the Russian amusement park and the global experience it offers visitors in form of a ride, featuring life-like replicas of iconic travel destinations such as Venice's Piazza San Marco[13] or the mill wheel of the Moulin Rouge in Paris (*DJ*, 259), highlights the connection between transnationalism and the (literally) constructed nature of contemporary reality. Inserted into the text at random intervals are photographs and drawings that correspond to episodes in the narrative in a documentary yet arbitrary fashion, creating what Dirck Linck et al. have described as "mediengenerierte Wirklichkeitseffekte" (media-generated reality effects) and underscoring the novel's engagement with the creation and perception of present-day reality and its "neuartige 'Globalität'" (new globality).[14]

Kathrin Röggla's "das recherchegespenst" tells the story of a brother and sister team of journalists, both in their mid- to late thirties, who have just completed a trip to several former Soviet Republics where they interviewed international aid professionals who had attempted to return home after extended sojourns abroad but ultimately could not bring themselves to do so.[15] Whereas the brother feels that they have enough good material to tell a coherent story, his sister, he believes, has joined the ranks of those who have made the transnational settings of the NGO-world their home, an environment characterized by the endless chase after information and pertinent social connections as well as the availability of Western-style amenities for those who inhabit it. Juxtaposing the current cohort of international aid workers' reluctance to return with the previous generation's groundedness in notions of *Heimat* (Home), Röggla's story explores transnationalism as a contemporary lifestyle that no longer seems to involve the need for a home.

Mobility, which here connotes a high degree of flexibility in response to the ever-shifting demands at the workplace in Germany as much as the willingness to travel abroad, is a defining feature of the characters in both von Steinaecker's novel and Röggla's short story. Neither demonstratively cosmopolitan in the tradition of the intellectual German travelers or "Bildungsreisende" (travelers in pursuit of education), such as Goethe or Alexander von Humboldt, nor mired in a conflicted post-Holocaust Germanness, the protagonists in these stories take moving in and out of Germany for granted, their cultural practices defined by work environments that require them to operate across the boundaries of German national culture. Unlike migrant workers, the characters portrayed in these texts practice a voluntary or privileged transnationalism that nevertheless echoes some of the disorientation and confusion concerning cultural belonging, especially regarding questions of home, we find in works such as Emine Sevgi Özdamar's *Brücke vom Goldenen Horn* (1998; *The Bridge of the Golden Horn*, 2007). Travel, instant communication, access to information at all times and from everywhere is routine for these literary characters. Family relationships, childhood memories, notions of home as well as references to the German past do play a role, but they no longer mark the protagonists as the heirs to a German history with whose legacies they have to grapple. Transnationalism thus also has a liberating quality not only for the protagonists but, we might speculate, for their authors as well, and, as such, these two texts represent a departure from those recent novels that explore German history through several generations of one family—including works such as Arno Geiger's *Es geht uns gut* (We Are Doing Well, 2005), Julia Franck's *Die Mittagsfrau* (2007; *The Blind Side of the Heart*, 2009), Uwe Tellkamp's *Der Turm* (The Tower, 2008), Eugen Ruge's *In Zeiten des abnehmenden Lichts* (2011; *In Times of Fading Light*, 2013), or Ursula Krechel's *Landgericht* (District Court, 2012). Through their travel, and even more so through their contemporary communication practices, the protagonists put before us ways of "being German" that are "transnationally polyvalent and performative" rather than "fixed, by nation and history." German history, Stuart Taberner has argued, is a major impediment nonminority German writers, as well as their characters, face in becoming transnational, one that plays a role in several of the titles listed above as well (626). At the same time, by introducing characters for whom the physical and mental mobility that defines transnationalism comes at a significant cost, both texts draw attention to the potential limitations of transnational polyvalence in regard to individual lives but also in regard to its power to rewrite and reconfigure notions of Germanness. The fact that both texts send their protagonists to the former Soviet Union is coincidence, but the authors' choice suggests that cultures and economies in such fundamental transition like Russia's or Uzbekistan's are particularly apt case studies for the workings of transnationalism not only for the people who live there but also for those who come to participate in and profit from these developments.

In contrast to what Stuart Taberner has termed an "ideal" (634) transnationalism that finds expression in the protagonists' ability to "move with ease within a plurality of cultures" (633), the texts under consideration here explore what I suggest we term "realist" transnationalism aimed at describing the limits and failures of the contemporary, highly mobile, information-driven lifestyles to which the protagonists aspire. Transnationalism, even though it has historical precursors in concepts such as cosmopolitanism and "Weltbürgertum" (citizenship of the world), is a phenomenon of the present age and thus one of the defining features of contemporaneity.[16] Germanist Frank Ruda, in an essay about the real in the contemporary novel, has argued that the realist project is "eine Frage der Zeitgenossenschaft" (a question of contemporaneity).[17] The present, he suggests in his analyses of Elias Canetti, Fredric Jameson, and Alain Badiou, instills in the observer "Ratlosigkeit und Desorientierung" (162; bewilderment and disorientation). This sense of disorientation, which has characterized realist writing since its inception in the nineteenth century and in response to the social changes it seeks to capture,[18] finds continued expression in experiences of transnationalism as a contemporary condition of profound transformation. In 2005, in response to a request by the German weekly *Die Zeit* to weigh in on the relevance of the novel as a literary form and its function in contemporary society, a group of four writers, among them Thomas Hettche and Thomas Politycki, rejected what they saw as the self-referentiality of "Popliteratur" (pop literature) demanding instead what they called "relevanter Realismus" (relevant realism) and identifying as its foremost task to engage with contemporary issues. Titled "Was soll der Roman?" (What Is the Purpose of the Novel?) the essay recognizes transnational contexts as one of the core issues of the contemporary period, albeit without using the term: "Und da sehen wir," the authors write, "jetzt und in Zukunft, Menschen, die von einem Ort zum anderen unterwegs sind" (And there we see, now and in the future, people moving from place to another). And they continue, "Dieser weite Blick für neue Gruppierungen und globale Zwischenräume ist gegenüber den engen Tälern und den technikfreien Naturreservaten zu reklamieren" (This broad outlook for new groupings and global interspaces must be claimed over narrow valleys and technology-free nature preserves). The emphasis on movement and technology as defining categories of contemporary life together with the rejection of closely circumscribed locations in favor of spaces and connections created by technological means identifies some central qualities of transnationalism as not only an appropriate but also a necessary topic of literature.

Thomas von Steinaecker's *Das Jahr, in dem ich aufhörte, mir Sorgen zu machen, und anfing zu träumen* centers on the workplace as its site of contemporary reality in a multicultural yet still male-dominated Germany in which men tend to have decision-making power both at the workplace and in personal relationships. Renate Meißner's daily routine, which involves the constant use of communication technology and is guided by the techniques she has learned in company-sponsored seminars with titles such as "Hunger nutzen" (*DJ*, 24; Harnessing Hunger), is shaped by attitudes and a vocabulary the reader will associate with American models of achievement-oriented conduct on the job: Giving in to hunger-induced "Food-Images" (*DJ*, 24–25) and buying a bar of chocolate from the on-site vending machine allows the contemporary employee to skip regular meals and keep working. With multiculturalism being an accepted element of contemporary German society, Renate's Turkish colleagues are entirely integrated into the office workforce. If anything, gender has a bigger influence on an employee's position and success than ethnic origin. The decision makers at CAVERE, the insurance company whose name in Latin means "to be careful," are German males; the secretary for Renate Meißner's office is a Turkish woman. Her colleague Serdar, a highly motivated young man with Turkish background, is the only one in her group who does not get fired as a result of the internal restructuring in response to the international financial crisis of 2008. "Schwanzvergleich" (dick comparison) is his somewhat apologetic explanation to Renate regarding the process of elimination (*DJ*, 27).

The novel's transnational aspects do not strictly follow the sociological definition of the "sustained linkages" across national borders suggested by Steven Vertovec but rather represent a network of circumstances, behaviors, and experiences that characterize the present as a time of hyperconnectedness and access to information from around the globe, some of which the protagonists process rather idiosyncratically. Renate's brother Erwin, for instance, who works for a TV station, relaxes every night by looking at the webcam transmission from an office in Tokyo's Fuji Center (*DJ*, 143), delighting in the fact that somewhere in the world people are working in an office. His mistaken claim that it is still Tuesday in Japan when it is already Wednesday in Germany only underscores that access to information does not always lead to correct interpretations (*DJ*, 144). Renate, by contrast, finds it difficult to relate to a Pakistani woman she sees on TV, wailing after an earthquake in that country. The poor quality of the footage shown on TV makes it hard to assess their authenticity, and, moreover, the disaster has no impact on her work since none of her clients own property in the region (*DJ*, 111). Broadly available documentation of every conceivable event or circumstance creates global connections whose effects and outcomes are inevitably erratic. Renate's dreams of adopting a three-year-old black girl from Africa, which she insists are "nicht abstrus, sie sind realistisch" (146; not absurd, they are realistic), are a contemporary and transnational adaptation of her desire to feel the unconditional love of a child. What makes these transnational fantasies realistic is not so much their feasibility but the fact that they are perceived and experienced as concrete possibility by the characters.

Realism, Gerhard Plumpe has argued in a piece titled "Realismus als Programm moderner Literatur" (Realism as Manifesto of Modern Literature, 2000) depicts the "Konstruktion von Wirklichkeit in einer sich selbst konstruierenden Wirklichkeit" (construction of reality in a reality that constructs itself).[19] Travel, border crossing, and the engagement with other cultures and their geographic sites, all of them core elements of transnationalism, underscore reality's constructedness and challenge notions of cultural or historical authenticity. No longer grounded in local space, culture, or history, the transnational settings and spaces depicted in von Steinaecker's novel are shown not only to be artificially created but open to misinterpretation, misrepresentation, or even incomprehensibility. The protagonist's often futile attempts at deciphering and mastering her environment serve to create ironic distance but also to convey critique. For instance, prior to her trip to Russia, Renate Meißner visits Munich's Alte Pinakothek, where she engrosses herself in a seventeenth-century painting titled "Moskau" (Moscow). Part of a multicanvas assembly labeled "Europe," in which portraits of several cities are grouped around a larger painting showing a female allegory of the continent, the city images, Renate learns from the catalogue, are copied from unreliable sources and should not be taken for accurate renditions (*DJ*, 236). The purpose of the arrangement, she concludes, is to depict "Europe" as a commercial enterprise, "das Gemälde selbst: Reklame" (*DJ*, 236; the painting itself: advertising). While the image of Moscow may not provide a mimetic depiction of that city but nevertheless can be appreciated and interpreted as a painting, the website for the Russian amusement park the protagonist accesses in preparation for her trip is utterly incomprehensible to her because of the translation software's inadequacy (*DJ*, 180). In this case, the message gets lost in the programming depths of cyberspace, calling into question the internet age's promise of border-less communication. In addition, the novel contains several passages featuring translations from Russian into German or German spoken by nonnative speakers. While the slight misapplication of terms adds to the novel's humor—"befriedigt" (satisfied) instead of "zufrieden" (*DJ*, 191; content)—the use of German instead of English in international settings draws attention to the German language's transnational clout but also reminds us that such breadth does come at the expense of nuance and precision. National emblems, to give a final example of culture on the move, can easily be transported into contexts where their meanings are no longer interpretable to those whom they are supposed to represent. Upon landing in Samara, Renate is taken aback by what she believes to be a display of German nationalism on the part of a young woman wearing a "Klose" sweatshirt and a scarf in the colors of the German flag—until she realizes that the woman is in fact Russian (*DJ*, 242).[20] Culture and its symbols are highly mobile in von Steinaecker's transnational scenarios; taken out of their original setting, they become open to a range of usages, undermining notions of authenticity and, in this case, losing the political connotations they carry within the national context to a transnational appropriation.

The amusement park itself is the novel's richest example of a transnationalism that at times distorts the world into caricatures of itself. Based on the model of Disneyland Paris, the Russian version, its representative admits, is perhaps not quite as elaborate but certainly worth a visit. A replica of a replica, the park features a twelve-minute tour of the world that includes places like Venice and New York City. Having never been to Venice, Renate Meißner fears that the flawlessness of the theme-park rendition might spoil any visit to the real city she might undertake in the future. Similarly, New York City, which still features the World Trade Center even though the novel is set in 2008 (*DJ*, 259), is an undamaged and therefore better version than the original. Her Russian host, whose fluent German and familiarity with German culture underscore his transnational credentials, mentions that business after 9/11 was strong because people no longer had the courage to travel to Paris for a Disneyland visit and the park's attractions allowed them to see the world without having to leave their home city. The park's version of sixteenth-century Nuremberg inspires him to inquire, "Wie gefällt Ihnen Ihre Heimat?" (*DJ*, 251; How do you like your homeland?) Applied to a display in an amusement park, the concept of *Heimat* is either stripped of its conventional meaning as a place of deep connections and familiarity or, perhaps appropriately, vastly expanded to satisfy the mobility requirement of transnationalism and no longer tied to authentic experience and notions of belonging. Yet Germany itself, Renate Meißner recalls her recently deceased mother having told her, is "ein bisschen wie ein großes Disneyland" (a bit like a huge Disneyland), passing off buildings as hundreds of years old that had in fact been rebuilt from rubble after the Second World War (*DJ*, 33). As Friedrike Eigler has argued in a recent article about "*Heimat* and the Spatial Turn," the concept of *Heimat* might be usefully explored in relation to the postmodern concept of space in addition to the more traditional notion of *Heimat* as grounded in memory and place.[21] The radical uncoupling of *Heimat* from authentic locations in von Steinaecker's novel not only abroad but also at home draws attention to the impact of transnationalism on the reconfiguration of geographical space. More important than the by now familiar blurring of reality and imitation are the emotions triggered by such replications of the real. A fake earthquake and a subsequent tsunami she witnesses in the amusement park instill panic but also a feeling of genuine satisfaction in Renate as she is able to lend a helping hand to a crying woman during what the protagonist herself knew to be a simulation (*DJ*, 280). From the seventeenth-century painting of Moscow that does not depict the city, to the theme-park version of a pre-9/11 New York City in a provincial city in Russia in the year 2008, the transporting and fusing of cultures into sites and time frames well beyond their original locations and histories are central to the novel's exploration of the contemporary period as transnational and of the often unsettling influence of the confluences of cultures on the protagonists' experiences and understanding of reality.

The Nazi past, which, as Stuart Taberner has argued, in recent literary texts either prevents the protagonists from entering into transnational spaces or, alternatively, compels them to do so,[22] must be considered the novel's most critical assessment of transnationalism and its function in German literature. Sofia Wasserkind, the amusement park's owner, was born in Samara to German immigrant parents and moved back and forth between Germany and Russia under the influence of the Russian Revolution and later the Nazi regime.[23] Unreliable as a narrator due to her very advanced age, she is a transnational German—albeit one who is unable to transform her knowledge of two cultures and languages into the progressive project that contemporary critics sometimes call for when they propose the creation of transnational identities as a countermeasure against nationalism.[24] Her life story, which she recounts at great length and to Renate Meißner's consternation, includes recollections about a plan to create a Germania theme park in Munich during the Nazi period, a project whose realness the novel keeps deliberately vague and that is abandoned after Sofia Wasserkind's husband, in an episode that pushes the mixing of reality and imagination to a disturbing limit, finds himself in an amusement park of sorts that resembles the Dachau concentration camp (370). Steven Spielberg's *Schindler's List* (1993), a film to which the novel repeatedly refers and to which the protagonist owes much of her awareness of the Holocaust, shows the Holocaust to be a transnational combination of German history and American filmmaking: The movie, she explains, allowed her to develop an emotional response to the Nazi crimes, something a school trip to the Dachau concentration camp prevented her from doing (364). Similarly, her Turkish colleague Serdar expresses fascination with an American TV series he is currently watching on DVD about a Jewish family during the Third Reich, for which the filmmakers had to build replicas of Auschwitz because at the actual site, he believes, "gibt es kaum noch was" (26; there is hardly anything left). Unlike the German audience in 1979, for whom the TV series *Holocaust* came as a revelation and an emotional shock, the Turkish-German insurance agent in 2008 credits the TV drama with preserving an aspect of history that otherwise could no longer be experienced. The authenticity traditionally attributed to notions of place can no longer be taken for granted but, significantly, is no longer required either. Von Steinaecker's novel affirms the importance of transnationalism as a central aspect of contemporary reality but also shows its limitations as a critical and progressive project expected to overcome chauvinism and to broaden cultural horizons.

Whereas Thomas von Steinaecker blends reality and imagination within the narrative frame of his fiction, at times leaving the reader wondering about an episode's realism, Kathrin Röggla's explorations of transnationalism as an aspect of contemporaneousness stay closer to empirical reality. Beginning with her account of 9/11 in *really ground zero*, a collage of observations, news coverage, and personal impressions about her time in New York City immediately after the attacks on the World Trade Center, Röggla has produced a number of texts that explore the connections between contemporary work life and notions of risk in international settings. *Wir schlafen nicht* (2004; *We Never Sleep*, 2009), her novel based on interviews with corporate employees, chronicles fast-lane lifestyles and their impact on the individual. Told in the subjunctive mode, the different chapters revolve around topics like coping with excessively long work days, crisis management both as job description and as experience on the job, and international work-related travel. With its nonplaces of offices and exhibition halls, the corporate work environment erodes connections to location and the local. Modeled after what perhaps once was perceived as an "American" way of working and today has become transnational in its ubiquity, her characters live in a reality that is no longer anchored in their immediate and physical environment. Even if they do not travel, their connection to a fixed territory or culture has become tenuous at best. Röggla's texts are based on copious research in the form of interviews but also attendance at conferences, allowing her to understand the concerns and the language of specific fields (environmental risks, legal issues, corporate world), which she transcribes and then uses as the foundation for her texts.[25] As a result, her writing conveys a high degree of linguistic and factual realism. The use of the subjunctive mode in most of her literary work and the arrangement of text elements into themes and topics reveal the author's voice and indicate to the reader the transformation of raw material into fiction.

In much of Röggla's recent work, transnationalism figures prominently in her analysis of risk and risk management, be it economic or environmental, as such concerns do not stop at national borders and increasingly involve multinational, nongovernmental teams of experts. Her recent film "Die bewegliche Zukunft" (The Flexible Future, 2012), for example, a documentary about high risk technologies in Eastern Europe and the people who manage the environmental but also economic hazards they pose, is a reflection on how local issues, such as the pollution caused by large-scale mining as well as the funding schemes available to such industries, become transnational concerns and pursuits. Traveling with a film crew and three experts on disaster management, Röggla, who made this film during her appointment as *Stadtschreiber* (writer-in-residence) in Mainz, visited sites in Eastern Germany, Kosovo, and Bulgaria. Risk and risk management are introduced as transnational concerns—certainly within the European Union, in which the site managers and interview partners have more in common than separating them despite their different nationalities and the clearly discernible economic differences between their respective countries. As such, Röggla's work responds to the arguments put forth by Ulrich Beck in his analysis of industrial nations developing from "*production* society" to "industrial *consequence* society" and the resulting "global surplus of risk" that stops at neither class nor national borders.[26] The risk technologies and their management that are the topic of *Die bewegliche Zukunft* result in transnational lifestyles for the film's protagonists in their pursuit of solutions to international problems. What is more, the shared concern over environmental issues and risks contributes to a sense of community and to an idea of what it means to live in a present whose challenges and solutions are shared across national borders. Röggla's interview partners, including the three German risk management experts, are not employed by government organizations, consistent with Steven Vertovec's insight that transnationalism involves nonstate actors.

"das recherchegespenst," one of several stories in the collection *die alarmbereiten* (People on the Alert) that explore transnational experiences, is a dialogue of sorts between a man and his sister, both of them in their mid- to late thirties, who work as journalists in international crisis settings. Using the subjunctive mode of indirect speech, the text conveys the brother's perspective on their cooperation through the narrative voice of his sister, who has somehow vanished from the story while her brother is sitting in the Tashkent airport waiting for his flight home. The story's first paragraph, one of the text's few passages related in the indicative mode, has the sister declare that her brother's letters, written or verbal, always reach her, suggesting that the following narrative is part of an ongoing exchange between the two of them that has taken a life of its own and no longer depends on an actual dialogue, because the siblings had these conversations many times before. Throughout the story, the brother questions his sister's approach and commitment to their project of interviewing European or American aid workers in former Soviet republics, such as Georgia and Uzbekistan. Specifically, the siblings had agreed to do a story on international aid professionals and the difficulties such people face if and when they return home, a topic that should not even have required the two to travel in the first place. The young man, who does not enjoy travel and, moreover, feels himself to be in charge of the pragmatic rather than the research aspects of reporting, accuses his sister of not following up on important leads and of pursuing new contacts without having made full use of those that already exist. In her brother's mind, she has turned into a "recherchegespenst" (research ghost)[27] or an "unheimlichkeitswesen" (*R*, 112; uncanniness creature), consumed by her pursuit of ever more information without producing the story the two of them set out to tell. A story about (not) writing a story about people who have lost their ability or will to return home, with paragraphs of notably different length and typically without transition, Röggla's text, through its content as well as its disjointed narrative structure, captures a lifestyle and mindset characterized by hypermobility and the creation of a "third space" that is neither a traditional home nor foreign. Kathrin Röggla develops further Steven Vertovec's argument about the "processes of formation and maintenance" of connections "across nation-states" (3), through characters for whom the creation of such linkages has become a pursuit and raison d'être in its own right and who refuse to be bound to a place they would have to call home, relying on mobility to replace the local with the global.

Central to Röggla's story is the question of home and the failure or unwillingness to return to it. Appropriately, the disagreement between brother and sister begins with the question from which physical location one can tell such a story. The brother, who is lured into the project by his sister's promise that this particular story, which, after all, takes place in "deutschen wohnzimmern und biergärten" (*R*, 93; German living rooms and beer gardens), would allow them to stay in Berlin or, in any case, not force them to travel beyond the "schengengrenzen" (*R*, 93; borders of the Schengen agreement). "allenfalls müssten wir nach bonn oder wien" (*R*, 94; at the most we would have to travel to Bonn or Vienna), he quotes his sister as having reassured him. While the brother feels that they have good material and could start their piece in a number of ways, his sister rejects all of his suggestions as either too insignificant (*R*, 96) or too personal (*R*, 97). Unlike their father, an engineer who worked abroad from the late 1960s through the early 1990s but always returned home from his trips to the same "wohnzimmertisch" (living room table), today's international experts can no longer claim this kind of a stable point of reference for themselves (R, 105).[28] Yet even during the 1980s, when the siblings were children, his sister insists, the living room did not offer shelter from the conflicts of the world because their father's work in crisis regions brought those struggles back to their "heimatstadt" (R, 97; home town). Their father was employed by a government organization, whereas people of their own generation work for international organizations or NGOs and thus no longer retain this particular connection to their nation of origin. As a result, far fewer people return and, furthermore, much prefer to talk about their "aufbrüchen . . . als von ihrer heim-kehr" (R, 105; departures . . . rather than their return). The connection to the homeland has been eroded through the emergence of a network of international organizations and the people who inhabit them. They have brought the medical care, schools, bars, and restaurants (100) they expect to have at their disposal with them, in the process creating transnational sites within the countries they came to serve. A case in point is the "sozialsöldner" (R, 111; social mercenary) who, having lost his job with his NGO, distributes his business card among the clientele of an international restaurant in the Kyrgyz capital Bishkek in the hope of finding a new job and to avoid having to return home. Home, for which the text suggestively rehabilitates the cliché of the German living room and the beer garden, is a center that no longer holds.

Absence of a center or a location from which the story could be told also plagues the organization of the narrative the brother-sister team set out to create. While the brother feels that they have plenty of material they could use to introduce "das abstrakte globale gesche-hen mit einer lokalen einstiegsluke" (R, 95; abstract global occurrences with a local point of entry)—he suggests a party in Tiflis for new NGO workers who arrived in the Georgian capital without the language skills needed to work with local populations—his sister seems dissatisfied with this approach, always chasing after weightier and more relevant information. Transnationalism here is not so much the emergence of cultural practices and exchanges across national borders but the creation of a culture that has lost its desire for home and place. Travel is a way of staying away from home rather than a means of experiencing different cultures. The two perspectives represented in this story, the brother with his attachment to place and his belief in the possibility of telling the story of those who no longer desire to return home, and the sister who he suspects vanishes into the depths of the airport to avoid having to board the plane back home, hint at the emergence of spaces and spheres of communication that are neither home nor foreign. Röggla's characters are migrants, not from one nation-state to another but from a nation-state into supranational organizations where they create their own transnational homes, however tenuous those might be.

In the two works of contemporary or relevant realism discussed here, transnationalism is an important marker of the present. The transnational realities depicted in these texts are characterized by an emphasis on mobility and instant communication in daily life, dwindling differences between cultures and a self-understanding of German society as multicultural, and the diminished importance of place and home in favor of environments that can be recreated in different locations. Affect, as a result, no longer depends on place or authentic locations but can be triggered by information, images, or narratives presented in various forms, at times taking surprising and unprecedented turns. In von Steinaecker's novel, moreover, transnationalism plays a central role in reconceptualizing German identity by referencing the Nazi past as transnational rather than German history, an undertaking the novel presents with a degree of scepticism. Importantly, both authors treat their protagonists and their transnational pursuits with a certain ironic distance, depicting them as people trying to react to the rapid and often confusing change that surrounds them rather than driving or controlling it. While neither of the texts mourns the loss of place and nation, acknowledging that there is no authentic culture of home, they also suggest that embracing contemporary reality as hyperconstructed and transnational may be a compelling answer to the provincialism of postwar Germany and its unfinished project of integrating the memory of the Nazi past into its identity, yet in the end raises more questions than it can solve. Ironizing the contemporary period rather than drafting the future, both works invite us to think critically about our transnational present. This is their most important contribution to contemporary German literature going forward.

Notes

[1] Steven Vertovec, *Transnationalism* (London: Routledge, 2009).

[2] Paul Jay, *Global Matters: The Transnational Turn in Literary Studies* (Ithaca: Cornell University Press, 2010), 6.

[3] Barbara Mennel, "Golden Bear for *Gegen die Wand* Affirms Fatih Akın as Germany's Preeminent Transnational Director," in *A New History of German Cinema*, ed. Jennifer Kapczynski and Michael D. Richardson (Rochester, NY: Camden House, 2012), 583.

[4] Claudia Breger, *An Aesthetics of Narrative Performance: Transnational Theater, Literature, and Film in Contemporary Germany* (Columbus: Ohio State University Press, 2012), 40.

[5] Anke Biendarra, *Germans Going Global: Contemporary Literature and Cultural Globalization* (Boston: De Gruyter, 2012), 9.

[6] Maria Stehle, "Transnationalism Meets Provincialism: Generations and Identifications in *Faserland*, *Kurz und schmerzlos*, and *Selam Berlin*," in *Generational Shifts in Contemporary German Culture*, ed. Laurel Cohen-Pfister and Susanne Vees-Gulani (Rochester, NY: Camden House, 2010), 270.

[7] Stuart Taberner, "Transnationalism in Contemporary German-Language Fiction by Nonminority Writers," *Seminar* 47, no. 5 (2011): 624–45.

[8] Michael Braun, *Die deutsche Gegenwartsliteratur: Eine Einführung* (Cologne: Böhlau, 2010), 20.

[9] Carsten Gansel and Elisabeth Herrmann, *Einwicklungen in der deutschsprachigen Gegenwartsliteratur nach 1989* (Göttingen: V&R unipress, 2013), 17.

[10] Paul Michael Lützeler, "Vorwort," *Gegenwartsliteratur: A German Studies Yearbook* 1 (2002): xv.

[11] If anything, Thilo Sarrazin's highly controversial anti-immigration book *Deutschland schafft sich ab* (Germany Does Away with Itself, 2010) and Angela Merkel's pronouncement that multiculturalism has failed, also in 2010, confirm that Germany is an immigrant society.

[12] An example here is Iranian-born writer Navid Kermani; in his essay "Grenzverkehr," he reflects on his layered local, national, and international identifications. Navid Kermani, "Grenzverkehr," in *Wer ist wir? Deutschland und seine Muslime* (Munich: Beck, 2009), 9–27.

[13] Thomas von Steinaecker, *Das Jahr, in dem ich aufhörte, mir Sorgen zu machen, und anfing zu träumen* (Frankfurt am Main: S. Fischer, 2012), 258. Hereafter *DJ* in the main body of the text.

[14] Dirck Linck, Michael Lüthy, and Martin Vöhler, "Zur Einführung: Realismus in den Künsten der Gegenwart," in *Realismus in den Künsten der Gegenwart*, ed. Dirck Linck, Michael Lüthy, Brigitte Obermayr, and Martin Vöhler (Berlin: diaphanes, 2010), 7.

[15] Kathrin Röggla uses small letters throughout her fictional work, including in titles. She retains the use of capitalization in her essayistic work, suggesting that small letters serve to underscore the distinct quality of the language of fiction.

[16] It is perhaps no coincidence that the cover blurbs on both Röggla's and von Steinaecker's books praise them as contributions to the understanding of "unsere Gegenwart" (our contemporary period).

[17] Frank Ruda, "Was ist das Reale des zeitgenössischen Realismus? Canetti, Jameson, Badiou," in *Realismus in den Künsten der Gegenwart*, ed. Dirck Link et al. (Berlin: diaphanes, 2010), 160.

[18] See Gerhard Plumpe, "Einleitung," *Theorie des bürgerlichen Realismus*, ed. Gerhard Plumpe (Stuttgart: Reclam, 1997), 9–40. Nineteenth-century realism is shaped by the tensions between political realism and an aesthetic that remains committed to idealism with the aim of harmonizing the uncertainties caused by political disillusionment (16).

[19] Gerhard Plumpe, "Realismus als Programm moderner Literatur," *Zeitschrift der Germanisten Rumäniens* 9, no. 17–18 (2000): 64.

[20] For a detailed discussion of German soccer nationalism see Maria Stehle and Beverly M. Weber, "German Soccer: The 2010 World Cup, and Multicultural Belonging," *German Studies Review* 36, no. 1 (2013): 103–24.

[21] Friedrike Eigler. "Critical Approaches to *Heimat* and the 'Spatial Turn'," *New German Critique* 39, no. 1 (2012): 33.

[22] Taberner, "Transnationalism," 626.

[23] The city of Samara does in fact have a significant population of German origin.

[24] For an insightful discussion beyond an understanding of multiculturalism as either failure or panacea to address cultural diversity in Germany, see Maria Stehle, *Ghetto Voices in Contemporary German Culture: Textscapes, Filmscapes, Soundscapes* (Rochester, NY: Camden House, 2012), 5–6. Transnationalism serves a similar function.

[25] Conversation with the author; see also Kathrin Röggla, "Stottern und Stolpern: Strategien einer literarischen Gesprächsführung, "in *besser wäre: keine* (Frankfurt am Main: S. Fischer, 2013), 307–31, especially 319.

[26] Ulrich Beck, "The Conflict of Two Modernities," in *Ecological Enlightenment: Essays on the Politics of the Risk Society*, transl. Mark A. Ritter (Atlantic Highlands, NJ: Humanities Press, 1995), 139.

[27] Kathrin Röggla, "das recherchegespenst," in *die alarmbereiten* (Frankfurt am Main: S. Fischer, 2010), 93–119; here, 119. Hereafter *R* in the main body of the text.

[28] In *besser wäre: keine*, her essay about the world of NGOs, Röggla refers to her father's work as an engineer in international crisis settings and the conversations the family had about this at the kitchen table (*besser wäre: keine*, 101). Several of the characters that appear in "das recherchegespenst" seem to be based on people Röggla interviewed during a trip to Kyrgyzstan and Uzbekistan she describes in this essay.

5: Transnationalism, Colonial Loops, and the Vicissitudes of Cosmopolitan Affect: Christian Kracht's *Imperium* and Teju Cole's *Open City*

Claudia Breger

THIS CHAPTER DISCUSSES transnationalism and cosmopolitanism against the backdrop of two recent novels, Christian Kracht's *Imperium* (Empire, 2012) and Teju Cole's *Open City* (2011; 2012). Kracht's novel about the turn-of-the-twentieth-century dropout and South Seas-colonizer August Engelhardt is thematically significant in this context, particularly insofar as colonialism—as a historical context marked by extremely asymmetrical transnational movements—constitutes a crucial backdrop for contemporary uses of the term. In contrast to Herrmann and Taberner in this volume, however, this chapter argues that Kracht's novel cannot therefore be called transnational in a more programmatic sense. As detailed below, the publication of *Imperium* unleashed a major feuilleton controversy in Germany. On the one hand, the author was accused of right-wing sympathies and racism; on the other hand, that charge was attributed to a lack of appreciation for the literary form of the novel, specifically its uses of irony. Critically engaging the terms of this debate (and thereby affirming the significance of aesthetics also for political readings of literature), my own close reading of the text suggests that the narrative voice, intertextual archive and rhetoric of *Imperium*'s literary fantasy return audiences into a colonial loop. The ironic inflections of its German narrator's voice, I demonstrate, do not translate into a clearcut intervention against the colonial mentalities he is evoking. Despite its thematic focus on transnational movements, *Imperium* thus does not resonate with the, in my view, most productive layer of transnationalism in its recent conceptualizations. As developed in the central section of this paper, I understand transnationalism (in the programmatic sense, and differing from its contextualization in the introduction to this volume) as a methodological perspective that foregrounds a critique of nationalist mythologies. This perspective does not imply the insignificance of nation-building, but it investigates the contingent historical processes through which nations came into being, and specifically the imperialist and racist mythologies supporting the process of German nation-building in the colonial era.

With its literary failure to effectively critique these mythologies, Kracht's novel is arguably indicative also of broader challenges for contemporary German literature as produced and read in a context still marked by these legacies of imperialist (and later fascist) nation-building. An alternative perspective, I suggest, is opened up by my second literary example, Cole's American debut novel about a young Nigerian-American doctor exploring the twenty-first-century cityscapes of New York and Brussels, where he hopes to reconnect with his German grandmother. Both thematically and in narrative form, *Open City* presents a counterpoint to *Imperium*: Set in the present, and in geographically different contexts, it indirectly connects to Kracht's world through its exploration of the histories of colonialism and the Holocaust, along with those of slavery. At first glance, Cole's novel is also not an altogether smooth fit with transnationalism in the outlined sense of a critical methodological perspective. Rather, it contributes to topical twenty-first-century discourses of *cosmopolitanism*. Explicitly quoting Kwame Anthony Appiah's philosophical essay on this topic, Cole's text engages a theoretical perspective which represents a new challenge to the notion of transnationalism spelled out in this chapter: a return to more "positive," in part universalist, in part culturalist paradigms of collective identification, which has gained prominence in theoretical as well as broader cultural discourses since the turn of our century. As my reading details, however, the narrative voice of Cole's character narrator (which differs starkly from that of Kracht's narrator) productively complicates Appiah's concept of cosmopolitanism by confronting it with the affective weight of the histories of colonialism, slavery, and the Holocaust. Thereby, the novel indicates how cosmopolitanism can be conceptualized in programmatically transnational terms: by engaging the contingent histories of the nation as important stumbling blocks for its project of overcoming the divisions between humans.

Colonial Loops: *Imperium*

When Georg Diez's *Spiegel* review of Kracht's *Imperium* accused both text and author of right-wing sympathies, or more specifically antidemocratic, antimodern aestheticism celebrating the protagonist's "exquisiteste Barbarei" (most exquisite barbarism; Diez, quoting the novel), a range of voices rallied to the novel's defense. An open letter signed by a group of renowned authors and critics (including Elfriede Jelinek) accused Diez of "denunciation" by way, not least, of attributing character and narrator utterances to the author.[1] Meanwhile, Jan Küveler, writing in *Die Welt* critically dismissed Diez's charges, and suggested that he was unable, or

unwilling, to decipher irony, and literary scholar Erhard Schütz praised
the novel as "glänzende Literatur" (magnificient literature) rather than
"Nazikram" (Nazi stuff).[2] I argue that both of these responses are unsat-
isfactory. Diez can in fact be charged with a lack of attention to the novel's aesthetic form and irony, along with all-too-substantial reliance on
contextual information that short-circuits the novel's implied author with
a flesh-and-blood Kracht reconstructed from a recently published set of
letters to David Woodard. However, the result of my own narratological
analysis dovetails less with Schütz's praise than, at least in some respects,
with the polemical counterpoint argued by yet other reviewers in response
to the debate, according to which Kracht's novel is "literarisch in jedem
Fall gründlich misslungen" (as literature, definitively thoroughly failed).[3]

Importantly (and beyond the polemics), I will develop my own assessment of the text's aesthetic quality in a self-reflexive frame of attending to
the ways in which such verdicts operate. As James Phelan has spelled out,
interpretative, ethical, and aesthetic judgments tend to overlap in the process of reading.[4] While inclined to agree with the skeptical assessments of
Kracht's prose, I am, in other words, aware of the ways in which my own
evaluations are also implicated in the larger ethical—and political—controversies (on racism, colonialism, and the legacies of the German nation)
stirred by the novel, even as I simultaneously strive to displace the oppo-
nents' contrary takes with a more differentiated analysis of the text. In
thus participating in the debate on Kracht's novel, I am interested in the
aesthetic (and political) limitations of his prose less for the sake of quality
judgments per se than insofar as those limitations can serve as indicators
about the novel's literary and discursive context.

Diez's reading of Kracht's novel as a celebration of its protofascist
protagonist, which would align with the author's nihilist worldview along
the coordinates of "Vernichtung" (destruction) and "Erlösung" (salvation), seems, as Küveler put it, in fact somewhat "böswillig" (mean-
spirited).[5] Rather, the narrator frames his story of Engelhardt, the radical
Lebensreformer (advocate of the "life reform movement") on his quest
for a colonial coconut utopia, as an analysis in the manner of Thomas
Mann's literary treatment of the genealogy of fascism through the biography of the composer Adrian Leverkühn in his *Doktor Faustus*.[6] Early on,
Kracht's narrator reflects on his allegorical project by announcing that he
will tell "stellvertretend die Geschichte nur eines Deutschen . . . , eines
Romantikers, der wie so viele dieser Spezies verhinderter Künstler war"
(representatively, the story of only one German . . . a romantic who like
so many among this species was a would-be artist) and adds (with a corny
aside at his hero's favorite fruit) that any parallels with "einem späteren
deutschen Romantiker und Vegetarier" (a later German romantic and
vegetarian) are intended and, "sinnigerweise, Verzeihung, *in nuce* auch
kohärent" (aptly, excuse me, in a nutshell also coherent).[7] The Hitler

comparison ambiguously suggested here is further unfolded—or perhaps, correctively adjusted—when the narrator later positions Engelhardt in a relation of metonymy (rather than, as in the first quote, simile) to Hitler by comparing him to "eines jener kleinen Wesen, die man Labrichthyini nennt, die anderen, größeren Raubfischen die Haut putzen" (77; one of these small beings called cleaner fish, who clean the skin of other, bigger predators). Said "predator" is then evoked as himself "ein kleiner Vegetarier, eine absurde schwarze Zahnbürste unter der Nase" (a small vegetarian with an absurd black toothbrush underneath his nose) climbing the steps to the Munich Feldherrenhalle, where the "Todessymphonie der Deutschen" (death symphony of the Germans) will be intonated (79). The narrator adds that the scenario would be "komödiantisch . . . anzusehen, wenn da nicht unvorstellbare Grausamkeit folgen würde: Gebeine, Excreta, Rauch" (79; look like a comedy, except that unimaginable cruelty was to follow: bones, excretions, smoke). Thus, the novel's title, *Imperium*, situates the colonial empire in the genealogy of Nazi imperialism and the Holocaust, to which the narrator alludes also in a note on his own grandparents pretending not to notice how "mit Koffern beladene Männer, Frauen und Kinder am Dammtorbahnhof in Züge verfrachtet und ostwärts verschickt wurden, hinaus an die Ränder des Imperiums, als seien sie jetzt schon Schatten, jetzt schon aschener Rauch" (231; men, women and children, burdened with suitcases, were freighted into trains at Dammtor station and sent eastwards, out to the margins of the empire, as though they were shadows already, already ashen smoke).

The trouble is that Kracht's narrator does not seem entirely equipped for the big task of analytically connecting colonialism and the Third Reich, which he has thus set for himself. To begin, I should note that my gendering of the narrator is the default move that most readers will probably perform, given the Thomas Mann associations, or simply the novel's male authorship. Kracht's narrator figure is, however, not explicitly gendered in the text, nor embodied in other ways. In the larger context of twenty-first century—German as well as, for example, US-American—literature, the large-scale ambitions of such an anonymous narrator indicate that *Imperium* participates in a trend which I have elsewhere discussed as the return of authoritative narration in twenty-first-century literature.[8] For Kracht specifically, this trend can be contoured by comparing *Imperium* to the author's early radical explorations of character narration: the thoroughly nonauthoritative, highly embodied narrators of *Faserland* (Fatherland, 1995) and *1979* (2001), whose loss of orientation and eventual self-effacement (ambiguously through disappearance or suicide in *Faserland*, and identification with a totalitarian collective in *1979*) arguably dramatized the loss of narrative authority in the postmodern condition. Now the narrator of *Imperium*, who reports on Engelhardt's similarly self-destructive (in fact, autocannibalistic) adventures from a distance, pretends to an overview that is, while not quite omniscient, certainly broad in that it encompasses more than one historical period; and as indicated, he claims more or less sovereign narrational authority in the ambitious setting of an analysis of colonialism and German fascism. The return to such authoritative forms in "post-postmodernist" literature has, however, more generally been haunted by the legacy of twentieth-century critiques of narrative authority. Most authors seem to find it difficult to straightforwardly reclaim the latter; and Kracht's narrator specifically does not very consistently assert the authority he claims.

Of course, these dilemmas of narrative authority as such are not new. The trajectory of Thomas Mann's narrators, from that of the *Buddenbrocks* to *Doktor Faustus*, demonstrates his own solution to the increasing questioning of narrative authority in the modernist era. With the design of Serenus Zeitblom, Mann's late novel beautifully confounded narratological system-building in that the authorial, presumably third person or heterodiegetic narrator became a character and first person narrator in his own right, allowing us to systematically evaluate his speech as an effect of his own socio-symbolic location. In contrast, Kracht's seemingly unembodied narrator is only vaguely positioned in time and space. Except for the above quotation about his grandparents (that stands out in the novel as a moment of reflective potentiality), he rarely ever uses the word "I" but prefers a nonpersonal "man" (one), or even passive constructions: "So wird nun stellvertretend die Geschichte nur eines Deutschen erzählt werden" (18; Thus, the story of only one German will be told representatively now). Compared to other fascinating experiments with the first person plural in contemporary fiction (for example, Jeffrey Eugenides's 1993 *The Virgin Suicides*), Kracht's narrator's occasional "we" also falls short of contouring an exercise in collective narration (as suggested by Lützeler). Rather, the narrator's "we" seems to rhetorically operate in part as royal conceit, in part as a gesture of pocketing his audience for an imagined community which attains its contours, in the diegetic context of colonial adventure designed by the narrator, primarily along the lines of the opposition between "uns Zivilisierte" (us, the civilized) and (their) "savagery" (66). It seems fairly safe to assume that this narrator pretends to speak from a majority-German position. This position, however, is not foregrounded to the reader as such (by way, for example, of an embodied narrator figure) to a degree that would invite critical reader engagement with the narrator's voice as such.

This diagnosis allows me to specify the use of irony referenced in the debate on the novel. To the degree that irony describes "a secret communion of the author and reader behind the narrator's back," as Wayne Booth puts it,[9] it remains rather fuzzy in *Imperium* in that we[10] get little to hold on to in the effort of clearly differentiating the narrator's voice from that of the (implied) author, which the reader needs to project in distancing herself from an ironized narrator. Although at moments we may be inclined to agree with Küveler's assessment that this narrator is "durchgeknallt" (nuts),[11] his overall lack of contours makes it difficult to construct a distinct presence "behind" him—in effect, we remain stuck with the narrator's voice. More clearly, distancing gestures to arguably ironic effect are developed in the interplay between the narrator and his protagonists, or the historical voices he quotes. When the narrator, for example (as highlighted by Diez), talks about how in its first half, the twentieth century looked "als würde es das Jahrhundert der Deutschen werden, das Jahrhundert, in dem Deutschland seinen rechtmäßigen Ehren- und Vorsitzplatz an der Weltentischrunde einnehmen würde" (as though it was to become the century of the Germans, the century in which Germany was to take her legitimate place of honor and presidency at the world table), he does so only after asking us, "die Zukunft im Auge [zu] behalten" (to keep an eye on the future), and thus, arguably, to weave our knowledge about Hitler and the Holocaust into the evaluation of the evoked turn-of-the-twentieth-century perspectives (18).

Short of fully claiming authority over his historical material, however, the narrator then refrains from spelling out any alternative view. And in a nutshell (no pun intended), this is the narrator's procedure throughout most of the book. Despite his repeated claims to a historical overview (see also, for example, 93, where he asserts his ability to "Überfliegen der Zeitzonen"; fly across time zones), his narrative practice mostly foregrounds the historical perspectives he references. (After the initial Hitler reference, for example, he immediately contracts the historical distance just established by suggesting that "im Augenblick," Hitler is still "ein pickliger, verschrobener Bub"; at the moment, Hitler is still a pimply, eccentric boy; 19.) All distancing gestures notwithstanding, *Imperium* thus significantly relies also on what I have described as narrative techniques of presencing, drawing us close to the narrated events through the use for example of the present tense and focalization (see *An Aesthetics*). Even the novel's extensive intertextual archive[12] does not effectively challenge its overall dominant historical restriction of perspective in that it presents what Richard Kämmerlings calls a "Bücher-Kosmos von Comic bis Conrad" (book cosmos ranging from comics to Conrad).[13] That is, it finds its center of gravity in the colonial period and, not least, the genre of the adventure novel, dem "Imperium der Knabenträume" (Empire of boys' fantasies), as supplemented by the belated colonial fantasies of postwar comics.[14]

In constituting his own fictive cosmos from these references, the narrator relies extensively on character perception: Variously, he focalizes through Engelhardt himself and, with the protagonist's descent into madness in the course of the novel, increasingly also through the people surrounding him. And contrary to Gérard Genette's insistence on categorically distinguishing "who sees" from "who speaks," focalization cannot be strictly differentiated from voice in this narrative situation. As we have already seen in the "Deutschlands Ehrenplatz" (Germany's place of honor) quotation, the historical perspectives explored infiltrate also the speech of the narrator, shaping his rhetoric as well as his perceptional positioning. (Thus, Georg Diez may have a point when he wonders whose voice this is: "Wer spricht da?"; Who is speaking there?).[15] When on the novel's very first page, "ein malayischer Boy schritt sanftfüßig und leise das Oberdeck ab" (a Malaysian boy was walking across the upper deck smooth-footedly and quietly), this highly racialized vocabulary is, on the following page, situated with the words "So oder ähnlich dachte der junge August Engelhardt" (12; Thus, or similarly, thought the young August Engelhardt), but the narrator never develops his "own," distinct way of talking about the novel's colonized peoples. Instead, he allows the frame of his own reflexivity to be circumscribed by the horizon of his diegetic world. When yet another page into the novel, the narrator traces Engelhardt's thoughts about "die dickleibigen Pflanzer" (the fat planters) dreaming "von barbusigen dunklen Negermädchen" (of bare-chested dark negro girls), he reports on Engelhardt musing that "das Wort *Pflanzer* traf es nicht richtig, denn dieser Begriff setzte Würde voraus . . . , nein, man mußte im eigentlichen Sinne von *Verwaltern* sprechen" (13; the word planter did not quite fit because this notion implied dignity . . . no, one had to speak of administrators in a literal sense).

Through this deployment of perspective, the narrator traces both Engelhardt's own utopian view, as unfolded through a critique of his society (in the last quote, his thoughts hint at a critique of instrumental reason), and the attraction it had, at least initially, for some of his contemporaries. My concern is not that this attraction was presented as an option for the novel's reader. When, for example, Engelhardt's imago appears "wie die eines radikalen neuen Menschen" (like that of a radical new human) to the local colonial official, Hahl, this idealization is quickly erased in the mental eclipse of Hahl's tropical fever (51). In that respect, the novel is fairly consistent (see, e.g., 61–63, 82)— thus, Diez's charge that Kracht celebrates his hero is clearly mistaken. Instead, *Imperium* unfolds an increasingly grotesque picture that invites our affective distancing also through the aesthetics of disgust dominating its second half, when Engelhardt starts to eat his toenails and eventually thumbs, and so forth.

My concern is that these techniques of distancing do not yet get us out of the discursive world of Engelhardt and his German contemporaries. The way in which the narrator, with Engelhardt, questions the notion "Pflanzer" (planter) in the above quote, but not the n-word used in the same sentence, is indicative of the ways in which the novel may present a critique of instrumental reason, but fails to contour a critique of colonial reason through its play of (predominantly European) perspectives. To be sure, the narrator occasionally focalizes through native characters, too, but the positional dialogicity conceit remains unconvincing. For example, the thoughts that the narrator ascribes to the "Tolaihäuptling" (Tolai chief) fascinated with the colonizer's piano confirm a grand narrative of European civilization, as the *Häuptling* grows out of, so to speak, "den ihm nun äußerst primitiv erscheinenden Trommeln und Pfeifen seiner Rasse" (188; the drums and pipes of his race that now seemed extremely primitive to him). A more promising moment, in which Captain Slütter "sich über den jungen Makeli [wundert], der . . . seine Rasse ähnlich beurteilt, wie es ein Kolonialbeamter täte" (222; [marvels] about the young Makeli who . . . assesses his race similarly to a colonial officer), is undone when the narrator himself shortly reiterates precisely the claim that triggered this surprise, namely the comparison of the "natives" with children (see 229).[16]

Along with the push and pull of attraction and distance vis-à-vis Engelhardt's utopia, the narrator thus presents an array of both positive and negative stereotypes of the—as we have to read again and again—"Eingeborenen" (natives), but he never questions the logic of race that grounds all of them. Importantly, that logic remains unaffected also by Engelhardt's initial dissent vis-à-vis the (negative) racisms of his era. As presented by the narrator, Engelhardt's early colonial enthusiasms include musings about the superiority of the "dunklen Rassen" (38; dark races), and at that point of his life, he clearly rejects the growing anti-Semitism of the era. When "der erste Adept" (121; the first adept) joining his coconut utopia from Germany turns out to be a hateful anti-Semite (as well as, in another highly unfortunate narrative cliché conjunction, homosexual), the narrator reports that "Engelhardt teilte nicht jene aufkommende Mode der Verteuflung des Semitischen" (127; Engelhardt did not participate in that emerging fashion of demonizing the Semitic). Blending his own perspective with that of the protagonist in free indirect discourse, the narrator adds, "Es war doch wohl strikt abzulehnen, über Menschen aufgrund ihrer Rasse zu urteilen" (127–28; After all, judging people by their race was to be strictly refused). While positive and neutral assessments of racial difference are thus granted a space in this novel, the underlying ordering principle of race as such remains not only unchallenged but prominently foregrounded throughout. Therefore it is on some level consistent when the narrator later reports the dramatic reversal through which Engelhardt himself was "unversehens [*sic*, CB] zum Antisemiten geworden, wie alle Mitglieder seine Rasse [*sic*, CB] war er früher oder später dazu gekommen, in der Existenz der Juden eine probate Ursache für jegliches erlittene Unbill zu sehen" (225; had suddenly turned anti-Semitic, like all members of his race he sooner or later had gotten around to seeing in the existence of the Jews a proven/appropriate reason for any incurred inequity). Possibly with the goal of preventing all-too-easy answers, the narrator confidently adds that there was no "kausalen Zusammenhang" (causal connection) between Engelhardt's mental illness and that hatred (225), but once more does not provide any further explanation of his own for Engelhardt's conversion to anti-Semitism. In the absence of such guidance, the novel's implicit theory of fascism disintegrates into a half-banalizing (fashion), half-mystical and fatalistic *Sonderweg*-narrative (like all members of his race . . . sooner or later) that confounds the novel's own premises in ultimately asserting more discontinuity than connection between the colonial world of the late nineteenth century and the emergence of Nazi ideology.[17] Rather than pursuing the explanatory task he set for himself, the narrator in the end performs yet another, decontextualizing historical swerve by declaring that the United States now represents "das Imperium" (240; the Empire).

Transnationalism and Cosmopolitanism: Theoretical Perspectives

As I suggested above, the novel's failure to account for the historical genealogy of racism in colonial Germany as an absolutely central part of the very *Imperium* that it set out to investigate means that the notion of transnationalism can be applied to Kracht's text only in a descriptive sense. Colonialism was obviously one of the constitutive forms of transnational traffic—or the flow of "people, things, knowledges, arts, and, not least, money . . . that reach across borders"[18] —throughout the modern era, and the novel thematizes such colonial traffic. At the same time, *Imperium* does not develop a transnational methodology, or unfold its world in ways that resonate with what I take to be transnationalism's most important conceptual layers. Underlining, namely, that the prefix "trans" is different from "inter" in that it connotes "developments cutting across" nations rather than "relations between" them,[19] I agree with Young-Sun Hong and Michael Geyer in identifying the "challenge" and "wager of transnational history"[20] as that of "deconstructing . . . the nation-state as one of the fundamental categories through which Western modernity is narrated."[21] As foregrounded here, this implies the task of denaturalizing Eurocentric oppositions between the modern nation-state and traditional communities, and "examining the racial regime on which the very idea of Europe"—as well as, more specifically, Germany—"rests."[22]

To avoid misunderstandings, "deconstructing" does not equal "dismissing the importance of"; and the move beyond the nation arguably connoted in the prefix "trans" does not imply that in the era of contemporary forms of globalization, nations have lost all their significance. Rather, in my own definition, "transnational" is opposed also to "global" in the sense that transnational flows attain their specificity in the ways they connect individual locales; the transnational operates on a smaller scale than the global. The prefix "trans" does, however, imply a methodological perspective that emphasizes the historical contingency of the nation, including its mythologies of race; it underlines the ways in which "exogenous 'forces and movements' condition the nation as a political space of decision, even if the latter is instantly historicized in being rooted in a millennial cultural or ethnic tradition," and the fact that "the formation of notions as discrete . . . is the product of accelerated interconnectivity."[23]

Rather than thus investigating the historical genealogy of the nation and the racialized concepts of the German, European, and the "native" constituting it in the colonial period, Kracht's novel effectively reinscribes these very concepts. My suggestion for the discussion in this volume is that this failure to develop a transnational perspective is dramatically highlighted by Kracht's literary choices—that is, his unevenly developed attempt at recuperating narrative authority through the play of historical voices. Simultaneously, however, this failure is indicative of two (interlocking) larger discursive conditions that present a broader challenge for the project of conceptualizing transnationalism through contemporary German literature. First, as many scholars have pointed out, the legacy of essentialist, racialized concepts of national belonging dating back to the colonial period is still very much with us in contemporary German majority—and, sometimes, minority—discourse.[24] More interestingly perhaps, this legacy, secondly, haunts twenty-first-century literature so adamantly in part because the slow process of challenging it at the turn of the twenty-first century (through increasing recognition of Germany's status as a country of immigration, the growing visibility of Black Germans, revised citizenship legislation, etc.) virtually coincided with emerging countermovements of closure in the wake of unification and 9/11.

Specifically, the argument I want to develop in the following is that these political countermovements intersected with and have been articulated through broader (not least, transnational) epistemological turns beyond "postmodern deconstruction." In the twenty-first century, not only mainstream political discourse but also a range of scholarly perspectives (with different political affiliations) have championed newly affirmative takes on collective identities on various scales. In other words, the trouble is that transnationalism in the outlined strong sense of a concept asserting the essential contingency of the nation is, in the second decade into the twenty-first century, essentially "out of fashion" again, violently so with Thilo Sarrazin and his followers, but more subtly also with the liberal advocates of a range of newly influential concepts, including universalism (if the latter is developed at the expense of detailed attention to the sociosymbolic differentials of race, class, or gender), or, similarly, of world literature and cosmopolitanism. Importantly, the renewed prominence of these concepts in twenty-first-century theory (including this overall volume) has been as manifold as it has been innovative; the critical contextualization undertaken in this chapter is not to deny their many crucial interventions. Thus, the return to cosmopolitanism has facilitated a shift in focus beyond the in fact sometimes stifling negativity of postmodern insistences on difference, violence, and (the "paranoid" methodologies of relentless) critique,[25] toward new investigations of ethics, conviviality, and the feelings that might sustain a living together beyond the nation in the age of planetary precarity.[26] The concern foregrounded in this chapter is only that in some developments of the notions of universalism and cosmopolitanism, this turn toward more "positive," affirmative perspectives threatens to facilitate a conceptual amnesia vis-à-vis—what, I believe, are in fact—crucial tenets of late twentieth-century critique.

Kwame Anthony Appiah's influential *Cosmopolitanism* provides a good example for the outlined turn beyond "postmodern," and here specifically postcolonial, insistences on the contingency and violence of identity formation within powerful socio-symbolic regimes of differentiation. Appiah's intervention combines a universalizing move with an affirmation of smaller-scale collective identities: His "partial cosmopolitanism"[27] tempers the plea for "universal concern" with what he calls the "respect for legitimate difference" (xv). Explicitly positioning his intervention against the War on Terror backdrop, Appiah sets out to make it "harder to think of the world as divided between the West and the Rest" (xxi) by affirming the essential contestability of value terms while simultaneously insisting on an ethics of conversation about values, without "a promise of final agreement" (44). His own promise, however, is not fully redeemed in the book: In line with mainstream Western representations of Islam, Appiah later identifies Muslim concepts of gender as one of the "roots" of Islamism (82), thus indicating that he himself remains trapped into a moderate version of the very notions of "culture clash" he set out to overcome. Although not essentialist in any narrow sense of the term, Appiah's "partial cosmopolitanism" also fails to fully commit to a transnational perspective in that he assigns relative closure and autonomy to cultural identities. He does so by theorizing culture (with Wittgenstein) as a matter of "deep *habits*" (84), not impossible to change, but requiring much patience to do so. In settling on that perspective, Appiah undertheorizes historical contingency, and specifically the crucial legacies of power, violence, and uprooting in the formation of cultural identities: he sidelines the histories of racism, colonialism, genocide, slavery, and migration.

The Vicissitudes of Cosmopolitan Affect: *Open City*

I chose Appiah's *Cosmopolitanism* as an example for these twenty-first-century trends also because of the ways the text figures in my second novel, Teju Cole's 2011 *Open City* (which appeared in German, with Suhrkamp, in 2012), the title of which itself metaphorically evokes notions of cosmopolitanism. Appiah's book is mentioned specifically when the character narrator Julius mails a copy of *Cosmopolitanism* to his Belgian acquaintance Farouq as a follow-up to their tense discussion in a smoky bar in Brussels, where Farouq and his Marxist friend Khalil had provoked Julius's New York sensibilities with their failure to fully distance themselves from Islamist radicalisms. This encounter in Brussels is positioned roughly at the center of the (otherwise New York–based) novel; and Brussels's Second World War status is explicated as the literal reference point of its title.[28] Pursuing this configuration in more detail, I claim that the intertextual relationship with Appiah is of central significance for the novel. Rather than just giving literary form to Appiah's concepts, however, the novel engages them critically, not to the effect of altogether abandoning cosmopolitanism, but to that of resituating it in a dialogue with more skeptical perspectives on cosmopolitanism's claims. Cosmopolitanism's critics have cautioned us about the concept's implication in the histories of colonialism and its association with "elite Western subjects" formed by "European bourgeois culture."[29] The novel echoes these concerns by confronting cosmopolitanism with the legacies of historical violence in uneven powerscapes, to the effect of opening up the concept toward more fully transnational perspectives.

Brussels was declared an "open city" in 1940, that is, effectively surrendered to the Nazis in the effort to protect it from destruction. In the play of metaphorical and literal meanings of the novel's title, this historical reference firmly establishes the histories of war as a backdrop for contemporary articulations of cosmopolitanism. In Julius's encounter with Farouq, Cole's novel dramatizes the effects of contemporary wars and juxtaposes Appiah's reliance on the "deep cultural habits" presumably constituting Muslim fundamentalisms with an emphasis on the ways in which radical affiliations are produced by histories of violence, power, and their affective legacies. Thus, Farouq has translated his experiences with European racism into an insistence on cultural "difference," that is: Muslim community (114), whereas Julius, who will try to stitch their failed conversation with his gesture of sending Appiah's book, answers his in some respects comparable experiences with the opposite move. Emphasizing the European elements of his own background, he develops a cosmopolitanism which, at moments, seems to constitute "an elite form of rootlessness and a state of detachment."[30] Julius's explicitly nonsovereign narration, however, enables a dialogue with the reader that productively continues the discussion about both response sets.

Since I discuss the conversation with Farouq itself in detail elsewhere, I will focus here on those aspects of the novel that connect it to the German *Imperium*, as explored by Kracht.[31] Namely, the encounter with Farouq takes the place of another encounter in the *Open City*, the hope for which has brought Julius to Brussels in the first place: he wanted to reconnect with his German grandmother who, he assumes, lives in Brussels but whom he fails to track down. The background for these difficulties is the double familial estrangement that has shaped his own growing up in Nigeria and subsequent life in the United States, where he has pursued a medical career with a focus, notably, on "affective disorders in the elderly" (7). Julius's "oma" (32) had come to visit the family in Nigeria only once during his childhood. While his mother had painted her as "a difficult and small-minded person" (34), Julius, who has faded memories of the grandmother's "quiet, puzzled affection" (35) during that visit, deems his mother's judgment to be inaccurate and colored by resentment (34). At the same time, he connects the estrangement between the two of them to his own subsequent estrangement from his mother, whom he remembers as having become "cold, frighteningly so," in a time of conflict with his father during his childhood (77).

Julius freely admits to the limits of his authority as a character narrator in speculating that his mother and grandmother "might have fallen out for reasons as inchoate as the ones that separated my mother and me" (34). However, he immediately begins to contextualize the situation by adding, "My mother had not returned to Germany since she left in the 1970s" (34). Later, he suspects that he is, "in some odd way, . . . the unaware continuation of" the "experiences, sensations, desires" that had shaped his mother's childhood in immediate postwar Germany (80). His report on her story relies on what she had told him, in a moment of attempted reconnection after the father's death, "in an abstracted . . . way" and "a faraway voice which, because it [*sic*, CB] could not talk about the death that had just shattered us, had begun to describe long-ago things" (79). The story is a majority German "story of suffering," of rubble, begging, and possibly experienced rape by Red Army soldiers, of a life overshadowed by the "rule" to "refrain from speaking" about the "horrors" of war, fascism, and the Holocaust: "nothing of the murders and countless betrayals, nothing of those who had enthusiastically participated in it all" (79–80). Julius concludes that his mother "was born into an unspeakably bitter world" and that it was only "natural . . . for her to displace the grief of widowhood onto that primal grief, and make the two pains a continuity" (80).

Julius's gesture of affirmation simultaneously highlights the contingency of the connection made by his mother. The transnational "continuity" at stake in this novel is not easily assimilated into any of the grand narratives with which we are familiar. If touching on the topos of a German "inability to mourn,"[32] this mother's story is more precisely perhaps about displaced mourning, in a postcolonial context that is not in direct continuity with the histories of German colonialism, even as her relocation to Nigeria in some respects may double Engelhardt's colonial desire to escape mainstream German realities. Unlike Kracht's novel, however, *Open City* refrains from grand gestures of ill-fated allegorization. Instead, the narrator configures what Leslie Adelson might call "touching tales" of violence in overlapping, but nonetheless crucially different contexts (21). Unfolding a dialogic play of different generational perspectives, Julius does so, not least, by reporting on his own experiences of unbelonging: Haunted by "a sense of being different" by virtue of his name, passport, and (lighter) skin color (78), the adolescent had tried to find "some sense of belonging" (81) at the Nigerian military school that he was attending at his father's wish. "Discipline: the word had the force of a mantra among Nigerian parents" (76). That one of the teachers there is nicknamed "Hitler" behind his back (82) does not create a straightforward continuity between Nigeria and Germany, or the larger transnational histories of (here British) colonialism, postcolonial culture, and German fascism, but it emphasizes contact, similarity, and counterpoint in the complex web of transnational histories that the novel unfolds through the voice of its nonsovereign narrator.

Without neatly mapping onto each other, the layered histories of sociopolitical violence shape contemporary (personal) lives. Readers of *Open City* know that it finds its climax in Julius's attempt to come to terms with a charge that threatens to undo his positive self-image: Moji, the sister of a childhood friend, tells him in New York that she was traumatized by the fact that Julius had raped her at a party as a drunk fourteen-year-old. The novel unfolds this turn of events, not least, as a drama of narration. "We are not the villains of our own stories" (243), Julius explicitly comments on his limits, but then proceeds to open up his nonsovereign account in a dialogue with Moji's voice—probing, if not authoritatively evaluating and affectively working through her charge by the (consequently open) ending of the novel. The reader as well, whose active involvement in the sensemaking process is explicitly called upon by the narrator's questioning of his own voice, may struggle with the challenge of sorting through Moji's claim against the background of the novel's larger sociopolitical stories. What exactly, if anything, connects this alleged rape to Julius's suspicions that his grandmother was raped by Red Army soldiers on the one hand, and his experiences with racism in contemporary Belgium, where, as he realized during his visit, his "presentation—the dark, unsmiling, solitary stranger—made" him a target for the inchoate rage of the defenders of Vlaanderen," so that he "could, in the wrong place, be taken for a rapist" (106)? How precisely do political histories translate into personal experience and accountability? And how would a cosmopolitan ethics, a sense of universal obligation supported by "a feeling that we belong to a world"[33] emerge from the layered positionalities and complications of unbelonging that characterize contemporary transnational lives?

Julius's narration does not answer any of these questions for us, and that may be for the better, given the complexity of his—and our contemporary—world. Attending to both gaps and links between the personal and the political, along with the heterogeneous political legacies of racism, colonialism, war, and fascism, the novel's rich, layered configuration confounds simple explanations. More promisingly than Kracht's presumably authoritative narrator, however, who fails to deliver the grand historical narrative he sets out to tell, Cole's nonsovereign character voice invites the reader to engage in the continued process of sense making herself. Specifically, the narrator's struggle with his own (personal-political) experiences of violence—as both victim and apparent perpetrator—dramatizes a call to rethink cosmopolitanism. Its ethics of reaching out to others needs to account not only for people's diverging values and "deep cultural habits" (as Appiah has it), but for the ways in which these values and habits are shaped by histories of trauma as well as public feelings in Ann Cvetkovich's sense: in a critical dialogue with trauma theory, Cvetkovich argues for foregrounding the "affective legacy of the racialized histories of genocide, slavery, colonization, and migration," a legacy which may have traumatic along with more everyday layers, but which has not been at the center of classical trauma theory (175).

Julius not only fails to ever reconnect with his own grandmother (who, for all the reader can suspect, might have died by the time of his visit to Brussels), but even his desire to do so is overdetermined by his struggles with positionality and belonging. In the novel, he first has the "feeling" that he "should make the effort to see her" at the occasion of a racist incident with two children interpellating him as a "gangster" in the New York subway (31–32). Read as an impulse to affirm his (white) European roots in this situation, which he has been cultivating also, for example, in his amply discussed preferences for classical music, this reaction could code his sophisticated cosmopolitanism as a gesture of flight and attempted detachment from those other parts of his background that are constantly projected (back) upon him in New York as well as Brussels. Repeatedly, Julius responds with indignation to the brotherhood interpellations offered to him by African-American cab drivers and postal clerks. When at one of these occasions, he describes the negative feelings provoked by such an interpellation as "the anger of a shattered repose" (41), however, his narration aids the reader in tracing how his (anxious) detachment operates, not least, as a defense mechanism. In a "less impatient" mood, Julius can later "admit" to himself that the "we blacks" plural makes sense as a gesture of recognizing racialized histories (55). In the face of the layered histories of violence that the novel touches upon, altogether discarding the impact of racialization is as inadequate a response as affirming race, in the way of Kracht's narrator, as a category of presumed autonomy.

In navigating beyond these alternatives, Julius's nonsovereign but ethically engaged narration enables us to probe an ongoing dialogue also about a possible cosmopolitanism that "is not one of rootlessness" but in fact might project "a universal circle of belonging"[34] in accounting for the complexities of transnational experience in the contemporary world. Short of fully sketching a positive image of such a different cosmopolitanism, the novel can thus be situated at the highly productive intersection that, I hope, our joint scholarly conversations in this volume map in a different key: the intersection between cosmopolitanism and transnationalism in the programmatic sense foregrounded in this chapter. To summarize more formally, my plea throughout these readings has been to hold on to a critically deconstructive layer in the notion of transnationalism. That is, I understand transnationalism (in the programmatic sense) as a methodological perspective which foregrounds a critique of nationalist mythologies in investigating the historical processes through which nations have come into being, not least in the processes of colonial traffic. As argued here, this critical concept of transnationalism attains its significance in response both to the lingering legacies of racialized notions of nationhood (that I detect in Kracht's novel) and to twenty-first-century returns to more affirmative perspectives on national as well as transnational connection, including concepts of cosmopolitanism. In some of its contemporary articulations, I have cautioned, the concept of cosmopolitanism threatens to set aside too quickly the historical legacies of violence and division haunting twenty-first-century societies. However, my reading of Cole's novel as a *critically* cosmopolitanism text simultaneously acknowledges the importance of cosmopolitanism's ethos of connection, which supplements transnationalism's analytical work on the historical contingency of the nation with an affirmative exploration of possible shared human futures.

Notes

[1] Elfriede Jelinek et al. "Offener Brief an die Spiegel-Chefredaktion zu Kracht," February 17, 2012, http://www.kiwi-verlag.de/news/17022012-offener-brief-an-die-spiegel-chefredaktion-zu-kracht/.

[2] Jan Küveler, "Kracht und die Bosheit." *Die Welt*, February 14, 2012.

[3] Andreas Fanizadeh, "Christian Kracht, Türsteher der Rechten," *Die Tageszeitung*, February 15, 2012. See also Sabine Vogel, "Hitler war kein Hippie," *Berliner Zeitung*, February 16, 2012, http://www.berliner-zeitung.de/literatur/neuer-roman-hitler-war-kein-hippie,10809200,11641656.html.

[4] James Phelan, *Experiencing Fiction: Judgments, Progressions, and the Rhetorical Theory of Narrative* (Columbus: Ohio State University Press, 2007).

[5] Küveler, "Kracht und die Bosheit."

[6] See, for example Erhard Schütz, "Kunst, kein Nazikram," *Der Freitag*, February 16, 2012.

[7] Christian Kracht, *Imperium: Roman* (Cologne: Kiepenheuer & Witsch, 2012), 18–19. Further references to this volume appear in the text.

[8] See Claudia Breger, "Like God's Voice? The Return of Authoritative Narration" in *An Aesthetics of Narrative Performance: Transnational Theater, Literature and Film in Contemporary Germany* (Columbus: Ohio State University Press, 2012). I situate this trend in a dialogue with Paul Dawson, who employs a more traditional narratalogical term in his diagnosis of a return of "omniscient" narration, while I prefer the (less totalizing) "authoritative." See also my article on Uwe Tellkamp's *Der Turm* (The Tower, 2008), for which I develop an argument resonant with the Kracht reading here, if in the context of post-GDR rather than transnational fiction. Breger, "On a Twenty-First-Century Quest for Authoritative Narration: The Drama of Voice in Uwe Tellkamp's *Der Turm*." *The Germanic Review* 86, no. 3 (2011): 185–200.

[9] Wayne C Booth, *The Rhetoric of Fiction*. 2nd ed. Chicago: University of Chicago Press, 1963), 300.

[10] In the attempt to methodologically reign in royal conceit, my use of "we" here and in the following designates the implied reader position that is projected by the formal design of the novel, and which should not be confused with empirical reader response.

[11] Küveler, "Kracht und die Bosheit."

[12] See, for example Paul Michael Lützeler, "Hitler und die Kokosnuss," *Die Welt*, February 11, 2012.

[13] Richard Kämmerlings, "Der einzig wahre Gott ist die Kokosnuss." *Die Welt*, February 13, 2012, accessed May 31, 2013. http://www.welt.de/kultur/literarischewelt/article13861894/Der-einzig-wahre-Gott-ist-die-Kokosnuss.html.

[14] Thus Schütz, although with a more generous inflection. The comics Kracht uses are Frank Le Gall's *Das Geheimnis des Kapitän Stien* (The Secret of Captain Stien; from the 1980s but set in the 1920s) and Hugo Pratt's Corto Maltese adventures (dating to the 1960s and 1970s), perhaps along with the prewar *Tim und Struppi im Kongo* (Tim and Struppi in the Congo, 1931; with thanks to Elisabeth Herrmann for the latter suggestion). Kämmerling tries to save the novel by suggesting that its extensive intertextuality indexes its "cannibalistic poetics" in the sense of postmodernist sign solipsism free of all referentiality ("Die deutschen Romane"). This is, however, not convincing: While the argument is theoretically limited in general (in that even the most self-reflexive texts still operate through some form of indirect referentiality), it becomes even more problematic when applied to a text like Kracht's that forcefully stakes out a claim to telling "grand" stories from the world of (actual) history.

[15] Georg Dietz, "Die Methode Kracht." *Der Spiegel*, February 13, 2012, accessed May 30, 2013. http://www.spiegel.de/spiegel/print/d-83977254.html.

[16] See also 66, where the play of (only presumably) diverging perspectives is ambiguously affirmed *and* historicized as "eines der Hauptmerkmale jener Zeit" (one of the main characteristics of that era)—namely that of modernist aesthetics.

[17] As the novel's configuration has it, the local colonial official, Governor Hahl, is not only rehabilitated as a "durchaus anständiger Mann" (by all means decent man) from the perspective of the positively coded Captain Slütter (202) but also joins an anti-Nazi resistance group (237).

[18] Michael Geyer, "Where Germans Dwell: Transnationalism in Theory and Practice," Luncheon Talk, GSA 2006.

[19] Konrad H. Jarausch, "Reflections on Transnational History," *H-Net Discussion Networks, Forum: Transnationalism,* http://h-net.msu.edu/cgi-bin/logbrowse. pl?trx=vx&list=h-german&month=0601&week=c&msg=LPkNHirCm1xgSZQK HOGRXQ&user=&pw.

[20] Geyer, "Where Germans Dwell."

[21] Young-sun Hong, "The Challenge of Transnational History," *H-Net Discussion Networks, Forum: Transnationalism,* http://h-net.msu.edu/cgi-bin/logbrowse. pl?trx=vx&list=h-german&month=0601&week=c&msg=Ug5gaQJIb0mI99%2b 4nOj7Ww&user=&pw.

[22] Hong, "Challenge of Transnational History."

[23] Geyer, "Where Germans Dwell." See also analogously Shelley Fisher Fishkin, "Crossroads of Cultures: The Transnational Turn in American Studies: Presidential Address to the American Studies Association, November 12, 2004," *American Quarterly* 57, no. 1 (2005): 17–57 for the context of American Studies, here in particular 22–23.

[24] See Fatima El Tayeb, "Dangerous Liaisons: Race, Nation and German Identity," in *Not So Plain as Black and White: Afro-German Culture and History, 1890–2000,* ed. Patricia Mazón and Reinhild Steingröver (Rochester, NY: University of Rochester Press, 2005), 27–60.

[25] See Eve Kosofsky Sedgwick, *Touching Feeling: Affect, Pedagogy, Performativity* (Durham, NC: Duke University Press, 2003) on the latter point.

[26] See, for example, David Held and Garrett W. Brown, eds., *The Cosmopolitanism Reader* (London: Polity, 2010); Paul Gilroy, *Postcolonial Melancholia* (New York: Columbia University Press, 2004); and Pheng Cheah, "Cosmopolitanism" *Theory, Culture, and Society* 23 (2–3): 486–96.

[27] Kwame Anthony Appiah, *Cosmopolitanism: Ethics in a World of Strangers* (New York: Norton, 2006), xvii. Further references to this volume appear in the text.

[28] Teju Cole, *Open City: A Novel* (New York: Random House Trade Paperbacks, 2012), 97. Further references to this volume appear in the text. A further intertextual association links, of course, to Rossellini's 1945 film *Roma, città aperta* (*Rome, Open City*).

[29] Aihwa Ong, *Neoliberalism as Exception: Mutations in Citizenship and Sovereignty* (Durham, NC: Duke University Press, 2006), 14, 17–18.

[30] Cheah, "Cosmopolitanism," 487.

[31] Claudia Breger, "Race, Cosmopolitanism, and the Intricacies of Belonging in the *Open City:* Teju Cole's Transnational Aesthetics," in preparation for *Narrative, Race and Ethnicity in the Americas,* ed. James J. Donahue, Jennifer Ho, and Shaun Morgan (under review with Ohio State University Press).

[32] Alexander Mitscherlich and Margarete Mitscherlich, *Die Unfähigkeit zu trauern: Grundlagen kollektiven Verhaltens* (Munich: Piper, 1967).

[33] Cheah, "Cosmopolitanism," 486.

[34] Cheah, "Cosmopolitanism," 487.

6: Writing Travel in the Global Age: Transnationalism, Cosmopolitanism, and the Reworking of Generic Conventions of Travel Literature in Ilija Trojanow's *An den inneren Ufern Indiens* and *Nomade auf vier Kontinenten*

Christina Kraenzle

Transnationalisms in Question

ILIJA TROJANOW'S LITERARY PRODUCTION provides an ideal case study with which to map the complicated relationships between transnationalism and cosmopolitanism. Trojanow's fiction and nonfiction works are profoundly concerned with historical and emerging transnational networks, from the history of colonialism and its attendant forms of migration and diaspora to more contemporary forms of global trade, commerce, and activism. This attention to diverse forms of transnationalism reminds us of the complexity and ambivalent nature of the concept: operating on multiple, and at times interconnected spatial scales, from the informal and private to the public and collective, transnationalisms can offer liberating spaces for dynamic exchange and cooperation but also further entrench old divisions—for example, of sex, race, or class—across, as well as within, national boundaries.

This point is underscored in Trojanow's best-selling historical fiction *Der Weltensammler* (2007; *The Collector of Worlds*, 2008), in which the figure of Sir Richard Frances Burton offers a powerful reminder that there is no direct correlation between transnationalism and cosmopolitanism. Burton's transnational existence fostered an admiration for other languages, customs, and religions, but this appreciation did not extend to all those peoples he encountered, nor did this admiration prevent him from utilizing his knowledge to advance British colonialism or the violence committed in its name. As Edward Said has noted,[1] while Burton's extensive travels and his knowledge of various cultures may have made him an exception to many of his peers, he was not simply a rebel against Victorian authority, but in many ways its most effective agent. Employing the figure of Burton, Trojanow reminds us that lives lived transnationally may produce transcultural competence, but they do not necessarily foster the respect for and openness to otherness associated with various strands of cosmopolitan thought (for example, in the forms of moral, cultural, romantic, or kynical cosmopolitanism discussed by Stuart Taberner earlier in this volume).

Nor should we see historical forms of transnationalism as exceptional; throughout his work, Trojanow shows that the relationship between transnationalism and cosmopolitanism remains fraught. In the opening passages of his travelogue, *Nomade auf vier Kontinenten* (Nomad on Four Continents, 2008), for example, he argues that old myths and misconceptions have persisted well into the present:

> Das 19. Jahrhundert ist in hohem Maße gegenwärtig. Viele unserer Vorstellungen von Differenz—bezogen auf fremde Länder und Kulturen—wurden damals geformt. . . . Wir sind weiterhin konditioniert von der Weltsicht des imperialen Zeitalters (wie selbst ein kursorischer Blick in die Medien und ihre Berichterstattung über Indien, Arabien und Afrika aufzeigt), weil wir sie nie umgeworfen, sondern nur korrigiert haben.[2]

> [The nineteenth century is to a high degree with us today. Many of our conceptions of difference—related to foreign countries and cultures—were formed then. . . . We continue to be conditioned by a view of the world from the age of imperialism (as even a cursory glance at the media and their reporting on India, the Middle East, or Africa will show) because we have never cast it off but have merely adapted it.]

In this and other travel writings, Trojanow challenges the myths and prejudices that continue to shape our understandings of self and other, even in a world increasingly connected through mass travel and technology. The fact that Trojanow so frequently employs the travelogue form is on the one hand unsurprising: with its emphasis on transnational mobility and transfer, the genre seems particularly well positioned to reflect on multidirectional relationships to place and community, thereby offering a primary site for the exploration and negotiation of concepts of transnationalism and cosmopolitanism. On the other hand, however, travel writing is a genre that has long been considered "tainted" by its association with European imperialism. As scholars such as Edward Said and Mary Louise Pratt have shown,[3] European travel and travel writing were fundamental to the production of knowledge of non-European spaces and helped to fuel the desire for further exploration and conquest. Founded on a system of asymmetrical power relationships in which mobile European observers assumed the authority to represent their non-European interlocutors, travelogues were essential to the production of Western knowledge about the rest of the world. Although regularly incorporating myth and fantasy, European travelogues were passed off as impartial truth, cementing alleged dichotomies of "the West" and "the Rest." In their production of imaginative geographies, travelogues implicitly legitimized colonization, either by depicting foreign spaces as *terra nullius* awaiting "discovery," or by casting foreign populations as savage, static, infantile, or irrational Others in need of European "civilization" and "progress."

The task Trojanow sets himself is therefore a difficult one, namely to challenge the history of European prejudices in the very genre most associated with empire, orientalism, and exoticism. In this chapter, I consider two of Trojanow's travelogues—*Nomade auf vier Kontinenten* and *An den inneren Ufern Indiens* (Along the Inner Banks of India, 2003; in English as *Along the Ganges*, 2005)—to investigate how they consider various forms of transnationalism and cosmopolitanism as well as the roles that narrative form and generic convention might play in perpetuating particular constructions of difference. Using formal strategies that attempt to eschew positions of narrative authority, Trojanow draws attention to the architecture of conventional travel writing while attempting to subvert it from within, challenging the forms through which meaning is negotiated.

Transnationalism and Travel Writing

Although best known for *Der Weltensammler*, Ilija Trojanow is also a prolific author of travel writing and reportage. Ranging in style from the journalistic, to memoir and essay, to complex experiments with the travelogue form, Trojanow's travel writings document his many sojourns and more extended periods of residence around the globe.[4] These texts provide excursions into local histories and culture, and contemplate how localities are transformed by the emergence of transnational spaces created through mass mobility (e.g., migration and tourism), international political organizations, global commerce, religious practices, or the circulation of information and ideas. While diverse in form, a common thread in Trojanow's travel writings is the desire to trace the origins of uninformed clichés, to debunk popular stereotypes, and to dispel notions of discrete and homogeneous national cultures. In this way, we can see Trojanow's travel writing as an extension of his larger oeuvre, in which he frequently draws attention to the syncretic nature of cultural practices. In texts such as *Kampfabsage* (Calling off the Fight, 2007), for example, Trojanow and his coauthor Ranjit Hoskoté counter growing discourses of the so-called clash of civilizations[5] by showing how what is often coded as inherently "Western" in fact has been shaped by cultural transfer with other parts of the globe. Rejecting notions of cultural purity or "container" models of identity, Trojanow and Hoskoté opt for the metaphor of the river to conceive of history as transnational flow and exchange:

> Je größer ein Fluß, desto irreführender sein Name. Unser geographisches Grundverständnis schreibt vor, daß die Quelle, die von der Mündung am weitesten entfernt ist, als Ursprung des Flusses zu gelten hat. Der gesamte Flusslauf trägt lediglich einen einzigen Namen. Aber kein Strom kann zu majestätischer Größe wachsen und den Ozean erreichen, ohne von Neben- und Zuflüssen gespeist zu werden. . . . Unsere Geschichte ist auch ein großer, fälschlich benannter Fluß. Über die Daten und Ereignisse der Geschichte definieren wir uns selbst und unsere Kultur. Dabei verwechseln wir meist eine Momentaufnahme des Flußes mit seinem gesamten Verlauf.[6]

> [The bigger a river, the more misleading its name. Our basic geographical understanding prescribes that the source that is the furthest from the river's mouth counts as its origin. The entire course of the river bears a single name. But no current can grow to a majestic size and reach the ocean without being fed by tributaries and streams. . . . Our history is also a great, misnamed river. We define ourselves and our culture according to historical dates and events. In this way we generally confuse a snapshot of the river with its entire course.]

Trojanow's own transnational ties have become an important part of his authorial persona. Born in Bulgaria, educated in Germany and Kenya, long-term resident of India and South Africa, now resident in Austria, his multilocational biography is often invoked in the promotion of his literary works, and some mention of these personal details often frames his travel writings.[7] The persistent emphasis on Trojanow's nomadic lifestyle seems a device designed to set him apart from his readers and thereby to establish his credentials as an ostensibly authoritative, cosmopolitan interpreter of foreign cultures. But it also places him within a new cadre of travel writers with similarly hybrid cultural backgrounds, such as Pico Iyer, Vikram Seth, and Amitav Ghosh, to name but a few authors who speak many languages, call several places home, and seek to explore complex networks of enduring transculturation through travel writing.

For Pico Iyer, this development marks a phase in the democratization of travel writing in which colonial legacies of the genre are giving way to more cosmopolitan visions of transnational intercultural exchange:

I think [travel writing has] evolved a great deal. Partly because even when I was growing up, travel writing was mostly white, nearly always male, often from England, and about going to Africa and Kenya and surveying the strange customs of the natives. And I think now it is more and more about a half-Thai, half-German girl living in Iowa City, going to an Afghanistan full of German aid workers and Japanese businessmen. And what used to be a very simple discussion between, in some ways, colonizer and colonized, is now a dialogue between a multi-cultural society and a multi-cultural person. All of which has made the texts much more interesting.[8]

Here Iyer posits a new beginning for travel writing in a contemporary world in which transnational flows of travel, labour, capital, and media have broken down the binary categories of colonizer and colonized or center and periphery that structured travel writing in the imperial era. Moreover, Iyer rejects old paradigms in which mobility is posited as the sole domain of the traveling observer who fixes his or her gaze on an allegedly static native population. In Iyer's example of contemporary travel writing, it is not only the traveling narrator who moves through transnational spaces, but also those residing in the places visited, either by virtue of their own physical mobility or their localized experiences of transnational aid and commerce.

Iyer's comments point to the potential for contemporary travel writing, in which the description of intensified transnational networks and the cultural hybridity, multipositional identities, and the border crossings they may afford offer new possibilities to reject past notions of essential cultural otherness. Some scholars of contemporary travel writing, however, are skeptical about the extent to which such potential has been achieved, highlighting instead the complex and often ambivalent relationships between the cosmopolitan and colonial visions they locate in contemporary travelogues. In *The Global Politics of Contemporary Travel Writing*, Debbie Lisle argues that the emergence of transnational authorial perspectives in no way guarantees a break with travel writing's colonial and patriarchal heritage. On the contrary, she argues that contemporary travelogues, constrained by readers' desires for sufficiently exotic locales, more often show continuities between a colonial past and an allegedly postcolonial present.[9]

Lisle's close readings of popular English-language travelogues reveal how generic conventions and the very act of writing about travel engender particular constructions of difference that are haunted by traces of orientalism, exoticism, and empire. Her study suggests that a successful jettisoning of imperial models of difference and encounter requires more than a cosmopolitan outlook; it necessitates a reworking of narrative convention and form. As Paul Smethurst similarly notes, "contemporary travelogues may be filtered through a self-reflexive, post-imperialist consciousness, but they may still reinforce an ordering of things, a *form*, that is still western in origin" and connected to the discursive formation of empire.[10]

Trojanow is equally skeptical that increased mobility, cross-cultural contact or multicultural, transnational author biographies can on their own escape old models of difference. In *Der entfesselte Globus* (The Unchained Globe, 2008), for example, he flatly rejects the notion that globalization has led to increased cultural awareness, showing instead how a Western imaginary continues to be constructed through colonial fantasies of the past.[11] Nor is Trojanow convinced that the emergence of more multicultural authors will necessarily diminish the exoticism and orientalism associated with the genre, a point made clear in an essay that describes his admiration for Amitav Ghosh. Here Trojanow argues that it is not Ghosh's multilocational biography that underpins the cosmopolitan worldview located in his literary production; it is instead a combination of content, formal treatment and Ghosh's "kulturelle Mehrsichtigkeit," (multiperspectival cultural outlook) that allows a cosmopolitan perspective to emerge.[12] This multiperspectival view is precisely what is missing from much contemporary travel writing, argues Trojanow in his praise of V. S. Naipaul's *India, A Million Mutinies Now*.[13] In Trojanow's opinion, Naipaul's travelogue overturns a troubling feature of the travel writing genre, namely what Mary Louise Pratt has termed "the-monarch-of-all-I-survey," in which the narrator assumes ultimate authority of knowledge and representation, as well as the power that accrues to such an omniscient position.[14] Naipaul, Trojanow insists, overcomes this tendency by allowing the residents of Bombay a voice within his travelogue, and an opportunity to assess their surroundings on their own terms, terms that may contradict the travel writer's (and the reader's) own view of the local environment.[15] In an interview about one of his own Indian travelogues, *An den innerern Ufern Indiens*, Trojanow discusses how he similarly tried to avoid a narrative position of authority in this text:

> Ich glaube, dass die übliche Reiseerzählung eines westlichen Autors aus zwei Sachen besteht: aus einem überragenden Ich, und aus einer Besserwisserei der Welt gegenüber. Und ich habe versucht, mich beider Sachen . . . zu enthalten, also das Ich möglichst zu reduzieren, also meine eigene Befindlichkeit nicht im Mittelpunkt stehen zu lassen, und die Besserwisserei auch völlig auszuschalten, sondern mich . . . auch in meinen Werturteilen überraschen zu lassen.[16]

> [I think that the usual travelogue written by a Western author consists of two things: a superior sense of self and a superior atttitude towards the world. And I tried to avoid both these things, that is to reduce my own self as much as possible, to not let my own attitudes

be the focus, and to completely turn off a know-it-all attitude. Rather I let myself be surprised by my own value judgments.]

Here Trojanow declares his awareness of the asymmetrical knowledge–power relationship that Pratt and others have located as a generic staple, along with his desire to overcome it. What Trojanow doesn't articulate, however, is through what literary devices he actually attempts this. In what follows, I consider the strategies Trojanow employs to both document transnational social spaces and to unsettle the discourses of exoticism, imperialism, or orientalism often associated with the genre of travel writing. I focus on two of Trojanow's travelogues, *An den inneren Ufern Indiens* and *Nomade auf vier Kontinenten*. Unlike his more conventional travel writings, these travelogues offer self-reflexive engagements with, and critiques of, the conventions of travel writing.

An den innerern Ufern Indiens

In his acclaimed travelogue, Trojanow provides an account of his voyage on foot, by boat, train, and bus along the Ganges to cities and villages from Gangotri, Haridwar, Benares, and Allahabad to Kanpur and Kalkutta. The narrative combines conventionally realist descriptions of the journey with highly lyrical passages based on Hindu mythology as well as citations from the Hindi poet Kabir. The resulting narrative allows Trojanow to document not only his travels and encounters with locals and other tourists, but also to reflect on Indian history and mythology as well as contemporary social and political issues, ranging from the globalization of manufacturing industries, to the impact of communications technologies, to the local effects of climate change.

It is in this Indian travelogue that Trojanow most overtly employs the spatial metaphor of the river (cited above), not only as a metaphor for the fluidity of history and cultural identity, but also as an unconventional way of thinking about space. By focusing on the meandering ebb and flow of the Ganges, Trojanow employs a mode of spatial representation that refuses what Bill Ashcroft has located as travel writing's tendency to present foreign spaces as sites to be accurately surveyed, mapped, and ultimately, controlled. In his essay, "Travel and Power," Bill Ashcroft notes that travel writing is not only about journeying; most often it is primarily about place, a place that is at once a geographical location, but also a space of the imagination, a distant world translated by the travel writer for an audience back home, "a strange world owned and domesticated."[17] Here Ashcroft references the knowledge–power relationship in the history of European travel writing, in which the travel writer invests him- or herself with an authority that comes from familiarity, alleged knowledge, and the power of representation, a power that is linked to a desire for control and possession. The connection between the desire to survey and the desire to control or possess foreign spaces finds its postcolonial expression in the trope of the map that links the act of travel and cartography to European colonialism. Given how deeply "travel writing has been implicated in the knowledge-power equation throughout history," how, Ashcroft asks, "can travel writing avoid colonizing the space of its journey? How can it avoid the invidious power relationship existing in the binary of surveyor/ surveyed, recorder/recorded, representer/represented?"[18]

Throughout his travels, Trojanow displays a similar postcolonial suspicion of maps. In his travels along the Ganges, Trojanow charts India's place in the European imaginary, initially fueled by inaccurate maps that nevertheless secured the desire to ultimately locate and conquer it.[19] In *An den inneren Ufern Indiens*, Trojanow avoids the position of the authoritative surveyor by structuring his route and narrative along the Ganges, a body of water that is constantly in motion. Trojanow thus complicates authoritative mappings of place, diffusing the tensions between stasis and mobility that exist in conventional travelogues in which place is conceived as a static location through which the narrator moves.[20] Instead, the travelogue presents the Ganges as unpredictable, unchartable, and defiant, challenging the travel writer's capacity to represent it.

From the very start of his journey, Trojanow depicts the Ganges as a dynamic force: even the riverbed is constantly on the move, eroding soil from the Himalayas and depositing it in the Bay of Bengal (*U*, 13–14). A farmer he meets along the way notes that his village has twice been relocated because of the Ganges' meandering route. "Ganga wandert," (*Ganga* wanders),[21] the farmer explains, predicting that the village will likely be shifted again within the next two years (*U*, 62). In other passages, this unpredictability takes on a menacing quality, for example when they encounter a shopkeeper whose tent and goods have been destroyed by flooding: "Um fünf in der Früh hatte ihn der Fluß überfallen" (*U*, 19; "at five in the morning, the rivulet had attacked him," *G*, 8). As Trojanow and his travel companion camp along the Ganges, bits of the bank break off and slide into the water, an unsettling reminder of the river's volatility (*U*, 63).

While the river's restlessness hinders human settlement, it also makes it difficult to navigate, especially for the narrator. Already at the outset of the narrative, the river thwarts his progress when he is unable to return across a flooded crossing point he had used earlier in the journey. Along with other stranded tourists, he is rescued and escorted across by locals who are better able to negotiate the currents. Later, Trojanow employs the metaphor of literacy to describe the ability to master the river's flow, as locals warn them of the river's unpredictability: "Die Männer grinsten und warnten uns vor dem launischen Sog der Ganga. Sie konnten die Strömung genau lesen, wir waren die Analphabeten." (*U*, 51; "The men grinned and warned us against the moody whirlings of the Ganges. They could read the flow precisely, we were the illiterates; *G*, 29) Traveling down the Ganges by an inflatable raft, Trojanow and his companion become disoriented and eventually lose their way, drifting into a tributary. Here maps prove unhelpful, providing only vague markings of the tributary and no clear direction back to their planned route (*U*, 53). Only with great difficulty, by following the sun, fighting currents and wading through the muddy swamp, are they able to finally make their way back to the safety of their planned route. In his struggles with the river, Trojanow is the very antithesis of the expert, male adventurer, instead showing his repeated failure to master the Ganges' unpredictable movements.

Most significantly, the river's restless movement not only thwarts the narrator's desire to read or survey, it also defies easy narration:

> Nichts wünschte sich der Dichter sehnlicher, als Gangas Fließen in Worte zu fasssen. Kaum hatten seine Strophen ihre Form gefunden, änderte sich der Fluß, diese Raga aus Strömung, Strudel und Sog, und er mußte ihn erneut besingen. Doch auch diese Hymne wurde umgehend weggeschwemmt, Ganga veränderte wiederum ihren Lauf, den es abzubilden galt. Der Dichter war verstrickt in ein ewiges Gedicht. Aber vielleicht würde Ganga ja antworten, vielleicht würde sie nach jeder Momentaufnahme, jedem Gedicht, jedem Gebet eine Stufe des Ghats hinaufsteigen, bis sie schließlich den Dichter umspülen, umarmen und befreien würde. (*U*, 135)

> [The poet yearns passionately to capture *Ganga's* flow in words. His strophes have barely found a form when the river, this raga of flow and undertow, changes its course, and he has to sing it again. But this hymn, too, is washed away soon after; *Ganga* has once again changed the course that he had to depict. The poet was caught up in a whirlpool of devotion. But perhaps Ganga would respond, perhaps she would climb the *ghat*, each step a frame, a poem, a prayer, until she laps around the poet, embraces and liberates him. (*G*, 88)]

Here, the identity of the poet is unclear: this may refer to the poet Kabir, whose poems precede the passage, but it may also extend to Trojanow himself. In this passage, the Ganges resists all attempts to capture or contain it linguistically, each snapshot ("Momentaufnahme") rendered obsolete by the river's ceaseless motion that, along with the ever-shifting narrative, threaten to engulf the poet. Together, these episodes construe place as constantly new and dynamic and reference the indeterminacy of representation. Trojanow thus offers a competing vision of space that contrasts with colonial attempts at mapping, naming, or possession. The river's unpredictability also thwarts the narrator's progress, forcing him from intended routes, slowing his pace and at times even stopping him in his tracks, facilitating what Ashcroft terms a form of "slow travel," a mode of reflection that offers an alternative to a more "aggressive form of knowledge-making."[22] Paul Smethurst refers to this as a form of "disorderly" mobility, which foregrounds mobility's potentially unruly and disorienting effects as well as the threat they pose to the travel writer's ability to impose order and meaning in his narrative of the journey.[23]

Disorderliness becomes a recurring theme in *An den inneren Ufern Indiens*, in which meandering, circuitous, or even thwarted motion offer multiple narrative possibilities: chance encounters with local interlocutors make for a polyphonic, multiperspectival text, while time spent waiting for the journey to resume offers space to reflect on India's history, on its place within a global imaginary, or on Hindu mythology of the Ganges. Disorderliness is therefore not only thematic, but also a narrative device that poses a challenge to representation itself.

But it is not just Trojanow's travels, or even the mobility of the Ganges, that is the focus of the travelogue. The narrative highlights multiple forms of mobility, ranging from international travel, to domestic tourism, to the movements of capital and electronic communications. Trojanow thus presents his own travels as far from unique, but as part of just one aspect of an Indian society marked by constant motion both within and across national boundaries.

As Martin Kämpchen notes, Trojanow's Indian journey is not exactly original, since it follows the ancient sites of Hindu pilgrimage.[24] Acts of pilgrimage feature prominently throughout Trojanow's writings: Richard Burton's infamous pilgrimage to Mecca comprises an important episode in *Der Weltensammler*, while Trojanow's own study of Islam and undertaking of the hajj is the focus of *Zu den heiligen Quellen des Islam* (To the Holy Sources of Islam, 2004; in English as *From Mumbai to Mecca*, 2007) and reappears in *Nomade auf vier Kontinenten*.[25] All four texts recall tourism's origins in religious acts of pilgrimage and that religions have a significant place in the history of transnationalism. As one of the oldest transnational institutions, religious affiliation helps diasporas maintain transnational ties with countries of origin or important religious centers. These ties are often strengthened through acts of pilgrimage that reconfirm collective identities that transcend nationality.

The focus on pilgrimage in *An den inneren Ufern Indiens* fulfills an additional function, precisely because the route is, as Kämpchen notes, unoriginal. Here Trojanow does not pose as the solitary traveler among an otherwise sedentary population, but as part of a network of fellow travelers. Along the route, Trojanow encounters locals as well as international tourists similarly on the move; India is presented as a highly mobile society, moving intricately between ancient traditions and modernity.

Trojanow also considers India's place within transnational circuits of commerce in his encounter with Yukti Sutwala, a young employee in a

General Electric call center in Kanpur, in which employees are trained to adopt flawless British, American, or Australian accents through exposure to popular TV and radio shows. Trojanow contemplates how one does not need to leave one's locality in order to participate in transnational spaces of capital, as he considers how the Indian call centers form a hub of international service calls, each floor devoted to another continent of the English-speaking world (*U*, 85). Here, transnationalism fuses with the imperatives of global capitalism, as employees are required to divest themselves of local identity or linguistic inflection to hide their distant location from their international clients. This episode also recalls Robert Halsall's contention that more functional forms of "corporate cosmopolitanism" do not facilitate "a utopia in which cultural difference and diversity is respected and celebrated, but a dystopia in which cultural difference is made superfluous by the establishment of a flexible transnational capitalist class with no attachment to or responsibility for place."[26] However, while Trojanow decries the erasure of difference and diversity demanded by transnational corporations as well as the precarious and unfulfilling work environments they promote, he does not see this erasure as inevitable or complete, and contrasts it with the strong civic engagement and attachments to place exhibited by many interlocutors. Yukti's father Gopal, for example, is a local activist who combats the growing sanitation problems in Kanpur, organizing community initiatives to take on the privatization of garbage removal (*U*, 79–80). Throughout the travelogue, Trojanow meets with numerous environmental activists, from scientists and engineers, to concerned citizens of humble means, who tackle the growing problem of environmental degradation, in particular the growing pollution of the Ganges. Transnational challenges of climate change and corporate influence are thus seen not as entirely homogenizing forces, but are instead regarded in their particular local contexts.

The emphasis on various forms of mobility—from the travels of other tourists and pilgrims to the movement of global capital—thwarts the travel writer's desire to construct himself as a solitary, exclusive traveler, and also complicates the mobility–privilege equation. Trojanow furthermore tracks the syncretism that marks the many destinations along his journey, noting the connections between global cultures that can be seen in the migration of cultural and religious traditions across continents. In India for example, Trojanow is astounded when on the last evening of Kumbh Mela he encounters Sadhus listening to qawwali, the music of Sufi Muslims. When the group dismisses his surprise with the explanation that qawwali will also bring them closer to God, Trojanow considers how such mixtures of religions can be found throughout India. A visit to the Pranami Temple in Panna provokes a digression on the history of the sect, from the seventeenth century to Mahatma Gandhi's religious education in rituals that drew equally from the Koran and the Bhagavadgita (*U*,

64–65). Through such examples, Trojanow historicizes transnationalism and cosmopolitanism, and also questions the tendency to see them as a primarily contemporary or Western phenomenon.

This syncretism is also tracked through the multiple allusions to Hindu mythology. Rather than use the mythology and poetry as a foil for his own perspective, Trojanow instead stresses the fluid nature of the Hindi texts, in particular the myths he cites:

> So wie sich Schauplätze und Handlungsstränge von Ort zu Ort und von Mund zu Mund ändern, wird auch der moralische und politische Gehalt des Stoffes variiert. Neben der klassischen brahmanischen Fassung von Valmiki existieren viele andere Versionen des Ramayana—ein Stoff, hunderte Autoren. (*U*, 77)

> [As scenes and plots change from place to place, from mouth to mouth, the moral and political direction of the myths also changes. Besides the classical, Brahmanical epic of *Valmiki*, there are many other versions of the *Ramayana*—one drama, one hundred authors. (*G*, 48)]

Trojanow goes on to list some of the alternative versions of the *Ramayana*—a Teluga feminist retelling, a Dalit version that emphasizes the oppression of the lower castes—as well as the transnationalization of the *Ramayana* as it traveled from India to Indonesia, Cambodia and Thailand (*U*, 78). The emphasis on the uses to which narrative is put, rather than its authenticity or truth-value, raises questions about the truth-value of Trojanow's travelogue. The poetic interludes should therefore not be seen as a counterpart to the presumably more factual prose and conversational styles of the travelogue. On the contrary, the poetic passages shed light on the subjective, introspective nature of the entire text. These passages also require considerable work on the part of the reader since, despite the presence of a glossary, the many connections and significances are not self-evident and can only be fully grasped through further investigations into aspects of Indian mythology and philosophy. This is the very opposite of exoticism, in which readerly desires to easily consume representations of difference and otherness are thwarted and readers are challenged to look beyond the travelogue itself. With this Trojanow refuses the role of cultural intermediary or authority, placing the focus not on his own intercultural competence, but on the many examples of local cosmopolitanism he encounters on his journey.

Nomade auf vier Kontinenten

In *Nomade auf vier Kontinenten* Trojanow traces the travels of the famous nineteenth-century explorer, linguist, diplomat, writer, and translator Sir

Richard Frances Burton. The subtitle and itinerary through the same locations featured in *Der Weltensammler*—India, Mecca, Medina, East Africa, Utah, and Trieste—might lead prospective readers to dismiss the text as simply a document of Trojanow's research for the novel. On the contrary, it is in fact Trojanow's most experimental travelogue and its self-reflexive engagement with and deconstruction of generic conventions of travel writing make it an important reflection on the relationship between travel, transnationalism, cosmopolitanism, and travel writing.

Here too we can locate Trojanow's desire to deconstruct the narrative authority associated with the genre of travel writing. In *Nomade auf vier Kontinenten*, this is achieved primarily through the travelogue's strategy of cross-genericism, a key feature noted by Sigrid Löffler in her review of the book, which she characterizes as simultaneously a travelogue, "Burton-Reader," biography, memoir, and "zweistimmige[r] Roman transkultuereller Bewegungen" (novel about transcultural movements told in two voices).[27] The narrative is curiously hybrid, interweaving Trojanow's account of his journey (printed in black font), with excerpts from Burton's writings (printed in green). Although color-coded, the two narrative voices are at times so complexly interwoven that readers may fail to distinguish between them. Menno Aden's German translation of Burton's poem *The Kasidah* is also included, printed alongside the English original as a header to the chapters describing Trojanow's (and Burton's) experience of the hajj, while photographs, drawings, and facsimiles of Burton's handwriting appear throughout the text. The narrative thus shuttles not only between locations, but also between centuries as it juxtaposes Trojanow's and Burton's impressions of the places visited. The travelogue can therefore be seen as a compendium of documents that together chart the evolution of particular locations and the changing nature of travel.

While *Nomade auf vier Kontinenten* documents the disjuncture that differentiates Burton's age from our present time, it more often draws attention to continuities, a point made forcefully in the narrative's opening pages. Here, Trojanow invokes the image of the archive to consider how our current worldview continues to be shaped by colonial constructions of difference:

Und heute, da imperiale Positionen mit einer frischen Frechheit bezogen werden und manch ein Intellektueller sich beeilt, sie mit seiner Bildung abzufüttern, ist es lehrreich, nachzuvollziehen, wie das "viktorianische Archiv" gefüllt wurde, von Männern—und einigen wenigen Frauen—wie Richard Burton (*N*, 16).

[And now, as imperial positions are adopted with a new brashness and many intellectuals rush to reinforce them with their edification, it is instructive to track how the "Victorian archive" was filled by men—and a few women—like Richard Burton.]

In this passage Trojanow rejects any notion of a clear break with the colonial past. Subsequently, one of his aims in *Nomade auf vier Kontinenten* is to document forms of neocolonialism that persist through global politics, media, and mass tourism. Throughout his African travels, for example, the narrator contemplates how Western myths of African landscapes are perpetuated through popular exoticism in global media that fuels safari tourism to places like Kenya and Tanzania, threatening local ecologies (*N*, 329–30). A trip to the Selous Game Reserve reveals continuities between contemporary wildlife preservation policies around the world that restrict indigenous populations from ancestral lands and colonial ideologies that envisioned foreign spaces as pristine landscapes devoid of human civilization (*N*, 327–29). Everywhere Trojanow is reminded of the local costs of mass tourism—from the influx of rowdy package tourists (*N*, 43–45), to the environmental damage and overcrowding in popular heritage sites (*N*, 88–89) and the uneven distribution of proceeds from tourism that accrue to developers but not local workers (*N*, 90).

While not explicitly stated, Trojanow's hybridization of the travelogue form can be seen as an attempt to also draw attention to the role that the genre of travel writing continues to play in neocolonial constructions of difference. Having already voiced his suspicion and rejection of the "Victorian archive," filled by Burton and his contemporaries and continually replenished in our present moment, we must ask how we should read the collection of impressions, citations, and images presented in *Nomade auf vier Kontinenten*. Is this an alternative, more authentic archive meant to replace a flawed, inherited one? Is its polyphonic nature in itself sufficient to overcome the authoritative narrative positions typically adopted in the genre? Trojanow suggests otherwise, constructing a narrative that continually points to its own fictional status as well the dubious truth-claims that have characterized the genre throughout its history.

Fiction, myth, and unreliable narrators play important roles from the very start of *Nomade auf vier Kontinenten*. The travelogue begins in the Himalayas with the incredible tale of Trojanow's visit to an antiquarian bookshop in Shimla that is eerily empty of customers, but brimming with rare volumes. Here, an encounter with the shop's peculiar owner is cast as the initial impetus for Trojanow's travels. Producing a mysterious index that purports to catalogue the world's destroyed manuscripts, the shopkeeper raises the narrator's hopes that some of Burton's diaries may still exist. It is at this stage that we might add another generic category to Sigrid Löffler's characterization of the text, namely the quest narrative. Burton's missing manuscripts serve as a kind of Holy Grail that leads the narrator to various individuals across four continents who provide guidance, documents, and anecdotes of their own family connections with Burton. The *Spuren* (traces) referred to in the travelogue's subtitle take on an additional meaning, referring not only to the traces of Burton's journey, but also to further evidence that might substantiate or authenticate existing biographical sources and solve the mystery of the manuscripts' whereabouts. The traces are from the outset marked as textual ones; although the quest for Burton involves a physical journey, material traces are sought primarily through Burton's (missing) diaries. Trojanow's travelogue becomes an archive of excerpts from Burton's surviving writings, drawings, and photographs, along with anecdotes, impressions, and opinions about Burton provided by Trojanow and his various interlocutors. Not all of these sources are useful or reliable, however: contacts relate stories of dubious veracity, archival documents are illegible, and many stories have been passed through countless translators and interpreters, undermining any notion of authenticity.

One example will serve here to underscore how Trojanow considers the conflation of fact and fantasy within the genre of travel writing. In Goa he stops to visit Carlo da Cunha, grandson of Burton's former acquaintance, Gerson da Cunha. During the course of his visit, Carlo submits Trojanow to a test of his gullibility. Recounting an unlikely story of his family's lineage, Carlo claims to be a direct descendent of the sixteenth-century Portuguese explorer and soldier Tristan da Cunha. Carlo relates how his ancestor fell in love with the local Rajah's wife and how, after the death of her husband, she was destined to perish on her husband's funeral pyre in the Sita ritual. With the help of local coconspirators, Carlo alleges, the explorer succeeded in saving the woman and the da Cunha line was born. When Carlo breaks into operatic song to embellish his story, Trojanow's initial suspicions about the truth of the account are confirmed. In response to Trojanow's utter disbelief, da Cunha explains the motive for his tall tale: "Ich wollte prüfen, ob Sie zu jenen Europäern gehören, die nur nach den Geschichten schürfen, die ihre eigenen Landsleute im fernen Boden vergraben haben" (N, 57; I wanted to test whether you belong to those Europeans who only hunt out those stories that your own countrymen have buried in distant soil).

Although the source of Carlo's story is never revealed, the plot and verses he sings stem from Louis Spohr's 1823 opera *Jessonda*. Representative of what James Parakilas[28] terms the "Age of Discovery" operas of the nineteenth century, *Jessonda* deploys the common trope of an interracial love story between a famous explorer and an exotic female. As Parakilas demonstrates, operas like *Jessonda* were set in the Age of Columbus and offered parallels to European colonial pursuits of the nineteenth century.[29] Exploring the possibilities of lasting relationships between colonizer and colonized, these operas offered narratives in which markers of difference—often religious difference—are conveniently erased. In *Jessonda*, religion, in the form of the Sita ritual, is posited as irrational and dangerous, and Jessonda's abandonment of her native culture is presented as reasonable. Operas like *Jessonda* thus functioned to cast the European colonial presence as a benevolent, civilizing influence, a notion that well suited imperial designs. The insertion of da Cunha's yarn thus references an entire repertoire of exoticism in the Western musical tradition that can be counted among the European archive of representations of otherness. It also serves as a warning to the traveler and, consequently, to the reader. As da Cunha suggests, while travel may offer the promise of first-hand experience and encounter, travelers may all too often "discover" what they set out to find, namely the myths and fantasies of previous journeys, both factual and fictional.

But the logical extension of this argument is that we must be equally skeptical of the truth-value of Trojanow's own account. Here again, attention to generic conventions is crucial. Ultimately Trojanow's quest fails: the missing diaries are never found and the travelogue's quest motif can only be registered as ironic. While the details of Trojanow's quest for Burton's missing notebooks may be pure invention, this only serves to prove a larger point. The parodic employment of the quest narrative pokes fun at travel writing's desire to produce the effects of authority and authenticity, showing instead that all travel writing is speculative, subjective, and comprised of partial representations.

This is not to say, however, that the travelogue has nothing substantial to relate. Invoking the figure of Burton raises provocative questions about the extent to which twenty-first-century global connections of tourism, trade, and technology have resulted in new, more cosmopolitan openness toward various forms of difference. For as Burton's biographer Dane Kennedy cautions, it would be a mistake to consider Burton's world as completely removed from a contemporary transnational reality. The Victorians, Kennedy argues, shaped their self-image from transnational encounters across the globe through military service, trade, and travel so that their world was also "a genuinely transnational and transcultural" one, "drawing inspiration and insight from wide-ranging, often unexpected sources."[30] By juxtaposing his travels with Burton's, Trojanow historicizes transnationalism, reminds us of its exploitative forms, and questions any direct connection between transnationalism and cosmopolitan attitudes toward various forms of otherness. Ultimately, he asks whether our world may not share more in common with the colonial era than we care to acknowledge. Conversely, he contemplates transnationalism's more liberating potential, in particular by pointing to non-European examples of pluralistic societies. Like *Der Weltensammler*, *Nomade auf vier Kontinenten* frequently highlights the cosmopolitanism of the spaces through which Burton traveled. In Zanzibar, for example, Trojanow admires the multilingualism and worldliness of the local residents he encounters there. He also cites Burton's reflections on the long history of cosmopolitanism in the region and the rich civilization that the Portuguese explorers found there at the close of the fifteenth century

(*N*, 286). In such passages, Trojanow not only reminds readers of earlier forms of transnationalism but also inverts the historical traditions of travel writing that locate cosmopolitanism as inherently European.

Conclusions

Unlike his more conventional travelogues and reportages, *An den inneren Ufern Indiens* and *Nomade auf vier Kontinenten* are experiments in form that seek to locate and deconstruct the architecture of what many deem the still "tainted" genre of travel writing. Employing various techniques— for example, the emphasis on disorderly narratives, inauthenticity, or generic hybridity—these travelogues attempt to unsettle the author's position of mastery and expertise. The engagement with form reinforces the notion that transnational author biographies and perspectives are not sufficient to wrest the genre from its colonial past, but also shows that Trojanow is not ready to abandon the genre altogether. Travel and travel writing still afford productive opportunities to investigate the ways in which diverse experiences of transnational encounter and exchange can be both emancipating and exploitative. Trojanow thus provides no simple answers to the relationship between transnationalism and cosmopolitanism, showing instead that each phenomenon exists in diverse array. If there is a recurring theme in these two travelogues, however, it is the question as to who counts as transnational or cosmopolitan and how this status continues to be conferred from privileged first-world positions that often ignore the many variants of local cosmopolitanism existing elsewhere. Trojanow's repeated references to non-European transnationalisms and cosmopolitanisms, both past and present, are perhaps the most effective thematic devices he employs to disrupt crude dichotomies of an imperial era that imagined worldly, European travelers in opposition to allegedly insular, immobile natives. Through his experiments with form, Trojanow attempts to recuperate the productive potential of travel writing, namely its ability to afford both a historical and transnational perspective that can disrupt the universalist pretentions of one's own point of view. With these two travelogues, Trojanow suggests that in order to approach a more cosmopolitan worldview, the transnational perspectives inherent to travel and travel writing must also be accompanied by innovations in narrative form.

Notes

[1] Edward Said, *Orientalism: Western Conceptions of the Orient* (New York: Vintage, 1979), 195–97.

[2] Ilija Trojanow, *Nomade auf vier Kontinenten: Auf den Spuren von Sir Richard Francis Burton* (Munich: Deutscher Taschenbuch Verlag, 2008), 16. Hereafter *N* in brackets in the main body of the text.

3 See in particular Said, *Orientalism*, and Mary Louise Pratt, *Imperial Eyes: Travel Writing and Transculturation* (London: Routledge, 1992).

4 For an overview of Trojanow's relationship to the European tradition of reportage, see Julian Preece, "From Kisch to Kapuściński: Trojanow and the European Tradition of Reportage," in *Ilija Trojanow*, ed. Julian Preece (Bern: Peter Lang, 2013), 171–86.

5 Samuel P. Huntington, *The Clash of Civilizations and the Remaking of World Order* (New York: Touchstone, 1996).

6 Ilija Trojanow and Ranjit Hoskoté, *Kampfabsage*, transl. Heike Schlatterer (Munich: Karl Blessing Verlag, 2007), 15.

7 See, for example, Ilija Trojanow, *Der entfesselte Globus* (Munich: Carl Hanser Verlag, 2008), 16. In one travelogue, Trojanow's transnational biography is even posited as a precondition for his ability to acclimatize to foreign surroundings. See Ilija Trojanow, *Gebrauchsanweisung für Indien* (Munich: Piper Verlag, 2006), 9.

8 Pico Iyer, cited in Matthew Davis, "On Travel and Travel Writing," *World Hum*, November 30, 2006, accessed November 30, 2014, http://www.worldhum.com/features/travel-interviews/pico_iyer_travel_writing_20061104/.

9 Debbie Lisle, *The Global Politics of Contemporary Travel Writing* (Cambridge: Cambridge University Press, 2006), 71.

10 Paul Smethurst, introduction to *Travel Writing, Form and Empire: The Poetics and Politics of Mobility*, ed. Julia Kuehn and Paul Smethurst (New York: Routledge, 2009), 10.

11 Ilija Trojanow, *Der entfesselte Globus* (Munich: Carl Hanser Verlag, 2008), 123.

12 Trojanow, *Der entfesselte Globus*, 143–47.

13 V. S. Naipaul, *India: A Million Mutinies Now* (New York: Viking, 1991).

14 Pratt, *Imperial Eyes*, 201–23.

15 Ilija Trojanow, "Voran ins Gondwanaland," in *Ferne Nähe: Tübinger Poetik-Dozentur 2007* (Künzelsau: Swiridoff Verlag, 2008), 90.

16 Claudia Kramatschek, "Hommage an Indien," Deutschlandfunk March 02, 2004, accessed June 20, 2014, www.deutschlandfunk.de/hommage-an-indien.700.de.html?dram:article_id=81635.

17 Bill Ashcroft, "Travel and Power," in *Travel Writing, Form and Empire: The Poetics and Politics of Mobility*, ed. Julia Kuehn and Paul Smethurst (New York: Routledge, 2009) 229–30.

18 Ashcroft, "Travel and Power," 235.

19 Ilija Trojanow, *An den inneren Ufern Indiens: Eine Reise entlang des Ganges* (Munich: Piper, 2008), 60–61. Hereafter *U* in brackets in the main body of the text.

20 Bill Ashcroft, "Travel and Power," 236.

21 All English citations have been taken from the published English paperback translation by Ilija Trojanow and Ranjit Hoskoté, *Along the Ganges* (London: Armchair Traveller at the BookHaus, 2011), 37. Hereafter *G* in brackets in the main body of the text.

[22] Ashcroft, "Travel and Power," 237.

[23] Smethurst, introduction, 6–9.

[24] Martin Kämpchen, "Wer der Ganga die Zunge löst," *Frankfurter Allgemeine Zeitung*, January 23, 2004.

[25] For a discussion of acts of pilgrimage in Trojanow's writing see Ernest Schonfield, "On the Road to Mecca with Trojanow and Burton," in *Ilija Trojanow*, 81–97.

[26] Robert Halsall, "The Discourse of Corporate Cosmopolitanism" in *British Journal of Management* 20, no. 1 (2009): 136.

[27] Sigrid Löffler, "Verschmelzungsgeschäfte auf vier Kontinenten," *Cicero*, accessed December 20, 2014, http://www.cicero.de//salon/verschmelzungsge-schaefte-auf-vier-kontinenten/43888. Trojanow is of course not unique: as Peter Hulme notes, generic hybridization is not new and has "periodically reinvigorated travel writing throughout its history." Peter Hulme, "Travelling to Write (1940–2000)," in *The Cambridge Companion to Travel Writing*, ed. Peter Hulme and Tim Youngs (Cambridge: Cambridge University Press, 2002), 95. For a more extensive analysis of *Nomade auf vier Kontinenten* and its investigation of ongoing links between transnationalism, cosmopolitanism, and colonialism, see Christina Kraenzle, "Rewriting Colonial Travelogues: Cosmopolitan Visions and Colonial Legacies in *Nomade auf vier Kontinenten*," in *Ilija Trojanow*.

[28] James Parakilas, "The Soldier and the Exotic: Operatic Variations on a Theme of Racial Encounter," *Opera Quarterly* 10, no. 2 (1993): 36.

[29] Parakilas, "The Soldier," 37.

[30] Dane Kennedy, *The Highly Civilized Man: Richard Burton and the Victorian World* (Cambridge: Harvard University Press, 2005), 271.

7: Europe's Invisible Ghettos: Transnationalism and Neoliberal Capitalism in Julya Rabinowich's *Die Erdfresserin*

Maria Mayr

> *Sie zogen durch Kleinasien nach Europa und nahmen ihre Schätze mit sich, und so lange diese dauerten, waren sie überall willkommen; wehe aber allen Armen in der Fremde.*
>
> [They wandered through Asia Minor and brought their treasures, and as long as these lasted, they were welcome everywhere; but woe to all the poor in foreign lands.]
>
> —Achim von Arnim, *Isabella von Ägypten*[1]

Introduction

IN HER TIMELY NOVEL *Die Erdfresserin* (The Woman Who Eats Dirt, 2012), Julya Rabinowich thematizes the confluence of a myriad of concerns affecting contemporary migrants in Europe, whose fates are shaped by matters of intersecting ethnic, religious, and gendered identities. Her novel thus engages issues also addressed by a now sizable body of Germanophone literature concerned with cultural transnationalism. However, Rabinowich's novel ultimately points to the fact that transnational social spaces are increasingly infringed upon by global capitalism. Her text thereby highlights that however important and interconnected matters of identity and its recognition are, they cannot be properly addressed if individuals' basic needs, such as food, shelter, and access to medication, have not been met. As Rabinowich's grim depiction of the fate of a transnational illegal sex worker clearly shows, for the estimated half-million illegal immigrants in contemporary Western Europe, they are not.[2] Forming part of a growing European precariat, these immigrants' plight is representative of the more wholesale failure of contemporary European nation-states to protect both denizens and citizens from globalization in its current shape of neoliberal capitalism.

Globalization, Transnationalism, and Neoliberalism

Much scholarship on the transnational stresses its distinctiveness from globalization. Victor Roudometof distinguishes between globalization and transnationalism, arguing that transnationalism is properly defined as the "emerging reality of social life under conditions of internal globalization or glocalization," here understood as the local manifestations of globalization in everyday life.[3] Taking a closer look at the nature of these transnational effects of economic globalization, it becomes clear that transnationalism describes a predominantly cultural phenomenon concerned with issues such as individual and community identity. Roudometof, for example, details that transnational social spaces include "spaces of transnational sexuality, popular music, journalism, as well as spaces fostering the construction of a multitude of identities (ranging from those based on gender to those based on race, religion, or ethnicity)."[4] Also emphasizing the cultural nature of transnationalism, Randall Halle concludes that globalization denotes "material economic processes" whereas transnationalism designates "socio-political ideational processes, or to put it more simply, the dynamic of culture."[5] Highlighting the difference between cultural transnationalism and economic globalization in this manner foregrounds that transnational phenomena are not antithetical to or somehow beyond the nation. Rather, as Sarah Mahler and Patricia Pessar point out, by virtue of their local manifestations or anchoring within nations, transnational processes in fact often affirm the importance of nation-states.[6]

Moreover, the ability to participate in transnational processes and social spaces to a certain extent presupposes the kinds of securities that have traditionally been provided by the nation-state. In her discussion of precariousness and precarity, Judith Butler emphasizes this enabling function of the nation-state. Premising that all living beings are in a state of precariousness, that is, that all lives "can be expunged at will or by accident," Butler holds that it is the task of "political orders, including economic and social institutions" to ensure that basic needs for survival are provided.[7] Failure to do so results in creating a state of precarity, which Butler defines as a "politically induced condition in which certain populations suffer from failing social and economic networks of support and become differentially exposed to injury, violence, and death."[8] In Europe and elsewhere, such protection is increasingly not only withheld from denizens, such as illegal immigrants, but also from European citizens, as the masses of unemployed young people in Greece and Portugal attest to.

This withdrawal of the nation-state from its role as the guardian of its citizens' welfare is a direct consequence of contemporary globalization, which is, according to Eric Cazdyn and Imre Szeman, simply a code for capitalism, "an ideological project—one that served to naturalize capitalism under its name."[9] According to David Harvey, neoliberal capitalist practices have become entrenched starting in the 1970s and were consolidated around the globe by leaders, such as Ronald Reagan in the United States, Margaret Thatcher in Great Britain, Helmut Kohl in Germany, Augusto Pinochet in Chile, and Deng Xiaoping in China.[10] According to Harvey's often-cited definition, neoliberalism is:

> A theory of political economic practices proposing that human well-being can best be advanced by the maximization of entrepreneurial freedoms within an institutional framework characterized by private property rights, individual liberty, unencumbered markets, and free trade. The role of the state is to create and preserve an institutional framework appropriate to such practices. . . . But beyond these tasks the state should not venture.[11]

As the 2008 financial and the ongoing Eurozone crises highlight, neoliberalism has indeed been detrimental to the welfare of populations around the globe, giving credence to Harvey's sinister assessment that the "destruction neoliberalization has visited across the globe is unparalleled in the history of capitalism."[12] In its neoliberal guise, capitalism permeates many nation-states pervasively, orienting them toward economic values, such as lower taxes and attracting investors and employers. By focusing mainly on the economic, the nation-states have turned away from their responsibility of preventing conditions of precarity to arise. For many, the Europe of austerity therefore entails a Europe of precarity.

Contemporary illegal immigrants, such as Rabinowich's main character Diana, an illegal sex worker from Dagestan, are representative of a much larger group both within and outside the "trans"-national Schengen zone and its individual nation-states, who suffer from the resulting conditions of precarity. Rabinowich's novel, to which I will now turn, highlights that there is very little room for participation in cultural transnationalism for this growing precariate. By means of her protagonist Diana, Rabinowich details a character who is barred from participation in transnational social spaces on account of her illegal and economically precarious status. Diana simply cannot afford to participate in what Roudometof calls "transnational interactions [that] involve such routines as international calls, faxes, emails, satellite TV broadcasting, simultaneous media access through Internet sources and TV stations, international conferences, the different varieties of international tourism."[13] While these are available to and shape the lived experience of many, they also are inaccessible for many others. Rabinowich's character Diana, for instance, simply cannot afford access to the internet or a cell phone. Johannes Voelz therefore argues that cultural studies scholars of transnationalism should "divest [them]selves of the urge to interpret the transnational as resistant and subversive" and instead ask questions, such as how "transnationalism [is] linked to the culture of consumption that is driving neoliberal globalization."[14]

Money, Money, Money

Julya Rabinowich was born in St. Petersburg and was, according to her website, "entwurzelt & umgetopft" (uprooted and transplanted) to Vienna in 1977.[15] In Vienna, she eventually studied simultaneous interpretation and art. For several years, she worked as an interpreter for psychotherapy sessions with refugees, which has greatly inspired her writing of *Die Erdfresserin*, her latest novel published in 2012. *Die Erdfresserin* is Rabinowich's third novel, preceded by *Spaltkopf* (Splithead, 2008), the semiautobiographical tale of a young Russian girl and her family immigrating to Vienna, and *Herznovelle* (Heart Novella, 2011), the story of a heart-sick patient becoming enamored with her heart-surgeon. She also has written numerous plays and writes a weekly column for the Austrian newspaper *Der Standard*.

Rabinowich's novel *Die Erdfresserin* traces and aesthetically mirrors the gradual disintegration of the main character Diana's body and psyche as she tries to make a living as an illegal sex worker in various, not always specified countries in contemporary Europe, periodically returning to her native Russian Republic of Dagestan to deliver remittances to her dependent family.[16] Working the streets all over Europe with the diminishing hope to eventually work in her professions as a stage director, the "Einzelwanderin" (lonely wanderer) Diana eventually finds temporary respite in Vienna due to a terminally ill Austrian client, the police officer Leo, and a stay in a charitable psychiatric institution, only to then plunge even more forcefully into poverty, eventual insanity, and finally, to what the reader has to assume to be her death.[17] Written after the financial crisis of 2008 and its consequences—or lack thereof—Rabinowich's novel illustrates how the often invisible structures but concrete material effects of neoliberal capitalism threaten any viable transnational present for Europe's non-European denizens.

Rabinowich's disturbingly bleak novel spans the years before the fall of the Iron Curtain up to 2012, and is set in 2011–12. For the first-person narrator, Diana, the rapid changes after communism in the East European cities she passes through are decidedly negative, described as so sudden and "brutal wie ein Schlag ins Gesicht" (Erdfresserin, 117; brutal like a smack in the face). For the illegal immigrant, the immediate postcommunist era is marked by a battle between the old, communist system and the new, capitalist one, in which people like her "gerieten den beiden Giganten ständig unter die Füße und in die geballten Fäuste" (117; fell constantly under the feet and into the clenched fists of both giants). For Diana, the eventual victory of the West, however, does not represent any kind of political or cultural triumph of democracy or the freedom to travel, but rather the end of a balance of powers. As a result, it is the "immer gleichen Global Players" (117; always the same global players) who now reign "im Bewusstsein ihrer Weltmacht, die anderen Weltmächte hatten ja zu existieren aufgehört" (117; fully conscious of their world power; the other world powers, after all, have ceased to exist). It is therefore not Europe over Russia, West over East, not one nation or ideology over another, but the capitalist global system itself, which has emerged as the winner in the twenty-first century. As Cazdyn and Szeman point out, after the Cold War "the globalization of one of the systems (capitalism) usurped the other system,"[18] leaving neoliberal capitalism free reign. As I will detail in the following paragraphs, Rabinowich's novel foregrounds this economic reality, which premises and affects all other areas of life, such as matters of ethnic, religious, individual, and familial identity.

Even though Europe and its borders figure prominently in the novel, Rabinowich's focus is on the economic essence of the union. Diana's native country Dagestan is rich in agricultural produce, part of the "Kornkammer" (grain basket) of Russia (*Erdfresserin*, 17). However, its produce is exported for giveaway prices. With what the novel depicts as acute unemployment in Dagestan and considering Diana's observation that one can earn ten times as much in Vienna than in Dagestan for the same amount of work hours (117), labor migration is not a choice but a necessity for many. Diana observes that ironically, the "fruchtbarste Gebiet von allen ist Westeuropa, das alle ernährt. Da gibt es Korn, da gibt es Arbeit." (17; The most fertile area of all is Western Europe, which nourishes everyone. There is corn, there is work.)[19] In Diana's view, postcommunist neoliberal economic realities have therefore forced her entire country to sell its produce, labor, and bodies, so that essentially, "das ganze Land begann, sich auf mannigfaltige und höchst legale Art und Weise zu prostituieren" (38; the whole country began to prostitute itself in diverse and highly legal ways). Alluding to Marx' famous dictum that "prostitution is only a *specific* expression of the *general* prostitution of the *laborer*" in the capitalist system,[20] Rabinowich's novel criticizes Europe's economic exploitation of former East Bloc countries, which was made possible by the latters' entry into the capitalist system.[21]

While such economic "prostitution" benefits global corporations, individuals like Diana do not necessarily profit from the post–Cold War capitalist system. As one of the illegal sex workers in Europe, the majority of which comes from non-EU Eastern Europe as well as Central Asia,[22] Diana clearly represents the flip side of globalization. She desired "nur einen Löffel vom Honig, ein Gläschen nur von der Milch, die in Europa fließt" (*Erdfresserin*, 17; only a spoonful of the honey, a little glass of the milk that flows in Europe), only to eventually realize that economic security is only possible for those "die hier geboren und aufgezogen wurden mit der warmen Milch der gesetzlichen Sicherheit" (92; who are born and raised here on the warm milk of legal protection). In the land of milk and honey, the milk does not flow in the same way for everyone, and rarely does it flow for those who lack the kinds of protection enjoyed by citizens of wealthy nations. However, national entities and quasi-national borders, such as the Schengen border zone, do not pose the major problem for Diana. While crossing borders is hazardous due to, for example, corrupt border guards, Diana does not experience the crossing as a significant obstacle, stating, "Ich habe [diese Straßen] unzählige Male ungestraft passiert und werde es wieder tun" (17; I have passed unimpeded through [these streets] countless times, and I will do it again). Oftentimes, the reader cannot even discern what country Diana finds herself in at a given moment, rendering considerations of national borders secondary because her situation neither improves nor worsens by crossing them. Instead, the novel foregrounds the more insurmountable borders as being those between poor and rich, which permeate European society much more pervasively. Thus, Diana's sense of exclusion is not experienced at a border crossing but rather in the middle-class neighborhood of a Dutch town where Diana observes a couple's quiet evening routine from the street through a curtainless window. While transparent, this glass border is impermeable for someone like her. Looking at Vienna's streets, Diana also observes, "dass es hier kein Ghetto gibt, das Ghetto muss nicht eingezäunt und abgegrenzt werden hier, es ist allgegenwärtig." (114; There is no ghetto here; the ghetto does not need to be fenced off and separated here. It is present everywhere.) The borders keeping Diana out are not necessarily national but rather economic borders, which are crisscrossing West European space.

This relativization of the inclusive or exclusive power of national borders in light of economic determinants becomes further apparent as the novel, in the form of a subplot, also highlights the precarious situation of Leo, an Austrian citizen. This terminally ill police officer, whom Diana cares for and sleeps with in exchange for food and rent, also is part of Europe's unbounded ghetto. He is, at least in part, himself a victim of the ideology underpinning the current economic system, in which individual worth is based on one's function in and contribution to the system. When he can no longer work due to his illness, his colleagues soon forget about him—a fact Leo finds even harder to deal with than not hearing from his still beloved ex-wife (*Erdfresserin*, 104). Not working, that is, not taking one's place in the capitalist system by commodifying one's labor, renders the individual irrelevant.[23] In his irrelevance, Leo to a certain extent resembles the invisible illegal immigrants, such as Diana (216), both inhabiting the nondemarcated ghetto of global capitalism that is not defined primarily by national and ethnic belonging but rather by economic status.

Just as there is no spatially locatable ghetto, Diana also lacks any apparent community, be it of kinship or an ethnic or religious nature. Instead, she is one of the many "Einzelwanderer" (lonely wanderer) traversing Europe "unsichtbar und allgegenwärtig" (*Erdfresserin*, 216; invisible and omnipresent). While both Judaism and Islam are gestured toward as forming part of Diana's background, religious identity is not fully developed as a theme in the novel. Diana's country of origin, Dagestan, is Russia's most ethnically diverse republic, not allowing for any conclusions to be drawn about Diana's religion or ethnicity. The narrator's use of "Gott ist groß und barmherzig" (God is great and merciful), a combination of the beginning of the Adhan (*Allāhu akbar*), the Muslim prayer call, and the first line of the first sura in the Koran, is more likely to depict cultural rather than religious belonging, on par with the Austrian Dr. Petersen's daily repeated "Grüß Gott" (167; greeting). Despite the prominence of the Golem legend that I will return to below, and a star-shaped piece of family jewelry her mother clings to, nothing in the novel allows for conjectures about Diana's religious background. In fact, the jewelry explicitly functions as a symbol of a lost era of the maternal family's "früherem Reichtum" (147; previous wealth), that is, as a sign of economic rather than religious or ethnic affiliation. Diana's situation thus resembles that of several other minority characters in contemporary German-language fiction. In her contribution to this volume, Anke Biendarra, for example, highlights Olga Grjasnowa's character Cem in *Der Russe ist einer, der Birken liebt* (2012; All Russians Love Birch Trees, 2014), who after a conflict ensuing a fender-bender does not want the incident to be turned into a matter of his ethnicity, stating that he needs "einen Anwalt und keine Kulturtheorie" (a lawyer, not cultural theory).[24] Like Cem, Rabinowich's character Diana ultimately refuses an analysis focused on cultural issues such as religious and ethnic affiliation.

Just as questions of national, ethnic, and religious belonging turn out to be absorbed by economic concerns, Diana's personal and psychological problems are ultimately eclipsed by immediate material, economic needs. When Leo and Diana's mutually beneficial relationship ends after a year because of Leo's death, Diana suffers a psychotic breakdown. Becoming the "Erdfresserin" or the "woman who eats dirt" of the novels' title, Diana gives in to an overwhelming urge to ingest and cover herself with soil.[25] As a result, Diana is institutionalized by a Viennese charitable organization, heavily medicated, and undergoes daily psychoanalytic sessions with Dr. Petersen, which frame the chapters in the first half of the novel. In the novel's opening paragraph, Dr. Petersen encapsulates the psychoanalytic process, telling Diana that he is interested in learning more about "Sie, Ihre Familie, Ihre Vergangenheit." (*Erdfresserin*, 9; you, your family, your past). Yet, while her absent father and troubled, often cruel mother figure prominently in her recollections during the psychoanalytic sessions, it becomes obvious that they are not the cause of her present problems. Instead, the present is overdetermined by the need to provide for her disabled son, the circumstances of whose conception and birth as well as whose father are never mentioned. In addition to her son, Diana also has to provide for her unemployed mother and sister who are taking care of him in Dagestan. On account of these responsibilities, Diana simply cannot afford to take care of her own psyche and mental health. Therefore, she answers Dr. Petersen's question of whether she has ever despaired by stating, "Das muss man sich leisten können" (87; You have to be able to afford that). In fact, she has to pay bitterly for the few weeks she stays in the hospital, since the lack of remittances puts her son's life in immediate danger. Out of touch with the reality of life in Dagestan, Dr. Petersen believes that Diana can simply return home and find a job if she addresses her psychological issues—an assumption to which Diana merely replies, "Aber mein Land kann das nicht, Herr Doktor" (183; But my country can't do that, doctor). Her reality is not primarily determined by her own individual past or roots, but rather by the present need to provide for her family, which constitute her "ausgedörrten Wurzeln, die [sie] tiefer ins Erdreich versenken konnte als [ihre] eigenen" (200; parched roots, which she was able to plunge deeper into the earth than her own). Economic necessities throw Diana back into a family network, in which taking care of oneself personally is an unaffordable luxury. Thus, Rabinowich's novel to some extent aligns with Chandra Mohanty's recent critique of the effects of "postmodern intellectual framings of transnational, intersectional feminist theorizing," in which oftentimes "all experience is merely individual, and the social is always collapsed into the personal."[26] While the psychoanalysis session provided for refugees in Vienna, which Rabinowich herself had interpreted for and that the novel's character undergoes, are certainly well intentioned, they seem to be ineffective as they reduce systemic economic problems to personal ones. Even though the destructive effects of neoliberal capitalism are certainly experienced at a personal and oftentimes physical level, as becomes glaringly obvious in the figure of the prostitute, these consequences cannot be addressed on a personal and individual level. In the face of precarity, psychoanalysis is impotent.

That Diana is first and foremost a victim of present economic realities transcending all other concerns becomes most apparent toward the end of the novel. While Diana is certainly afraid of representatives of the state on account of her illegal status (*Erdfresserin*, 128), the novel does not contain any scenes in which Diana is physically brutalized by one of its agents, such as a police officer or border guard. In fact, none of the Austrian police, the doctors, or the immigration officer are depicted as very powerful but rather as being weak personalities. While both Leo and Dr. Petersen certainly could have done more to help Diana, Dr. Petersen simply has no legal power to help her obtain legal status in Austria, and the illness her lover Leo is suffering from has made him physically dependent on her. Power in the form of brutal violence instead is exerted by the private security guards of a fancy department store in an unidentified country, in which Diana seeks shelter from the snow on her attempted final journey back to Dagestan (218). Wishing one of the beds on display had her name on it, just like the ones apparently reserved for Mr. Armani and Mr. Hilfiger, Diana cuddles up in one of the soft beds to be promptly and forcefully removed by private security guards. Out of the sight of customers, "hinter all der Pracht und dem Glanz" (222; behind all the magnificence and splendor), Diana is violently beaten by the guards, reduced to howling like a "verzweifeltes Tier" (222; desperate animal). Thrown back into the cold winter streets, Diana no longer remembers where she was supposed to go and how to get there. Confused both on account of her abruptly ceased psycho-pharmaceutics and the violence of the guards, it is in this capitalist private "Reich" (empire, 218) that Diana is dehumanized, loses all memories of her family, and forgets the fact that her son will most likely die if she does not find her way back home as soon as possible (223). Presenting the reader with a private bedroom in a public department store that is guarded not by a publicly funded police but rather by private security forces, this scene points to a system in which everything is for sale at the expense of the private and the rights formerly associated with it. While Austrian authorities and institutions are certainly depicted as impotent and at least passively complicit in Diana's ultimate demise, the overwhelming share of the blame lies with the current economic system that is represented by a private corporation.

No Golem without a Ghetto

Diana's fate as a transnational illegal sex worker brings current neoliberal realities into sharp focus, illustrating that the economic system has come to permeate all aspects of physical and mental life, leaving no room for participation in transnational social spaces and interactions. As *Pictures of a Reality* (2012), a collection of interviews conducted by the INDOORS project with sex workers from nine European cities shows, the majority of the (mostly female) sex workers in Western Europe are all driven by economic necessity rather than war or human and natural catastrophes.[27] Yet, Western countries fail or refuse to acknowledge the urgency and consequences of this economic labor migration. In the novel, an immigration officer contacted by Dr. Petersen explains to Diana. "Sie kommen aus keinem Kriegsgebiet. . . . Sie gehören nicht einmal einer ethnisch verfolgten Minderheit an. Das ist ein Problem. . . . Sind Sie politisch aktiv gewesen? . . . Heimlich religiös? . . . Sind Sie denn wenigstens vergewaltigt worden?" (*Erdfresserin*, 179; You don't come from a war zone . . . you don't even belong to a persecuted ethnic minority. That is a problem. . . . Were you politically active? . . . Secretly religious? . . . Were you at least raped?) Never having been raped, Diana is once more unable to buy herself membership in what Terri Tomsky calls the present trauma economy, in which even trauma has become implicated in economics by being turned into a currency in "international circuits of mediation and commodification."[28] Neither an immigrant, recognized refugee, nor a demure victim to be easily sympathized with, Diana instead is condemned to a life in transit and illegality, which come to define her ontologically. Diana's body itself thereby becomes marked by economic necessity, so that she follows "nur der einen Straße, die aus meinem Herzen in die Welt hinausführt, . . . meine Arterien und Blutgefäße und Nervengestränge hängen fest verbunden an diesem Weg, es ist keine Frage, ob ich folge, ich muss folgen." (*Erdfresserin*, 195; Only the one street which leads from my heart into the world . . . my arteries and blood vessels and nerve fibers are attached tightly to this way. There is no question about whether I follow; I must follow.) Her way of life as well as the cause for her psychotic breakdown is the result of economic pressures, her body and mind reduced to precariousness and the need to survive.

This need for survival is moreover gendered as feminine. In part, this reflects the nature of the sex industry, in which 93% of all migrant sex workers in Europe are female.[29] In addition, this gendering also highlights the particular vulnerability of the maternal body, which is thematized by the novel's use of the golem legend.[30] Desperate to return to Dagestan to save her son, who has been institutionalized by the authorities and is now in danger of dying from neglect and abuse unless the staff can be bribed, Diana flees from the psychiatric institution in Vienna and thus also abruptly stops her antipsychotic medication. Trying to find her way back home on foot, as she had done many times before, she becomes increasingly disoriented, losing her way, her sense of the past and future, and eventually her sense of identity. Instead, she blindly follows the golem who she believes is accompanying her since her mental breakdown and whom she initially believes herself to have command over. However, this golem instead leads her to her death in an unspecified country.

The golem's eventual failure to help Diana can be attributed to the realities of her embodied female existence in a world marked by global capitalism. After all legal and illegal channels are exhausted, Diana clings to this folkloristic creature that she calls out of the earth to take care of her, chanting, "Der Vater, den ich nie kannte. / *Ein Atemzug hinaus.* / Das Geschenk, das ich bereit bin, an seiner statt anzunehmen." (*Erdfresserin*, 203; The father whom I never knew. / *Exhale one breath.* / The present that I am prepared to take in his place.) Meant to substitute for her disappeared father, the version of the many golem tales invoked here is one in which a wise man commands a golem to protect his family and community (169), a duty her father as well as the unknown and never-mentioned father of her own child neglect. Even as a child, Diana wishes to be "dieser gelehrte Mann . . . dessen Hand die Zeichen in die leere Golemstirn geritzt hatte, um ihn so zum Leben zu erwecken, wie eine Frau es niemals tun könnte" (this learned man . . . whose hand carved the symbols on the empty forehead of the golem in order to bring him to life as a woman never could, 50). However, the act of male imaginative creation based on learned wisdom is sharply contrasted with female procreation, because whereas a golem is useful and ready to serve from the moment of its inception, a mother has to tend to her child for "eine ermüdend lange Zeit" (50; for a exhaustingly long time) and is "durch das von ihr geschaffene Wesen gebunden" (50; tied to this being of her own creation). For women and outside of the realms of the intellect and imagination, the act of creation is not necessarily empowering but rather a physically messy act and a child a lifelong responsibility. Whereas the rabbi of the legend can simply terminate the golem's existence by wiping a letter from his forehead, Diana is bound by her mentally and physically ill son's material needs, no matter how often she asks him, "Wann stirbst du denn endlich" (100; When are you finally going to die). Ultimately let down by matters of the intellect and imagination, Diana throws the books she had kept with her on her travels into a river at the end of the novel, stating that books "stillen weder Not noch Hunger" (229; satisfy neither need nor hunger).

Since she is reduced to matters of existence and survival, the novel puts Diana's bodily needs into sharp focus. Such a focus on the body can also be observed in other recent German-language literature written by women. In her analysis of Charlotte Roche's *Feuchtgebiete* (2008; *Wetlands*, 2009) and Helene Hegeman's *Axolotl Roadkill* (2010) provided in this volume, Hester Baer for instance shows that in pop-feminist texts, a similar focus on bodily experiences constitutes an attempt to "map subjectivity" due to "the absence of stable identity constructs." In the case of Rabinowich's Diana, such a mapping fails because of the lack of the necessary material preconditions for such an endeavor. Whereas in pop-feminism, a phenomenon driven by white, middle-class Western writers, the protagonists are reduced to focusing on the body as a last refuge from neoliberal structures, they at least can seek such refugee.[31] Members of the class of denizens and illegal sex workers that Diana belongs to, however, are deprived even of that last resource, their bodies having become fully co-opted as a commodity. In a last effort to resist the golem leading her astray, Diana creates herself what she calls her little "Adam" in the final pages of the book. She forms this little clay figure from the soil into which she empties her menstrual fluids and the blood she squeezes from a self-inflicted wound in her breast. Diana, whose mental illness seems to have taken over by that point, proudly and joyfully insists that this is *her* Adam, the fruit of what she views as an act of boundless generosity (*Erdfresserin*, 227–28). However, the fact that the figure does not come alive and therefore cannot accompany her on her journey, as she had intended, shows that this act of creation is not a moment of female empowerment. Rather, it highlights Diana's acute state of disenfranchisement, in which all that she has left to give is her infertile menstrual blood.

The only thing Diana does own, therefore, is the reality of her displacement as an "Einzelwanderer" (*Erdfresserin*, 216; lonely traveler). In her study of golem legends, Cathy Gelbin points out that despite its "heterogeneous cultural origins, [the golem] has become a signifier of globalized Jewish cultural identity."[32] Yet, as above-mentioned, "Einzelwanderer" like Diana are not part of any ethnic or religious diaspora, epitomized by global Judaism. Nor is the novel's protagonist part of any kind of the transnational diasporas and communities enabled by modern technological advances in communication. Without economic means, cell phones and the Internet are out of reach for both Diana and her family in Dagestan.[33] From Diana's point of view, in Western cities one therefore has to wait "lange, lange . . . auf den Golem" (115; for a long, long time for the golem). While a superman-like golem defends and protects the Jews of the Prague Ghetto[34]—and by default, the city's prostitutes who were also located there—against adversaries, any distinct and geographically locatable community as well as easily identifiable enemy are missing in Diana's present-day Western Europe. And without a ghetto or community, there also cannot be a golem.

While much literature and scholarship on migration and transnationalism focuses on questions of culture and identity, Rabinowich's novel echoes critiques of such an emphasis. The novel thereby is in implicit agreement with scholar Nancy Fraser, who argues that a focus on matters of culture, ethnicity, and identity often deflects from economic issues by focusing on recognition rather than redistribution.[35] *Die Erdfresserin* illustrates the negative effects of a lack of economic redistribution. Foregrounding her main character's justified anxiety about meeting basic material and bodily needs, Rabinowich draws attention to the problematic fact that one's participation in cultural transnationalism and related issues, such as questions of identity and recognition, is premised on one's economic status in the current era of neoliberal capitalism. In fact, the novel here also echoes Fraser's comprehensive critique of second-wave feminism, which resonates with the above-mentioned critique of transnational feminism by Chandra Mohanty. Fraser argues that on account of its focus on identity politics and struggles for recognition, second-wave feminism came to sideline critiques of the political economy and matters of redistribution at a critical historical moment when a "turn to recognition dovetailed all too neatly with a rising neoliberalism that wanted nothing more than to repress all memory of social egalitarianism."[36]

Moreover, Fraser adds that second-wave feminism and its role in encouraging women to enter the labor market across the globe has "unwittingly provided a key ingredient of the new spirit of neoliberalism."[37] In its support for the two-earner family model, second-wave feminism failed to recognize that the need for two incomes arises, in the first place, from the adverse effects of neoliberal capitalism, such as lower wages and increasing job insecurity. Second-wave feminism thereby has unintentionally become complicit in the project of neoliberal capitalism when it left behind its focus on a "fully three-dimensional account of injustice" that encompasses redistribution, recognition, and representation.[38] It effectively severed the connection between feminist critique and a critique of capitalism. Reminiscent of Diana's golem, this truncated "'feminism' has gone rogue," representing a "strange shadowy version of itself, an uncanny double."[39] Whereas Fraser is hopeful that feminism can recuperate its emancipatory agenda in face of the current crisis of neoliberal capitalism, Rabinowich's novel ends on a bleaker note by gesturing toward a crisis in imagination. In his analysis of the various versions of the Prague golem legend, Alfred Thomas argues:

> The theme of the double made prominent by Freud and Otto Rank coincided with the emergence of the modernist treatment of the golem. Both the doppelganger motif and its manifestation in the golem legend were the result of a philosophical and religious crisis brought about by the Enlightenment. . . . What characterized this moment in central Europe was the post-Enlightenment crisis of liberal thought.[40]

In light of an extended scene in which Diana watches the 2011 funeral procession of Otto von Habsburg in the streets of Vienna, the prominence of psychoanalysis, and the just outlined economic focus of the novel, it stands to reason to suggest that the golem figure in this text points to yet another moment of crisis, this time the one brought about by neoliberal global capitalism in a Europe of austerity. In addition, the golem's failure, the novel's hopeless ending with Diana's death and the lack of a hope for the future embodied by her terminally ill son suggest that there also is a marked lack of an alternative, positive vision of the future. There is not yet any imaginative creation, no golem, to save its people by pointing to the future. As Ulrich Beck points out in a recent EUROPP interview,[41] this lack of a creative response is what distinguishes what he calls "first modernity" from the present moment:

> First modernity, which lasted from around the 18th century until perhaps the 1960s or 1970s, was a period where there was a great

deal of space for experimentation and we had a lot of answers for the uncertainties that we produced: probability models, insurance mechanisms, and so on. But then because of the success of modernity we are now producing consequences for which we don't have any answers, such as climate change and the financial crisis.[42]

While Dr. Petersen stresses the past and Diana the present, the future is not imaginable in this novel on account of a system that imprisons Diana in the present, denying her the luxury to think about the future.

In its lack of vision for the future, Rabinowich's novel echoes current anxieties of what is supposed to come after or replace globalization in its current neoliberal guise. In *After Globalization*, Cazdyn and Szeman argue that globalization as a project to render neoliberalism invisible, has ended due to the 2008 financial crises, which has drawn renewed and due attention to issues like capitalism and class. Yet, alternative visions for what comes after have yet to be formalized, a process impeded by the fact that, by its very nature, "globalization involves a certain configuration of time—one that cannot imagine an 'after.' Modernity could have a post-modernity to follow it. But globalization? Post-globalization sounds like some dystopian coda to everything, not a new phase of human existence."[43] As Fraser points out, the response to the financial crises of 2008 consequently has been one of individuals or small groups, a bunch of Rabinowich's "Einzelwanderer," rather than a movement.[44] In view of the lack of any "broader, transnational alternatives," one is left to wonder with Fraser why "'society' [does] not organize politically to protect itself from 'economy'."[45]

Indeed, in light of most nations' collaboration with neoliberalism and as is hinted at by the character of Leo, even citizens of Western nation-states can no longer necessarily rely on receiving such protection from their own nation-states. Rather, the nation-state today has become complicit in global capitalism. As Cazdyn and Szeman argue, the territorial divisions maintained by the nation-state are in fact necessary for the latter's continued existence. Without our current political divisions, global capital would have no "differential zones of labor, no spaces to realize profit through the dumping of overproduction, [and] no way to patrol surly populations who might want to resist capitalism," and therefore, "we don't need the nation —capital does."[46] Until there is an alternative to neoliberal nation-states, then, migrants like Rabinowich's Diana are in danger of being lost in transit. Unable to participate in and benefit from the positive and creative sociocultural aspects a transnational life could afford, they face the consequences of neoliberalism capitalism, the only alternatives to which, the novel pessimistically seems to suggest, presently are only found in insanity or death.

Notes

[1] While Rabinowich does not explicitly refer to Achim von Armin's golem tale, the novel echoes von Armin's thematic preoccupations, such as economic and sexual exchanges. However, whereas his heroine Isabella's final journey ends in her being crowned the queen of her people, Julya Rabinowich's character's final journey merely leads her to insanity and her death. Achim von Arnim, *Achim Von Arnim, Isabella von Ägypten und andere Erzählungen (1812)* (Zurich: Manesse Verlag, 1959), 5–12.

[2] Given the very nature of their status, it is of course difficult to assess the number of illegal or undocumented workers, making this number an estimate only. See Hans Riebsamen, "Illegale Arbeiter: Deutschlands Schattenpersonal," *Frankfurter Allgemeine Zeitung*, November 21, 2006, accessed June 14, 2014, http://www.faz.net/aktuell/politik/inland/illegale-arbeiter-deutschlands-schatten personal-1384170.html.

[3] Victor Roudometof, "Transnationalism, Cosmopolitanism, and Globalization" *Current Sociology* 53 (2005): 118.

[4] Roudometof, "Transnationalism," 119.

[5] Randall Halle, *German Film after Germany: Toward a Transnational Aesthetic* (Champaign: University of Illinois Press, 2008), 5.

[6] Sarah Mahler and Patricia Pessar, "Gendered Geographies of Power: Analyzing Gender Across Transnational Spaces," *Identities: Global Studies in Culture and Power* 7, no.4 (2001): 444.

[7] Judith Butler, *Frames of War: When Is Life Grievable?* (New York: Verso, 2010), 25.

[8] Butler, *Frames of War*, 25.

[9] Eric Cazdyn and Imre Szeman, *After Globalization* (West Sussex: Wiley-Blackwell, 2011), 1.

[10] David Harvey, *Seventeen Contradictions and the End of Capitalism* (New York: Oxford University Press, 2014), x.

[11] David Harvey, "Neoliberalism as Creative Destruction," *Annals of the American Academy of Political and Social Science* 610 (March 2007): 22–23.

[12] Harvey, "Neoliberalism as Creative Destruction," 22–23.

[13] Victor Roudometof, "Transnationalism," 119.

[14] Johannes Voelz, "Utopias of Transnationalism and the Neoliberal State," in *Reframing the Transnational Turn in American Studies* (Hampshire: Dartmouth College Press, 2011), 356.

[15] See Julya Rabinowich's website, accessed July 29, 2013, http://www.julya-rabinowich.com/leben.html,.

[16] Julya Rabinowich, *Die Erdfresserin* (Vienna: Deuticke, 2012).

[17] Diana's death, while not narrated due to the novel's first-person narrative, is indicated by the similarities and differences between the novel's opening and final pages. For instance, Diana does not allow herself to look back on her path at the beginning of the novel, arguing that one is only allowed to do so when one has

arrived at the place from which there is no return (*Erdfresserin*, 9). At the end, she states that she is now allowed to look back, suggesting that she has arrived at the place of no return, going deeper and deeper into some figurative "Erdreich" or underground (235). There, she literally disappears from the text, with the subject "I" being omitted from the final two sentences: "Ich gehe. Ich gehe. Gehe. Gehe" (236; I am. I am going. Go. Go). The impression that the narrator dies in the end is confirmed by Rabinowich herself in an interview with Michael Granner. See Michael Granner, "Interview: Julya Rabinowich: *Die Erdfresserin*," *Vienna Rama*, accessed September 30, 2012, http://viennarama.at/2012/09/30/ interview-julya-rabinowich-die-erdfresserin/#more-7446.

[18] Cazdyn and Szeman, *After Globalization*, 59.

[19] As a 2009 study of immigrant sex workers in Europe shows, for both new and non-Europeans, "Western Europe still offers the best working and earning potential" despite increasingly restrictive immigrant legislation. Lucia Brussa, *Sex Work in Europe: A Mapping of the Prostitution Scene in 25 Countries* (Amsterdam: TAMPEP, 2009), 17.

[20] Emphasis in original. Karl Marx, "Private Property and Communism," in *Karl Marx: Selected Writings*, ed. Lawrence H. Simon (Indianapolis: Hackett Publishing, 1994), 68–78, 72.

[21] Marx's dictum has been widely criticized and discussed. For an overview of the debate surrounding the relationship between prostitution and capitalism, see Marjolein Van Der Veen, "Rethinking Commodification and Prostitution: An Effort at Peacemaking in the Battles over Prostitution," *Rethinking Marxism* 13, no. 2 (2001): 30–51.

[22] Brussa, *Sex Work in Europe*, 18.

[23] In her discussion of the treatment of unemployment in contemporary German literature, Anke Biendarra discusses literary works such as Jakob Hein's *Herr Jensen steigt aus* (Herr Jensen Drops Out, 2006) or Annete Pehnt's *Mobbing* (2007), which thematize the psychological effects of unemployment. As Biendarra shows, these literary connections between precarious work situations and psychiatric illness are based on real-life medical studies that evidence "a clear correlation between rising unemployment and mental problems . . . as well as between levels of unemployment and higher psychotic morbidity." Anke Biendarra, *Germans Going Global: Contemporary Literature and Cultural Globalization* (Boston: De Gruyter, 2012), 131.

[24] Olga Grjasnowa, *Der Russe ist einer, der Birken liebt* (Munich: Hanser, 2014), 158. Olga Grjasnowa, *All Russians Love Birch Trees*, trans. Eva Bacon (New York: Other Press, 2014).

[25] As an interviewer in the Austrian newspaper *Kurier* points out, "Es geht ums Überleben. Da frisst man schon manchmal Erde, um nicht ins Gras zu beißen." (It's about survival. One sometimes eats dirt in order not to bite the dust). Interview: Julya Rabinowich über *Die Erdfresserin*," August 4, 2012, accessed June 14, 2014, http://kurier.at/kultur/literatur/julya-rabinowich-ueber-die -erdfresserin/806.937.

[26] Chandra Mohanty, "Transnational Feminist Crossings: On Neoliberalism and Radical Critique," *Signs* 38, no.4 (2013): 967, 971.

[27] The INDOORS project was organized by members from Austria, Bulgaria, France, Finland, Germany, Italy, the Netherlands, Portugal, and Spain and took place from January 2011 to December 2012. Its goal was to assess the situation of female sex workers in Amsterdam, Genoa, Hamburg, Helsinki, Madrid, Marseille, Porto, Sofia, and Vienna and was financed by the European Union. Veronica Munk, *Pictures of a Reality: Sex Workers Talk about Their Life and Work Experiences within the Indoor Sex Work Setting in Nine European Cities* (Marseille: Autres Regards, 2012), accessed June 14, 2014, http://www.indoors-project.eu /documents/Pictures _of_a_reality-Indoors_2.pdf.

[28] Terri Tomsky, "From Sarajevo to 9/11: Travelling Memory and the Trauma Economy," *Current Sociology* 17, no.4 (2011): 50.

[29] Brussa, *Sex Work in Europe*, 14.

[30] The multiple functions of the golem figure in the text are complex, and exploring all the intertextual allusions and thematic connections hinted at by the novel are outside of the scope of this paper.

[31] See also Hester Baer, "German Feminism in the Age of Neoliberalism: Jana Hensel and Elisabeth Raether's *Neue deutsche Mädchen*," *German Studies Review* 35 (2012): 371–72.

[32] Cathy Gelbin, *The Golem Returns: From German Romantic Literature to Global Jewish Culture, 1808–2008* (Ann Arbor: University of Michigan Press, 2011), 2.

[33] After Leo's death, Diana has to rely on a prepaid phone card handed to her by Dr. Petersen, who attempts to assuage his bad conscience when he is unable to help Diana obtain legal status. She also steals a cell phone once but can only make one phone call before having to destroy it, apparently due to fear of the phone being traced.

[34] That is according to Yudl Rosenberg's popular 1909 adaptation of the legend. See Alfred Thomas, *Prague Palimpsest: Writing, Memory, and the City* (Chicago: University of Chicago Press, 2010), 51–52.

[35] See Nancy Fraser and Axel Honneth, *Redistribution or Recognition? A Political-Philosophical Exchange* (New York: Verso, 2003).

[36] Nancy Fraser, "Feminism, Capitalism, and the Cunning of History," in *Re-Framing the Transnational Turn in American Studies*, ed. Winfried Fluck, Donald E. Pease, and John Carlos Row (Hampshire: Dartmouth College Press, 2011): 383.

[37] Fraser, "Feminism, Capitalism," 384.

[38] Fraser, "Feminism, Capitalism," 388.

[39] Fraser, "Feminism, Capitalism," 387.

[40] Thomas, *Prague Palimpsest*, 55.

[41] "EUROPP: European Politics and Policy" is an established multidisciplinary academic blog run by the London School of Economics and Political Science. The blog provides accessible academic research with the goal of furthering the public's understanding of European politics.

[42] Beck, "Five Minutes with Ulrich Beck: 'Germany Has Created an Accidental Empire'," *EUROPP*, March 25, 2013. Accessed June 14, 2014, http://blogs.lse.

ac.uk/europpblog/2013/03/25/five-minutes-with-ulrich-beck-germany-has-created-an-accidental-empire/.

[43] Cazdyn and Szeman, *After Globalization*, 2.

[44] As Fraser put it, "Popular opposition fails to coalesce around a solidaristic alternative, despite intense but ephemeral outbursts, such as Occupy and the *indignados*, whose protests generally lack programmatic content." Nancy Fraser, "Triple Movement? Parsing the Politics of Crisis after Polyani," *New Left Review* 81 (2013): 121.

[45] Fraser, "Triple Movement," 127.

[46] Cazdyn and Szeman, *After Globalization*, 49.

8: Precarious Sexualities, Neoliberalism, and the Pop-Feminist Novel: Charlotte Roche's *Feuchtgebiete* and Helene Hegemann's *Axolotl Roadkill* as Transnational Texts

Hester Baer

THE TRANSNATIONAL TURN IN LITERARY STUDIES has drawn attention to literature's increasing engagement with economic and cultural globalization, as well as to the breakdown of national paradigms for understanding literature.[1] Transnationalism has become a pervasive term in recent scholarship, but its analytical valence is often hard to pin down, especially when compared to similar or related concepts, including globalization and neoliberalism. Scholars have often relied on a distinction between transnationalism as a signifier of spatial mobility and cultural interconnectedness, and globalization as an economic process concerned with the operations of capital (and thereby connected to the ideologies of neoliberalism).[2] Whether invoked in the context of cultural or economic relations, transnationalism predates the rise of neoliberalism in the second half of the twentieth century. Nonetheless, as David Harvey notes, "there has undoubtedly been a deepening as well as a widening of these transnational connections during the phase of neoliberal globalization, and it is vital that these connectivities be acknowledged."[3] Harvey emphasizes the connections of the transnational ruling class and the global elites who have deliberately enacted neoliberal policies; transnational connectivities have also developed in response to the increasingly predominant structures of insecurity arising from neoliberalization, seen for example in the emergence of the precariat.[4]

Critics of neoliberalism have pointed to the fact that it is increasingly hegemonic and yet rarely named, so that its concepts have come to seem like common sense or second nature.[5] This imperceptibility of neoliberalism, together with the impossibility of imagining the scale of transnational networks or grasping the abstraction of the global financial system, creates a context in which the contemporary world often appears incomprehensible or unrepresentable.[6] Such indecipherability is crucial to the ideology of neoliberalism, which operates via an illusion of political neutrality.

The notion of precarity has emerged as one way of making intelligible a central paradox of neoliberalism: it creates a situation of permanent insecurity that disproportionately affects minority groups, but at the same time its emphasis on individualism, flexibilization, and mobility offers unprecedented opportunities for destabilizing normative roles and eroding traditional social formations in ways that appear empowering, not least to women and gender and sexual minorities.[7] Theorists of precarity therefore emphasize both the endemic insecurity of the contemporary world and the way this instability gives rise to potential for change. As Rosalind Gill and Andy Pratt describe precarity, it "signifies both the multiplication of precarious, unstable, insecure forms of living and, simultaneously, new forms of political struggle and solidarity. . . . This *double meaning* is central to understanding the ideas and politics associated with precarity: the new moment of capitalism that engenders precarity is seen as not only oppressive but also as offering the potential for new subjectivities, new socialities, and new kinds of politics."[8] That is, precarity as a paradigm seeks to subvert the dynamics of neoliberal ideology by unmasking its apparent neutrality, mining its potential for opening up new social formations, and foregrounding its paradoxes. In this context, literature provides a crucial space for making visible the dynamics of precarity, including both its oppressive quality—insecurity as the key structure of experience today—and the potential it offers for envisioning something new.[9]

In this essay, I examine the way two of the most widely circulated and discussed texts of recent German-language literature make visible aspects of the contemporary world through their deployment of precarity, in particular precarious sexualities. The popfeminist novels *Feuchtgebiete* (Wetlands, 2008) by Charlotte Roche and *Axolotl Roadkill* (2010) by Helene Hegemann investigate key facets of life in neoliberal capitalism, including sexual deregulation, privatization, and new configurations of the family. By emphasizing precarity, they also open up spaces for thinking about statuses, such as gender, sexuality, class, race, and ethnicity, that no longer form the basis for an oppositional politics today, and yet continue to inform the subjective lives of individuals and their ability to survive or thrive in the present.

Because of how they envision the contemporary world and engage with the frameworks of neoliberalism and precarity—an engagement that drove and is also reflected by the worldwide circulation and reception of both novels—I contend that *Feuchtgebiete* and *Axolotl Roadkill* should be viewed as aesthetically sophisticated and politically meaningful works of contemporary transnational literature. Transnationalism has been taken up by scholars of German-language literature to analyze works by migrant and minority authors, or to investigate texts that engage with Germany's (post)colonial history or with travel. My focus on neoliberalism and precarity suggests another line of inquiry for thinking about how works of German literature "interact creatively with contemporary processes of cultural interpenetration."[10] If Charlotte Roche and Helene Hegemann can both be considered what Stuart Taberner has referred to as "nonminority German writers," then both their authorship and their texts raise some questions about nonminority status and its relation to transnational cultural production.[11] Specifically, women and sexual minorities pose a challenge both to an authorial status ("nonminority") that is conceptualized primarily in racial and ethnic terms and, in a larger sense, to static identity categories in general. In this way, texts like *Feuchtgebiete* and *Axolotl Roadkill* expand our conception of German transnational literature and how and why it travels.

In *Minor Transnationalism* (2005), Françoise Lionnet and Shu-mei Shih make the case for "an awareness and recognition of the creative interventions that networks of minoritized cultures produce within and across national boundaries" including networks of transnational migrants, diasporic populations, or, I would add, transnational feminist and queer connectivities.[12] Lionnet and Shih problematize the binary logic that has driven many theories of transnationalism, including the transnationalism/globalization binary and the binary of "transnationalism from above" (hegemonic operations of finance capital and global media) and "transnationalism from below" (counterhegemonic sites of resistance by the nonelite).[13] Instead, they argue that "transnationalism is part and parcel of the process of globalization, but also that the transnational can be less scripted and more scattered."[14]

Emphasizing transnationalism's productive potential to make visible aspects of the present, Laura Briggs, Gladys McCormick, and J. T. Way draw on an analogy with feminist theories of gender to propose a specific conceptual genealogy of the term: "We want to suggest that 'transnationalism' can do to the nation what gender did for sexed bodies: provide the conceptual acid that denaturalizes all their deployments, compelling us to acknowledge that the nation, like sex, is a thing contested, interrupted, and always shot through with contradiction."[15] As an analytical category that problematizes "the natural frame of the nation," transnationalism has a long, cross disciplinary scholarly history (in area studies, postcolonial theory, and cultural studies, among others),[16] but Briggs, McCormick, and Way specifically emphasize the contributions of transnational feminist and queer theory and critiques of neoliberalism in denaturalizing more recent constellations of nation to "diagnose the neoliberal moment."[17]

As these approaches suggest, transnationalization and neoliberalization can be viewed as mutually constitutive processes that contribute to the precarity of contemporary life. As Maria Mayr notes in this volume, "Many aspects of transnational existence are threatened by the capitalist system, the powerful existence of which has arguably become more real to many since [the financial crisis of] 2008."[18] Similarly, Katharina Gerstenberger proposes here the term "realist transnationalism" to characterize texts that describe contemporary states of mind and aim to convey the disorientation of the present, thereby participating in the project of diagnosing the neoliberal moment.[19] Considering the imbrication of transnationalism and neoliberalism, this essay examines how depictions of nonnormative and thus precarious sexualities in *Feuchtgebiete* and *Axolotl Roadkill* make visible aspects of the imperceptible present.

Feuchtgebiete and *Axolotl Roadkill* as Transnational Texts

Chronicling the hospital stay of teenage protagonist Helen Memel to repair an anal fissure, self-inflicted while shaving, *Feuchtgebiete* captured worldwide attention for its depiction of female sexuality and its critique of compulsory beauty and hygiene culture. Even before it was translated into twenty-seven languages and became a worldwide bestseller, Roche's novel was the first (and so far only) German-language work to top Amazon.com's global bestseller list, becoming, in the words of *The Economist*, "the world's biggest-selling novel" in the original German.[20] *Feuchtgebiete* has sold a whopping 1.3 million copies domestically, and in August 2013, it was released as a major motion picture, debuting at the Locarno Film Festival. *Axolotl Roadkill* also skyrocketed to the top of the bestseller list in Germany, where it was shortlisted for the prestigious Leipzig Book Prize. Narrating the story of Mifti, a teenage dropout, Hegemann's novel presents a kaleidoscopic pastiche of Mifti's experiences in the Berlin drug and club scene. Like *Feuchtgebiete*, *Axolotl Roadkill* captured attention for its transgressive depiction of female sexuality, though its initially positive reception was eclipsed by the revelation that its 17-year old author had lifted some passages of her novel from other original sources, including a little-known text by a Berlin blogger named Airen. Fueled by this plagiarism scandal, *Axolotl Roadkill* has been translated into at least sixteen languages and has sold approximately half a million copies domestically.

Feuchtgebiete and *Axolotl Roadkill* can be understood as key works of German transnational literature: along multiple vectors, these are traveling texts. Both novels engage global pop style in their formal language, frames of reference, idiomatic expression, and stories.[21] Both novels participate in the transnational project of rethinking feminism in an age of global connection, when media culture exerts a pervasive influence on gender roles, beauty standards, and conceptions of sexuality.[22] At the level of form and content, both novels also venture into world literature, resignifying literary tropes and employing intertextuality and montage in their self-reflexive literary practice. Mobility—of subjectivity, identity, and status—is a central theme of both novels, especially Hegemann's. Finally, *Feuchtgebiete* and *Axolotl Roadkill* have also been widely translated, achieving widespread international recognition and commercial success, and their transnational dissemination has taken place through a number of channels, including both traditional and new forms of media.

Though perhaps not in ways conventionally associated with German transnational literature, these works "have traversed and translated foreign cultures while probing fixed notions of 'Germanness,'"[23] simultaneously denaturalizing conventional conceptions of both nation and sex. Significant here is the fact that both novels arise from and participate in the recent movement of pop-feminism, which resignifies global feminisms under the sign of performativity and with recourse to the subversive, antihierarchical, and antiorderly strategies of pop.[24] As Carrie Smith-Prei has observed, "Popfeminism utilizes the symbols of global pop culture in order to create a critical, local, and individual subculture, a new public and visible space of resistance defined, not constrained by gender."[25] Because of their pop-feminist alignment with discourses of self-stylization and empowerment that are "individual, personal, self-fulfilling, and based in everyday experiences," *Feuchtgebiete* and *Axolotl Roadkill* have been targeted by feminist critics as lacking an explicitly feminist-political message, especially in comparison to second-wave feminism.[26] For example, Christa Binswanger and Kathy Davis view *Feuchtgebiete* to be "unsuited as a critical feminist perspective on sexual empowerment," while Christina Scharff sees pop-feminist texts as devoid of the critical and empancipatory potential of feminist and queer politics.[27] While these readings are well taken—especially for their examination of white privilege in popfeminist texts—a primary focus on feminist history and generational conflict has meant that critics sometimes overlook the very salient frameworks of transnationalism and neoliberalism in understanding these texts.[28]

Both *Feuchtgebiete* and *Axolotl Roadkill* share in common the fact that their status as transnational media events relied strongly on a conflation of the novels' chief protagonists with their authors. Both works were read as largely autobiographical (despite some evidence to the contrary) and both authors drew on this perception when engaging widely with various media, creating playful and self-confident performances that influenced the reception of their books. As Maria Stehle has pointed out, these media performances follow a tradition of feminist art whereby female authors take risks, employing their bodies in performative ways to "force change" in the public sphere. However in the case of young popfeminists, as Stehle shows, this strategy is double-edged, for "in the process of mainstream media reception the female body is fragmented, disciplined, and controlled."[29] Thus, Roche's and Hegemann's authorial presence in the transnational dissemination and reception of their works emerges as emblematic of their precarity, exposing the ongoing insecurity of female authorship and the subjugation of the female body in neoliberalism while simultaneously signalling a new form of pop-feminist political engagement. Echoing key themes of their texts, Roche's and Hegemann's performative authorship makes visible the sense in which gender and sexuality continue to affect individual lives, including subjective and bodily experience, as well as cultural production and reception, although these statuses no longer form the basis for feminist politics, not least due to their inherent instability as identity categories.

Crucial in this regard is the novels' representation of sex and sexuality, which has been key for the transnational literary production, translation, marketing, and reception of many German-language works of literature and cinema, both historically and at present. In the case of *Feuchtgebiete* and *Axolotl Roadkill*, the specific engagement with precarious sexualities—including queer, S-M, and nonmonogamous scenes and practices—proves salient for understanding how and why these works travel.[30] The term "precarious sexualities" was coined by Volker Woltersdorff to describe the erosion (but not disappearance) of gender and sexual norms in neoliberalism. As Woltersdorff argues, neoliberalism is characterized by a paradoxical ambivalence between destabilizing and strengthening heteronormativity: "It is merely the site of femininity and masculinity that has become increasingly precarious, for the neo-liberal flexibilization of gender and sexual identities allows traditional and flexible gender roles to coexist."[31] Woltersdorff suggests that the neoliberal discourse of mobility and deregulation appears to open up spaces for nonnormative gender identifications, sexual practices, and affective ties, but the institutional sex-gender system is still an imperative, creating a situation of permanent insecurity. To put it another way, "Sexuality is therefore simultaneously an agent and a resource of precarity."[32]

Both Roche and Hegemann emphasize precarious sexualities through their representation of sex, gender roles, and body politics, including thematization of female sexual fantasies and lived sexual experiences; exploration of mother-daughter relationships; and in general a critical framework regarding the possibilities of emancipation from the explicit misogyny and heteronormativity of life in late capitalism, especially as practiced through the family unit. Precarious sexualities are crucial to the novels' representation and critique of "new femininities" and to their intervention into pop-feminism.[33] Angela McRobbie has pointed out that in neoliberal societies self-management and good planning emerge as social norms of contemporary femininity, and that "conversely the absence of such styles of self-organization becomes an indicator of pathology, a signal of failure, or a symptom of some other personal difficulties."[34] By foregrounding precarious sexualities, Roche and Hegemann make visible this paradoxical dimension of contemporary femininity, whereby the prevailing neoliberal discourses of choice and empowerment mean that the absence of a well-planned life emerges as a sign of personal failure, even pathology (regardless of whether this "poor planning" was caused by underlying structural factors such as economic disparity, racism, or misogyny, or by illness, chance, etc.).

Moreover, precarious sexualities in these novels constitute a primary vector for generating affect. As affect theorists have argued, individuals perceive the present largely via affective responses; affect becomes a way of tracking adjustments to transformations in society, politics, and the economy that can augment or diminish "a body's capacity to act, to engage, and to connect."[35] In the case of *Feuchtgebiete* and *Axolotl Roadkill*, critics and readers have emphasized the way both novels generate feelings of discomfort and even disgust, elements that certainly played a role in both texts' widespread translation and media dissemination.[36] By the same token, their ability to generate affect speaks to the ways in which they make palpable for readers otherwise imperceptible aspects of the neoliberal everyday.

Feuchtgebiete

Roche's *Feuchtgebiete* chronicles the diverse sexual practices of protagonist Helen Memel, who trains her vaginal muscles by masturbating with avocado pits, takes pleasure in eating bodily excretions (both her own and others'), crafts open-crotched DIY underwear to attract male lovers, and regularly patronizes female prostitutes. Helen's narration begins with a description of her devotion to anal sex, for which she engages in elaborate rituals of preparation, including shaving her anus and performing an enema by inserting a shower head in her rectum. "Solange ich denken kann, habe ich Hämerrhoiden" (As far back as I can remember, I've had hemorrhoids),[37] asserts Helen in the opening sentence of the novel, and it is while shaving around a large, cauliflower-shaped external hemorrhoid that she inflicts the wound that lands her in the proctological division of the hospital: "Weil ich mich innerlich sehr gegen das Rasieren wehre, mache ich das immer viel zu schnell und zu dolle. Genau dabei habe ich mir diese Analfissur zugefügt, wegen der ich jetzt im Krankenhaus liege. Alles das Ladyshaven schuld. Feel like Venus. Be a goddess!" (*F*, 10; Since I'm always conflicted about the idea of shaving, I always rush it and end up pressing too hard. Which is exactly how I caused the anal lesion that's the reason I'm lying here in the hospital now. Blame it all on lady-shaving. Feel like Venus. Be a goddess. [3]) Here, the Venus razor plays a double-edged function, as it were, that is emblematic of the text's deployment of precarity: the citation of Gillette's ubiquitous global marketing slogan humorously and ironically makes visible the power of the beauty industry in the production of contemporary femininities, but Helen's razor-inflicted injury simultaneously highlights that industry's damaging corporeal effects. Roche's opening passage references the marked shift in attitudes toward female body hair in Germany over the past two decades, a topic that has been taken up by pop-feminists as an index of the transnationalization of hegemonic femininity.[38]

Throughout *Feuchtgebiete*, Helen takes delight in challenging the compulsory beauty and normative hygiene that are key components of this hegemonic femininity: "Ich benutze mein Smegma wie andere ihre Parfümflakons" (*F*, 19; I use my smegma the way others use their vials of perfume, 14), she explains. Helen does not wash her genitals, revels in strong smells, rubs her bodily fluids around in public spaces, and derives pleasure from spreading bacteria in novel ways. An exhibitionist, she also enjoys both exposing her body and revealing her sexual fantasies to strangers.

Helen drinks her best friend's vomit (*F*, 59; 63), fantasizes about squeezing out and eating the pus from a visible pimple in her male nurse Robin's ear (131; 133–34), and engages in incestuous fantasies about sex with her father (164–65; 168). She also describes gynosocial practices, such as exchanging used tampons with her best friend in the bathroom at school: "Und als wir fertig waren mit Pinkeln und Abtupfen, hatte jede den Tampon der anderen reingestopft. So waren wir durch unser altes, stinkendes Blut verbunden wie Old Shatterhand mit Winnetou. Blutschwesternschaft" (*F*, 114; And then, when we were finished with peeing and dabbing ourselves dry, we each shoved in the other's tampon. Through our old, stinky blood, we were bound together like Old Shatterhand and Winnetou. Blood sisters. [114]) Helen's graphic descriptions engage the reader with pop citations (such as the reference to Karl May) and idiomatic language, but they are also calculated to elicit disgust, thereby calling attention to "the disappearance of the old idea of perversion in a deregulated sexual market," one of the key paradigms Woltersdorff identifies as characteristic of neoliberal sexuality.[39] Not coincidentally, this strategy also proves to be integral to the transnational appeal of *Feuchtgebiete*.[40]

As Woltersdorff suggests, just as neoliberalism resolves conflicts within Fordist capitalism by absorbing critical social and political forces, within the realm of sexuality it has largely co-opted emancipatory demands of the feminist, gay liberation, and free love movements; "sexual deregulation" describes both the empowerment to pursue individual sexual desires and a concomitant increase in insecurity, resulting from economic changes as well as the decline of social and family networks. Helen's nonnormative sexual and bodily practices push the boundaries of "the old ideas of perversion," making visible by provoking laughter or disgust the erosion and co-optation of some (but not all) sexual norms in neoliberalism.

Critics have suggested that Helen's sexual framework remains largely heteronormative, because her sexual encounters with women are driven by her quest "zur Erforschung des weiblichen Körpers" (*F*, 114; to explore the female body, 115) rather than by desire: "Nowhere in the book does she express a sexual *desire* for women, other than her 'scientific' interest in their genitals and bodies. . . . Helen's experience of orgasms with women does not mean she identifies as lesbian or bisexual."[41] Indeed, Helen is characterized as omnisexual: a voracious teenager who explores all possible avenues for erotic pleasure, she is more like a cipher for female desire. And while it is certainly true that the novel ends with a "conventionally romantic twist" in which Helen plans to move in with Robin, her nonnormative bodily and sexual practices throughout the novel ultimately eclipse any straightforward subsumption into a heteronormative framework.

Roche has explained in interviews that her primary objective in writing *Feuchtgebiete* was to articulate a language of desire for women: "Viele Frauen können nicht gut über ihr Geschlechtsorgan, ihre Lust und ihre Fantasien beim Sex sprechen. Daher sind viele Szenen ins Absurde gedreht, um zu zeigen, wie viel falsch läuft bei uns, wie wenig Sprache es gibt für diese ganzen weiblichen Sachen."[42] (Many women can't speak well about their sex organs, their desire, and their fantasies during sex. That's why many scenes are twisted to the point of absurdity, in order to show how much has gone wrong with us, how little language there is for all these female issues.) While she originally conceived of writing an essayistic critique focused on the hazards of the beauty industry and the impoverishment of women's sex lives, she ultimately turned to literature because it offered both imaginative possibilities for giving voice to female sexual fantasies and a space for linguistic experimentation. Over and over again, Roche uses words that are rarely named in everyday speech, including *Smegma*, *Schleimhaut* (mucous membrane), *Schamlippen* (vaginal lips), *Klitoris*, *Poloch* (bumhole), and so forth. Moreover, Helen invents her own names for female genitalia, drawing attention to the way that neither scientific words nor idiomatic expressions adequately convey women's relationships to their own bodies:

> Ich kratze zwischen den inneren Schamlippen, von mir Hahnenkämme genannt, und den äußeren Schamlippen, von mir Vanillekipferl genannt, feste hin und her, und irgendwann klappe ich die Hahnenkämme nach rechts und links weg, um genau in der Mitte das Jucken wegzukratzen. . . . Wenn ich kurz vorm Kommen bin, kneife ich mir fest in die Klitoris, von mir Perlenrüssel genannt. Das steigert meine Geilheit ins Unermessliche. Ja, so wird's gemacht. (*F*, 22)

> [I scratch up and down between the inner labia—which I call the dewlaps—and the outer labia—which I call the ladyfingers—and at

some point I fold back the dewlaps to the right and left so I can scratch right down the middle. . . . Right as I'm about to come, I pinch my clit—which I call my snail tail. That makes me come so much harder. Yep, that's how it's done. (16–17)]

By emphasizing Helen's attempt to invent a language for female desire, Roche connects *Feuchtgebiete* to the aesthetic and political tradition of women's literature, as well as to the transnational feminist movement's longstanding concern with sexual empowerment and body politics.

In this regard, Binswanger and Davis compare *Feuchtgebiete* to Verena Stefan's second-wave feminist classic *Häutungen* (Shedding, 1975), arguing that, whereas Stefan's earlier text engages "women's collective experience of becoming sexual subjects" and creates identification and solidarity among readers, Roche's work addresses readers as autonomous individuals and engages a "new femininity organised around self-confidence and autonomy."[43] However, while the kind of collective solidarity that characterized second-wave feminist politics and literature is certainly lacking in the style and address of Roche's novel, Binswanger and Davis overstate the degree of self-confidence and autonomy exhibited by Helen, whose story in fact emphasizes the precarity of the neoliberal everyday in terms of the body, sexuality, and family relations. Roche's pop-feminist resignification of language, grounded in the sexual organs of the female body, suggests the creative potential that inheres in this position of precarity.

To be sure, Helen illustrates the potential empowerment for young women offered by sexual deregulation, which opens up spaces for sexual mobility, nonmonogamy, and reproductive choice. For example, Helen's defiance of conventional gender roles and familial inheritance extends to her decision to undergo elective sterilization surgery as soon as she reached majority age, to guarantee her ability to enjoy all forms of sexual pleasure without the possibility of reproduction, thereby insuring her permanent refusal of motherhood. However, despite her autonomy in sexual and reproductive choices, Helen makes visible how the female body is still constrained by social gender norms, including the hegemonic femininity perpetuated by the beauty industry, and she is also haunted by the precarity of her own family relations. Critics have pointed out that *Feuchtgebiete* is framed by Helen's quest to restore her heteronormative family of origin: "Als Scheidungskind wünsche ich mir wie fast alle Scheidungskinder meine Eltern wieder zusammen" (*F*, 7; I'm also a child of divorce, and like all children of divorce I want to see my parents back together, n.p.). In the course of the narrative, Helen seeks unsuccessfully to stage a reunion of her mother and father in her hospital room; when this does not happen, she goes so far as to intentionally tear open her surgical wound in a gruesome scene of self-harm, hoping to prolong her hospital stay and eventually bring her parents together. Helen's simultaneous refusal of motherhood and quest for a heteronormative family unit has been viewed by critics as paradoxical, but it makes visible the disintegration of traditional social structures in neoliberalism as well as the precarity of contemporary family relations and lacking provisions for caregiving.

As Woltersdorff writes, "Not having children, or the privilege of being able to outsource support and caretaking, are not necessary conditions, but they certainly represent enormous advantages for non-monogamous lifestyles."[44] For in neoliberalism, the state increasingly promotes nonmonogamy as a way of delegating to new kinds of alliances support and caretaking formerly provided by social welfare. While this brings the advantages of sexual mobility and choice as well as the possibility of new social formations and domestic partnerships, "social lack of solidarity proves to be a historical condition for the recognition and normalization of non-marital lifestyles and moves within the neo-liberal constellation of gains in industrialization and risk growth."[45]

Throughout the narrative, Helen references a traumatic episode from her childhood, when she came home to discover a suicide attempt by her mother, who sought to gas herself and her young son, Helen's brother. Repressed and never discussed within the family, this episode is at first mentioned by Helen as something "von der ich mir nicht sicher bin, ob sie eine Erinnerung ist" (F, 63; that I've never been sure is even a memory, 60), but in the course of the novel it is increasingly desublimated. Helen first articulates the story to herself in detail and then later verbalizes it to her brother when he visits her in the hospital, telling him a story he has never heard spoken before.

Toward the very end of the novel, Helen reenacts her mother's traumatic suicide attempt by creating a kind of installation art piece out of her mother's clothing and her own hair before she leaves her hospital room: "Büschelweise rupfe ich [Haare] aus der Kopfhaut raus und lege sie auf das Kissen, bis ich finde, dass man sie gut genug erkennen kann. . . . Jetzt wird klar, dass dort eine Frau und ein Junge liegen. . . . Ich gehe ein paar Schritte zurück und begutachte, was meine Verwandtschaft gleich vorfinden wird. Mein Abschiedsbrief. Der Grund, warum ich sie verlasse. Das Schweigen." (F, 219; I yank hair out of my scalp in bunches and lay it on the pillow until I think you can make it out well enough. . . . Now it's obvious that a woman and a boy are lying there. . . . I step back and take a good look at what my relatives are about to discover. My good-bye letter. The reason I'm leaving. Silence. [228]) Helen's representation of her childhood trauma marks her escape from the circuit of abuse and self-harm perpetrated by her family. Reminiscent of feminist performances by artists like Valie Export, Carolee Schneemann, and Yoko Ono, it also constitutes a pop-feminist resignification of the traces of hegemonic femininity that Roche has played with throughout the text, this time in a darker vein.

As Gill and Scharff write of neoliberalism, "Secure and stable self-identity no longer derives automatically from one's position in the social structure, and in its place some argue that we are seeing attempts to ground identity in the body, as individuals are left alone to establish and maintain values with which to live and make sense of their daily lives."[46] Helen's choice to undergo elective sterilization can be understood in the double-edged context of this precarity: by making reproduction impossible for herself, she puts an end to the traumatic family past that haunts her while also underscoring her investment in nonmonogamous and nonreproductive sexuality.

Axolotl Roadkill

In *Axolotl Roadkill*, Hegemann's sixteen-year-old protagonist Mifti inhabits a range of precarious subjectivities and sexualities, all chronicled in her diary, which comprises the text of the novel. From the first page on, the diary proclaims (in corporeal metaphors) Mifti's ambivalent aspirations for it as literature: "O.k., die Nacht, wieder mal so ein Ringen mit dem Tod, die Fetzen angstgequälten Schlafes, mein von schicksalsmächtigen Orchestern erbebendes Kinderzimmer. . . . Früher war das alles so schön pubertär hingerotzt und jetzt ist es angestrengte Literatur." (OK, so it's night, and once again that grapple with death, the snatches of fearful sleep, my bedroom shaking with daemonic orchestras. . . . In the old days it all got spewed up in finest adolescent style and now it's seriously intense literature).[47] Mifti introduces herself by describing her inability to masturbate to hardcore porn, or to look at her fingernails and then in the mirror; her exczema and broken eyelashes; and the way she dries off after a shower by pulling from the dirty laundry a sheet, "das die letzten beiden Monate gemeinsam mit zwei vollgekotzten Kleidungsstücken in einem großen Behälter verbracht hat" (*A*, 12; [that] spent the last two months in a large basket in the company of two puke-encrusted items of clothing, 4). Like *Feuchtgebiete*, *Axolotl Roadkill* makes visible the extent to which, in the absence of stable identity constructs, individuals increasingly focus on bodily experience in order to map subjectivity or make sense of everyday life. The novel's detailed descriptions of bodily functions—eliciting recognition, discomfort, and disgust on the part of the reader—are crucial to its literary success in this regard.

Both the radical subjectivity and pastiche style of her narration reflect on a formal level the precarity exemplified by Mifti:

1. Ich habe meine von Analsex, Tränen und Leichenschändung geprägte Patchworkgeschichte verloren.
2. Ich habe eine offene Entzündung im Rachen.

3. Meine Familie ist ein Haufen von in irgendeiner früh-
kindlichen Allmachtsphase steckengebliebenen Personen mit
Selbstdarstellungssucht. Im äußersten Fall wird von deren Seite
aus mal ein popkultureller Text über die Frage verfasst, weshalb die
Avantgarde TROTZDEM bauchtanzt, aber das war's dann auch
schon. (*A*, 12)

[1. I've lost my patchworked personal history which is marked out
by anal sex, tears, and necrophilia.
2. I've got an open sore in my throat.
3. My family is a bunch of pathological self-promoters stuck in some
early childhood omnipotence phase. In the most extreme case, they
might write a pop-culture essay on the issue of why the avant-garde
belly dances DESPITE IT ALL, but that's about it. (4)]

This statement, which ends the novel's first chapter, sets the tone for its
literary self-reflexivity as well as its thematization of precarious sexualities,
bodies, and families. Mifti characterizes herself in this passage in nonnormative terms, emphasizing her atypical family background; the insecurity
that marks her psychological and corporeal health; and the provisional
quality of her own creative practice.

Critics have commented on Hegemann's remarkable style:
"*Axolotl Roadkill* ist sowohl hemmungslose, halluzinatorische
Entladung eines traumatisierten Bewusstseins. Als auch dessen kalku-
lierte, ziemlich komische Parodie mit postmodernem Beigeschmack."
(*Axolotl Roadkill* is both an unrestrained, hallucinatory unloading of
a traumatized consciousness and also a calculated and rather amusing parody of itself, flavored with a touch of postmodernism.)[48] This
double-edged quality—the inverse of Roche's tone, which begins with
parody and tips into trauma—is crucial for Hegemann's mapping of
the present. "Vor lauter mit Angstanfällen gekoppelten Magen-Darm-
Exzesse will ich mich aus dem dritten Stock stürzen, schalte stattdes-
sen jedoch RTL II ein und da läuft eine super Tiersendung" (*A*, 10;
What with all my gastric excesses coupled with panic attacks, I feel like
launching myself from my third-floor window. But instead I switch
on trashy TV and watch a great nature documentary, 1–2), remarks
Mifti, capturing the way that the banality of pop culture contributes to
the flattening of experience in the contemporary world. "Ich will ein
Kinderheim in Afghanistan bauen und viele Anziehsachen haben" (*A*,
11; I want to build a children's home in Afghanistan and own loads
of clothes, 2), Mifti further proclaims, in a statement that embodies
this double-edged quality by highlighting the paradoxical coexistence
of global activist ambitions and individual consumerist fantasies in the
formation of neoliberal subjectivities.

Characterized by liminality, both Mifti and her text defy socially constructed binaries, including child and adult, heterosexual and homosexual, and chronicle and fiction. Throughout the novel, Mifti's body literally resists consensus culture, through both the excessive consumption of alcohol and drugs (including cocaine, ketamine, and heroin) and nonnormative sexual practices. Mifti is in love with a forty-six-year-old DJ named Alice, with whom she had a fling at the age of fifteen, and whom she pursues throughout the novel as both a sexual partner and an ersatz mother figure. At the same time, she has an occasional sexual relationship with her older friend Ophelia. Ophelia and Mifti watch the trailer for a film about the rape of an eight-year-old boy, which turns Ophelia on. She wonders aloud why she desires brutal sex with men when she only loves women, and she comments to Mifti, "Wir sind beide so geschlechterverwirrt, Schatz" (*A*, 45; We're both so gender-confused, honey, 38). Mifti also has sex with men, including a brutal encounter with a taxi driver who rapes her (though this rape is represented in somewhat ambiguous terms, perhaps as sadomasochistic role play). Violent sexual fantasies and acts are thus recurrent themes of the novel, and are linked to the disintegration of conventional binaries of sex and gender.

Though sex and desire comprise a central theme of *Axolotl Roadkill*, they are rarely linked to pleasure, instead providing a focal point for Mifti's anxiety and liminality: "Ich funktioniere nicht einfach fröhlich vor mich hin, ich funktioniere halt einfach nicht. Besitzgier, Gewohnheiten, Eifersucht, mangelnde Privatsphäre, Begehren, Begehren, Begehren." (*A*, 65; translation modified: I don't just function properly like a happy little bunny, I don't function at all. Material greed, rituals and habits, jealousy, a lack of privacy, it's all desire, desire, desire. [58–59]) In this sense, Hegemann employs Mifti's precarious sexuality as the signifier of a wider cultural critique, which *Axolotl Roadkill* articulates at the levels of both form and content—a critique of advanced capitalism, of privatization, of the family as the central unit of Western culture, and of heteronormativity in all facets of social life.

Like Helen Memel in *Feuchtgebiete*, Mifti articulates a critique of globally ascendant hegemonic femininity, lambasting "Heidi Klum und die Tatsache, dass meine komplette Generation von dieser Bitch mittelalterliche Standards vermittelt kriegt" (*A*, 56; Heidi Klum and the fact that that bitch is imparting medieval standards to my entire generation, 49). Invoking in her investigation of female subjectivity well-known signifiers of transnational third-wave feminism, such as the riot grrrl band L7 and the actress Gena Rowlands, Hegemann's pop-feminist pastiche recalls Katja Kauer's description of German pop-feminism:

> Popfeminismus bietet . . . die Möglichkeit für popkulturell sozialisierte Frauen, ein feministisches Bewusstsein und die eigene

Weiblichkeitsvorstellung, die gesellschaftlich produziert wurde, in Einklang zu bringen, ohne dabei zwangsläufig alle weiblichen Performanzen ablehnen zu müssen.[49]

[Popfeminism offers . . . the possibility for women socialized by pop culture to reconcile their feminist consciousness with their own socially determined notions of female identity, without having to forcibly reject all performances of femininity.]

However, Kauer emphasizes pop-feminism's contribution to a "positive weibliche Identitätsbildung" (positive female identity formation).[50] By contrast, Hegemann makes visible the precarity of female identity, and identity categories more generally, through her depiction of Mifti, who simultaneously refuses to inhabit any mode of conventional femininity but also has trouble establishing any stable counterhegemonic status. Mifti's mapping of "new femininities" thus overlaps with Gill and Scharff's description of neoliberalism, where "the capacity to invest in 'alternative' or counterhegemonic modes of femininity is contingent and unstable, as well as based in particular sets of material conditions and cultural advantages that are not available to all."[51] The precarious sexualities and body politics represented by Roche and Hegemann make visible the way that the neoliberal promise of female empowerment, gender and sexual mobility, and individual choice is conjoined with a simultaneous disciplining of female bodies through hegemonic femininity, a pervasive insecurity, and a lack of provisions for caregiving.

Mifti is a teenage dropout who lives with her two older half-siblings in the gentrified center of Berlin. Her siblings Annika, a brilliant creative director at a marketing firm, and Edmond, a slacker with ambitions to become an experimental-theater impresario, are exemplars of the self-absorbed "Berlin Generation," described by sociologist Heinz Bude:[52] characterized by their entrepreneurial spirit and their status in the globalized "knowledge economy," they are part of a postnational, postpolitical creative intelligentsia that the younger Mifti utterly rejects. Occasionally her siblings try to intervene in Mifti's life by forcing her to go to school or eat a good meal, but generally she is left to her own devices.

Their father, an art dealer, who lives nearby with his young wife, also doesn't have much time for or interest in Mifti, whose mother died of an overdose when she was thirteen. Like Helen, Mifti is haunted by the traumatic experience of her mother's violent and neglectful behavior (culminating in her eventual death). In a central passage, Mifti recalls an episode that took place when she was ten years old, when she was locked out of her apartment and feared that her mother was dead. In fact, her mother was on a bender, and Mifti witnesses her drug-induced rampage when the authorities forcibly open the apartment. This experience of insecurity presages her mother's death and forms the core of Mifti's personal history and of the novel; as Mifti points out, "Dass ihr Tod diese Ebene der Finsternis zu meiner Wahrnehmung addiert hat, ist ein zu hoher Preis für den Satz: 'Meine Mutter ist gestorben, als ich dreizehn war.' Trotzdem ist dieser Satz eigentlich alles, was ich noch habe." (*A*, 146; The fact that her death added this level of blackness to my perception is too high a price for the words, "My mother died when I was thirteen." But still, those words are actually all I have left now. [141]) Mifti's story, like Helen's, typifies the precarity of contemporary family relations, illustrating the waning of affective and familial ties in neoliberalism.

However, Mifti's individual trauma is framed by an awareness of the structural inequalities that surround the death of her mother, who was a single parent and welfare recipient. Mifti recalls the prejudice of the ambulance crew dispatched to her mother's dilapidated apartment, who stood around debating the Hartz IV social welfare reform instead of saving her mother's life (*A*, 124; 119). With well-chosen details, she describes the financial disparity and gender inequality between her parents, naming the objects her father bought for himself while her mother was living in destitution: "Ein Originalfoto von Leni Riefenstahl, ein Plasmabildschirm, indische Wandgehänge, die aussehen, als hätte sie jemand von einer Elefantenreise mitgebracht und ein Salzstreuer für dreiundsiebzig Euro" (*A*, 122; An original Leni Riefenstahl photo, a plasma screen, Indian wall hangings that look like someone brought them back from a wildlife safari, and a seventy-three-euro salt cellar, 117). By highlighting this inequality, Mifti's framing of her mother's story runs counter to the postfeminist "current of individualism that has almost entirely replaced notions of the social or political, or any idea of individuals as subject to pressures, constraints or influence outside of themselves."[53] Instead, Mifti's story exposes the contradictory role requirements to which women in particular are increasingly subjected, and the toll this takes on the individual struggling to balance paradoxical expectations. Indeed, as Mifti proclaims later about herself, "Es ist megahart, ein Individuum zu sein" (*A*, 161–62; It's mega-tough being an individual, 157).

Hegemann's use of language echoes this self-reflexivity regarding neoliberal individualism; it reflects on a formal level a key thematic concern of the novel, which maps insecurity as the representative experience of neoliberalism, while also emphasizing the mobility it facilitates. The novel is comprised of a pastiche of citations reflecting its transnational milieu, including global pop language (especially musicians and song texts) and intertextual literary references. Entirely referential, eminently self-reflexive, and yet ultimately substantial rather than derivative, *Axolotl Roadkill* makes visible the precarity of literature itself in a transnational and intermedial age (something that the plagiarism scandal surrounding the book reiterated). As Mifti's brother Edmond tells her, "Ich bediene mich überall, wo ich Inspiration finde und beflügelt werde . . . , weil meine Arbeit und mein Diebstahl authentisch werden, sobald etwas in meine Seele berührt. Es ist egal, woher ich die Dinge nehme, wichtig ist, wohin ich sie trage." (*A*, 15; I steal from anywhere that resonates with inspiration or fuels my imagination . . . , because my work and my theft are authentic as long as something speaks directly from my soul. It's not where I take things from—it's where I take them to. [7]) In the aftermath of the scandal, Hegemann repeated in interviews again and again the idea that what is important for her work is what she does with things ("wohin ich sie trage" [where I take them to]), not where she takes them from. She might also have cited Mifti, who explains, "Mir wurde eine Sprache einverleibt, die nicht meine eigene ist. Diese Sprache ist sehr lebendig obwohl einige Worte extrem überstrapaziert werden." (*A*, 49; They've imbued me with a language that is not my own. That language is very lively, although certain words are put to extreme overuse. [42]) Hegemann both denaturalizes this imbued language and invents new words in order to make visible aspects of the neoliberal present. Like Roche, she exemplifies in this way the creative potential signaled by precarity.

One of its most inventive features, the organizing trope of Hegemann's novel is the axolotl, an unusual amphibian of the salamander family. The axolotl is a biological outlier for a number of reasons. Not only can it regenerate lost limbs entirely, but it also presents a rare example of neoteny: it never metamorphoses but instead always remains in a larval state. Strangely, in the case of the axolotl, this neoteny is entirely genetic rather than environmental; despite never reaching adulthood, axolotls do reach sexual maturity in larval state and are able to reproduce. Axolotls grow in a range of bright colors, and are notable for their grotesque appearance, including coral-colored external gills, transluscent larval skin, through which they breathe, and large grinning faces with glowing blue or gold eyes, which give them the aspect of comic book characters. An endangered species today, the axolotl is native to Mexico City (its name derives from the Aztec language Nahuatl), though it is extremely rare in the wild.

In employing the axolotl as a literary trope, Hegemann borrows from a much-discussed tradition in Latin American literature, where the creature has served as a symbol of ambiguity, a metaphor of arrested development, and an allegorical figure highlighting postcolonial relations.[54] In Julio Cortázar's 1956 short story "Axolotl," for example, the first-person narrator visits the Jardin des Plantes in Paris to observe the caged axolotls there, until one day he turns into one.[55] The narrator's obsession with the axolotls derives from his attempt to comprehend their difference despite his dawning understanding that they are quite similar to humans: "The eyes of the axolotls spoke to me of the presence of a different life, of another way of seeing" (5). It is only when he is transformed into an axolotl that the narrator begins to understand the cognitive paradox occupied by the caged animal (a.k.a. the colonial subject). Writing after his transformation, the narrator explains: "Only one thing was strange: to go on thinking as usual, to know. To realize that was, for the first moment, like the horror of a man buried alive awaking to his fate. . . . I am an axolotl for good now, and if I think like a man it's only because every axolotl thinks like a man inside his rosy stone resemblance" (7–8). At the end of Cortázar's story, the narrator's sole, ironic consolation is to be found in the promise of representation, specifically literature: he remarks hopefully on the possibility that the man outside the cage, with whom he has switched places, will write a story about axolotls.

In Hegemann's novel, the axolotl serves as a metonym for multiple themes in the text, including adolescence, bisexuality, the city of Berlin, and the arrested development of both the political Left and the cultural avant-garde in Germany. Drawing intertextually on Cortázar's story, Hegemann's axolotl is both a potent symbol of ambiguous identity and a curiosity that demands representation in literature. The figure of the axolotl first appears in the second half of *Axolotl Roadkill*, directly following a break in the narrative, illustrated by a blank white page on which only one sentence is printed: "Ich traue mich nicht, an morgen zu denken, ich traue mich eigentlich überhaupt nicht zu denken" (*A*, 137; I don't dare to think about tomorrow, in fact I don't even dare to think at all, 132). Like Cortázar's protagonist, Mifti pursues the notion of achieving enlightenment and/or permanently arrested development via transformation into an amphibian. Just before she encounters the axolotl, Mifti experiences a crisis: "Ich höre zu laut Musik, ich tanze zu viel, ich übertreibe in allem, um mir selbst nicht mehr auffallen zu müssen. Ich warte. Darauf, dass ich einschlafe, dass ich wahnsinnig werde, dass ich wieder aufstehe und in die Küche gehe, um mich dort auf dem Fensterbrett in eine kolumbianische Schwarznabenkröte zu verwandeln." (*A*,138; I turn up my music too loud, I dance too much, I go over the top in everything I do just so I don't attract my own attention anymore. I wait. Wait to fall asleep, to go crazy, to get up again and go in the kitchen, to turn myself into a Columbian black-spined toad on the kitchen windowsill. [133]) She visits a friend whose apartment is filled with forty aquariums containing animals for sale. There, she is immediately drawn to a very pink axolotl. After her friend explains to her that the axolotl "bleibt sein gesamtes Leben lang im Lurchstadium, das heißt, es wird einfach nicht erwachsen" (*A*,138; it reaches sexual maturity without ever undergoing metamorphosis out of the amphibian stage—it just never grows up, 133), Mifti buys it, carrying the axolotl out in a plastic bag filled with water. Hegemann writes, "Meine Lunge verabschiedet sich, und ich renne weiter, mein Herz überschlägt sich, und ich renne weiter, die Schleimhäute quillen mir aus den Nasenlöchern, nachdem sie sich schmerzhaft von den mechanisch abzugrenzenden Organoberflächen gelöst haben" (*A*, 138–39; My lung says its farewells and I keep on running, my heart skips a beat and I keep on running, the mucous membranes start coming out of my nostrils, having painfully separated from the mechanically delineated organ surfaces, 133–34). Like Cortázar's narrator, Mifti appears to turn into an axolotl at this point in the text, and although her appearance does not change, this transformation signals her precarity, understood as a defiance of conventional identity categories—in subsequent pages she explores her adolescence, her bisexuality, and, in connection with her drug use, also refers to herself as a zombie, locating herself between childhood and adulthood, heterosexuality and homosexuality, and life and death.

If I have dwelled at length on the trope of the axolotl and the way it intertextually evokes Julio Cortázar, it is to illustrate, first of all, Hegemann's sophisticated citation of transnational literary influences. While condemnations of the novel have revolved around Hegemann's "stealing" from Airen's novel and other plagiarized material, critics have largely failed to remark upon the way that she reworks citations, updating and embroidering on them, though this mode of resignification is a central strategy of pop literature and pop-feminism. Under fire for copyright infringement, Hegemann's publisher Ullstein Verlag issued a lengthy bibliography, downloadable by PDF from its website and included in subsequent published editions of the novel, which documents many of the source texts that Hegemann drew from in composing *Axolotl Roadkill*.[56] While the list includes Airen's blog and the lyrics of numerous pop songs, it does not include Julio Cortázar. Yet, Hegemann quite self-reflexively employs Cortázar and foregrounds in the construction of her novel practices of intertextuality and montage. Indeed, from its very inception, the novel signals to readers that they are about to enter a collage world of intertextual references and recycled language: the epigraph reads, "We love to entertain you," a quote, in English, from the private German television broadcaster Pro 7.

When, at the end of *Axolotl Roadkill*, Mifti's family attempts to stage an intervention into her drug use, she learns that her brother has stolen the magenta notebook in which she has recorded her experiences—the text that, in turn, makes up the novel *Axolotl Roadkill*. Hegemann writes:

Mein Körper reißt Edmond das Heft aus der Hand und rennt zur Tür. Edmond hält meinen Arm fest und sagt: "Eins muss man dir lassen."
"Was denn?"
Mit diesem Satz sind wir wieder eine Einheit, dieser Körper und ich, komisch, das alles.

"You write like a roadkill."
"Like a what?"
"Ein angefahrenes Tier" (*A*, 190).

[My body tears the notebook out of Edmond's hands and runs to
the door. Edmond grabs my arm and says, "I'll say one thing for
you."
"What?"
The words bring us back into a single entity, my body and me—odd.
"You write like a roadkill."
"Like what?"
"Like a dead animal squashed against the road." (186)]

In this metatextual passage, which invokes the novel's title, Hegemann
demonstrates that Mifti, by performing the role of the author, here
"becomes one" with her body again, transforming from an axolotl back
into a girl. At the same time, this highly self-conscious passage foregrounds Hegemann's project to "write like a roadkill," harvesting the
dead remains of the pop cultural avant-garde—including Julio Cortázar
(most famous in Europe as the author of the story filmed by Antonioni
as *Blow-Up*)—and reanimating them for a new cultural experiment. As
Hegemann herself describes *Axolotl Roadkill*, "Das ist ja kein Tagebuch
oder ein aus Überdruck entstandener Bekenntnisroman. Das ist ein
Experiment." (It is not a diary or a confessional novel generated by excess
pressure. It is an experiment.)[57] Indeed, Hegemann is a sophisticated
author well versed in world literature, whose experiment seeks to push
the boundaries of performative writing.[58]

As I have suggested, the pop-feminist texts of Roche and Hegemann
make visible the insecurity of contemporary experience, particularly sexuality and gender roles, as well as the precarity of literature itself in an era
of hegemonic transnational media cultures. At the same time, they renew
the idea of literature and its transformative powers—to convey subjectivity, to undermine our perception of reality, to critique the status quo, and
in so doing to create change. Through their inventive use of language,
including neologisms, intertextual references, and global pop citations,
many of them connected to female sexual organs, Roche and Hegemann
exemplify the creative potential of precarity for imagining new subjectivities and social relations. The phenomenal worldwide resonance of both
novels derives not least from the way they engage transnational connectivities by expanding our perception of neoliberalism and by addressing
feminist and queer networks both within and across national boundaries.
As traveling texts that explore mobile identities, *Feuchtgebiete* and *Axolotl
Roadkill* suggest new frameworks for considering transnationalisms in
German literature.

Notes

[1] See Paul Jay, *Global Matters: The Transnational Turn in Literary Studies* (Ithaca, NY: Cornell University Press, 2010).

[2] Neoliberalism refers to the idea that the market can and should serve as the guiding principle of all human activity. The doctrine of neoliberalism was advocated by economists and politicians in the West throughout the twentieth century and came to prevail around the turn of the millennium, when the New Economy of technologically driven global capitalism replaced other forms of socioeconomic and political organization throughout much of the world. See, for example, David Harvey, *A Brief History of Neoliberalism* (Oxford: Oxford University Press, 2005); Lisa Duggan, *The Twilight of Equality? Neoliberalism, Cultural Politics, and the Attack on Democracy* (Boston: Beacon Press, 2003); and Raewyn Connell, "Understanding Neoliberalism," in *Neoliberalism and Everyday Life*, ed. Susan Braedley and Meg Luxton (Montreal: McGill-Queen's University Press, 2010), 22–36.

[3] Harvey, *Brief History of Neoliberalism*, 35.

[4] Precariat, a neologism that combines the words "precarious" and "proletariat" refers to an emergent class of people worldwide whose lives and work are shaped by structures of insecurity engendered by neoliberal policies. On the precariat, see, for example, Guy Standing, *The Precariat: The New Dangerous Class* (London: Bloomsbury, 2011).

[5] See for example Harvey, *Brief History of Neoliberalism*, 3.

[6] See also Hester Baer, "Affectless Economies: The Berlin School and Neoliberalism," *Discourse* 35, no. 1 (2013): 72–100.

[7] On the concept of precarity, see Pierre Bourdieu, "Job Insecurity is Everywhere Now," in *Acts of Resistance: Against the Tyranny of the Market*, trans. Richard Nice (New York: New Press, 1998), 78–87; Robert Castel and Klaus Dörre, eds., *Prekärität, Abstieg, Ausgrenzung: Die soziale Frage am Beginn des 21. Jahrhunderts* (Frankfurt: Campus, 2009); and Irene Götz and Barbara Lemberger, eds. *Prekär arbeiten, Prekär leben: Kulturwissenschaftliche Perspektiven auf ein gesellschaftliches Phänomen* (Frankfurt: Campus, 2009).

[8] Rosalind Gill and Andy Pratt, "In the Social Factory? Immaterial Labour, Precariousness and Cultural Work," *Theory, Culture, and Society* 25, no. 7–8 (2008): 3.

[9] On insecurity as the key structure of experience today, see Lauren Berlant, *Cruel Optimism* (Durham, NC: Duke University Press, 2011), Kindle file, Intro. Berlant points to how the imperceptibility of neoliberalism along with its inherent contradictions leads to a situation in which individuals become complicit with ideologies that harm them, a situation she labels "cruel optimism."

[10] Stuart Taberner, "Transnationalism in Contemporary German-Language Fiction by Nonminority Writers," *Seminar* 47, no. 5 (2011): 627.

[11] Both Roche and Hegemann are white and hail from privileged backgrounds. Though Roche is bicultural (with British and German heritage, and having migrated from the UK to Germany as a child), her race and class privilege align her with other "nonminority" writers considered by Taberner.

[12] Françoise Lionnet and Shu-mei Shih, "Introduction: Thinking through the Minor, Transnationally," in *Minor Transnationalism* (Durham, NC: Duke University Press, 2005), 7.

[13] Lionnet and Shih, "Introduction," 5–6.

[14] Lionnet and Shih, "Introduction," 5.

[15] Laura Briggs, Gladys McCormick, and J. T. Way, "Transnationalism: A Category of Analysis," *American Quarterly* 60, no. 3 (2008): 627.

[16] Paul Jay also identifies in the transnational turn a "shift in our attention from sameness to difference" that he attributes to the crucial role of social and political movements outside the academy in the second half of the twentieth century, including the feminist, gay rights, and anticolonial movements, as well as to "the rise of theoretical and critical practices within the academy dominated by a sustained and critical attention to difference," such as ethnic studies and feminist and postcolonial theory. See Jay, *Global Matters*, 17.

[17] Briggs, McCormick, and Way, "Transnationalism," 636. For example, Myra Marx Ferree points out that feminists have highlighted the dangers inherent in neoliberalism's incursion on the nation-state, demonstrating how neoliberalism limits the state's ability to realize social justice. See Myra Marx Ferree, *Varieties of Feminism: German Gender Politics in Global Perspective* (Stanford: Stanford University Press, 2012), 16.

[18] See Maria Mayr, "Europe's Invisible Ghettos: Transnational Existence and Neoliberal Capitalism in Julya Rabinowich's *Die Erdfresserin*," in this volume.

[19] See Katharina Gerstenberger, "'im flugzeug nach bischkek oder im flughafen von taschkent': Transnationalism and Notions of Home in Recent German Literature," in this volume.

[20] "Fiction in German Makes It to Pole Position," *Economist*, April 3, 2008, accessed March 10, 2012, http://www.economist.com/node/10952281.

[21] On globalization and its effects on German authorship and literature, especially German pop literature, see also Anke Biendarra, *Germans Going Global: Contemporary Literature and Cultural Globalization* (Berlin: De Gruyter, 2012).

[22] See Rosalind Gill and Christina Scharff, introduction to *New Femininities: Postfeminism, Neoliberalism and Subjectivity* (New York: Palgrave Macmillan, 2011), 10.

[23] Taberner, "Transnationalism," 626.

[24] Feminism experienced a resurgence in Germany beginning around 2006, in response to the so-called demography debates, which blamed women for the declining German birthrate. Young feminists responded with a groundswell of publications and interventions, referred to under the umbrella term pop-feminism because many of them aimed at resignifying pop culture and reframing media representations of feminism. While pop-feminism has its origins in the specific national context of German politics, its influences are broadly transnational, and it resonates widely with contemporary feminist movements around the globe. See for example the website *Mädchenmannschaft.org*, the publication *Missy Magazine*, and books including Sonja Eismann, ed., *Hot Topic: Popfeminismus heute* (Mainz: Ventil, 2007), which helped popularize the term, and Meredith Haaf, Susanne

Klingner, and Barbara Streidl, *Wir Alphamädchen: Wie Feminismus das Leben schöner macht* (Hamburg: Hoffmann und Campe, 2008).

[25] See Carrie Smith-Prei, "'Knaller-Sex für alle': Popfeminist Body Politics in Lady Bitch Ray, Charlotte Roche, and Sarah Kuttner," *Studies in 20th & 21st Century Literature* 35, no. 1 (2011): 20.

[26] Smith-Prei, "Knaller-Sex für alle," 29.

[27] Christa Binswanger and Kathy Davis, "Sexy Stories and Postfeminist Empowerment: From *Häutungen* to *Wetlands*," *Feminist Theory* 13, no. 3 (2012): 259; Christina Scharff, "The New German Feminisms: Of Wetlands and Alpha-Girls," in *New Femininities: Postfeminism, Neoliberalism and Subjectivity*, ed. Rosalind Gill and Christina Scharff (New York: Palgrave Macmillan, 2011), 275.

[28] On the way that pop-feminist discourse often dovetails with neoliberal ideology, especially in its neglect of white privilege, see also Hester Baer, "German Feminism in the Age of Neoliberalism: Jana Hensel and Elisabeth Raether's *Neue Deutsche Mädchen*," *German Studies Review* 35, no. 2 (2012): 355–74.

[29] Maria Stehle, "Pop, Porn, and Rebellious Speech," *Feminist Media Studies* 12, no. 2 (2012): 235.

[30] In this sense, my discussion of the representation of precarious sexualities in *Feuchtgebiete* and *Axolotl Roadkill* constitutes one response to Taberner's call to examine "the extent to which there is a German *Sonderweg* within contemporary world literature and the degree to which nonminority German writing is doubly coded, for a domestic audience on the one hand and for an international public on the other." See Taberner, "Transnationalism," 641.

[31] Volker Woltersdorff, "Paradoxes of Precarious Sexualities," *Cultural Studies* 25, no. 2 (2011): 173.

[32] Woltersdorff, "Paradoxes of Precarious Sexualities," 167.

[33] Rosalind Gill and Christina Scharff suggest that, in contrast to the many studies of hegemonic masculinity, gender theorists have not adequately attended to "hegemonic femininity." They use the term "new femininities" to refer to the increasingly pervasive forms of hegemonic femininity that emerge in neoliberalism. See Gill and Scharff, *New Femininities*, 2.

[34] Angela McRobbie, *The Aftermath of Feminism: Gender, Culture, and Social Change* (London: Sage, 2009), 77.

[35] Patricia Ticineto Clough and Jean Halley, eds., *The Affective Turn: Theorizing the Social* (Durham, NC: Duke University Press, 2007), 2.

[36] According to the *Berliner Zeitung*, for example, audience members at Roche's readings of *Feuchtgebiete* regularly passed out, closed their eyes tightly, and turned their faces away, physical reactions that manifest discomfort, disgust, and shame. See Sabine Rennefanz, "Aufklärung für Fortgeschrittene," *Berliner Zeitung*, April 15, 2008, accessed July 27, 2013, http://www.berliner-zeitung.de/archiv/wenn-charlotte-roche-aus-ihrem-bestseller--feuchtgebiete--liest--fallen-leute-in-ohnmacht--vielleicht-sagt-das-mehr-ueber-dieses-buch-als-vieles-andere-aufklaerung-fuer-fortgeschrittene,10810590,10552128.html. See also Decca Aitkenhead, "It Should Make You Blush," *The Guardian*, January 16, 2009,

accessed July 29, 2013, http://www.theguardian.com/books/2009/jan/17/interview-charlotte-roche-debut-novel-wetlands.

[37] Charlotte Roche, *Feuchtgebiete* (Cologne: Dumont, 2008), 8; *Wetlands*, trans. Tim Mohr (New York: Grove, 2009), 1. Further references to this work are given in the text using the abbreviation *F*; citations refer to the page numbers from the German original followed by Mohr's translation.

[38] For example, Li Gerhalter writes, "Ausgehend von den USA haben sich in den letzten Jahrzehnten auch in Europa kanonisierte Ästhetik-Standards durchgesetzt, die von den größten Teilen der Bevölkerung akzeptiert und reproduziert werden. Beeinflusst werden diese 'Standards' in gegenseitiger Wechselwirkung von einer immens gewachsenen Kosmetikindustrie, die sich wiederum vor allem auf die Argumente vermeintlicher Hygiene stützt." See Li Gerhalter, "Wie Angora: Körperbehaltung ist out—und krause Politik," in *Hot Topic: Popfeminismus heute*, ed. Sonja Eismann (Mainz: Ventil, 2007), 91. See also "Dossier Haarige Angelegenheiten," *Missy Magazine* 2 (2012).

[39] Woltersdorff, "Paradoxes of Precarious Sexualities," 165.

[40] See for example Nicolas Kulish, "Germany Abuzz at Racy Novel of Sex and Hygiene," *New York Times*, June 6, 2008, accessed May 15, 2012, http://www.nytimes.com/2008/06/06/world/europe/06taboo.html?pagewanted=all&_r=0.

[41] Scharff, "The New German Feminisms," 271.

[42] Stephan Loichinger, "Gegen die Hygiene-Diktatur: 10 Fragen an Charlotte Roche," *Frankfurter Rundschau Magazin*, February 25, 2008, 32.

[43] Binswanger and Davis, "Sexy Stories," 250, 257.

[44] Woltersdorff, "Paradoxes of Precarious Sexualities," 177.

[45] Woltersdorff, "Paradoxes of Precarious Sexualities," 177.

[46] Gill and Scharff, *New Femininities*, 8.

[47] Helene Hegemann, *Axolotl Roadkill* (Berlin: Ullstein, 2010), 9; *Axolotl Roadkill*, trans. Katy Derbyshire (London: Corsair, 2012), 1. Further references to this work are given in the text using the abbreviation *A*; citations refer to the page numbers from the German original followed by Derbyshire's translation, unless otherwise noted.

[48] Ursula März, "Literarischer Kugelblitz," *Die Zeit*, January 21, 2010, accessed June 16, 2013, http://www.zeit.de/2010/04/L-B-Hegemann.

[49] Katja Kauer, *Popfeminismus! Fragezeichen! Eine Einführung* (Berlin: Frank & Timme, 2009), 138.

[50] Kauer, *Popfeminismus!*, 103.

[51] Gill and Scharff, *New Femininities*, 9.

[52] Heinz Bude, *Generation Berlin* (Berlin: Merve, 2001).

[53] Gill and Scharff, *New Femininities*, 7.

[54] See, for example, Roger Bartra, *The Cage of Melancholy: Identity and Metamorphosis in the Mexican Character* (New Brunswick, NJ: Rutgers University Press, 1992).

186 ◆ HESTER BAER

55 Julio Cortázar, "Axolotl," *Blow-Up and Other Stories*, trans. Paul Blackburn (New York: Collier, 1974), 3–8.

56 See Ullstein Verlag, "Quellenverzeichnis," *Axolotl Roadkill*, accessed September 10, 2010, http://www.ullsteinbuchverlage.de/media/0000461234.pdf.

57 Tobias Rapp, "Das Wunderkind der Boheme," *Der Spiegel*, January 18, 2010, accessed July 9, 2013, http://www.spiegel.de/spiegel/a-672725.html.

58 Hegemann's biography provides one justification for this argument. The daughter of *Volksbühne* dramaturg Carl Hegemann, she grew up in a highly literate milieu. Before writing the novel, she had already written a play, "Ariel 15," and directed a film, "Torpedo." Both the play and the film have shown widely in Germany.

9: Dislocation, Multiplicity, and Transformation: Posttransnationalism in Antje Rávic Strubel's *Kältere Schichten der Luft* and *Vom Dorf*

Faye Stewart

THOSE WHO ASSOCIATE THE WORK of contemporary German writer Antje Rávic Strubel with transnationalism might have in mind her debut, *Offene Blende* (Open Aperture, 2001), in which an East German woman reinvents herself in New York City, or award-winning novel *Tupolew 134* (Tupolev 134, 2004), the fragmented tale of a plane hijacking between Cold War era Eastern Europe and West Berlin. Strubel's novels are transnational not only because their characters and settings cross, question, and trouble national and cultural boundaries, but also because they participate in the ongoing processes of negotiating contemporary German identities beyond the political borders and bounded histories of the former East and West. This chapter investigates the affinities between the categories of East German and transnational literature and identifies Strubel's novels as engaging in a new posttransnational German project: thematizing the East–West boundary and its dissolution while acknowledging the variety of experiences, affiliations, and narratives that are intertwined with and separated by the border that once divided these now unified nations.

A comparative study of two ostensibly very different books published by Strubel almost two decades after the fall of the wall, *Vom Dorf: Abenteuergeschichten zum Fest* (From the Village: Adventure Stories for the Holiday, 2007) and *Kältere Schichten der Luft* (Colder Layers of Air, 2007), locates a shared set of themes and concerns linking narrative indeterminacy with citizenship, mobility, and transformation. Emphasizing the novels' representations of little brothers, surveillance, and gendered and generational belonging, I argue that these two recent works can be read as transnational in both conventional and innovative ways. This analysis serves as the foundation for my argument for a characterization of postwall East German literature as posttransnational. I propose an interpretation of Strubel's narratives that stresses the *trans* of *transnationalism*, demonstrating what such an approach can reveal by examining the interconnections among depictions of transgressions, transformations, and transgenderedness, and the texts' poignant confrontations with national boundaries and their legacies.

Transnationalism in East German and Postunification Literature

Though Antje Rávic Strubel is a German-born author of German heritage and a native speaker of German, her biography and her literary output qualify her as a quintessentially transnational writer. Born and raised in Potsdam, East Germany, and having lived in Berlin, the United States, and Sweden, Strubel crosses myriad national borders in her life and writing. Not only do her novels consistently thematize interconnections between place, positionality, and culture, but in so doing they also traverse other kinds of boundaries, challenging paradigms of singular identity, binary gender, and coherent narrative voice. However, a classification of Strubel's work as transnational may seem counterintuitive to those who think of such literature as the exclusive domain of writers with minority or hyphenated identities (i.e., Afro-German or German-Turkish). Until recently, scholarly discussions of transnationalism in German-language writing have focused primarily on minority and bicultural authors, apparently motivated by the unspoken assumption that members of a nation's majority culture do not produce transnational works. In his 2011 study of contemporary transnational literature, Stuart Taberner enumerates the fallacies of the assumption that transnational equals bicultural, which effectively ghettoizes minority authors as outsiders and suggests that they alone are capable of possessing a transnational gaze.[1] While I do in fact argue for an understanding of postwall East German literature as exemplifying a kind of minority writing—one that neither numerically nor sociopolitically represents the mainstream (in other words, West or unified) German experience—I nonetheless submit that a perhaps more fruitful line of inquiry, following in Taberner's footsteps, would "make the case for a broader conceptualization of transnationalism," namely one that includes nonminority authors.[2] Taberner's examination of works by nonminority authors suggests that textual politics are of greater significance than authorial identity and proposes a new understanding of transnational literature as encompassing texts in which national boundaries interface with representations of locatedness and dislocatedness. In accordance with the kind of approach Taberner advocates, recent years have witnessed an increasing consideration of transnationalism in the work of nonminority writers of West German origin that brings borders, positioning, and mobility into focus. I suggest, in keeping with Taberner's interest in the textuality of space and belonging, that the category of transnational literature can also include texts in which inner-German boundaries, particularly the former East–West divide, play a critical role. This line marked the border between nations as well as ideologies, doubling as the fault line separating spheres of international influence during the Cold War, and its significance continues to resonate long after its erasure from world maps. Dislocatedness, often appearing in conjunction with disappointment, nostalgia, reevaluation (as well as revaluation), and transformation, is perhaps one of the most frequently recurring themes in contemporary East German writing. Taberner neither mentions the East–West boundary nor examines primary texts that explore it, though he does suggest that historical conflicts involving territory and ethnicity, in particular colonialism, the Holocaust, and post-1990 refugee arrivals, have surfaced as central concerns in the transnational German-language output of nonminority writers. A consideration of the present-day literary production of former East German authors who probe the constructedness of statehood, history, and identification could, however, bring new perspectives and insights to the discussion of transnationalism.

A view of postunification East German authors as transnational also resonates with more traditional understandings of the descriptor, which emphasize biculturalism and biography. Erika Nelson's definition is illustrative of this perception: "The term *transnationalism* suggests that both an author's persona and his or her work encompass experiences of two or more cultures and national contexts, and that the writer is able to draw upon both literary and linguistic traditions."[3] The work of writers from the German Democratic Republic is especially well suited to such analyses because it belongs both to the majority culture of German-identified speakers of German, and to the minority GDR culture in today's unified Federal Republic of Germany. (Former) East Germans are a minority: not only are they fewer in number than West Germans, but they are also at the margins of the unified state due to the dissolution of the GDR and its absorption into the FRG, which critics have characterized as a "colonization."[4] Unified Germany is, as its name and Basic Law indicate, essentially an expanded version of the Cold War era FRG: incorporating *die neuen Bundesländer* (the new federal states) entailed the abandonment, or at best reconstruction, of longstanding socialist institutions and practices in favor of Western alternatives. As Paul Cooke intimates in his monograph on postunification representations of East Germany, feelings of ethnic and cultural identity have clearly shifted due to global events since 1990—namely, the sense of "'east Germanness' as an identity marker" distinct from west Germanness has intensified.[5] Germans from both sides are still working through their divided and united histories. Recent scholarship in German studies provides ample evidence that categories such as "GDR literature" and "East German culture" do not refer only to the past but remain relevant in contemporary cultural production, and will continue to do so as long as intellectuals and writers continue to identify as East German, as long as society deems the labels East and West German to be meaningful.[6]

With these critical and historical contexts in mind, I propose the concept of *posttransnationalism* to describe German texts narrated from postunification points of view and in which the East–West divide plays a pivotal thematic and structural role. The term *posttransnational* applies to literature in any cultural context where a no longer existing national border has significant hermeneutic force. While much of the way in which I use the word here refers specifically to recent and contemporary German contexts, the term could be useful to describe works whose production is marked by shifting or disappearing geographical boundaries, such as those of Alsace-Lorraine, the historical Kingdoms of Prussia and Bavaria, and the Mongolian People's Republic, as well as colonial and postcolonial territories like British North Borneo and the Cherokee Nation of the United States. The characteristics of posttransnational literature as I outline them below—such as transience and transformation—are definitive for the genre and can also be located in other posttransnational texts. The line separating the former GDR from the FRG may no longer function as a national boundary, but the *Mauer im Kopf* (wall in the head) still influences the experiences of East and West Germans today, and these divided perceptions shape perspectives on Germany and Europe's pasts, presents, and possible futures.[7] I offer the term *posttransnational* to characterize cultural forms that emphasize the crossing of national borders that no longer exist, where the prefix *post* references tension among conceptions of unification, projected on the one hand as a geopolitically complete process, and widely understood on the other hand to be socioculturally ongoing. The *post* of *posttransnational* is therefore both real and imaginary. Posttransnational literature explores the history of a boundary and highlights its physical absence together with its psychological and social traces. A key characteristic of this genre is that it marries these themes with representations of transience, ethereality, and above all, evolution. In the case of unified Germany, posttransnational literature examines vestiges of the inner-German boundary while envisioning new possibilities after and beyond the wall. Katharina Gerstenberger and Jana Evans Braziel point out that such themes are not uncommon in postwall culture, which testifies to "the continued engagement with East Germany as a state that no longer exists but whose memory reverberates in sometimes unexpected ways, not only today but as a projection into the future."[8] What I describe as *posttransnational* culture investigates these "unexpected ways" of remembering, being, and becoming. In posttransnational narratives, we witness a complex intermingling of voices and points of view, verb tenses and moods, and gestures of self-reflection and social critique. Such literature brings to the fore the dislocations accompanying the disappearance of a state border that aggressively shaped its citizens' experiences and memories, as well as their ambitions and fantasies. It reflects on the wall's past significance and subsequent legacy, but also celebrates the opportunities its collapse opens up, and it does so from multiple perspectives, destabilizing attempts to fix Cold War era and unified German history from any singular or hegemonic point of view. Posttransnational German literature is introspective, reevaluating biography and rethinking identity; however, it also looks outward through a socially critical point of view that challenges dominant paradigms and proposes radical alternatives to ideologically correct historical narratives. It thus has an important social purpose in advancing both the *Vergangenheitsbewältigung* (coming to terms with the past) of German division and the reconceptualization of what German identity, in its diverse forms, means today. Posttransnational literature not only accentuates borders and border crossings, but also performs the transgression of boundaries through narrative gestures that are themselves mobile, transitional, and indeterminate.

In the introduction to this volume, Elisabeth Herrmann, Carrie Smith-Prei, and Stuart Taberner remark that fiction is—and always has been—about crossing and transgressing boundaries. There are few writers whose work so steadily calls attention to boundaries and their dissolution as Antje Rávic Strubel. Her seven novels and numerous short stories play with identity, language, and reality to such an extent that readers will often find themselves working to comprehend what is actually happening in the text. For many of Strubel's protagonists, crossing national borders, be they imagined or real, leads to transformative experiences: her characters experiment with language, discover new pleasures, unlearn old behaviors and adopt new ones, reinvent themselves, rewrite collective narratives, or disappear altogether, sometimes dissolving into thin air. In these processes, one set of cultural and conceptual boundaries that consistently figures centrally in her writing is the blurry lines dividing commonly accepted binary categories of gender (male or female) and sexuality (heterosexual or homosexual)—as well as the margins of white space between these and other established categories. My focus on gender and sexuality in Strubel's transnational work is intended in part as an addendum to Taberner's sidelining of women writers and his omission of the consideration of gender in his article on transnational literature by nonminority authors.[9] In addition to Strubel, we might add such figures as Christa Wolf, Kathrin Schmidt, Irmtraud Morgner, Jana Hensel, Sarah Kirsch, and Monika Maron to the growing list of transnational—and even posttransnational—authors whom we can also identify as East German and feminist. All of these writers critically engage and intertwine notions of gender and sexuality, geopolitics, citizenship, and belonging.

In this analysis of Strubel's fiction, I examine the dimensions of transnationalism that interface with further possible meanings of the prefix *trans*, which include, in addition to the aforementioned practice of transgressing boundaries, the processes of transporting, transforming, and transgendering. A consideration of these themes as interconnected highlights the ways in which new and unprecedented entities emerge in the posttransnational narrative. Helen Finch remarks that Strubel's novels are "informed by a longing to go beyond gender liberation into the realm of corporeal dissolution or transcendence into nothingness."[10] Indeed, boundary crossing and self-dissolution are crucial steps in Strubel's novels, but these destabilizing works of literature also go on to offer new, adaptable, and mobile forms of identity. As Emily Jeremiah notes in a comparative reading of *Kältere Schichten der Luft* and *Vom Dorf*, protagonists Anja and Antje "represent . . . a set of transformative possibilities, a productive nomadism" that is linked explicitly to queer gender and sexuality.[11] I similarly read the radical transformations that Strubel's characters embody as enabled by their androgyny and unconventional desires. I take cues from Finch, Jeremiah, and from Beret Norman, who also locates Strubel's portrayals of ambiguous and shifting positionalities in the context of the historical ruptures of the late twentieth century, namely the dismantling of the GDR and its incorporation into the Federal Republic. "Deconstruction and reconstruction," Norman maintains, "appear as choices her fictional characters make: their self-determination and creation of identity become central."[12] These studies of Strubel's writing point to the significance of the production, dissolution, and transformation of identity, which I explore further in connection with national histories and boundaries on the one hand, and gender and sexuality on the other.

Dislocation and Multiplicity

On the surface, Antje Rávic Strubel's two 2007 novels, *Kältere Schichten der Luft* and *Vom Dorf*, could not seem more different. In comparison with *Vom Dorf*, *Kältere Schichten* is a relatively straightforward story about a group of East German thirtysomethings who work in a summer canoe camp by the shores of Lake Foxen, in southwestern Sweden. The heart of the novel is a love affair between first-person narrator Anja, a camp employee, and a waiflike woman she meets who lives in a dilapidated house nearby—we never learn the lover's name, but Anja christens her "Siri."[13] The intense emotional bond between these two characters, which evolves primarily through language and narrative, transforms Anja into a boy named Schmoll. Their courtship elicits jealousy and ridicule on behalf of other camp employees, and these tensions climax in the allegedly accidental death of Ralf, an older coworker who pursues and attempts to rape Anja/Schmoll. As summer draws to a close, Siri vanishes and Anja-turned-Schmoll plans to return to the hometown of Halberstadt, in the former GDR. By contrast, *Vom Dorf* appears, by virtue of its multilayered narrative structure, more convoluted. A framing device written in the voice of a "Herausgeberin" (editor) identifying herself as author Antje Rávic Strubel presents the inner narrative as a fictional manuscript that has falsely been attributed to her authorship.[14] The manuscript includes a cycle of magical realist short stories, several letters to Antje, and ten numbered, diary-like "Protokolle" (protocols) allegedly written by an unidentified aspiring writer, an older East German man. The first-person "Protokolle" chronicle the man's four-year obsession with and surveillance of "ARS," the abbreviation he uses to refer to his idol, Antje Rávic Strubel. The short stories, characterized by editor Antje as unsuccessful attempts to imitate her literary style, are set in Brandenburg and Berlin during the winter and narrate endeavors to write a "Weihnachtsgeschichte" (Christmas story) devoid of clichés. The book concludes with the disappearance of the male writer after the publication of the anonymously authored manuscript under Strubel's name.

Though these novels are ostensibly quite different, under their diverging surfaces we can locate a set of shared themes and concerns. As the above synopses demonstrate, both texts engage in playful negotiations of identity on interconnected levels: gender, sexuality, nationality, and perhaps most significantly, fictionality. These themes come to the fore not only in *Kältere Schichten* and *Vom Dorf*, but also in Strubel's other novels, in particular *Unter Schnee* (Snowed Under, 2001) and *Fremd gehen* (Going Strange, 2002). At a glance, *Kältere Schichten*—a chronological narrative with fewer alternations in voice and point of view—might sound more straightforward than *Vom Dorf*, but the two stories achieve comparable levels of complexity by mixing diegetic reality with fantasy: in neither novel is it clear whether the events narrated are real or merely imagined by the characters, and any attempt to distinguish between diegetic realities and fantasies will face considerable challenges. *Kältere Schichten* and *Vom Dorf* narrate posttransnational experiences of dislocation from gendered—and yet shifting and indeterminate—points of view. The two novels feature East German characters of different genders and generations who come to terms in different ways with their personal histories and the circumstances of their present lives in postunification Europe. Both novels have as their protagonists queer women who narrate in the first person, and the two texts also share changes of narrative voice that unsettle or destabilize the female narrator, intermingling her voice with that of a male doppelgänger. Several further parallels can be found among the two constellations of characters: older male stalkers, younger brothers, ethereal female lovers, and figures that vanish into thin air. Moreover, although *Kältere Schichten* is set in rural Sweden and *Vom Dorf* in postunification Brandenburg and Berlin, both novels are heavily invested in exploring the troubling notions of what it means to be German and how to deal with recent historical ruptures. Even as Siri in *Kältere Schichten* sarcastically comments that any authentically German narrative includes the requisite reference to National Socialism—"ohne Nazis würde man als Deutsche etwas vermissen" (*KSL*, 165; without Nazis, as a German you would be missing something)—it is unmistakably the East German past that looms much more tangibly over these stories.

One of the most striking similarities between *Kältere Schichten* and *Vom Dorf* is the dislocatedness and multiplicity of the queer main characters Anja and Antje. *Kältere Schichten*'s Anja is also known as Schmoll, and shifts in the main character's identity are signaled by abrupt changes in narrative point of view: the first-person singular "ich" corresponds to Anja, and interruptions come from a third-person perspective designating Schmoll with the masculine pronoun "er." In addition to the gendered, grammatical, and narrative boundaries that, as Norman demonstrates, this "linguistic rupture" questions, it also performatively conveys Anja's disorientation and the reconstruction of her identity, whereby Schmoll emerges, through language, in reaction to a set of border crossings and dislocations.[15] The causes for these dislocations are various in nature, ranging from geopolitical factors such as the fall of the wall and the ensuing spike in German unemployment, Anja's voluntary exile to work in Sweden, and the camp's lakeside location near the Norwegian border; to social conflicts precipitated by Anja's liminal position as a late arrival and outsider to the camp staff's inner circle, the circulation of homophobic sentiments within the camp, an attempted rape by Ralf, and camp director Svenja's effort to subject Anja to sexual blackmail. The origin of the moniker "Schmoll," however, can be attributed to none of these factors; it is invented by Anja's ethereal lover Siri, who christens her Schmoll upon their first encounter, thereby bringing about perhaps the most forceful dislocation of all. Though the narrator initially dismisses the misnomer and misgendering as honest mistakes, the play on identity is extended for the reader, who only has the name Schmoll to go by at first; only later do we learn that the narrator's given name is Anja (*KSL*, 32). In Siri's eyes, Anja already is "ein kluger Junge" (*KSL*, 10; a smart boy) whom she can transport, with childlike innocence, into a dreamworld where they recreate themselves and experience falling in love for the first time. Anja gradually comes to identify with masculinity and youth, and as she appropriates Siri's fantasies, she derives power from imagining herself as a boy. Threats to Anja's agency and well-being trigger Schmoll's appearance, for example after Ralf tries to force himself on her in the middle of the night, or when Ralf attacks her and Siri near the story's conclusion, a confrontation that culminates in Ralf's death (the narrative presents his demise as an accident, but there is ample evidence that Schmoll premeditates killing Ralf). Were it not for the active role that Siri plays in producing Schmoll's identity, one might be tempted to read the boy's emergence as a traumatic reaction, and trauma does in fact appear to be one of the factors contributing to his continued existence. But Schmoll is more than a defense mechanism or an effect of repression; he is also an active source of strength and self-knowledge: through him, Anja reinvents herself and acquires a sense of belonging that displaces the feelings of disconnectedness and purposelessness dominating her memories of young adulthood in unified Germany. Significantly, the very name of Anja's East German hometown, Halberstadt (Half-city), signals marginality and incompletion, suggesting a fragmentary origin that Anja must leave behind in order to come of age and achieve wholeness. The initial dislocatedness that accompanies Anja's departure from Halberstadt and arrival in the Swedish Dalsland initiates a progressive locatedness, whereby she gains confidence in embracing androgyny, disorientation, and liminality.

Antje in *Vom Dorf* is also a complex and fragmented character. The book playfully presents three distinct narrative perspectives, and Antje takes shape through the juxtaposition of these voices and the conflicting stories they tell. The reader first encounters "Antje," the editor-narrator of the framing device, written from the point of view of a character who shares the full name of the book's actual author.[16] The unnamed male impostor's letters and diary-like entries also introduce us to Antje as "ARS," an abbreviation I use to denote the character as the impostor imagines her and as she materializes in his first-person accounts. To these character names from the book, I add one of my own inventions, "Narrator," to designate the first-person narrator of the nine Christmas stories written by the imposter but attributed to Antje. None of these is to be confused with the male narrator-writer of the "Protokolle," letters, and short stories, whom I call "Writer," or the real-life author of *Vom Dorf*, who shall heretofore be referenced by the surname Strubel. Though Antje sets up an interpretive context for the story in the "Vorwort der Herausgeberin" (*VD*, 7; Editor's Foreword), she has no control over the internal narrative outside of the choice to publish it or not. She clarifies that her only editorial intervention entailed reordering the short stories by placing them in alternation with the "Protokolle" according to shared motifs and themes (*VD*, 11). Writer controls the rest of the narrative, and because Antje's frame story consists only of a foreword and is not reprised at the end, it is Writer and not Antje who has the final word. Antje's first-person perspective is therefore dislocated in that it remains external to the story, the rest of which is dominated by the alternating first-person perspectives of the older male Writer and the younger female Narrator. Writer belongs to an older generation of formerly state-employed East Germans whose careers faltered after the fall of the wall, and he has struggled to find a sense of belonging and connection with his new countrymen. Plagued by feelings of inadequacy resulting from an unfulfilling job and a failed relationship, he attempts to redefine himself as a man of letters, seeing in ARS a potential ally. ARS is also East German, though she is two decades younger than Writer and does not share his feeling of alienation, nor does she reciprocate his conviction of their intellectual affinity. The disappointed Writer retaliates against these perceived injustices by ridiculing and stalking ARS, mimicking her prose style, and recasting her in the figure of the impotent Narrator who suffers from writer's block. Because Narrator struggles to pen a praiseworthy story without reiterating common clichés, it might seem that Writer ultimately triumphs with the successful completion and publication of his provocative manuscript. However, Narrator also has special powers: she inhabits a magical-realist realm where it is possible to fly, become invisible, teleport, and time travel. And in the end, Writer calls his own accomplishments into question, shirking responsibility for his actions by suggesting that "ein Fremder" (*VD*, 196; a stranger) is to blame—or to credit, as the case may be. Despite this, Writer's success is most poignantly evident in that his manuscript unsettles Antje, so much so that she launches an investigation into his identity. But he has disappeared without a trace and those who know him refuse to help Antje find him, so all that remains to testify to his existence is his written work.

Little Brother Is Watching: Validating Narratives

Another theme shared by *Kältere Schichten* and *Vom Dorf* is intergenerational constellations of troubled and troubling East German male characters: the stalkers Ralf and Writer, and Anja's and Antje/ARS/Narrator's unseen younger brothers.[17] Though Ralf and Writer embody the novels' most visible forms of social pressure and surveillance, these themes are also linked with the unnamed little brothers, who represent living connections to family histories, traditions, and expectations. And unlike Ralf and Writer, the brothers additionally function as pivotal incentives for the narrators' self-censorship and transformations: they drive the impetus to script new posttransnational trajectories. By recasting the metaphorical "big brother" as a younger sibling, the stories interrogate the vestiges of invasive mechanisms of social control and consider possibilities for overcoming their influence over the production of identity and narrative.

Anja's two younger brothers in Halberstadt are tied up with her feelings of belonging and social alienation. In *Kältere Schichten*, these male relatives largely personify a moralizing superego: they typically receive mention at junctures when Anja is weighing decisions or measuring her own success. She grew up close to her siblings and identified strongly with them as a child; this, she suggests, explains her tomboyishness and homosexuality: "Durch ihre Nähe kam mir gar nichts anderes in den Sinn, als Frauen zu lieben" (*KSL*, 18; Because of their proximity, nothing else occurred to me than to love women). Paradoxically, Anja's queerness comes across not as a deviation but as a logical result of maintaining the status quo and internalizing the influence of male relatives. She and her brothers later grew apart, a dissonance signaled by their employment and relationship status: while the brothers find stability in postunification Germany by working in sales and getting steady girlfriends, the only constants in Anja's life prior to camp are joblessness, bar crawling, and one-night stands. Anja reacts with ambivalence to this divergence from her siblings' path: "Ich beneidete sie nicht und wußte doch, daß meine Flucht in ihren Augen ein Versagen war" (*KSL*, 22; I didn't envy them, and yet I knew that my flight was a failure in their eyes). Uninterested in living the monotonous lifestyle her brothers adopt and anxious to get away from the high unemployment, incessant construction work, and right-wing machinations that make life in Halberstadt unbearable for her, Anja escapes to Sweden. Living in Sweden liberates her from the social expectations her brothers exemplify. Norman argues that Strubel "assert[s] that reality is malleable" and "embraces the flexibility of societal boundaries," which can also be said of Anja, as she reinvents herself and her consciousness multiplies.[18] Schmoll is more self-reliant and confident, but Anja wonders what her siblings would think of her transformation, and these thoughts assign her brothers the ultimate authority to validate Schmoll's existence, which she hopes—perhaps in vain—to receive upon returning home at the end of the summer. Though the brothers would probably still see Anja in her, this perception could potentially be destabilized if they were to acknowledge her male alter ego: "Vielleicht werden mich meine Brüder manchmal, verunsichert, *Schmoll* rufen, wenn ich sie darum bitte, und dann ihre Klappe halten" (*KSL*, 188; Maybe my brothers will sometimes, unsettled, call me *Schmoll*, when I ask them to, and then keep their mouths shut). By imagining the brothers' recognition and possible acceptance of Schmoll, Anja begins to revise the scripts of social expectations in the former GDR. Because this move is tentative, it cannot be considered a fait accompli, but it opens up a possibility for the dislocated East German subject to shed burdens of the past and rewrite narratives about normalization and marginalization.

In *Vom Dorf*, the unnamed younger brother plays an even more substantial role as an instance of suppression and internalized control. The brother figure who comes to life through Writer's and Narrator's perspectives is quite different from the one editor Antje introduces briefly. Antje's brother is an ally, partnering with her in the investigation into Writer's identity: though the endeavor is futile, her brother helps search for the counterfeiter (*VD*, 9–10). We also learn from Antje that the Christmas tradition, which figures as the impetus for storytelling in the manuscript, is a real, secret family ritual: every year, she gives her brother the gift of a story to be read before the entire family underneath the Christmas tree (*VD*, 10). For Narrator, however, the brother and the tradition he upholds pose challenges, because not only does everyone already know all the Christmas stories, but her tales must be original and plausible enough to pass muster with the larger family audience. The brother represents an incentive and a social obligation: it is he who initiated and encourages the tradition, and if Narrator does not continue it appropriately, she risks earning his disappointment, or worse even, his rejection. This character constellation supports a reading of the novel as a commentary on the place of literature in supporting and interrogating social order in postunification Germany—as Finch argues, "Strubel mobilizes concepts of haunting, trauma, and repression to question whether the German past (Nazism and the communist regime of the GDR) can be overcome."[19] Several dimensions of the brother–sister relationship recall censorship and surveillance in East Germany, implying continuity with contemporary mechanisms of cultural production. Narrator's brother is a propaganda minister–like authority figure who urges the production of narratives that conform to social expectations: he decides which resources and stylistic elements she is permitted to use, pressures her to write and demands updates on her progress, and has the final say in whether the stories are permissible. He thus preserves tradition, while notably also facilitating a breach of confidentiality. It is from ARS's brother, via his ex-girlfriend, that Writer learns about the secret family ritual, which he then uses to exact revenge upon ARS. The ex-girlfriend stands in as a modern Stasi informant, transmitting intelligence to someone who is undertaking extended surveillance of ARS. The end of the novel offers relief to Antje and ARS because the surveillance operation ends with the stalker's departure, but more importantly, Narrator claims a right to greater control over the conditions of literary production. At the end of the final Christmas story, "In die Wüste geschickt" (Sent into the Desert), Narrator resolves to revise the terms of her familial obligation: "Die Bedingungen für die nächsten Jahre [sind] mit meinem Bruder noch einmal zu verhandeln" (*VD*, 189; The conditions for the coming years are to be renegotiated with my brother). This optimistic moment suggests increased agency and promises future innovations on narrative traditions, evoking literature's important social role in creating a forum in which to break with the past.

Posttransnational Transformations

In Strubel's novels, processes of creating narrative give rise to dislocations and multiple identities and highlight the transformative potential of transnational shifts. A reading of *Kältere Schichten* and *Vom Dorf* from this standpoint complements and extends existing interpretations of Strubel's fiction. In the most comprehensive existing study of Strubel's novels, Jeremiah links gender and sexuality with nationality, asserting that the writer's novelistic "disorientations" develop "queer nomadic" perspectives on German identity: "Strubel depicts the troubled homelessness of the East German subject, but also suggests the liberating potential of this condition."[20] I wish to push Jeremiah's reading a step further to contend that the dislocations these stories portray are transformative, offering new possibilities for representing and theorizing postunification East German identity. These new possibilities are transgressive posttransnational subjects, who both do and do not exist, can appear and disappear, and inhabit both a dream world and the real one, but whose presence can only be confirmed in and through narrative. They are highly mobile and often ghostly subjects, which makes them difficult to locate and pin down. *Kältere Schichten* and *Vom Dorf* thus produce new and adaptable figures capable of moving forward rather than only hesitating, looking back, or stagnating.

Anja/Schmoll's gender identity, which might best be described as queer, androgynous or transgendered, emerges as a hybrid form that answers questions about Germanness after unification. In view of discourses about German unification as a gendered contract between a feminized East and a masculinized West, it seems significant that Anja develops and embraces a masculine ego before returning home.[21] *Kältere Schichten* concludes with a final shift to the third-person "er" voice, suggesting that Schmoll survives; this ending may be reminiscent of the gendered struggle for control of the narrative in Ingeborg Bachmann's *Malina* but is more ambivalent.[22] The reader is left to decipher a puzzling narrative mosaic: as Finch points out, "Strubel's ironic dialogical poetics . . . refuses to give authority to any one voice."[23] It is unclear whether Anja or Schmoll emerges at the end, or whether, as Finch implies, they decouple and lead separate lives, or, as I suggest, they continue to coexist as multiple psyches residing in the same body.[24] The final passage presents possibilities rather than events: it imagines that Anja, when she eventually goes back home, may be perceived as "ein bißchen gaga" (*KSL*, 188; a little gaga), while assigning to Schmoll a different "Geschichte" (*KSL*, 189; a double entendre meaning both "story" and "history") than the one shared by Halberstadt's inhabitants, one that has nothing to do with the fall of the wall. Anja/Schmoll therefore multiplies rather than being reduced or fragmented, and she/he occupies the past and present as well as the future. This conclusion resists a reading as a decisively gendered allegory about East and West, instead indicating an understanding of postunification GDR identity as dynamic and hybrid, resonating with Claudia Breger's claim, in her study of Strubel's *Unter Schnee*, that "East German articulations of gender may be constituted through strategies of partial, sometimes ironically hyperbolic, adaptation to the West."[25] If Schmoll signifies a masculinized adaptation to the West, then he also denotes the disavowal of another type of masculinity in the "Toter, der uns verbindet" (*KSL*, 189; dead man who connects us): Ralf, who represents an older,

discontented East German generation that acquired a feeling of importance under socialism and faces greater challenges in coming to terms
with unification.[26] Though Ralf is crucial to Schmoll's evolution because
he acknowledges the boy's existence, and by extension Siri's too, he also
poses a hindrance to Schmoll's development by seeking to subjugate him.
Schmoll's victory over Ralf imagines, along the lines of Breger's theory
of feminine masculinity, the adaptable mixing of gender attributes as a
promising direction for the reformulation of German identities.[27]

As a "Toter," Ralf can also be understood as a metaphor for East
Germany as a whole, embodying both continuity and rupture. Such a
reading encourages an interpretation of Siri, the catalyst for Schmoll's
emergence and Ralf's demise, as an embodiment of the *Wende* ("turn,"
referring to the transitional period between the 1989 fall of the Berlin
Wall and the 1990 unification of East and West). Siri's existence may
be ephemeral and altogether uncertain—she inexplicably vanishes soon
after Ralf dies, and a possible interpretation is that Siri is not real, merely
an apparition born of the deceptive Nordic light—but it is nonetheless transformative, fundamentally altering Anja's being and opening up
posttransnational avenues for further development. Siri reassures Anja
that nothing is preordained or unchangeable, even when there are only
two options: "Man kann sich jederzeit entscheiden" (*KSL*, 42; One can
choose at any time). The novel's final line, expressing the "Wunsch, sich
aufzulösen, hinein in die kälteren Schichten der Luft" (*KSL*, 189; wish
to dissolve away, away into the colder layers of air), celebrates mobility
and the dissolution of the identity, witnessed most forcefully in Siri's
agency, imagination, and ability to dematerialize and escape categorization. After she disappears, some circumstances seem to revert to prior
conditions—the chaotic state of Siri's rundown old house, for example,
and Anja's renewed decision to return to Germany instead of staying in
Sweden—while other circumstances endure, such as the Anja/Schmoll
duality and the death of Ralf. In contrast with Finch, who asserts that
"Anja's escape . . . fails because the Nazi past and its echo in the GDR
regime catch up with her," I advocate a writerly perspective that finds
in *Kältere Schichten*'s last pages a more ambiguous, if not hopeful and
productive, movement.[28] While there is unmistakably a glance into
personal and political histories, this reflective and hypothetical gaze is
coupled with a consideration of potential paths forward. The narrative tense, which alternates between present and future, leaves open to
speculation and interpretation the question of what really happens in
the diegesis and what may or will happen after its end (*KSL*, 188–89).
Closure therefore entails a partial return to the past, to the homeland,
and a partial departure into something new and unknown.

The rotation among three narrators who are also all writers invites a
reading of *Vom Dorf* as a reflection on literary production and criticism.[29]

Together, the "Vorwort," "Protokolle," and "Weihnachtsgeschichten" forcefully decouple authorial and narrative voices. Antje's unsuccessful attempts to track down Writer and her insistence on the dissimilarity between their styles suggest that the manuscript could be a fictionalized variation on Roland Barthes's "The Death of the Author." According to Barthes, who advocates an approach to reading that refrains from assigning authority to the presumed intentions of a text's creator, "the removal of the Author . . . utterly transforms the modern text."[30] In *Vom Dorf*, the removal of the author takes figurative and literal forms: Narrator traverses the bizarre fantasy worlds of offbeat Christmas stories, Writer implies that "ein Fremder" (*VD*, 196; a stranger) is responsible and then disappears, Antje denies authorship, and the entire "forgery" is published as a book under Strubel's name. Rather than simplify the question of the text's origins, these acts of distancing cause the author-narrator to proliferate, transforming her/him from a singular instance into a multifaceted posttransnational self.[31] As characters, ARS and Writer both represent affirmative answers to the question she asks him, "Hadern Sie denn nicht manchmal mit dem, der Sie sind?" (*VD*, 43; Aren't you sometimes at odds with the one who you are?) Like author Strubel, who herself claims multiplicity—"Ich bin viele" (I am many)[32]—so is Antje also a malleable and mobile figure who takes on many forms. I suggest that perhaps Antje is indeed the author of the manuscript, and that Writer is a narrative instance who exists only in the moment of writing, which explains why he cannot be located afterward. The transgressive act of writing from the points of view of variously gendered "ich" figures inhabiting different narrative dimensions transforms Antje into the male counterfeiter and the female short story writer-narrator, while also allowing her to emerge from the transgendering and transnarrativization process as the "dead" author.

This distancing also enables the expression of cultural criticism in the historical context of early twenty-first-century Germany, particularly through the Writer's first-person perspective. His journal entries and letters to Antje provide glimpses into the wide-reaching social and psychological impacts of the historical *Wende*. Writer comes from an older generation than Antje, and unlike her, he had already built a comfortable life and career as an economic engineer in the GDR, where he had been "Teil einer Idee" (*VD*, 76; part of an idea). But he no longer feels a sense of purpose in his postunification bureaucratic job; now he just kills time, waiting for retirement. In a symbolic parallel to *Kältere Schichten*'s Anja, who hails from "Half-city," *Vom Dorf*'s Writer possesses only "die Hälfte eines Hauses" (*VD*, 176; half of a house) and struggles to divest himself of this domestic fragment, though the implications of this incompleteness link him much more clearly with Ralf than with Anja: Writer is lonely, unfulfilled, and envious of Antje's success. The half-house signals both his inability to identify with sentiments of German unity, and his longing for a unity of purpose in contemporary German society. Writer bemoans the changing cultural landscape since the fall of the wall, expressing nostalgia for a literature with a unifying (that is, socialist) message: in a letter to Antje, he writes that he would be incapable of speaking about "den Wert, . . . den deine Bücher für die Gemeinschaft besitzen, . . . die bewußtseins-bildende Rolle, die Literatur in einer Gesellschaft spielen kann, besonders in einer so herausgeforderten und zerriebenen wie der unseren" (*VD*, 74; the value that your novels have for the community, the consciousness-building role that literature can play in a society, particularly in one so challenged and bruised as ours). In his view, literature, like all other cultural products in the capitalist marketplace, has become superficial and meaningless, and though he has a deep conviction that ARS is different, he cannot change the means of production of her novels in a system that inherently devalues them. Writer nonetheless seeks to escape his torpor and overwhelming sense of dislocatedness through an imagined connection to ARS, whom he meets for the first time at a reading of her work on October 23, 2001. This historical date, exactly six weeks after 9/11, saw the announcement of Apple's first iPod, a notable step in the accelerating global electronic pop-culture revolution.[33] Since *Vom Dorf* so heavily stresses media of communication, such as oral storytelling, email messages, and cell phones, it seems meaningful that Writer first hears ARS on the same date that Apple launched its digital music player. The fraudster resembles the iPod in that he is unable to create new poetry: obsessed with ARS and the idea of copying her style so precisely that the deception is imperceptible, he can only shuffle and replay what he has already read. We can recognize in him a critique of plagiarism and copyright violations, among other contemporary abuses of rapidly proliferating technologies of reproduction. Perhaps Strubel's novel, which narrates the period between 2001 and late 2005 and appeared in late 2007, was reacting in part to the European Pirate Party movement, which began with the foundation of the Swedish Pirate Party in January 2006, followed by the establishment of similar parties in Austria and Germany later that year. The Pirate Party platform promotes open content and supports copyright law reform. However, the increased electronic availability and unlimited reproducibility of longer texts has undoubtedly contributed to the rising number of literary plagiarism accusations and controversies, which Antje openly criticizes in her "Vorwort" (*VD*, 11).

Vom Dorf's ARS inspires and embodies the transformative possibilities that her counterfeiter attempts to harness. Like Anja's first encounter with Siri in *Kältere Schichten*, Writer's first meeting with ARS causes a profound dislocation, one that in this case may seem at first to hold the potential of transformation but eventually fails to deliver on that promise. Unlike her stalker, ARS in not held captive by the national history and reproduction compulsion that have such a powerful grasp on him.

In response to a fan's question about what entitles her to appropriate a history that is not her own by writing about events she did not herself experience, ARS claims that her East German biography does not bind her, but rather frees her to experiment with new possibilities:

> Ob es angesichts der Tatsache, daß ein Land, das ihn viele Jahre geprägt habe, eines Tages verschwinden könne, ohne daß er mit verschwunden sei, nicht ein Trugschluß wäre, anzunehmen, solche Prägungen würden die Identität eines Menschen tatsächlich so stark beeinflussen, wie alle glaubten. Ob nicht vielmehr das Flüchtige daran deutlich würde. Für sie sei das Verschwinden all der Verhaltensregeln, Glaubenssätze und des für sicher erachteten Wissens geradezu eine Aufforderung, sich zu ändern, vielleicht sogar, sich neu zu erfinden. (VD, 43)

> [If it wouldn't be a false conclusion, in light of the fact that a land that had shaped him for many years could disappear one day without him disappearing along with it, to assume that such effects would actually influence a person's identity as strongly as everyone believed. If it weren't instead the ephemerality of it that became apparent. For her, the disappearance of all the rules of conduct, doctrines, and the knowledge that had been considered certain was actually an invitation to change, perhaps even to reinvent oneself.]

Antje experiences the posttransnational moment as "an invitation" (the German word Aufforderung can also translate more forcefully as "order" or "challenge"), one that she enthusiastically accepts, for it allows her to continually redefine herself on her own terms. It also gives her occasion to celebrate the transience, not just of the East German past, but also of everything that follows. Upon hearing this, Writer zealously takes ARS's appeal to heart, imagining that he becomes unfettered from historical burdens—"Ich fühlte mich frei von mir" (VD, 44; I felt free of myself)—only later to arrive at the conclusion that he cannot let go because "zu viele Dinge passiert sind" (VD, 196; too many things have happened). He opts to preserve his real memories instead of inventing new ones, which not only makes him an ill-suited writer of fiction but also implies a misplaced conviction in the impartiality of historical and biographical narratives.[34] In the social ruptures of the Wende and the void of identity that ensues, it would seem, for Writer at least, that "such a lack of stability does not spell liberating transformation, but madness," as Jeremiah contends.[35] However, if we read Writer as one of Antje's many literary creations, then in view of the above citation we can understand him not as a failure, but rather as a success: he is another ephemeral embodiment of a possible response to these historical changes, one that the narrative ultimately dismisses as untenable and unproductive. Ironically, the languishing Writer becomes a social specimen in the novel's investigation of the opportunities opened up by envisioning diverse postwall subjectivities.

Writer additionally functions as a character foil for the dynamic figures that the quirky Christmas stories introduce, especially Narrator and her lover Berenice. Even as Narrator repeatedly struggles to find creative inspiration, several short stories find her undergoing transformations, rescripting her postunification life, and imagining gravity-defying escapes from daily conundrums. As Jeremiah points out, Strubel's novel transports us into "a queer time and place"—referring to Judith Halberstam's theory of the challenges transgender lifestyles pose to dominant cultural forms—where "the associative logic of the dream dominates."[36] Not only do these stories enact radical breaks with narrative traditions, but they also have their protagonists accomplishing geographically impossible feats that depict the American West, Berlin-Mitte and Brandenburg, and Siberia as if they were contiguous spaces, stops on a virtual train route where passengers could embark and disembark at whim. Norman argues that Strubel's characters "travel in search of exits and loopholes and take on different identities," and in *Vom Dorf* transportation and transformation are intertwined processes.[37] Adventure goes hand in hand with masquerade and self-discovery: Narrator, Berenice, and the other enigmatic figures populating the hybrid fantasy–reality tales they traverse play diverse roles as angels and devils; sloganeers and salespeople; hostages and terrorists; tourists and spies; and murder victims and detectives. In so doing, they become self-aware producers of and participants in "Text*entropie*" (*VD*, 168; text entropy, emphasis in the original). The motivating and magical Berenice can be read as a personification of literary inspiration. She encourages Narrator to envision unprecedented ways of being while maintaining consciousness of her own status as a fictional character existing in language; this awareness, however, does not stop her from claiming agency and naming the terms of her embodiedness and mobility. Because Berenice changes her accent at will, sometimes talking in thick Berliner dialect and at other times using standard German, she decides whether to play the East German or just the German in evolving contemporary contexts. By thusly dismissing and displacing Writer's complaints about literature's lost social significance since the fall of the wall, *Vom Dorf* comes across as an ode to the fertile ground of postunification identity and narrative in their many possible posttransnational forms.

Conclusion

Antje Rávic Strubel's posttransnational fiction works through German pasts from a range of perspectives and envisions multiple possible futures. In *Kältere Schichten der Luft* and *Vom Dorf*, the author depicts older men as delusional East Germans unable to adjust to changing social circumstances, younger brothers as moralizing superegos and defenders of tradition, and queer androgynous women as adaptable citizens of unified Europe who break free from social expectations. These are themes that Strubel's two 2007 novels share, in varying forms, with her other five books, from the first, *Offene Blende* (2001), to the most recent, *Sturz der Tage in die Nacht* (When Days Plunge into Night, 2011). Through these themes, Strubel not only develops critiques of contemporary culture but also offers posttransnational subjects that unfetter themselves from the burdens of recent German history and transport readers into alternate realms. In so doing, Strubel rewrites the stakes of twenty-first-century German literature, celebrating the proliferation of identity and the creation of unconventional narratives.

Strubel's work demonstrates the significance and potential of posttransnational literature in revisiting and revising accepted narratives about nation, citizenship, and belonging in a rapidly globalizing world. Labels and identifications such as East and West German did not simply dissolve or become obsolete with the disappearance of the national border that separated the two Germanies for four decades, but rather gained additional meaning after unification. For Strubel's characters, as well as for many Germans, the assertion of an East German identity is today as important as the formation of a unified German identity: maintaining both positionalities can involve adaptation, playfulness, and evolution. As national boundaries continue to disappear and shift, and as new nations and transnational entities are founded, citizens are actively renegotiating the terms of their belonging in and through literature. For Strubel's protagonists, this may present challenges, but it is also an opportunity. The dynamic and transformative figures that *Kältere Schichten* and *Vom Dorf* offer are more than fictions of mobility and creativity: they embody ways of envisioning global citizenship in the twenty-first century, with all of the possibilities and limitations that this entails.

Notes

1 Stuart Taberner, "Transnationalism in Contemporary German-Language Fiction by Nonminority Writers," *Seminar* 47, no. 5 (2011): 625.

2 Taberner, "Transnationalism," 641.

3 Erika M. Nelson, "A Path of Poetic Potentials: Coordinates of German Lyric Identity in the Poetry of Zafer Şenocak," in *German Literature in a New Century: Trends, Traditions, Transitions, Transformations*, ed. Katharina Gerstenberger and Patricia Herminghouse (New York: Berghahn, 2008), 158–59, emphasis in the original.

4 See, for instance, Paul Cooke, *Representing East Germany since Unification: From Colonization to Nostalgia* (Oxford: Berg, 2005); and Wolfgang Dümcke and Fritz Vilmar, *Kolonialisierung der DDR: Kritische Analysen und Alternativen des*

Einigungsprozesses, 3rd ed. (Münster: Agenda, 1996). Katrin Sieg's characterization of unified Berlin as a postcolonial space also resonates with this discourse. See Katrin Sieg, "Postcolonial Berlin? Pieke Biermann's Crime Novels as Globalization Critique," *Studies in Twentieth and Twenty-First Century Literature* 28, no. 1 (2004): 152–82.

[5] Cooke, *Representing East Germany*, 7.

[6] See, for instance, Paul Cooke, "'GDR Literature' in the Berlin Republic," in *Contemporary German Fiction: Writing in the Berlin Republic*, ed. Stuart Taberner (Cambridge: Cambridge University Press, 2007), 56–71; and Stuart Taberner, *German Literature of the 1990s and Beyond: Normalization and the Berlin Republic* (Rochester, NY: Camden House, 2005), especially 33–67.

[7] The oft-cited claim that the "Mauer im Kopf" will persist long after the German border disappears originated in Peter Schneider's 1982 novel *Der Mauerspringer*. See Peter Schneider, *Der Mauerspringer* (Darmstadt: Luchterhand, 1982), 102. Schneider argues that the process of dismantling the mental wall will last for another generation after the destruction of the physical wall, and further asserts that this process is a two-way street: "It is not merely about Westerners bringing Easterners into the fold; there is also what I call the 'Easternization' of the West going on." Peter Schneider, "Tearing Down Berlin's Mental Wall," *New York Times*, August 12, 2011, *New York Times: The Opinion Pages*, accessed May 10, 2013, http://www.nytimes.com/2011/08/13/opinion/tearing-down-berlins-mental-wall.html?_r=2&. For a recent perspective on this phenomenon and the persistence of stereotypes about East and West Germans, see Anja Goerz, *Der Osten ist ein Gefühl: Über die Mauer im Kopf* (Munich: Deutscher Taschenbuch Verlag, 2014).

[8] Katharina Gerstenberger and Jana Evans Braziel, "After the Berlin Wall: Realigned Worlds, Invisible Lines, and Incalculable Remnants," introduction to *After the Berlin Wall: Germany and Beyond*, ed. Katharina Gerstenberger and Jana Evans Braziel (New York: Palgrave Macmillan, 2011), 2.

[9] Taberner does not name a single woman among the historical writers who, he asserts, "have traversed and translated foreign cultures while probing fixed notions of 'Germanness'"; this oversight is likely unintentional—but does merit mentioning and correction. Taberner, "Transnationalism," 626. However, Taberner does begin his essay with an analysis of Judith Hermann's "Rote Korallen," in which both the narrator's femininity and her ancestors' East–West migrations carry critical weight, and he mentions texts by a few other female authors, including Herta Müller, Kathrin Röggla, Dagmar Leupold, Katrin Dorn, Juli Zeh, Karin Duve, and Elke Naters. These references notwithstanding, women writers represent a small minority in comparison to the dozens of male writers and texts Taberner cites in this article.

[10] Helen Finch, "Gender, Identity, and Memory in the Novels of Antje Rávic Strubel," *Women in German Yearbook* 28 (2012): 93.

[11] Emily Jeremiah, *Nomadic Ethics in Contemporary Women's Writing in German: Strange Subjects* (Rochester, NY: Camden House, 2012), 115.

[12] Beret Norman, "Antje Rávic Strubel's Ambiguities of Identity as Social Disruption," *Women in German Yearbook* 28 (2012): 67.

[13] Antje Rávic Strubel, *Kältere Schichten der Luft* (Frankfurt am Main: S. Fischer, 2007). The mysterious girl never tells Anja her name, instead suggesting that she wants Anja to make one up (59). Anja decides to call her Siri (88), but then questions whether she got the name right, believing it should have been Iris (94). Further references to this volume appear in the text with the abbreviation *KSL*. All translations from German to English are my own.

[14] Antje Rávic Strubel, *Vom Dorf: Abenteuergeschichten zum Fest* (Munich: Deutscher Taschenbuch Verlag, 2007), 7–11. Further references to this volume appear in the text with the abbreviation *VD*. All translations from German to English are my own.

[15] Norman, "Antje Rávic Strubel's Ambiguities," 75.

[16] My interpretation differs from that of Jeremiah, who reads Antje as identical with the book's author. See Jeremiah, *Nomadic Ethics*, 120–21.

[17] The affinities between Ralf and Writer have already been discussed by Emily Jeremiah, who reads these melancholy, anxious, and disturbed figures as suggestive of a problematic concept of older East German masculinity. See Jeremiah, *Nomadic Ethics*, 115–22.

[18] Norman, "Antje Rávic Strubel's Ambiguities," 67.

[19] Finch, "Gender, Identity, and Memory," 82.

[20] Jeremiah, *Nomadic Ethics*, 98, 102.

[21] See, for instance, Ingrid Sharp, "Male Privilege and Female Virtue: Gendered Representations of the Two Germanies," *New German Studies* 18, no. 1/2 (1994): 87–106; and Ingrid Sharp, "To the Victor the Spoils: Sleeping Beauty's Sexual Awakening," in *Women and the "Wende": Social Effects and Cultural Reflections of the German Unification Process*, ed. Elizabeth Boa and Janet Wharton (Amsterdam: Rodopi, 1994), 177–88.

[22] In *Malina*, which also includes a final shift from the "ich" to the "er"-perspective, the male ego kills the female narrator, and it is with him that the novel ends. Ingeborg Bachmann, *Malina* (1971; reprint, Frankfurt am Main: Suhrkamp, 2004), 337–38.

[23] Finch, "Gender, Identity, and Memory," 93.

[24] Finch, "Gender, Identity, and Memory," 94.

[25] Breger, Claudia, "Hegemony, Marginalization, and Feminine Masculinity: Antje Rávic Strubel's *Unter Schnee*," *Seminar* 44, no.1 (2008): 167.

[26] As a former soldier in the NVA (*Nationale Volksarmee*; the National People's Army of East Germany), where he worked as a border guard, Ralf is complicit in maintaining oppressive forms of order under socialist rule. After unification, he lost his job and his wife, experienced long periods of unemployment, and viewed his daughter a living link to "seiner sozialistischen Heimat" (*KSL*, 38; his socialist homeland).

[27] See Breger, "Hegemony, Marginalization."

[28] Finch, "Gender, Identity, and Memory," 93.

[29] Many aspects of the production and reception of literature come into play in *Vom Dorf*. Though I am unable to discuss them all here, it bears mention that the

novel touches upon everything from creative inspiration, writing, research, archival work, editing, and translation; to legalities, rejections, marketing, and fandom. The story is also replete with intertextual references to many forms of writing, from the nineteenth-century literature of Eichendorff and Dickens, to contemporary pop culture texts, such as Madonna songs and advertising slogans.

[30] Roland Barthes. "The Death of the Author," in *Image—Music—Text*, trans. Stephen Heath (New York: Hill and Wang, 1977), 145. In this seminal text from 1967, Barthes praises the likes of Bertolt Brecht, whose self-conscious distancing makes it difficult to locate the author in his texts.

[31] A similar playfulness with proliferating narrative voices characterizes Strubel's earlier novel, *Tupolew 134*. For discussions of the various voices and narrative layers in that novel, see Norman, "Antje Rávic Strubel's Ambiguities"; and Lea Müller-Dannhausen, "'. . . scheiß neue Lust am Erzählen!': Untersuchungen zum Erzählen in Terézia Moras *Alle Tage* und Antje Rávic Strubels *Tupolew 134*," in *Zwischen Inszenierung und Botschaft: Zur Literatur deutschsprachiger Autorinnen ab Ende des 20. Jahrhunderts*, ed. Ilse Nagelschmidt, Lea Müller-Dannhausen, and Sandy Feldbacher (Berlin: Frank & Timme, 2006), 197–214.

[32] Antje Rávic Strubel, "Die Übersetzerin der Übersetzerin," Workshop (Women in German Conference, Shawnee Inn, Shawnee on Delaware, PA; October 26, 2013). Here, "ich" could refer to the author Strubel, to her writing persona, or to her use of the "ich" narrative voice; the context of the citation leaves all of these possibilities open.

[33] From the point of view of 2015, it is also tempting to read Strubel's Siri in *Kältere Schichten* as a navigator not unlike Apple's Siri, the personal assistant introduced in 2010.

[34] In this novel as in others, particularly *Tupolew 134*, Strubel conveys her theory that "memory is always a story" by using rotating narrators and a multilayered structure: "We construct every event by way of talking about it." Antje Rávic Strubel, "'Memory Is Always a Story': An Interview with Antje Rávic Strubel," interview by Beret Norman and Katie Sutton, *Women in German Yearbook* 28 (2012): 103–4. See also Müller-Dannhausen, ". . . scheiß neue Lust"; and Norman, "Antje Rávic Strubel's Ambiguities."

[35] Jeremiah, *Nomadic Ethics*, 122.

[36] Jeremiah, *Nomadic Ethics*, 116. See also Judith Halberstam, *In a Queer Time and Place: Transgender Bodies, Subcultural Lives* (New York: New York University Press, 2005).

[37] Norman, "Antje Rávic Strubel's Ambiguities," 76.

10: Cultural Dichotomies and Lived Transnationalism in Recent Russian-German Narratives

Anke S. Biendarra

TRANSNATIONALISM IS A SLIPPERY CONSTRUCT that means different things in different contexts and academic disciplines. The expansion of the semantic field of the concept, both geographically and theoretically, has also led to a loss of specificity.[1] Originally, the term was used as a by-product of economic globalization and referred almost exclusively to multinational corporations whose commercial and financial activities transcended national boundaries and the controls exerted by the nation-state.[2] Over the last twenty-five years or so, the concept of transnationalism has gained traction especially in the social sciences and in interdisciplinary fields, such as international relations, gender studies, and cultural studies.

As a manifestation of the processes of globalization,[3] which mobilizes capital, people, goods, and energies across national boundaries, transnationalism identifies the tensions that globalizing processes mean for the nation-state and its inhabitants. This is especially true in the German context, where inclusion into and exclusion from the nation have been historically volatile and continue to be fraught, despite new legislation, such as the Nationality Act (2000) and the Immigration Act (2005). Transnationalism, then, opens up issues of territoriality and nationality for renewed questioning.

Transnational literature—for a start understood as texts dealing with characters, movements, and forces that cross national boundaries, translate identities and cultures, and complicate the political, social, and cultural fabric of nations and people—has experienced a growing popular and critical attention in Germany, Austria, and Switzerland. In terms of the literary market place, we might suggest that the literature of the "transnational turn"[4] was for the first millennial decade what *Fräuleinwunder* (Miss Miracle), new realism, and New German Pop Literature were for the late 1990s.[5] This positioning has not only altered the societal discourse about literature, but also the internal, linguistic, and thematic topography of the literatures of the German-speaking countries since the 1990s.[6]

This is especially due to the many authors who write in languages different from their mother tongues and have brought about structural changes of the literary scenes by breaking open incrusted categories. Hyphenated authors, that is, migrant, minority, and nonethnic German-language writers, were the primary focus of literary criticism in analyzing issues of transnationalism. In recognition that nonminority writers also experience and write transnationally, as Stuart Taberner has suggested,[7] and might transcend national, ethnic, and cultural boundaries, imaginaries, and identities, the category of transnational writing has now become quite inclusive.

Not limiting transnational writing to texts that speak of deterritorialization and displacement and employ aesthetic means that are indebted to an author's transculturality also makes it possible to redefine an important aspect of transnational writing. Transnational literature in a German-language context today might still speak primarily for those "paranational" communities that exist alongside the citizens of the host country. But it does not still operate outside the national canon, contrary to what Azade Seyhan posited in her 2001 seminal study *Writing Outside the Nation*.[8] After over fifty years of immigration history and through the conceptual permutations of "Gastarbeiterliteratur," "Secondo-Literatur," "interkulturelle Literatur" or "Chamisso-Literatur," transnational literature has challenged notions of what constitutes German-language literature, both in the public sphere and in institutions.[9] By disrupting the orderly systems of national canons and national literatures and taking seriously multicultural realities and complexities, it thus lives up to the tasks of a new World Literature[10] that Elke Sturm-Trigonakis has identified.[11] A continuously changing canon will handle the addition of more openly hybrid texts dealing with displacement, war, mobility, identity issues, a globalized world and often, but not exclusively, the "processes by which immigrants forge multistranded social relations that link together their societies of origin and settlement."[12]

To exemplify how transnational identities and experiences, multiculturalism, and plurilingualism map onto the literary sphere and how they are appropriated thematically and aesthetically, this essay focuses on recent Russian-German prose texts. Its main proposition is the introduction of "lived transnationalism"; a category that demonstrates the permutations of transnationalism as a workaday phenomenon in autobiographically inspired, realistically narrated texts. My analysis starts from the observation that many of the narratives in question pick out the differences between Russian and German cultures as a central theme. The study identifies these cultural dichotomies between the German mainstream and the Russian minority and the ways in which they are constructed, overcome, or elided. Moreover, it illustrates the ways in which the literary characters—many of them migratory and transnational—struggle to bridge the gulf between two cultures. Often, cultural stereotyping by the host culture undermines the process of social integration and establishing a meaningful and contented existence in the new home. Yet it also appears as a commonplace strategy of the migratory characters themselves. It is used as a primary textual means to characterize *both* German mainstream society *and* the Russian minority and their respective understanding.

On a cultural macro level, focusing on disparities between the two cultures might to some extent reflect an ambivalence that has characterized the relationship between Russia and Western Europe for centuries. For example, Boris Groys has demonstrated that Russian (intellectual) history is defined by a lack of its "own" tradition and is a compound of elements taken from Western culture; consequently, it appears as "the other of the West."[13] On a textual micro level however, stressing dichotomies begs the question to what extent transnationalism in these texts truly appears as a "*facility*," that is, the ability to move easily between different cultures.[14] My goal is to illustrate how cultural oppositions are negotiated and to mark different positions on the broad spectrum of transnationalism as a lived reality in selected texts.

The degree to which the texts rely on binary categories with regard to national belonging, integration, and identity building varies considerably. However, two distinct positions will be highlighted. The first, encountered here in Lena Gorelik's *Meine weißen Nächte* (My White Nights, 2004) and Alina Bronsky's *Scherbenpark* (2008; *Broken Glass Park*, 2010) respectively, presents immigrant and host culture as innately dichotomous. The two narratives rely openly on cultural stereotyping as a means of characterizing both German mainstream society and the Russian minority. This choice begs the question whether identities continue to be constructed in opposition to one another or whether the separation is overcome through the characters' conscious effort at "integration" into mainstream German society or through an ironic stance that undercuts cultural binaries. In a second, less common position, exemplified here by Olga Grjasnowa's *Der Russe ist einer, der Birken liebt* (2012; *All Russians Love Birch Trees*, 2014), the characters skip a few of the usual steps of integration and transgress notions of origin and transnational belonging altogether, thereby creating what B. Venkat Mani has called "cosmopolitical claims"[15] and identities that resist binary identification.

Russian-German Literature in the Aughts and Beyond

Wladimir Kaminer (born 1967 in Moscow) is a very popular and—with about twenty books to his name in about as many years—one of the most prolific writers in Germany today. He has become the figurehead of Russian-German literature and cornered its market, not least because he has managed to make his binational identity into a brand. He also has led the way in using clichés and cultural stereotypes about Germans and Russians alike as an aesthetic strategy, which is not only something that has brought him a fair share of criticism,[16] but also an aspect most Russian-German narratives continue to play with. Literary scholars have analyzed the ways in which Kaminer performs both his German identity and his Russian persona[17] and added to our understanding of his ubiquitous presence in the German public as a Russian who can always be counted on for a quip about his compatriots.

While Kaminer put Russian-German literature on the map, in recent years female writers have emerged as more interesting literary voices, such as Alina Bronsky (born 1978 in Yekaterinburg/Sverdlovsk, Ural), Marjana Gaponenko (born 1981 in Odessa, Ukraine), Lena Gorelik (born 1981 in Leningrad), Olga Grjasnowa (born 1984 in Baku, Azerbaijan), Eleonora Hummel (born 1970 in Tselinograd, Kazakhstan), Olga Martynova (born 1962 in Krasnoyarsk, Siberia), Katja Petrowskaja (born 1970 in Kiev), Julya Rabinowich (born 1970 in Leningrad), and Nellja Veremej (born 1963 in Leningrad). Many of their debuts are what I will call "arrival narratives," that is, partially autobiographical literary accounts of the immigration experience. The texts illustrate personal attempts to navigate an unknown language and often unwelcoming host culture, as well as the need to come to terms with the loss of former lives in which discrimination (often due to their Jewish heritage) or ethnic conflicts loomed large. Living between languages and cultures implies, at least for a while, negotiating alliances and dichotomies between the Russian home culture and the German host culture. The relationship between the two and the aesthetic forms a lived transnationalism takes are the heuristic points of departure in the following reading of three different debut novels.

"Ab da wird alles gut"—*Meine weißen Nächte*

On the varied spectrum of a lived transnationalism, Lena Gorelik's 2004 debut signifies a position that advocates for a conscious bridging of binary oppositions between Russian home and German host culture by means of integration, which in Gorelik's understanding denotes a process that involves and challenges immigrant and host in equal measure.[18] Considerably lighter in both tone and subject matter than Bronsky's and Grjasnowa's novels, *Meine weißen Nächte* is the first-person arrival narrative of Anja Buchmann, a Jewish "Kontingentflüchtling" (quota refugee[19]) from Leningrad (since 1991 called Saint Petersburg again) who settles with her family in Germany in 1992. She studies in Munich and lives with her German boyfriend Jan in a content and well-rehearsed, if somewhat conventional relationship. When her first love and boyfriend, fellow

Russian Ilja, appears back in her life and offers her a job alongside him as a guide for Russian tourists, it throws Anja into emotional turmoil, mostly because charming and flamboyant Ilja is the opposite of nonromantic, clearheaded Jan. The ensuing conventional love conflict between Anja and Ilja makes up one strand of the narrative; the other (much more interesting one) presents her interspersed memories of growing up in the crumbling Soviet Union in the late 1980s and her early experiences as a child immigrant in Ludwigsburg.[20]

Anja's narrative illustrates a common problem of transnational characters, whose identity cannot easily be defined via origin or national belonging. Identity in general is a relational matter that implies alterity; it is constructed both from the anticipatory expectation of others and the desires of the individual. While this observation is somewhat of a topos, transnational characters in particular need to find a balance between social integration and their own identity beyond preconfigured societal roles and models. In Anja's case, as in most other arrival narratives, social integration is facilitated or hindered by formative experiences in school. Contrary to the characters in the other novels discussed here, Anja encounters little discrimination. She first attends a remedial class specifically for Russian quota refugees before moving on to the regular class in a German elementary school, which contains a number of immigrant students from Eastern Europe. The educators are for the most part helpful and understanding; her first teacher Herr Wolf even makes her part of a writing club and encourages her to write a story she titles "Meine weißen Nächte," foreshadowing her later profession of "Shriftstela" (writer).[21]

Russian culture is primarily represented through Anja's close-knit family, which consists of her older brother Andrej, their parents, and their eighty-seven-year-old grandmother, who lives with them. Anja's stories about her loud and boisterous family correspond with and confirm Western notions of Eastern European culture. The family is closer-knit than the typical German family (as exemplified in Jan) and unconditionally supportive of one another, interested in high culture and social advancement, hardworking, plucky, and thrifty. Food plays a major role as a token of mutual appreciation and love and as a catalyst for social bonding experiences (*MwN*, 69–71). The book even includes a recipe for Russian potato salad in the end, showing how "ethnicity has taken on the form of a consumable food item."[22] Especially Anja's mother fits the cliché of the Russian-Jewish mother who is so focused on the well-being of her loved ones that she regularly alienates her adult children with her overprotectiveness, inquisitiveness, and bossiness (*MwN*, 30–34). In *Meine weißen Nächte*, Russian culture is reduced to those folkloristic and cultural elements that can easily be juxtaposed with German culture, despite the fact that Anja herself is annoyed with the German attitude of taking "Russen für Außerirdische" (*MwN* 25; Russians for aliens). While the book's goal seems to be the undermining of Russian clichés, the character herself uses her Russianness when it suits her purposes, for example, when she is flirting with German men (*MwN*, 24–29). Gorelik—much like Kaminer—exploits clichés in the narrative to a certain point, although she lacks his ironic stance.

Attempts at social integration lead to an omission of vital factors that have shaped and constitute the identity of the migratory character. Anja avoids talking about her Russian background and the fact that she was a quota refugee, even with her best friend Lara. Only Jan knows certain aspects his girlfriend has shared with him, but when he references her experience as a refugee, she is generally not pleased: "Kannst Du deine verdammte Klappe nicht halten? . . . Ich will nicht über das Wohnheim reden. Das Wohnheim führt zu unangenehmen Fragen. Es setzt mich ab, macht mich von einer russischen Exotin zu einem Fremdkörper." (*MwN*, 17–18; Why can't you just shut your damn trap? I don't want to talk about the residence hall. It leads to uncomfortable questions. It sets me apart—instead of being an exotic Russian, it makes me into a foreign body.) In order to avoid being singled out, Anja decides early on to leave her Russianness behind and become German: She quickly learns the language perfectly, observes holidays, and adapts to customs and idiosyncrasies. The often unpleasant memories of Russia, such as food shortages and endless standing in line; the experience of poverty and economic and social differentiation as the Soviet Union begins to unravel; and discrimination and anti-Semitism are nevertheless not forgotten. They are instead "vergraben" (*MwN*, 140; buried) and not even discussed with close family members. Whenever Anja's parents speak about the past and reveal how their values and interests are inflected by their Russianness, she is easily annoyed and disengages. The use of the present tense in Anja's St. Petersburg memories might primarily be an artistic device to create a more dynamic narrative, but it also illustrates the staying power of those memories.

Anja's attempt to extinguish part of her own identity also leads to a conflict with Ilja and is a big part of her ultimately deciding against her Russian side. Ilja accuses her of wanting to be as "unrussisch" (non-Russian) as possible, of neglecting her double heritage and ensuing hybridity, to which she replies that the bigger part of her simply is German (*MwN*, 193). After going through a stocktaking process of her present and former relationships with Jan and Ilja that involves an amorous Parisian adventure with the latter, a conscience-stricken Anja decides to return to her somewhat boring, but content Munich life with Jan. Choosing the ethnic German boyfriend is the adult cementation of her efforts at integration that began as a child of eleven years old.

Gorelik's arrival novel in the end turns out to be "the quintessential immigrant success story."[23] Anja's decision-making process is interspersed with memories of her family's successful inclusion into a middle-class life in Germany, which entails the family's own four-bedroom apartment, a solid career for both parents, and friendships of all family members with ethnic Germans: "Ich veranstalte an meinem Geburtstag eine große Party in unserer Wohnung, zu der ich alle meine deutschen Freunde aus der Schule einlade. Zum Wohnheim gehe ich nie wieder." (*MwN*, 260; On my birthday, I throw a big party in our apartment and invite all my German friends from school. I am never going back to the residence hall.)

Entertaining stories of contented integration into German society, such as those by Kaminer and Gorelik, are rare in this subcategory of transnational writing. The relative simplicity with which both authors describe complex processes of deterritorialization and negotiating old and new identities might be owed to the category of *Belletristik*, that is, plot-driven, not overly literary fiction.

A World Divided—*Scherbenpark*

Alina Bronsky's widely acclaimed debut *Scherbenpark* (2008; *Broken Glass Park*, 2010)[24] tells the story of Sascha Naimann, a teenage Russian immigrant. The setting is a public housing development inhabited by Russian immigrants, ironically called "Solitär" (Solitaire),[25] on the outskirts of Frankfurt am Main. Two years prior to the time of the novel's action, Vadim—Sascha's mother's abusive second husband and father of her younger siblings Anton and Alissa—had shot and killed her mother and her German boyfriend Harry. The children have continued to live in the apartment where their private horror took place, being watched over by Vadim's cousin Maria from Novosibirsk. Sascha's only goal is to revenge her mother's death and kill Vadim, captured in the startling opening paragraph: "Manchmal denke ich, ich bin die Einzige in unserem Viertel, die noch vernünftige Träume hat. Ich habe zwei, und für keinen brauche ich mich zu schämen. Ich will Vadim töten. Und ich will ein Buch über meine Mutter schreiben." (*S*, 9; Sometimes I think I'm the only one in our neighborhood with any worthwhile dreams. I have two, and there's no reason to be ashamed of either one. I want to kill Vadim. And I want to write a book about my mother. [*BGP*, 11])

When Sascha sees a newspaper article sympathetically describing Vadim's life in jail, she seeks out and confronts the newspaper's editor Volker Trebur, who recognizes that the young woman is in crisis and offers help. She requests to stay with him for a while in order to escape Maria and her affair with a neighbor. At his home, she meets his son Felix who suffers from a chronic lung condition, making him somewhat of an outsider. Sascha eventually has sex with him, even though she also has feelings for his father. While Volker and Felix are on vacation, Sascha meets a young man, who turns out to be a right-wing extremist. After she has sex with him, she takes him to a group of young Russians from the neighborhood, led by her nemesis and neighbor Peter, who beat him up. She then skates around town in a self-destructive daze. When the newspaper subsequently reveals that Vadim has committed suicide in jail, thereby thwarting Sascha's fantasy to avenge her mother and Harry, Sascha takes out her frustration in a violent fight with her neighbors, which leaves her unconscious and hospitalized.

The novel presents the Russian home and the German environment as two separate spheres that do not interconnect, constructing dichotomies that are almost impossible to bridge. Sascha is intensely critical and full of contempt for her social environment. She cannot relate to the aspirations of her fellow Russian immigrants, avoids hanging out with the resident youth at the nearby "Scherbenpark" and has little understanding for the problems of other Russians to integrate into German society: "Ich hasse den Solitär. Ich hasse diese Leute. Ich kann nichts dafür, und sie können noch weniger dafür. Alles arme Schweine." (S, 199; I hate the Emerald. I hate the people here. There's nothing I can do about it, and nothing they can do either. They're a bunch of impoverished pigs. [BGP, 154]) At the same time, she does not shy away from verbal and physical confrontation in an attempt to "ward off trauma instead of working through it and to access codes of masculinity to cover her own vulnerability."[26] When she gets into a physical altercation with fellow Russian Peter who threatens to rape her, she challenges him in front of his cronies, ironically commenting on Peter's broken German and joblessness: "'Ich kann nur mit Männern, die lesen können,' presse ich zwischen den Zähnen hervor. . . . 'Daran wird es scheitern, Peterchen. Hartz IV und gebrochenes Deutsch machen mich einfach nicht an. Da habe ich Orgasmus-Probleme.'" (S, 195; 'I only sleep with men who can read,' I sneer. . . . 'Which means you're out, dear Peter. I'm afraid welfare checks and broken German just don't get me off' [BGP, 152]). Here and in other scenes, Russian maleness is coded negative as dark, violent, even degenerate.

Bronsky appropriates stereotypes with which Russia has been connected since the sixteenth century, when Western travelers described both the splendor and wealth of the Muscovite Empire, as well as alcoholism, debauchery, cruelty, rudeness and xenophobia, alongside piety and superstition, as central to Russian character culture.[27] Yet in her description of Russian masculinity, Bronsky also activates contemporary global pop culture, an aspect that surely contributed to her novels being quickly translated and globally successful. Samples from international bestsellers, such as Stieg Larsson's *Millennium Trilogy* (2005–7, featuring the fearless heroine Lisbeth Salander and subsequently made into very successful movies), or cinematic blockbusters, such as *Eastern Promises* (2007, dir. David Cronenberg), show that stereotypes of reckless and violent Russians are not only very much alive in the Western imagination, but also equal commercial success.

The novel presents social stratification as a key determinant for positive integration. Sascha is the only non-German student in her class at a private catholic *Gymnasium* that accepted her, in Sascha's words, "um ein bisschen Integration zu proben" (*S*, 14; to try to create a little diversity, *BGP*, 15). Although she is acutely aware how different she is from the well-heeled middle-class German students frequenting the school, she has no problems fitting in. Everyone is nice to her because they do not have any contact with immigrants, which makes her the token foreigner, so to speak. But instead of feeling victimized by her status as an outsider, Sascha seizes the opportunities of a free education, which she recognizes as her ticket to a better life. Like Gorelik's main character, she learns German in record time and becomes a straight-A student, recognizing that language skills are the key to everyday survival. Consequently she has little understanding for her Russian neighbors' lack of discipline and ambitiousness in school: "Wir sprechen Russisch miteinander, aber ihres ist fast so schlecht wie ihr Deutsch. Ich finde es eh merkwürdig, in welchem Kauderwelsch die Leute hier manchmal daherreden. Na gut, die neue Sprache können sie nicht lernen—aber wie schaffen sie es, auch die alte zu vergessen?" (*S*, 208; We speak Russian to each other, but her Russian is almost as bad as her German. It's strange, the gibberish people around here speak in. Okay, so they can't learn the new language. But how do they manage to forget the old one? [*BGP*, 161])

In contrast to the dilapidated, hopeless environment of the Russian ghetto, the German mainstream appears to the narrator as one of material wealth, orderliness, spaciousness, and cultural literacy, mirrored in the comfortable middle-class world of Volker and Felix. Their house is full of books and smells of dust and vanilla; thus becoming aligned in Sascha's imagination with the happiness and warmth of her early childhood. Volker's role in the narrative oscillates between father figure and love interest; Sascha reveals that she thinks of him as her savior. He also promises to help find a new apartment for her and her siblings and takes care of her when she is in the hospital. In the end, it even becomes possible to integrate Volker and Felix into the existing family, which suggests that the trauma of the violent family history can eventually be overcome. In the last scene of the novel, Sascha steals away from the ensuing idyllic family scene to travel to Prague and follow in her mother's footsteps: "Ich werfe mir die Tasche über die Schulter, schiebe den Schirm meiner Kappe in den Nacken und trete hinaus in die Sonne" (*S*, 289; I throw my backpack over my shoulder, turn my baseball cap backwards, and head out into the sun, *BGP*, 221). While the departure of the hero at the end of the ghetto narrative constitutes a staple genre convention,[28] the plot development and happy ending also suggest that this immigrant can only experience happiness and contentment when she assimilates into German society and accepts living by the standards set by the mainstream, which are embodied by the liberal journalist Volker and his son Felix, aptly named the "lucky one."

Like Kaminer's and Gorelik's works, *Scherbenpark* also participates in the discourse on *Leitkultur* and assimilation, that is, the question how Germany should integrate its citizens with a migratory background and grant them political rights, but in quite a different way. Kaminer stereotypes both Russians and Germans in a hyperbolic way, thereby creating an ironic distance that might motivate the reader to question the problematic nature of superficial judgments of other cultures. The first-person narrator in *Scherbenpark*, on the other hand, stereotypes only her fellow Russians and thus inadvertently assumes a point of view that is critical of minority cultures and often advanced in the German mainstream press.

"Ich bin weder hier noch dort"— *Der Russe ist einer, der Birken liebt*

The novels by Gorelik and Bronsky provide interesting counterpoints to a breakout debut in the literary spring of 2012. Olga Grjasnowa's[29] *Der Russe ist einer, der Birken liebt* (2012; *All Russians Love Birch Trees*, 2014) is a novel of transgression on multiple levels. It combines a personal history of displacement and trauma with narratives of war and ethnic conflicts in Baku and Israel, while destabilizing notions of fixed sexual and national identities. The novel puts up an active resistance to nostalgia and identification with national origins in its depiction of various strong characters. This is especially true of the first-person narrator Maria (Mascha) Kogan who is a compound, a literary poster child of national, ethnic, and linguistic diversity. An Azerbaijani refuge from Baku who as a child fled the ethnic war in Nagorno-Karabakh that lasted from 1988 to 1994, Mascha grew up as a Jewish quota refugee in Hesse. Now twenty-something, Mascha speaks German, Russian, Azerbaijani, French, and English, studies Arabic and translation science in Frankfurt, and has plans for an ambitious career as an interpreter with the UN. How her past defines her is one of the central questions of the novel, and it remains a blind spot until the very end. Trauma, deterritorialized identities, and an arbitrary cosmopolitanism are the dominant themes of the novel.

In the first part, the unexpected death of Mascha's live-in boyfriend Elias causes the trauma of her war-torn childhood to come rushing back, leading to her complete mental and physical breakdown. Unable to put her life back together, Mascha decides to take a translating job in Israel, which makes up the novel's second part. Her sexual adventures with both Tal, a former elite female Israeli soldier, and Tal's brother Ori thrust her into the conflict between Israelis and Palestinians. Mascha experiences hostile Israelis because she speaks Arabic but not Hebrew and works for a German organization that supports NGOs (a mission called *Arab-Hugging* in Hebrew-inflected English).[30] The omnipresent security measures, weapons, and the day-to-day stressor of living in a war zone bring up Mascha's suppressed trauma of seeing an Armenian woman being pushed out of a window and witnessing the ethnic cleansing of the Baku pogrom on January 13, 1990, and lead to panic attacks and depression. In the final section of the novel she enters the West Bank with Tal and a group of activists, but ends up wandering the streets, bleeding, disoriented, and lost in memories of Baku, before calling a friend in Germany for help to rescue her from her self-imposed exile.

Grjasnowa abandons the dichotomous setup of German mainstream and Russian-Azerbaijani culture previously discussed. Yet instead of integrating the two, German mainstream culture is in fact largely omitted from the novel altogether. Apart from Elias, only few ethnic German characters appear who are by and large depicted negatively, such as Mascha's professor, aptly named Windmühle (Windmill), for whom multiculturalism means "weniger Kopftücher und mehr Haut" (*DR*, 33; fewer hijabs and more skin, *AR*, 31) or Daniel, a fellow student who treats her as an extension of the Israeli state and his personal "Teddyjuden" (*DR*, 64; pet Jew, *AR*, 65). While there is no clear indication that Elias's parents, East Germans from Apolda in Thuringia, resent Mascha for not being an ethnic German, a considerable distance between them is repeatedly thematized, which only deepens after Elias's death.

The textual elision of positive images of German mainstream society[31] is testament to the characters' exasperation of being singled-out, questioned, and discriminated against (not always just by the mainstream but also by other immigrants), despite being German citizens and, by all policy standards, models of "successful integration" to boot. That Mascha's tolerance generally does not extend to ethnic Germans thus needs to be read as a reaction to her own marginalization by them. As an aside to this literary finding, the irritation of transnational immigrants about the slow-changing political and social status quo has deepened in Germany in recent years, especially following the Sarrazin debate and other populist critiques of Islam.[32] Books, such as Zafer Şenocak's *Deutschsein: Eine Aufklärungsschrift* (Being German: An Educational Pamphlet, 2011) or Lena Gorelik's *Sie können aber gut Deutsch! Warum ich nicht mehr dankbar sein will, dass ich hier leben darf, und Toleranz nicht weiterhilft* (But Your German Is So Good! Why I Don't Want to Be Grateful Anymore That I'm Allowed to Live Here and Tolerance Doesn't Help, 2012), establish a nonfictional counter discourse to positions advanced in the popular mainstream and question societal concepts of identity, citizenship, and culture; Grjasnowa's novel writes back via her feisty main character.

Der Russe ist einer, der Birken liebt furthermore acknowledges findings of sociological studies about the realities of immigrant communities in Germany, according to which immigrants show a high degree of cultural integration, yet continue to rely on their own networks in which ethnic Germans do not play a role.[33] In their private lives in Germany, Mascha and her family move almost exclusively in "paranational" networks, which Azade Seyhan defines as "communities that exist . . . alongside the citizens of the host country but remain culturally or linguistically distanced from them."[34] As Mascha's narrative makes amply clear, her parents have not overcome the collapse of the Soviet Union and have never begun to feel at home in their new environment, not least because of the Holocaust, in which family members perished. Her father, an aerospace engineer and former high-ranking ministry official, gave up when he came to Germany because "Deutschland hatte für meinen Vater keine Verwendung. . . . Er freundete sich nicht mit anderen Menschen an, ging kaum kaum aus dem Haus, nur manchmal, um an den Tankstellen die Benzinpreise zu vergleichen." (*DR*, 53; Germany had no use for my father. . . . He didn't befriend other people. He rarely left the house, and if so, it was mostly to compare prices at gas stations. [*AR*, 54]) Mascha's mother, a former concert pianist, has managed to secure a teaching position and supports the family but is alienated by the cultural differences she perceives in her German students. Her social life revolves around the Russian-Jewish community and the synagogue.

Different from Anja's positive account of her experiences in school in *Meine weißen Nächte*, different also from Sascha's academic overachieving as a means of social advancement in *Scherbenpark*, Mascha remains an outsider and even thinks about committing suicide after moving to Germany. She is being blamed for anything that goes wrong in her *Gymnasium* class, despite the fact that she hardly speaks for the first three years. When she finally physically attacks a teacher in a class discussion about immigrant juvenile delinquents, she is thrown out of school. Life for her only takes a turn for the better after she moves to Frankfurt, a more tolerant environment.

Mascha and Elias live in Frankfurt's multicultural *Bahnhofsviertel* among other immigrants.[35] Her transnational friends are integrated, cosmopolitan, and highly educated, thus defying stereotypes—especially of Southern European immigrants—that circulate in the populist public discourse. They also give testimony to the complexities of the immigrant experience in the aughts. Cem, a gay German-Turk who grew up bilingually in Frankfurt, studies with Mascha to be an interpreter and speaks better Turkish than his parents. Mascha's ex-boyfriend Sami, a Lebanese who grew up in Paris and Frankfurt, pads his Arabic with French words and went to high school in the United States. In the first part of the novel, he is a PhD student in German at an unnamed American university but has been denied the renewal of his student visa, and thus the return to the United States, due to his Arabic-sounding name, which brings the political realities of post-9/11 America squarely into the novel. Then there is Sibel, a young German-Kurdish woman, who flees from her devout and violent brothers and an arranged marriage into a lesbian relationship with Mascha before disappearing with her passport, insurance card, and cash.

As these complex story lines suggest, *Der Russe ist einer, der Birken liebt* integrates the German sociopolitical discourse on immigration and minorities throughout. While a few passages consequently seem a bit con- trived and read like a polemic thesis play (especially *DR*, 135–37; *AR*, 150–53, in which Cem reports on the experience of his Turkish father when attending an election rally of the CDU, the Christian Democratic party), including them still makes for a more political and interesting text. Mascha and her friends embody identity politics that react to the social and political realities of living as immigrants in an environment that often deliberately ignores those realities. The characters are cognizant of fixed national and sexual categories while at the same time seeking to defy and transgress them. Mascha does not feel at home in Germany, yet her memories of Baku are free of nostalgic childhood memories, attesting to how "diasporic memory detaches itself both from the homeland and the host land."[36] Her memories center on the atrocities witnessed, indicat- ing that the ethnic cleansing and war she experienced have made a sense of national belonging impossible: "Der Begriff Heimat implizierte für mich stets den Pogrom" (*DR*, 203; To me, the term *homeland* always implied pogrom, *AR*, 229). Only personal relationships provide a sense of belonging and familiarity, first and foremost in the connection to Elias and secondly, her mother. Interestingly, Elias as an East German is tex- tually aligned with the "other/ed" immigrants in the text (for example, see *DR*, 110–16; *AR*, 120–28). After Elias dies and Sami returns to the United States, the ties that have connected Mascha to Germany unravel completely and the transnational space they have inhabited collapses; this is rendered in the visceral experience of packing boxes and moving out of the apartment once shared with Elias (*DR*, 146–51; *AR*, 153–58).

Mascha is Jewish without relating to religion, she is Azerbaijani without relating to her country of origin, and she is German without relating to the culture. When Elias is having surgery, Mascha spots an injured rabbit outside the hospital and decides to strike a bargain with God—he can have the rabbit but not Elias. Not being religious, Mascha makes up her own makeshift ritual—"Ich wiegte mich im Gebet, wie ich es bei den religiösen Juden auf *Arte* gesehen hatte" (*DR*, 24; I swayed in prayer as I had seen the Orthodox Jews do on one of the public chan- nels, *AR*, 20)[37]—and smashes the rabbit's skull with a stone. Having a German passport is insignificant because Mascha's postnational identity is arbitrary and flexible. This is especially visible in the second half of the novel and the relative ease with which Mascha navigates the day-to-day political, linguistic, and psychological complexities of living in Israel.[38] In conversation with the Palestinian photographer Ismael she is confronted with the question whether she is German, Jewish, Arabic, or Russian, because she does not look, act, or speak like either. Then again, Mascha asks back, how do Russians look anyway, and the answer, borrowed from Chekhov's play *Three Sisters* is, of course, another stereotype: "Wie Leute, die Birken lieben" (*DR*, 265–65; Like people who love birch trees, *AR*, 301–3).

Grjasnowa employs many German clichés throughout the novel (a doctor cannot pronounce Mascha's "difficult" name; Elias's petit-bourgeois parents collect wall clocks without ever questioning why, *Tatort* is on TV, etc.), explaining in an interview that she finds them manifested in language and thus useful as aesthetic devices.[39] For example, when Cem and Mascha get into a fender bender with an ethnic German, the incident quickly turns into a stereotypically racist altercation, in which the man calls Cem "Kanake" (*DR*, 155; *kanack, AR*, 173) and suspects that he has no residency permit. Yet Cem's reaction, expressed in an enraged phone conversation with his boyfriend, shows again that national belonging is not a conflicted concept for the character:

> "Alter, ich habe keine Probleme mit meiner nationalen Identität. . . . Komm mir nicht mit dem Scheiß. Nationale Identität. Ich gehe vor Gericht, ich habe ihn angezeigt. Steck dir deine Nation also sonst wohin. Ich brauche einen Anwalt und keine Kulturtheorie." (*DR*, 158)

> [Dude, I don't have a problem with my national identity. . . . Don't give me this crap again. National identity. I am pressing charges. I'll go to court. I don't care about this nation bullshit. . . . I need a lawyer, not a lecture in cultural theory. (*AR*, 176)]

Cem's recourse to being stereotyped and insulted as one who does not belong is to fight back the legal way and insist on a pragmatic application of his citizenship status as German.

Transnational and Cosmopolitan Identities

In summary, the characters in the respective novels share the burden of negotiating memories of their culture of origin, which are tainted by discrimination, loss, even war; of coming to terms with the trauma of displacement, and adapting to the culture of arrival. Due to her negative memories of growing up in the late Soviet Union and her positive experiences in Germany, Gorelik's Anja Buchmann attempts to divide her Russian and Jewish heritage from her German identity and life. Where this is not possible, she reduces Russian culture to its folkloristic elements, making cultural assimilation her strategy of choice. In Sascha Neimann's estimation, which is tainted with the violent and traumatic loss of her mother, Russian culture has no positive attributes whatsoever—all Russian men are violent drunks and Russian women are at fault for living with them.[40] While German culture is characterized as exclusionary toward immigrants, it also exhibits a strongly Western, almost American, notion of the pursuit of happiness that suits Sascha's character. Like Anja, she ultimately also opts for integration, albeit not out of enthusiasm for German culture, but a sense of necessity.

Grjasnowa's debut transcends the dichotomies between Russian-Azerbaijani and German culture in the complex character of Mascha Kogan. She embodies a culture of "in-between" that resists binary placing while signifying an uneasy and somewhat arbitrary cosmopolitanism. Despite the fact that the character's fate remains open, the text nevertheless presents an acceptance of hybridity, complexity, and provisional identities and seems comfortable with all. This includes an ongoing, playful, and open negotiation of cultural identity constructions and has been identified as a decisive characteristic of New World Literature.[41]

The cosmopolitanism displayed in the novel can also be linked to Ulrich Beck's concept of a new cosmopolitan world order.[42] It is based on the premise of difference, alienation, and foreignness, yet encourages a construction of mentalities and imaginations in the "cosmopolitan gaze." The "dialogic imagination" Beck calls for leads to an acknowledgment of the clash of cultures within one's own life and the active acceptance of difference and tolerance for the other, who is dissimilar, yet fundamentally an equal.[43] This new cosmopolitanism replaces the logic of "either/or" with the logic of *Sowohl-als-Auch* (as well as), and Mascha Kogan might well be its literary poster child.

Notes

[1] For an overview, see B. Venkat Mani and Elke Segelcke, "Cosmopolitical and Transnational Interventions in German Studies," *TRANSIT* 7, no. 1 (2011): 1–27.

[2] Imre Szeman, "Cultural Studies and the Transnational," in *New Cultural Studies: Adventures in Theory*, ed. Gary Hall and Clare Birchall (Athens: University of Georgia Press, 2006), 200.

[3] Steven Vertovec, *Transnationalism* (London: Routledge, 2009), 2.

[4] See Paul Jay, *Global Matters: The Transnational Turn in Literary Studies* (Ithaca, NY: Cornell University Press, 2010).

[5] See the first chapter of my book *Germans Going Global: Contemporary Literature and Cultural Globalization* (New York: De Gruyter, 2012).

⁶ Bettina Spoerri, "Deterritorialisierungsstrategien in der transnationalen Literatur der Schweiz—ein aktueller Paradigmentwechsel," in *Diskurse in die Weite: Kosmopolitische Räume in den Literaturen der Schweiz*, ed. Martina Kamm (Zurich: Seismo, 2010), 31.

⁷ Stuart Taberner, "Transnationalism in Contemporary German-Language Fiction by Nonminority Writers," *Seminar* 47, no. 5 (2011): 626.

⁸ Azade Seyhan, *Writing Outside the Nation* (Princeton, NJ: Princeton University Press, 2001).

⁹ One manifestation of the institutional impact of transnational writing in academia is the Internationales Forschungszentrum Chamisso-Literatur which was inaugurated in June 2014, is housed at the University of Munich, and cofinanced by the Robert Bosch Foundation.

¹⁰ See also Emily Apter, who uses the upper-case "World Literature" to stress its character as a "disciplinary construct." Emily Apter, *Against World Literature: On the Politics of Untranslatability* (London: Verso, 2013), 2.

¹¹ Elke Sturm-Trigonakis, *Global Playing in der Literatur: Ein Versuch über die Neue Weltliteratur* (Würzburg: Königshausen & Neumann, 2007), 99.

¹² Linda Basch, Nina Glick Schiller, and Christina Szanton Blanc, *Nations Unbound: Transnational Projects: Postcolonial Predicaments, and Deterritorialized Nation-States* (London: Routledge, 1994), 7.

¹³ Boris Groys, *Die Erfindung Russlands* (Munich: Hanser, 1995).

¹⁴ Taberner, "Transnationalism," 633.

¹⁵ B. Venkat Mani, *Cosmopolitical Claims: Turkish-German Literatures from Nadolny to Pamuk* (Iowa City: University of Iowa Press, 2007).

¹⁶ The limitation to offering amusing anecdotes led *Die Zeit* critic Ursula März to state acidly: "Seit zwanzig Jahren lebt Wladimir Kaminer davon, so zu tun, als habe er just vor einer Woche in Moskau den Zug bestiegen und sei vor fünf Tagen in einem Land gelandet, in dem er alles ungeheuer erstaunlich, ungeheuer seltsam und ungeheuer witzig findet." (For the last twenty years, Wladimir Kaminer has made his living by pretending that he got on the train in Moscow just a week ago and landed five days later in a country where everything strikes him as utterly surprising, utterly strange, and utterly funny). Ursula März, "Der Dauerwunderer," *Die Zeit*, October 13, 2011, Kultur Feuilleton.

¹⁷ See Adrian Wanner, "Wladimir Kaminer: A Russian Picaro Conquers Germany," *The Russian Review* 64 (October 2005): 590–604, and *Out of Russia: Fictions of a New Translingual Diaspora* (Evanston: Northwestern University Press, 2011). See also Kathleen Condray, "The Colonization of Germany: Migrant and German Identity in Wladimir Kaminer's *Mein deutsches Dschungelbuch*," *Seminar* 42, no. 3 (September 2006): 321–36.

¹⁸ Lena Gorelik, "Interview mit Lena Gorelik," interview by Alexej Kinder, *East-Talk*, October 6, 2008, accessed August 30, 2013, http://easttalk.de/articles/show/interview-lena-gorelik.

¹⁹ Germany distributes refugees according to quotas to the sixteen federal states. These refugees, accepted for humanitarian reasons by the Ministry of the Interior, do

not need to undergo asylum or other acceptance procedures, but cannot freely chose where they want to reside. Between January 9, 1991, and December 31, 2004, the Quota Law governed the immigration of Jews from countries in the former Soviet Union. The new Immigration Act revoked the Quota Law on January 1, 2005.

[20] There are obvious parallels between the character and Gorelik herself, who has confirmed as much (in Lena Gorelik, "Petersburger Kartoffelsalat: Lena Gorelik über ihre Erinnerungen an Russland," interview by Teresa Grenzmann, *Münchner Merkur*, November 7, 2004, accessed August 30, 2013, http://www.lyrikwelt.de/hintergrund/gorelik-gespraech-h.htm). Gorelik was born in Leningrad in 1981 and immigrated with her Russian-Jewish family to Germany when she was eleven years old. She completed the Deutsche Journalistenschule in Munich before studying Eastern European studies there. For her debut she received the Bayerischer Kunstförderpreis in 2005 and has since published various nonfiction and fiction books, most recently the novel *Die Listensammlerin* in 2013.

[21] Lena Gorelik, *Meine weißen Nächte: Roman*, 2nd paperback ed. 2009 (Munich: Schirmer Graf, 2004), 226. Hereafter MwN in parentheses after quotations in the main body of the text. Translations from the novel are my own.

[22] Wanner, *Out of Russia*, 74.

[23] Wanner, *Out of Russia*, 72.

[24] Alina Bronsky is a pseudonym. Born in 1978 in Sverdlovsk (now Yekaterinburg), she spent her childhood "at the foot of the Ural mountains in Central Russia" (http://www.alinabronsky.com/about, accessed January 17, 2015) and moved to Germany when she was thirteen. She grew up in Marburg and Darmstadt, went to and dropped out of medical school and worked as a copywriter for an ad agency. *Scherbenpark* was nominated for the Ingeborg Bachmann Prize in 2008 and later adapted into a play and made into a movie. Bronsky's second novel *Die schärfsten Gerichte der tartarischen Küche* (2010) was nominated for the Long List of the *Deutscher Buchpreis* in 2010 and translated into English in 2011. Her third novel, *Nenn mich einfach Superheld*, was published in 2013 and appeared in English in 2014.

[25] Alina Bronsky, *Scherbenpark: Roman*, 3rd ed. 2010 (Cologne: Kiepenheuer & Witsch 2008); *Broken Glass Park: A Novel*, trans. Tim Mohr (New York: Europa Editions, 2010). All English quotes are drawn from Mohr's translation. Subsequent citations refer to page numbers from the German original (*S*), followed by the English translation followed by the page numbers from the translation (*BGP*).

[26] Barbara Mennel, "Alina Bronsky, *Scherbenpark: Global Ghetto Girl*," in *Emerging German-Language Novelists of the Twenty-First Century*, ed. Lyn Marven and Stuart Taberner (Rochester, NY: Camden House, 2011), 164.

[27] Elisabeth Cheauré, "Infinite Mirroring: Russia and Eastern Europe as the West's 'Other'," in *Facing the East in the West: Images of Eastern Europe in British Literature, Film, and Culture*, ed. Barbara Korte, Eva Ulrike Pirker, and Sissy Helff (Amsterdam: Rodopi, 2010), 29.

[28] Mennel, "Alina Bronsky," 175.

[29] Grjasnowa was born in 1984 in Baku, Azerbaijan, grew up in the Caucasus, and spent extended periods in Poland, Russia, and Israel. She moved to Germany

at the age of twelve and finished *Gymnasium* in Frankfurt. In 2005 she began to study art history and Slavic studies in Göttingen, later switching to the *Deutsches Literaturinstitut Leipzig*, from which she graduated in 2010. For her debut novel she won the Klaus-Michael Kühne Prize of the Hamburg Harbour Front Festival and the Anna Seghers Prize (both 2012). Her second novel *Die juristische Unschärfe einer Ehe* was published in 2014.

[30] Olga Grjasnowa, *Der Russe ist einer, der Birken liebt: Roman* (Munich: Hanser, 2012), 183; *All Russians Love Birch Trees*, trans. Eva Bacon (New York: Other Press, 2014), 207. All English quotes are drawn from Bacon's translation. Subsequent citations refer to page numbers from the German original (*DR*) followed by Bacon's translation followed by page numbers from the translation (*AR*).

[31] For example, "Heiligabend lief ich durch den Park, . . . Es war der perfekte Abend, um draußen Sport zu treiben. Auf der Straße waren nur Moslems, Juden und ein paar einsame Christen." (*DR*, 118; On Christmas Eve I strolled through the park . . . It was the perfect night for outdoor exercise. The only people out on the streets were Muslims, Jews, and a few lonely Christians. [*AR*, 131]).

[32] This is also visible in the growing alliance between feminists and the political right with regard to Muslim practices. See my article "The Headscarf in Germany: A Critical Reading of the Feminist Debate," in *Visions of Europe*, ed. Gail K. Hart and Anke S. Biendarra (Berlin: Peter Lang, 2014), 83–94.

[33] Regina Römhild, "Confronting the Logic of the Nation State: Transnational Migration and Cultural Globalisation in Germany," *Ethnologia Europaea* 33, no. 1 (2003): 63.

[34] Seyhan, *Writing Outside the Nation*, 10.

[35] According to the Statistical Yearbook 2012 of the City of Frankfurt, 37% of the inhabitants of Frankfurt's Bahnhofsviertel are quantified as "ausländisch" (foreign) and 65% have a "Migrationshintergrund" (migrant background). Accessed August 2, 2013, http://www.frankfurt.de/sixcms/media.php/678/J2012K02x.pdf.

[36] Azade Seyhan, "Unfinished Modernism: European Destinations of Transnational Writing," in *Migration and Literature in Contemporary Europe*, ed. Mirjam Gebauer and Pia Schwarz Lausten (Munich: Martin Meidenbauer, 2010), 14.

[37] The translation "one of the public channels" does not quite capture the specific qualities of *ARTE*, a Franco-German channel that promotes programming in the areas of culture and art and is generally watched by people who might consider themselves part of a cultural elite.

[38] The focus on rarely thematized political conflicts in contemporary German-language literature makes Grjasnowa an example of what Sturm-Trigonakis has called *Neue Weltliteratur*. In order to be part of this corpus, texts need to fulfill the criteria of "Mehrsprachigkeit . . . die andere Aufnahmebedingung betrifft die Handlungsebene und besteht in der literarischen Verarbeitung eines wie auch immer gearteten Globaliserungsdiskurses in den narrativen und poetischen Zusammenhängen" (20; Multilingualism . . . the other condition of admission has to do with plot and lies in the literary treatment of a discourse of globalization, however, this might be rendered within the narrative and poetical contexts).

[39] In Oya Erdogan, "'Mich erschrecken und faszinieren diese Strukturen.' Olga Grjasnowa: *Der Russe ist einer, der Birken liebt,*" Deutschlandradio, June 6, 2012, *Büchermarkt.*

[40] The negative attributes or Russian culture are portrayed even more starkly in Alina Bronsky's second novel, *Die schärfsten Gerichte der tartarischen Küche* (Cologne: Kiepenheuer & Witsch, 2010).

[41] Sturm-Trigonakis, *Global Playing,* 200.

[42] Ulrich Beck, *The Cosmopolitan Vision,* trans. Ciaran Cronin (Cambridge: Polity Press, 2006).

[43] Ulrich Beck, "The Cosmopolitan Society and Its Enemies," *Theory, Culture, and Society,* 19, no. 1–2 (2002): 17–44, esp. 20, for a summary of "dialogic imagination."

11: "Wo geh ich her? . . . Wo komm ich hin?": Delineating Transnational Spaces in the Work of Juli Zeh

Lars Richter

"BEI DER GESCHICHTE," Juli Zeh writes in *Treideln* (Towing),[1] her 2013 poetics lecture at the Goethe University in Frankfurt, "gibt es ein Außerhalb. Sie ist ein (fiktives) Stück Lebenswelt mit einer anderen Lebenswelt drumherum. . . . Wer schreibt, schwingt sich auf zu einem Gott, der Welten erschafft, um sie erkennend überdauern zu können."[2] (A story has an outside. It is a [fictional] piece of a lived-in world with another lived-in world around it. . . . An author soars to be a God, a creator of worlds who outlives them while seeing through them.) Part of any narrative created by an author, whether a deity or not, is its spatial and, more specifically, geographical and territorial setting. Although Zeh in her self-proclaimed antipoetics does not mention this aspect of literature—she focuses predominantly on the narrator's perspective and narrative time—it is still useful to examine more closely the spaces she creates in her fictional and nonfictional texts. More specifically, I propose to have a closer look at what Barbara Piatti in her 2009 study *Die Geographie der Literatur* (The Geography of Literature) has categorized as "Handlungsraum"[3] (space of action), that is, the linguistically created space inhabited by the personnel of any text. While this space will be the focus of the analysis, I propose that, to once again borrow Piatti's terminology, the "durchlässige Membran zwischen den Welten" (*GdL*, 19; permeable membrane between worlds), that is, the intersection between the geographical world we inhabit and the geographies within narrative works, is of equal importance. According to Piatti, geography is a point of contact between inner-textual and extra-textual worlds (*GdL*, 19). If we accept this claim, I would like to argue that it is this point of convergence that allows for the inclusion of Juli Zeh's work, even though her texts are generally not situated in a discourse devoted to a negotiation of what the term *transnationalism* might mean at the beginning of the twenty-first century. Conventionally, Juli Zeh is read as an author who with great persistence comments on current sociopolitical developments both within and outside of her literary and nonfictional texts, a reading confirmed by her recent involvement in the international protest against NSA-surveillance, to give but one example. I suggest that it is precisely this situatedness of her work—both inside and outside of the literary realm—in the realities of the early twenty-first century that allow for an inclusion of Zeh's work in this volume because she not only actively shapes discourses on politics through her essays and participation in talk shows and so forth, but furthermore reflects on said discourses in her literary work. In other words, the situatedness of Zeh's work that I speak of is constituted by the fact that her texts, and consequently the diversely shaped spaces of action Zeh creates therein, mirror the "andere Lebenswelt drumherum"—our lived-in world—mentioned in the introductory quote from *Treideln*. While some authors might choose to create intra-textual spaces without referents in the geographical realities of our world—many works from the fantasy genre may serve as example—, Zeh belongs into the category of writers who firmly anchor their narratives in the lived-in world her readers inhabit. Therefore, Zeh's texts can be read as literary representations of a world characterized by an increasing mobility, migration flows, and, not the least, a dialectical relationship between deterritorialization and reterritorialization. In simplified terms, while—at least for those with the financial and technological means—space and its demarcation in the form of geographical borders appears to be losing its meaning due to advances in transportation or mass communication, we are at the same time also witnessing the reemergence of the significance of borders as means of controlling flows of migration as well as an increase in populist national rhetoric across the world, as discussed in the introduction to this volume.[4] This dialectic relationship echoes in Juli Zeh's texts as well through a reemergence of the nation even in texts that cannot straightforwardly be associated with a precise geographical framework.

While space and time have gained new significance in the course of contemporary globalization processes, they have of course always been a condition for any text, fictional or nonfictional. "Jede Fiktion," Barbara Piatti reminds us, "baut Handlungsorte und – räume auf, wobei die Skala von gänzlich imaginären bis hin zu realistisch gezeichneten, präzise lokalisierbaren Schauplätzen mit hohem Wiedererkennungswert reicht." (*GdL*, 16; Every fiction creates spaces and places of action that range from those that are completely imaginary to those that are realistically drawn, precisely locatable, and highly recognizable.) While this may appear to be self-evident and not worthy of any further elaboration, the spatial conditions of literature—that is, the complex interrelation between topographical realities both writer and reader populate, their literary representation and potential transformation, the nation as a concept that frames and confines these topographical realities within borders, and potential literary endeavours to transcend them—become more complicated if we consider that, in the globalized world of the

early twenty-first century, literature is written in a time in which national
borders are diffused and crossed frequently and easily by those who are
privileged enough to do so. The same is true for literary texts which
circulate across the globe through an increasingly globalized economy
and, more traditionally, through translation. In response to these processes German-language literature of the twenty-first century has, in
part at least, increasingly looked beyond national borders and become
more globalized in various configurations as well.[5] These configurations
come in all shapes and forms and range from texts dealing with migrant
flows and the need to cross borders in order to find work like Julya
Rabinowich's *Die Erdfresserin* (The Woman Who Eats Dirt, 2012, discussed by Maria Mayr in this volume) to texts who reflect on Germany's
history "written abroad" like Christian Kracht's *Imperium* (Empire,
2012, discussed by Claudia Breger) to texts that utilize the movements
of traveling in a foreign country to reflect on German identity, as is
the case in Zeh's *Die Stille ist ein Geräusch* (Silence Is a Sound, 2002),
which I will discuss in this chapter. Conventionally, however, the traversing of geographical, linguistic, and cultural borders has been examined
with respect to the discussion of what the term *world literature* might
mean in the context of globalization as well as with regard to authors
with a migration background. For the former, David Damrosch and
Elke Sturm-Trigonakis, for example, strive to readapt the term *world
literature* for today's globalized world, either by offering the metaphor
of world literature as "windows on the world"[6] or by developing an
elaborate catalogue of criteria to come to terms with a new set of texts
that no longer fit established categories in the case of Sturm-Trigonakis.
For the latter, scholars like Karl Esselborn directly link the migration
flows of the late twentieth- to early twenty-first century with the literary
success of "minority" authors like Wladimir Kaminer.[7]

As outlined in the introduction to this volume and further examined by Stuart Taberner, however, the textual borders in the works of
what Taberner terms "nonminority writers"[8] like Daniel Kehlmann (*Die
Vermessung der Welt* [Measuring the World, 1995] and *Ruhm* [Fame,
2009]), Christian Kracht (*Imperium*), and Juli Zeh have proven to be
permeable as well. As Taberner puts it, "Nonminority Germans, in short,
are as itinerant as anyone else."[9] While Zeh's work may not necessarily
fit the ways in which transnational crossings find their way into the categories devised by Taberner,[10] reading Zeh's work through the lens of
transnationalism may shed light on conceptualizing the term transnationalism through emphasizing the vital importance of the term's inherent
meaning of going beyond the borders of the nation. Zeh's texts serve
as prime examples for a kind of literature that highlights the *trans* in
the term *transnational* by effortlessly traveling across geographical borders or creating deterritorialized spaces and can thus be read as forms of

*trans*nationalism in literature. At the same time, they also serve as examples of texts that are very much aware of the compound's second part, namely the nation. As my reading will show, the nation proves to be a concept a text cannot elude quite as easily, even if it manages to diffuse geographical borders. Therefore, the selected texts by Juli Zeh serve to problematize the term *transnationalism* itself by emphasizing its intrinsic ambiguity. Seen this way, the concept of transnationalism is not limited to a tool of analysis that, at least within German studies, is almost exclusively applied to authors with a migration background.[11]

Within the broader framework of German-language literature of the early twenty-first century, Zeh's literary output furthermore affirms that Ottmar Ette's prediction from 2001 has at least partially become true:

> Denn nicht nur aufgrund der nicht abreißenden Migrationsströme . . . werden die Literaturen des 21. Jahrhunderts zu einem beträchtlichen Teil Literaturen ohne festen Wohnsitz sein, Literaturen, die sich Versuchen eindeutiger (Re-)Territorialiserung entziehen.[12]

> [Not only because of the ongoing flows of migration . . . literatures of the twenty-first century will be to a large extent literatures without a fixed place of residence, literatures that elude any attempts of a clear-cut (re-)territorialization.]

In fact, this quote accurately describes Zeh's more recent publications, especially *Corpus Delicti* (*The Method*, 2009) that ask for an active participation on the part of the reader if they are to be linked to a specific national background at all. The widespread perception of Zeh as a very German author in the sense that she continues the long-established tradition of the author as public intellectual notwithstanding, a surprisingly large number of the author's texts have been on the move from the outset and can thus be classified as "itinerant" in the sense that Taberner applies the term to a set of German-language literature. In Zeh's acclaimed debut *Adler und Engel* (Eagles and Angels, 2001), for example, the protagonists embark on a journey that takes them from Germany to Austria to former Yugoslavia, thus integrating extraliterary political and military conflicts of the late 1990s into the narrative of the plot. The Balkans are of special importance for Zeh's works;[13] indeed, she not only sets parts of her debut in the war-torn region but, in 2002, published a travelogue based on her own journey to Bosnia-Herzegovina. While *Adler und Engel* and the travelogue *Die Stille ist ein Geräusch* are characterized by a high mobility paired with great geographical accuracy, her more recent works *Corpus Delicti* and *Nullzeit* (*Decompression*, 2012) appear to follow a trend toward deterritorialized literary spaces, that is, spaces that defy clear geographical determination.

The quotation in this chapter's title is borrowed from *Adler und Engel*. In a conversation between two of the novel's protagonists, Max and Clara, the latter describes it as the "ultimative Frage" (ultimate question) and continues with what we can regard as the ultimate question of literary studies: "Und was zum Teufel soll der ganze Scheiß?" (And what the fuck is it all about?).[14] Even though Clara's question in the context of the novel aims at the increasing erosion of norms, values, and reliable meaning in the early twenty-first century,[15] I intend to transpose her inquiry to the question of what function does literature have and what kind of literary spaces are created to what purpose in selected works by Juli Zeh. Going back to Piatti's assertion cited above, I will argue through the analysis that the continuum of possible literary spaces also includes imaginary ones that are highly recognizable as well as realistically drawn locations nowhere to be found on a map.

"Wo geh ich her"—
Die Stille ist ein Geräusch

"Der Reisebericht," Ottmar Ette claims in his 2001 study *Literatur in Bewegung*, "ist im Grunde jene Art des literarischen und wissenschaftlichen Schreibens, in dem sich das Schreiben seiner Raumbezogenheit, seiner Dynamik und seiner Bewegungsnotwendigkeit am deutlichsten bewußt wird" (*LiB*, 25; The travelogue is indeed the kind of literary and scientific writing in which writing becomes most aware of its own spatial connection, its dynamic and its need to move). Accordingly, Zeh's 2002 travelogue *Die Stille ist ein Geräusch* is arguably the text within her body of work that most explicitly deals with movement within and across geographical borders. As mentioned above, Zeh had already incorporated the war in Bosnia and Herzegovina in the mid-1990s as the broader backdrop into *Adler und Engel* before embarking on a journey to the region herself. Accompanied by a comprehensive and informative website,[16] the textual result of this journey is the documentary travelogue *Die Stille ist ein Geräusch*. Zeh describes the objective of her journey as the desire to find out whether or not Bosnia and Herzegovina is indeed a geographically locatable space. In other words, her objective was to match the lines drawn on the set of maps she takes along with geographical realities she is about to explore. While preparing for the trip, Zeh attempts to explain her motivation to her traveling companion, her dog: "Ich will sehen, ob Bosnien-Herzegowina ein Ort ist, an den man fahren kann, oder ob es zusammen mit der Kriegsberichterstattung vom Erdboden verschwunden ist" (I want to find out if Bosnia-Herzegovina is a place you can visit or if it is a place that vanished from the face of the earth with the war reports).[17] Her expressed discomfort with mass media coverage of the war, a feeling that will reemerge throughout the text, leads to a desire to counter the "facts" of media coverage and concomitant preconceptions with a subjective experience tightly connected to questions of territoriality.[18] Before leaving Zagreb for Sarajevo and into what she has grown up to know as the "Blackbox hinter dem Eisernen Vorhang" (*SiG*, 61; black box behind the Iron Curtain), Zeh one last time assures herself of her own spatial location by inscribing herself on an imaginary global map: "Vor dem Bahnhof lege ich mich auf die Wiese, breite Arme und Beine aus, bis ich ein Kreuz bilde, mit mir selbst die Stelle auf dem Erdball markiere, an der ich liege" (*SiG*, 17; I lay down in the grass in front of the train station, arms and legs spread wide until I form a cross, marking the spot on the globe on which I'm lying). Once on the road, Zeh's experiences and observations no longer guarantee such certainty at all times. They can rather be described as a mixture of striving for geographical accuracy, the desire for spatial anchoring in uncertain territory, and, after some initial resistance, the eventual willingness to become lost on the map.

On the way to Sarajevo, Zeh encounters a landscape that corresponds to her own uncertainty as to what to expect in Bosnia and Herzegovina at the beginning of the journey: "Je weiter wir uns der Grenze nähern, desto unentschiedener wird das Gelände" (*SiG*, 23; The closer we get to the border, the more indecisive the terrain becomes). Whereas the first destroyed buildings she encounters match mediated images of the country during and in the aftermath of the war, the border, a seemingly fixed and clear-cut line on a map, reveals itself as being surprisingly elusive: "'Das ist die Grenze,' sagt Dario, aber zwischen was und was? Gerade noch sehe ich das Schild vorbeiflitzen: Auf Wiedersehen in der Republik Srpska." (*SiG*, 25; "That's the border," Dario says, but the border between what and what? Out of the corner of my eye, I see the sign flying by: See you again in the Republic of Srpska.) Repeatedly, Zeh expresses her amazement toward the velocity with which topographies alter. This makes it all the more difficult for her to get a steady and reliable grip on the country: "In diesem Land wechseln die Städte sekundenschnell das Gesicht, genau wie Landschaft und Wetter" (*SiG*, 70; In this country, cities change faces rapidly, just like the landscape and the weather). Consequently, and contrary to her expectations, Zeh expresses relief when she does not lose the ground beneath her feet upon first setting foot on Bosnian soil in the town of Jajce. For one brief moment at least, Zeh reexperiences the comforting feeling of spatial grounding: "Meine Füße, tastend beim ersten Kontakt mit bosnischem Boden: Alles klar. Trägt." (*SiG*, 26; My feet, carefully making first contact with Bosnian soil: nothing to worry. It carries.) More importantly, though, this quotation demonstrates the distrust with which Zeh approaches the country at first, a distrust clearly informed by the media coverage of

the war she intends to verify. Shortly after arriving in Jajce, Zeh enters
a potential minefield and immediately finds herself confronted with her
own preconceptions of the region that result from the above mentioned
media coverage: "Ein seltsames Gefühl, diese ersten Schritte auf mögli-
chem Minenfeld, die Beine reagieren mit Verspätung. . . . Es ist friedlich,
besonders im Maisfeld zur Rechten. Trotzdem sehe ich mich alle zwei
Minuten um, ob mein Rucksack noch da ist, ob doch noch etwas in
die Luft fliegt oder ein Mörder sich nähert. . . . Es ist halt mein erster
Tag." (*SiG*, 27–28; An unsettling feeling, these first steps on a potential minefield, my legs react delayed. . . . It is peaceful, especially in the
cornfield to my right. Nevertheless, I turn around every two minutes to
check if my backpack is still there, if something is exploding, or if there
is a murderer approaching. . . . It's my first day, after all.) As shown in
the last sentence, Zeh is all too aware of her own presumptions, which
she has to constantly face, reject, and renegotiate throughout her stay
in Bosnia and Herzegovina. By extension, the author also renegotiates
conceptions of the self, and thus Zeh's travels in the "Blackbox" both
illuminate and become a reconfiguration of her own West German identity. By being constantly reminded of her own national background in a
foreign country, Zeh enters a state that mirrors the transnational realities of the globalized early twenty-first century characterized by a constant crossing and reformulation of borders, be they geographical or
those of identity conceptions that might be tied to a national framework. As far as Zeh's own biographical background is concerned—she
was born in 1974 in Bonn to an upper middle-class family—it is within
the German context as nonminority as it gets. Her upbringing in the
capital of peaceful and affluent post–Second World War West Germany
makes the immediate confrontation with the impacts and hauntings
of the Bosnian war all the more problematic: "Ich kenne das Gefühl
nicht, durch alles, was man braucht, einem anderen etwas wegnehmen
zu müssen, Nahrung, Wasser, Kerzen, Brennholz, Öl." (*SiG*, 75; I do
not know the feeling that taking what you need means to take something away from someone else, food, water, candles, fire wood, oil.)
Visiting a geographical region scarred by the effects of military conflicts not only reminds Zeh of her own upbringing in a prosperous
and peaceful society established in the aftermath of a devastating war.
It furthermore is a reminder that the crossing of geographical borders
more often than not go hand in hand with a reformulation of one's
own identity demarcations through experiences gained while moving
through previously unchartered territories. Accordingly, Ette describes
the travelogue as an "inszeniertes Erfahrungsmodell" (enacted mode
of experience) that allows the reader to retrace the "Bewegungen des
Verstehens im Raum" (*LiB*, 22; movements of understanding in space)
inscribed in the text.

Still, at no point does Zeh give in to the illusion that she might be able to comprehend the people she meets or the country through which she travels. Toward the end of the text, her distrust of the country turns into a distrust of the supposed transformative effects traveling is said to have on identity construction: "Wie ein Kind sitze ich da und verstehe nichts, muss den Menschen vertrauen, wie sie sind. . . . Immer meint man auf Reisen, sich völlig verändert zu haben. Dass nichts mehr ist, wie es war. Zu Hause wartet das alte Selbst im Sessel und bereitet einen gierigen Empfang." (*SiG*, 220–21; Like a child, I do not understand anything and have to trust the people as they are. . . . We always believe to completely change by traveling. At home, the old Self is sitting in an armchair, giving an eager welcome.) The childlike trust she invests in the people is transposed to topography as well—and turns out to be an unexpected source of bliss. Zeh resignifies the above-mentioned problematic instability of seemingly fixed geographies into a way of encounter:

> Das Gefühl, sich verirrt zu haben, in die falsche Richtung voranzustreben, sich sonst wo zu befinden und nirgendwo anzukommen, habe ich auszuhalten gelernt. Gerade im Moment, wenn ich innerlich aufgebe, wenn es zum Umkehren zu weit ist und ich die verbleibende Zeit bis zur Dämmerung zu berechnen beginne, taucht das nächste Schild auf. Oder ich stelle fest, dass ich schon da bin. (*SiG*, 163)

> [The feeling of being lost, to go the wrong way, to be who knows where and getting nowhere anyway is something I got used to. Just when I am about to give up, when it is too late to turn around and I start calculating the time until dusk, the next sign appears. Or I realize that I am already there.]

Whereas Zeh on the outset of her journey was keen on demarcating herself on the map, she now gives in to freely floating across it, paired with a trust in arriving where she wants to or even being already there. On an imaginary free-floating map like this, it is practically impossible to get lost, and Zeh has managed to transfer this feature to the uncertain geographic realities of Bosnia and Herzegovina. Consequently, once the location markings are set loose, her perception of the country—and in fact the whole European continent—changes profoundly. If location markers are no longer reliable—and this is most impressively exemplified when she encounters a village demarcated on a map but completely eradicated by war—it is no longer feasible to cling to the idea of a fixed home:

> Dieser Kontinent lässt keine Ruhe mehr, wenn man einmal begonnen hat, sich auf ihm zu bewegen. Heimweh wäre schön, es bewiese, dass es ein Zuhause gibt. Aber Heimweh stellt sich nicht ein. Nur

das Gefühl, weg zu wollen, weiter. Woandershin. Das ist nicht das-
selbe. (*SiG*, 198)

[This continent does not leave you alone once you have started moving on it. Homesickness would be nice, it would prove that there is
in fact a home. But there is no homesickness. Just the itch to get
away, onwards. Someplace else. That is not the same.]

Arguably, these passages emphasize the *trans* in *transnationalism* to the
greatest extent in the texts examined here. The loss of the notion of home,
that is of a fixed space situated within the boundaries of a nation, results
in a longing for permanent movement that is unfazed by the concept of
geographical and political borders. In addition, if read in conjunction
with the previous quote that described the unreliability of geographical markers as rather enjoyable, these passage can also be read as how
to put theoretical conceptions of *trans*nationalism into practice. At the
same time, they echo the ambiguity of the term *transnationalism* itself.
While the text describes the free floating across the map as positive, these
passages are also a reminder that the nation is a concept not easily abandoned; quite literally, as Zeh puts it herself, the old self is waiting at home
in an armchair for the newfound transnational self to return. Moreover,
the text—and this goes back to Zeh's realization that she was brought up
in prosperous West Germany—reminds us that the blissful free-floating
movement across borders is of course a very idealized and privileged idea.
Regardless of theoretical and literary depictions of a pleasurable transnational state of mind, there *are* national borders out there that form an
impassable barrier for those not lucky enough to be able to return home,
not because they choose not to do so but because it is no longer existent
in a much more literal sense than described in the quote above.

In the end, it is a matter of debate whether Zeh has succeeded in
achieving her goal, which she has declared prior to her journey, namely
to determine whether Bosnia and Herzegovina is a "real" location one
can visit. The text itself hints at a reading that leaves the country in an
indeterminable—and in the truest sense of the word: transnational—
state: "Bosnien, fällt mir ohne Zusammenhang ein, ist ein Land wie jedes
andere, weil nichts auf der Welt sich mit etwas anderem vergleichen lässt.
So etwas wie Bosnien gibt es nirgendwo sonst, aber auch Frankreich gibt
es nicht. Nicht mal in Frankreich." (*SiG*, 125; Bosnia, I start thinking
out of context, is a country like any other because nothing in this world
is comparable to anything else. There is no place like Bosnia anywhere
else, but there is also no place like France. Not even in France.) In light
of the fleeting nature of the geographical realities Zeh encounters during
her time on the road, one might consider the possibility that, within the
context of the travelogue, Bosnia and Herzegovina remain geographical

spots that are just as oscillating and blurry as Zeh has described her own feeling while traveling through them.

"Wo komm ich hin"—
Corpus Delicti and *Nullzeit*

Corpus Delicti is not only Juli Zeh's first stage play—it was originally written for the Ruhrtriennale in 2007—but also a first step toward incorporating literary spaces into her body of work that defy easy geographical localization. While all her previous novels, *Adler und Engel, Spieltrieb* (Gaming Instinct, 2004), and *Schilf* (*In Free Fall*, 2007) are very specific with regard to their temporal and geographical setting, this is—at least to some extent—less the case with *Corpus Delicti*. Set in the near future, the novel tells the story of biologist Mia Holl who gets entangled in a confrontation with the governmental system called the "Methode" (method). Based on a synthesis of biologist principles and scientific rationality, the system depicted in the novel replaces health for personal freedom as one if not the highest good in society, thus resulting in what critics have labeled a "Gesundheitsdiktatur" (health dictatorship).[19]

While her previous novels had been firmly anchored in both space and time, the temporal and spatial framework of *Corpus Delicti* is of a discernibly vaguer nature. Moreover, when comparing the text's initial form as a play and its figuration as a novel, there are a number of significant changes toward a further deterritorialization of the setting. The script of the play[20] clearly defines both time and space of the action. After a preface—an excerpt from a fictional text that serves as an introduction to the ideological foundations of the "Methode"—the novel starts with the verdict of the trial against Mia Holl, which forms the central part of the play. Showcasing her professional training as a jurist, Zeh fastidiously presents the case including the names of defendants, plaintiffs, and jurors. The date of the trial, while in the chapter title indistinctly given as "Mitten am Tag, in der Mitte des Jahrhunderts" (Midday, Midcentury), is defined as April 11, 2057. The stage directions suggest to alter this date according to the day of subsequent performances. It prescribes an intonation which creates a juncture of the intra-textual date with the extra-textual date of performance: "Hier kann das Datum der jeweiligen Vorstellung eingefügt werden; es müsste dann betont gesprochen werden: zum Beispiel für die Premiere 15. September Zweitausendsieben . . . undfünfzig." (Here, one may choose to insert the date of the respective performance; this should be stressed by intonation, in case of the premiere September 15 Two thousand and fifty . . . seven).[21] *Corpus Delicti* is thus marked to bridge the gap between its future setting and the temporary present of its performance. With respect to geography, the script clearly localizes the court as being the "Schwurgericht Essen" (Jury Court Essen) and sets the action in the city of the play's premiere at the Maschinenhaus Zeche Carl. With this distinct location in mind, the ensuing descriptive passages that present the geographical surroundings of the action guide the reader's perception in a way that further anchors the plot in the Ruhr area. Imitating the establishing shot of a movie camera, the text first presents a panorama view of the landscape before zooming into the actual place of the first scene, an office in the district court. The script lists "stillgelegte Kies- und Kohlegruben, vor vielen Jahren geflutet" (*CDP*, 8; gravel pits and quarries, now abandoned and flooded) as well as abandoned factories and industrial complexes that are, just like the actual Maschinenhaus, now used as arts and performance centers. The clearly delineated temporal and geographical references in the stage version confront the audience with a plot that takes place right where they are—only within a temporal framework geared toward an emphasis of its contemporary relevance by projecting discourses on health and personal freedom of the late 2000s into the near future.

The novelization of the play published two years later presents a version of the setting which is—at least after a first, cursory reading—less specified with regard to both time and space and thus arguably a more transnational one. In addition to accentuating the omnipotent power of the governmental system by changing the formula "Im Namen des Volkes" (In the Name of the People; play) to "Im Namen der Methode" (In the Name of the Method; novel) and in this manner even further emphasizing the political impetus of the text,[22] the novelization omits all detailed information on its temporal location. Instead, it leaves the reader with the deliberately vague "Mitten am Tag, in der Mitte des Jahrhunderts."[23] Consequently, the text makes no mention of its geographical location either. While the novel contains the same descriptions of the setting as the play—and indeed they appear to be much more at home within the context of a prose text—the reader is no longer able to effortlessly associate the abandoned factories and industrial sites with the Ruhr area since the distinct reference to Essen has been omitted. In fact, the novelization requires some effort on the part of the reader if one is to determine the action as being set in Germany at all. If not for the characters' names and the notable exception of characterizing protagonist Mia as a "deutsche Staatsangehörige" (*CDP*, 9; German national), the text offers only very few references to its localization—and even this clear-cut national affiliation does not play a significant role for the plot that will unfold because its political impetus transcends national borders. Just like in the play, the action, following the above-mentioned zoom of the camera, quickly moves and stays inside. The greater part of *Corpus Delicti* takes place in courtrooms, interrogation cells, and Mia's apartment, in short, indoor spaces that provide no clues to their larger locality.

In sum, the novelization of *Corpus Delicti* cuts the ties of temporal and spatial reference previously established in the stage version. While keeping yet slightly blurring the temporal frame, it situates the action in a geographically deterritorialized place that can only be determined as being set in Germany by associating the "stillgelegte Kies- und Kohlegruben, vor vielen Jahren geflutet" (*CDP*, 8; gravel pits and quarries, now abandoned and flooded) with the Ruhr-area—and this only provided that the reader already has a knowledge of that particular landscape. In my reading of the novelization of *Corpus Delicti*—while still pushing the reader to transfer discourses of the present to the future setting of the novel—the geographical space of our lived-in world is no longer of significant importance for its reception. By omitting distinct location markers and thus entering a space beyond discernible borders, the text manages to emphasize its focus on its general themes that are not tied to a specific spatial setting. At the same time, this assertion has to be read with a fair amount of caution. Just as the nation is very much present in the term "trans*nation*alism" itself, there is always the possibility of a reinscription of the nation into a literary work on the part of the reader. Regardless of the author's efforts to eradicate any hints toward a specific spatial setting and, especially in the case of *Corpus Delicti*, to pursue a political agenda that could be labelled "global," or even "universal," the reader might easily be tempted to reintroduce the nation based on the knowledge that the author comes from a certain background—and of course based on the fact that any literary text is written in a language that is usually tied to a national background. Additionally, there might be a desire to reinscribe the nation in order to give any given text a specific locality. Therefore, the nation, even in markedly transnational fiction or in fiction that is, to repeat Ette's term, "on the move," remains a concept that looms in the background of literary texts.

This is also true for Zeh's most recent fictional publication *Nullzeit* from 2012, even though she has continued to set her narratives in deterritorialized spaces. While the novel falls into the category of texts that are set abroad like, to give but one example, Judith Hermann's *Nichts als Gespenster* (Nothing but Ghosts, 2003), *Nullzeit* can also be classified as a text in which the nation looms in the background—this time, as my reading will show, in a very literal sense. Like *Die Stille ist ein Geräusch* and *Corpus Delicti*, *Nullzeit* stresses the ambiguities of the term transnationalism in that it is set in a deterritorialized space and a text that cannot escape national reterritorialization.

Moving away from the starkly political content of her previous novel, *Nullzeit* tells the story of scuba diving instructor Sven, who has left Germany fourteen years prior to the novel's plot to open a business on what is only referred to as the "Insel" (island). Germany, on the other hand, is referred to by Sven as "das Kriegsgebiet" (the war zone), to which he has burned all bridges. The reason for Sven's self-chosen exile is laid out clearly. A humiliating experience during his final oral exam before achieving a degree in law results in his disgust for the legal trade as well as in being fed up with permanently being labeled and judged. As a consequence, Sven has decided to lead a life that is consciously detached from emotional entanglements and demonstrates disinterest in if not ignorance of politics: "Mit Deutschland, das ich seitdem das 'Kriegsgebiet' nannte, wollte ich nichts mehr zu tun haben. Als ich wenig später auf der Insel ein neues Leben began, war 'Raushalten' das Fundament, auf dem ich meine Weltsicht erbaute." (I wanted nothing more to do with Germany, which I've thought of as "the war zone" ever since. When I began my new life on the island not long afterward, the fundamental expression of my worldview was "Stay out of it.")[24] The affiliation of Germany as a nation with his identity construction has been severely scarred and leads to a radical rejection of his country of origin. Sven goes so far as to extend his weariness of Germany to society and politics in general. However, his firmly established worldview to "stay out of it" is profoundly challenged by the arrival of his customers Theo and Jolanthe, which sets in motion a series of events that eventually leads to Sven's departure from the island and a return to "the war zone," Germany, as I will elaborate later on.

The geographical setting of the novel, the "Insel" is, even if the text avoids any mentioning, clearly recognizable as Lanzarote. In Piatti's terms, the setting can be described as a "transformierter Handlungsraum" (*LiB*, 361; transformed space of action), that is, a space of action that is based on an actual geographical location but slightly altered to fit the framework of the narrative. While the frequent references to the volcanic landscape and the works of art scattered across the island—a reference to César Manrique and his profound influence on Lanzarote—already hint toward the Canary Island, the island in *Nullzeit* is fully elevated from its feigned anonymity by demarcating cities, towns, and villages. On his way home from the airport where he had picked up Jolanthe and Theo, Sven passes the actual towns Arrecife and Tinajo before reaching the fictional Lahora where Sven lives with his girlfriend Antje, an imaginary location of greater significance for the characters than the island's realistic counterparts. In more than one sense of the word, Lahora is a place at the end of the world. In addition to being situated in the midst of a volcanic area, Sven describes the spot as unfinished and devoid of any amenities of civilization: "Lahora besitze keinen Bauplan. Keine Straßennnamen. Keine Kanalisation. Genau genommen besitze Lahora außer mir und Antje auch keine Einwohner. . . . Ein Ort des Stillstands. . . . Das Ende der Welt." (*N*, 15; Lahora had no building plan, I told them. No street names. No sewer systems. All in all, except for Antje and me, Lahora didn't have any inhabitants either. . . . A place where everything came to a halt. . . . The ends of the earth.) Not only does the barren volcanic landscape mirror Sven's equally desolate emotional state of mind, the fact that it is situated on an island, that is, a geographical configuration detached from the mainland, further stresses Sven's attempts to stay away from social commitments. However, it also has to be mentioned that Lanzarote, the blueprint for the transformed space of action in *Nullzeit*, is traditionally one of the most popular travel destinations for German tourists, and it is more than debatable how likely it is from the outset for Sven to escape his national affiliation if he decides to settle on an island heavily flocked by Germans every year. The characteristic of an island as being removed from society, however, is of course the perfect setting for creating new identity and social configurations and can be traced back in literary history to Jonathan Swift's *Gulliver's Travels* (1726) and Thomas Morus's *Utopia* (1516). In the end, Sven's personal utopia will crumble, and he is forced to recreate a new identity for himself that pushes him toward a reintegration into society. Significantly, his moment of epiphany occurs in a realm even further removed from human society, in a realm that is considered by Sven to be his true—and arguably a truly transnational one as well—home, namely underwater. While the topography of the ocean is of course just as mapped and charted as the rest of our world, my point here is that subaqueous environs are generally not perceived as such. When thinking of the borders of a nation, we usually do not include the sea borders, not the least because we often are not aware of their exact route. The underwater territory of any given nation is thus a peculiar space that geographically and politically belongs to a nation while it is at the same time not necessarily associated with a specific national territory. In addition to being uninhabitable to humans, it is also a realm in which our standard means of communication, the spoken language, is of no use. For the protagonist, the underwater world of the Atlantic therefore serves as an idealistic transnational mirror image of the world above the surface and constitutes a perfect haven for his world-weariness. As mentioned above, the crossing of the easily permeable boundary between the ocean and dry land leads to a turning point in *Nullzeit*. During a scuba diving trip, Jolanthe attempts to kill her despised partner Theo and pushes him into the ocean. She thus invades Sven's realm where he is, because of both his profession and his attachment to his perfect kingdom, in control. Sven encounters the drowning Theo who is under the influence of alcohol and is forced to decide between either helping Theo or letting him drown in order to start a new life with Jolanthe. This way, and quite contrary to her intentions, the calculating Jolanthe confronts Sven with his own indifference and concept of "staying out of it" in a matter of life and death. After a moment of hesitation, Sven helps Theo who, together with Jolanthe, shortly thereafter leaves the island for Germany.

Nullzeit utilizes both the island and the underwater world as deterritorialized, borderless, transnational, and—at least for a while—utopian spaces in the sense that they are, in the case of Sven's home in Lahora, left in a state of geographical vagueness and devoid of any boundaries in the case of the underwater realm. Especially with regard to Sven's safe haven below the ocean's surface, a world beyond human society and with a specific code of behaviour and language that bears little to no meaning on land, the mere notion of geographical borders loses its meaning entirely. In simplified terms, there are no checkpoints under water. Both spaces serve as playgrounds in which the protagonist Sven not only seeks refuge but is able to try out new identity figurations, figurations that eventually fail because of the inevitability of social entanglements that force him to resurface.

"Und was zum Teufel soll der ganze Scheiß?"—Conclusion

Juli Zeh's texts, I argued earlier, can be read as literary reflections of today's globalized world, a world characterized by accelerated mobility, migration, and an oscillating relationship between deterritorialization and reterritorialization. It is this firm anchoring in our lived-in world that allows for a reading of Zeh's work against the backdrop of broader transnational discourses, especially in light of Ottmar Ette's claim that literatures in the twenty-first century will be increasingly "on the move" and Taberner's assessment that nonminority writers are as itinerant as minority writers, who are traditionally the focus of analysis of transnational literature. In general, Juli Zeh in her fiction creates spaces of action beyond German national boundaries that allow her protagonists to be highly agile, thus echoing the broader economical, sociopolitical, and cultural framework of the globalized world in which they are both set and written.

The concrete configurations of spatial references within the respective texts, however, defy any tidy categorizations. As my reading of *Die Stille ist ein Geräusch* has attempted to show, it can range from distinct references to geographically determinable locations—each chapter names at least one town, village, or landmark that Zeh visits—to passages in which seemingly fixed topographies appear much more vague and elusive. The unreliability of location markers and geographical borders, however, is made productive by giving in to their fluctuation. This submission eventually results in a pleasurable, if temporarily limited, movement on the map that can be read as truly *trans*national in the sense that it is no longer tied to, and even oblivious to national boundaries. Consequently, Zeh's more recent works have abandoned the idea of fixed geographies to an even higher extent. In both *Corpus Delicti*, especially in its novelized form, and *Nullzeit*, Zeh creates deterritorialized literary spaces of action devoid of distinct referents on geographical maps. In the case of *Corpus Delicti*, this can be read as a deliberate move to emphasize and

heighten the agenda of the novel which is not bound to geographic specificities. At the same time, and this mirrors the relationship between deterritorialization and reterritorialization on a textual level, readers might be
tempted to reinscribe the geographical background into the novel to give
it a spatial anchoring. On the level of reception, such potential reinscription counters the transnational practice of eradicating all references to a
geographic background and reintroduces territorial certainty into a previously undetermined text. Similarly, the admittedly thinly veiled deterritorialized space of the island in *Nullzeit* is implemented as a testing ground
for a new identity construction for the protagonist against which the
clearly defined geographical—and national—space of Germany appears all
the more negative. All utopian ideas of creating an identity not connected
to a national background, as exemplified through the novel's protagonist
Sven, is shown to be bound to fail because no matter to which deterritorialized spaces Sven retreats, he is eventually forced to resurface by realizing
that his self-declared motto to "stay out of it" is not a feasible disposition
in today's world. The character's return to the surface of the Atlantic—
quite literally a return from borderless to chartered territory—can be read
as analogous to the resurgence of the nation as a clearly defined place to
which one is able to return as well, regardless of whether one is very fond
of this place or not.

Thus the idea of a nation with more or less rigid borders looms on
all three texts. With this in mind, I propose to read Zeh's work as literary negotiations of the very concepts of "nation" and "transnationalism" in contemporary German-language fiction. Just like transnational
practices are presented as desirable, even blissful, Zeh's texts classify the
nation as an ever-present, if somewhat elusive construction nonetheless.
In her travelogue *Die Stille ist ein Geräusch*, Zeh rather pessimistically
writes that, no matter how profoundly we think we change during our
travels, the "old self" is always waiting for us at home. This seems to be
a fitting metaphor for how the nation in transnational fiction, and this
arguably applies not only to Zeh's texts, is not all that easily overcome.
For just like the "old self" waiting at home rids the traveler of all delu-
sions of impactful change, the nation looming on transnational discourse
rids the concept "transnationalism" of an overtly optimistic outlook on
the realities of the twenty-first century. Rather, texts like Zeh's travelogue
remind us that the traversing of borders is only an option for those who
are privileged enough to do so. This insight is, as outlined above, already
included in *Die Stille ist ein Geräusch* when Zeh is repeatedly reminded of
her privileged position of her West German identity. In addition, transnational practices like the deterritorialization of texts on the part of the
author may be countered by a reterritorialization on the part of the reader
who potentially reinscribes a geographical background and thus helps to
bring the nation back to the front.

While the nation reemerges in Zeh's texts, there is however no textual evidence that creates a hierarchy of the nation *over* the concept of transnationalism. In other words, while the nation is present in her texts, this presence does not result in a dominating position and therefore provides no evidence of a resurgence of nationalist ideas. Rather, it seems that Zeh's texts simply acknowledge the nation as a still intrinsic part of today's sociopolitical and economic configuration in the sense of a worldview based in "Realpolitik" that serve as a counter weight to overly optimistic perceptions of the reality and possibilities of transnationalism. That being said, it is all the more important to remember that the nation has an elusive, that is, not fixed, quality to it. Transnational experiences and practices can still have an impact on the nation and help to keep its lines blurred. In other words, if the nation as the "old self" is sitting at home waiting for the traveler's return, it will do well to be interested to learn what happened abroad.

Notes

1 A note on the translation: The English translation of the passages quoted from *Nullzeit* (*Decompression*) and *Corpus Delicti* (*The Method*) are taken from the translation by John Cullen and Sally-Ann Spencer respectively. Juli Zeh, *The Method*, trans. Sally-Ann Spencer (London: Harvill Secker, 2012); Juli Zeh, *Decompression*, trans. John Cullen (London: Harvill Secker, 2014). Unless otherwise indicated, all other translations are my own.

2 Juli Zeh, *Treideln: Frankfurter Poetikvorlesungen* (Frankfurt am Main: Schöffling, 2013), 102–3. Further references are given in parentheses in the text in the form (*T*, page number).

3 Barbara Piatti, *Die Geographie der Literatur: Schauplätze, Handlungsräume, Raumphantasien* (Göttingen: Wallstein, 2009), 361. All further reference are given in parentheses in the text in the form (*GdL*, page number).

4 For an overview of these trends and countertrends, see the entries "Deterritorialization and Reterritorialization" in *Encyclopedia of Global Studies* (Los Angeles: SAGE, 2012).

5 See Stuart Taberner, *The Novel in German Since 1990* (Cambridge: Cambridge University Press, 2011), also Katharina Gerstenberger and Patricia Herminghouse, "German Literature in a New Century: Trends, Traditions, Transitions, Transformations: An Introduction," in *German Literature in a New Century: Trends, Traditions, Transitions, Transformations*, ed. Katharina Gerstenberger and Patricia Herminghouse (New York: Berghahn Books, 2008), 1–11.

6 David Damrosch, "Introduction: All the World in the Time," in *Teaching World Literature*, ed. David Damrosch (New York: Modern Language Association of America, 2009), 5.

7 Karl Esselborn, "Neue Zugänge zur inter/transkulturellen deutschsprachigen Literatur," in *Von der nationalen zur internationalen Literatur: Transkulturelle*

deutschsprachige Literatur und Kultur im Zeitalter globaler Migration, ed. Helmut Schmitz (Amsterdam: Rodopi, 2009), 43–44. For an overview of literature and migration, see Heinz L. Arnold, *Literatur und Migration* (München: Edition Text + Kritik, 2006). For a broader discussion of transnationalism and world literature, see Doris Bachmann-Medick, "Multikultur oder kulturelle Differenzen? Neue Konzepte von Weltliteratur und Übersetzung in postkolonialer Perspektive," *Deutsche Vierteljahrsschrift für Literaturwissenschaft und Geistesgeschichte* 68, no. 4 (1994): 585–612; Elke Sturm-Trigonakis, *Global Playing in der Literatur: Ein Versuch über die Neue Weltliteratur* (Würzburg: Königshausen & Neumann, 2007); John Pizer, *The Idea of World Literature: History and Pedagogical Practice* (Baton Rouge: Louisiana State University Press, 2006); and *Teaching World Literature*, edited by David Damrosch (New York: Modern Language Association of America, 2009).

[8] Stuart Taberner, "Transnationalism in Contemporary German-Language Fiction by Nonminority Writers," *Seminar* 47, no. 5 (2011): 624.

[9] Taberner, "Transnationalism," 625.

[10] In addition to reminding us of the transnational tradition of German literature with reference to canonical authors like Schiller and Goethe, Taberner discusses contemporary German fiction's transnationality with respect to a reimagination of a German diaspora in South America and the former African colonies, travels from the German province to metropolitan areas, and, lastly, the "'transational value' of German culture" (Taberner, "Transnationalism," 627).

[11] In fact, Sonja Klocke has taken the first step in applying the term *transnationalism* to Zeh's second novel *Spieltrieb* (Gaming Instinct, 2004) in her 2011 article that analyzes the impact of transborder exchanges on the novel's protagonists: Sonja Klocke, "Transnational Terrorism, War, and Violence: Globalization and Transborder Exchanges in Juli Zeh's *Spieltrieb*," *Seminar* 47, no. 4 (2011), 520–36.

[12] Ottmar Ette, *Literatur in Bewegung: Raum und Dynamik grenzüberschreitenden Schreibens in Europa und Amerika* (Weilerswist: Velbrück Wissenschaft, 2001), 17. Further references are given in parentheses in the text in the form (*LiB*, page number).

[13] See also Juli Zeh, *Die Diktatur der Demokraten: Warum ohne Recht kein Staat zu machen ist* (Hamburg: Körber-Stiftung, 2012), an edited version of her dissertation that addresses nation-building in the Balkan region in the aftermath of the war.

[14] Juli Zeh, *Adler und Engel* (Frankfurt am Main: btb, 2001), 221.

[15] For an analysis of *Adler und Engel*, see Stephen Brockmann, "Juli Zeh, Spieltrieb: Contemporary Nihilism," in *Emerging German-Language Novelists of the Twenty-First Century*, ed. by Lyn Marven and Stuart Taberner (Rochester, NY: Camden House, 2011), 62–74. Also, see Patricia Herminghouse, "The Young Author as Public Intellectual: The Case of Juli Zeh," in *German Literature in a New Century: Trends, Traditions, Transitions, Transformations*, ed. Katharina Gerstenberger and Patricia Herminghouse (New York: Berghahn Books, 2008), 268–84.

[16] http://www.stille-ist-geraeusch.de. For an analysis of Zeh's travelogue with respect to notions of orientalism, see Karoline von Oppen, "Nostalgia for Orient(ation): Travelling Through the Former Yugoslavia with Juli Zeh, Peter Schneider, and Peter Handke," *Seminar: A Journal of Germanic Studies* 41, no. 3 (2005): 246–60.

[17] Juli Zeh, *Die Stille ist ein Geräusch: Eine Fahrt durch Bosnien* (München: btb, 2003), 11. Further references are given in parentheses in the text in the form (*SiG*, page number).

[18] To some extent, this discomfort and the resulting journey can even be read as an act of resistance—for an analysis of the relationship between media coverage, resistance, and agency, see Arjun Appadurai, *Modernity at Large: Cultural Dimensions of Globalization* (Minneapolis: University of Minnesota Press, 1996), 7.

[19] Evelyn Finger, "Das Buch der Stunde," *Die Zeit*, March 1, 2009.

[20] While the script has not been published, it is available upon request from the Rowohlt Theaterverlag.

[21] Juli Zeh, *Corpus Delicti*, play (Reinbek bei Hamburg: Rowohlt-Theater Verlag, 2007), 7. Further references are given in parentheses in the text in the form (*CDP*, page number).

[22] Even though Zeh is commonly perceived as a politically committed writer, she claims that *Corpus Delicti* is her only "true" political novel: "Ich selbst habe mich erst einmal im Leben an einen politischen Roman gewagt. Er heißt *Corpus Delicti*." (*T*, 133; Personally, I have only once in my life dared to write a political novel. It is called *The Method*.)

[23] Juli Zeh, *Corpus Delicti: Ein Prozess* (München: btb, 2010), 11. Further references are given in parentheses in the text in the form (*CD*, page number).

[24] Juli Zeh, *Nullzeit* (Frankfurt am Main: Schöffling, 2012), 40. Further references are given in parentheses in the text in the form (*N*, page number).

12: Transnational Politics in Friedrich Dürrenmatt's *Der Auftrag* and Wolfgang Herrndorf's *Sand*

Tanja Nusser

> *Die Wüste änderte die Anschauungen rasch.*
>
> [The desert altered perceptions rapidly.]
>
> —Wolfgang Herrndorf[1]

IN WOLFGANG HERRNDORF'S NOVEL *Sand*, published in 2011, the reader's attention may be drawn to the following line: "Der Beobachter ist der Beobachtete" (*S* 117; The observer is the observed). This line resonates with another text written twenty-five years earlier, set like *Sand* in an unnamed North African country: Friedrich Dürrenmatt's 1988 *Der Auftrag oder Vom Beobachten des Beobachters der Beobachter: Novelle in 24 Sätzen* (The Assignment, or On the Observing of the Observer of the Observers). On the one hand, both texts depict economic interests like arms deals between Western nations and North Africa, along with political interventions, such as espionage. On the other, they posit North African countries as corrupt, terrorist states that are key players in international weapon deals with Western countries. Both texts utilize the particular geographical space of North Africa and the associated sociocultural and political stereotypes to turn the gaze back on Western countries and to critically question their investment in global transnational relations.

In the following chapter, I will examine two themes: the motif of sand as a representation of the instability of identity, and transnational political conflicts that are present in the Middle East. Relating to the first of these, I will analyze how a concept of subjectivity is constructed in the two texts, formed in one sense by a panoptical structure, and in another by power structures as developed by Foucault. In examining the second, I will evaluate the political implications of the two texts, with reference to Giorgio Agamben, Noam Chomsky, and other key thinkers. The analysis will focus on the figure of the terrorist and the definition of terrorist acts, demonstrating that in actuality, both texts question how terrorism and legal and nonlegal violence are defined or point toward the construction of certain political images. Finally, I will bring the two strands together to argue that the instability of identity in the texts is mirrored by the instability of political-identity positions.

In *Der Auftrag*, the protagonist is the film director F., who is famous for her film portraits, and "sich vorgenommen hatte, neue Wege zu beschreiten und der noch vagen Idee nachhing, ein Gesamtporträt herzustellen, jenes unseres Planeten nämlich" (had resolved to explore new paths and was pursuing the still vague idea of creating a total portrait, namely a portrait of our planet).[2] She is asked by Otto von Lambert to investigate the murder of his wife, Tina, by terrorists in North Africa. Directly after her arrival in an unnamed North African country, different political groups intervene to put a stop to her investigation. Following a clue into the desert, she uncovers that not Tina but a Danish journalist, Jytte Sörensen, was killed (not by terrorists as originally was assumed, but rather by a Vietnam veteran named Achilles), and also learns that the desert is the space in which the Western nations are observing each other and arming themselves for the next war. This undefined region is vital to the transnational economy of war because it is the market of the present and the future, as the protagonist Polyphem in *Der Auftrag* asserts:

> Die Haupteinnahme sei ein Krieg, den das Land mit dem Nachbarstaat um ein Gebiet in der großen Sandwüste führe . . . ein Krieg der nun schon seit zehn Jahren dahinmotte und längst nur noch dazu diene, die Produkte aller waffenexportierenden Länder zu testen . . . , der Krieg suche sich immer neue Schauplätze, folgerichtig, weil nur durch den Waffenexport die Konjunktur einigermaßen stabil bleibe . . . , die Fundamentalisten sähen in diesem Krieg eine westliche Schweinerei, was ja stimme. (*A*, 97–98)

> [Its principle source of revenue was a war with a neighboring country, a war for control of an area in the great sand desert . . . a war that had been creeping along for 10 years now and no longer served a purpose except to test the products of all the weapons-exporting countries . . . , the war effort was constantly seeking out new battlefields, quite logically, since the stability of the market depended on weapon exports . . . , the fundamentalists regarded the war as a criminal plot of the part of the West, which was true.]

The crime—the novella argues—is not the murder of a woman, but the interests of transnational companies and the countries that invest in North African countries to sustain their armament-based economy.

Herrndorf's *Sand* makes a similar point and seems indirectly to answer a question that Dürrenmatt's novella poses on the discursive level, namely, who is allowed to buy and own weapons of war. Herrndorf himself describes his novel in a blog entry as an "in der Wüste spielende[r]

Krimi mit B-Picture-Plot" (a crime novel in the desert with a B-Picture-Plot) (Herrndorf 2010, paragraph 30).³ Set in 1972 (and naming the massacre in Munich as one of the reference points for transnational terrorism), the main protagonist, Carl Gross, seeks to reconstruct his identity after waking up in a barn in the middle of the desert with amnesia. He is helped in this endeavor by Helen Gliese, whom he meets in the desert when he stops her car for help. He does not know how he came to the barn, he has no idea what happened, he does not know who he is, and the reader experiences the same disorientation that he does because he or she has no more knowledge at that point of the story than the unnamed protagonist (*S*, 91–94). The plot centers on the search for his personal identity and intertwines it with the recurrent topic of a "Mine" (Landmine) that Helen Gliese searches for and that she believes Carl Gross can locate. Before he dies, he is tortured by Helen and three men, all agents of an unnamed Western organization, to give up all his secrets—which he cannot do because he does not remember his identity. Ultimately, he is shot by an old man who believes him to be someone else; this means that even his violent death is based on an affirmation (even if it is incorrect) of his identity through the other. Carl's relationship to Helen throughout the novel is solely based on a Foucauldian power of knowledge—who is Carl Gross, what does he know, who are the players in this international spy situation in the middle of the desert—and on power over the weapons of war, in the case of the novel, the nuclear bomb. Helen Gliese, in fact, is an agent who represents the Western nations and their ambition to distribute this power to their own interests. This means not distributing it to North African nationalists with "Nationalstolz, Idealismus, religiöse[m] Dogma, de[m] ganze[n] Tand und Flitter, mit dem der geistig Unterbelichtete sein Weltbild möbiliert und der im Erwachsenenalter erfahrungsgemäß so schwer abzuwerfen ist" (*S* 427; national pride, idealism, religious dogma, the whole bric-a-brac and tinsel with which the intellectually underexposed person furnishes his perception of the world and which is empirically proven to be difficult to abandon in adulthood). The only definite fact that remains is that a man loses his memory in an unnamed country in North Africa and is tortured because Western agents believe he knows where the nuclear bomb is. Indeed, even the blurb on the book cover fails to provide any illumination as to the novel's content: "Während in München Palästinenser des 'Schwarzen September' das Olympische Dorf überfallen, geschehen in der Sahara mysteriöse Dinge. In einer Hippie-Kommune werden vier Menschen ermordet, ein Geldkoffer verschwindet, und ein unterbelichteter Kommissar versucht sich an der Aufklärung des Falles. Ein verwirrter Atomspion, eine platinblonde Amerikanerin, ein Mann ohne Gedächtnis—Nordafrika 1972" (*S*, 247). While the Palestinians of the Black September attacked the Olympic village in Munich, mysterious occurrences transpired in the Sahara. In a hippie commune four people were murdered, a suitcase full of money disappeared and an underexposed commissar attempts to solve the case. A confused atomic spy, a bleach-blonde American woman, a man without a memory, North Africa 1972).[4]

Even if *Sand* and *Der Auftrag* do not directly thematize globalization or transnational actors, they can nevertheless be read usefully within this conceptual framework, since they depict a multiplicity of actors whose interests are not solely bound to or defined by a nation-state, even as they highlight the extreme violence that nations commit in pursuit of their interests.[5] Whereas the transnational turn is mainly based on migration and globalization theories, few theorists focus on other forms of transnational movements.[6] My approach to reading Dürrenmatt's and Herrndorf's texts are informed instead by theories about terrorism as a key form of contemporary transnationalism. Despite the fact that terrorism in the 1980s was generally understood as a threat to particular nation-states, Ulrich Beck argues that today's terrorism operates transnationally.[7] In the context of this chapter, the differences in the definition of terrorism and inter- as well transnational politics are interesting insofar as both texts span the timeframe of 1972 to 1986. While it can be argued that both texts deal with a perception of terrorism as a threat to nations, I would like to argue that they are also informed by politics contemporary to the era in which the texts were written. This means (taking up Beck's argument) that although *Sand* is set in 1972, terrorism appears in this novel of 2011 as a *transnational* threat and no longer as a threat to one nation. Terrorists are depicted as the new global political actors. and the distinction between different political and economic interests becomes much more difficult to make. In contrast to Dürrenmatt's novella that seems to be able to identify its crime and the actors involved in the crime—financial and political interests—*Sand* shows that the contemporary situation is far more diffuse and that nowadays it is more or less impossible to grasp either the political agendas of the different parties or, indeed, what the goals of the terrorist act are.

This Nihilistic Desert[8]

At the same time, these stories also focus on a second concern that may be even more precarious than the political situation of North Africa and the West's response to the presumed threat of terrorism. The two texts use the genre of the crime novel in this geographically undefined space to question fundamentally the Western belief in a subject that is able to solve or control a situation. In the traditional crime novel, the plot moves toward solving the crime at the end of the story, even if the crime is sometimes revealed at the beginning of the narration. The classical crime novel is based on the belief that truth can be uncovered by the protagonist in the story. This "discovery or unearthing of truth" follows a narrative logic because, at the beginning of the plot, all the obvious signs of the crime are part of a speculation and reconstruction of the sequence of events. Only through the narrowing down and exclusion of irrelevant things does the "truth" of the crime emerge. In *Der Auftrag* and *Sand*, this possibility of truth and an answer to the question, who's done it?—or, who is the criminal?—is fundamentally questioned, since the multitude of interests and intersecting stories show the arbitrariness of an exclusionary logic. This means that the description of the texts as crime novels is deceptive to a certain extent, and sets the stage for a one-dimensional reading, focusing on the crime plot and neglecting the other themes and genres developed throughout and represented through the texts.[9] But if the traditional crime novel can be perceived as the literary place where a kind of enlightened subject is moving the plot along toward some kind of unquestionable knowledge of the truth, then Dürrenmatt's novella as well as Herrndorf's novel use this genre to question exactly the subject of definite knowledge production and the possibility of one definite truth out there.[10]

In scrutinizing the Western belief in the enlightened subject (embodied by the figure of the truth seeker and quasi detective, the filmmaker F., as well as by Carl Gross's search for identity), both texts question the construction of Western identities based on concepts of rationality, as I will argue later in this chapter. Both texts play a game of confusion with their readers with regard to the identities of their protagonists. On a content level, the narratives are centered on a misinterpretation or contestation of individual identities and biographies that moves the plots forward: in the case of Dürrenmatt's novella on a doubling or copying of Tina; in the case of Herrndorf's *Sand* on a false identity ascription. Confronted with texts that question knowledge and truth itself (and not only in regard to political situations), it has to be questioned how both texts link espionage, terrorism, and only vaguely specified North African nations—in *Der Auftrag* the country's acronym is M; in *Sand* the setting is the Maghreb, with hints at Morocco—to thematize transnational politics and globally operating economies on the discursive level, as well as to demonstrate the precariousness of the individual subject in transnational and global times.

Focusing firstly on the subject positions in both texts, I want to show how the texts present their readers with subjects whose existence is fundamentally dependent on the confirmation of their subject status by someone else. While the topic of the subject position seems to be in the first instance connected to the psychodynamic of the protagonists, it becomes clear while reading the texts that it is intertwined with a political dimension right from the very beginning of both texts. Identity is positioned as psychodynamic and political. In the fifth chapter of Dürrenmatt's text, F. visits a friend, the logician D., to talk with him about "the case" before she leaves on the trip to find Tina. D. reacts in a lengthy monologue, in which he contests the status of the subject, highlighting the subject's dependence upon an observer who simultaneously affirms and threatens the fundamental existence of the subject:

> D. . . . meinte, . . . kein Mensch sei mit sich identisch, weil er der Zeit unterworfen und genau genommen zu jedem Zeitpunkt ein anderer sei als vorher . . . womit sich nur die logische Feststellung bestätige, zu jedem Beobachteten gehöre ein Beobachtendes, das, werde es von jenem Beobachteten beobachtet, selber ein Beobachtetes werde, eine banale logische Wechselwirkung . . . jeder fühle sich von jedem beobachtet und beobachte jeden, der Mensch heute sei ein beobachteter Mensch. (*A*, 18–20)

> [D. . . . remarked . . . there was no self-identical person anywhere, because everyone was subject to time and was therefore, strictly speaking, a different person at every moment . . . an empirical confirmation, in short, of the logical conclusion that anything observed requires the presence of an observer, who, if he is observed by what he is observing, himself becomes an object of observation, a banal logical interaction . . . everyone observed and felt observed by everyone else, so that a very suitable definition of contemporary man might be that he is a man under observation.]

While at this point of the novella the monologue shifts the story into a new level, it later becomes obvious how D.'s words tie the subject constitution (as observer and observed) to the political theme of the text (the desert as the space in which one nation observes the other nation). It essentially embeds subject constitution within a structure of surveillance that brings subject theories (the affirmation as subject through the other) together with Bentham's Panopticon and Foucault's interpretation of it in *Surveiller et punir: Naissance de la prison* (Discipline and Punish: The Birth of the Prison; 1975). Whereas subject and object are positioned as relational and interdependent concepts on a logical, psychological, and political level in *Der Auftrag*, the subject(-position) is thematized in *Sand* via amnesia of Carl Gross, who "borrows" his name from the label of his jacket (since he is not only unable to remember his identity but also has no reference for his nationality) and whose existence as a psychological and political subject is dependent upon the recollection of his personal and national identity. Additionally, he requires approval of his identity by the other (the observer), or disavowal of his memory loss and insinuation of an identity that he cannot confirm for most of the story. Even if the subject positions are constructed completely differently and hint at different discourses, they both share the dependence on a person that (re)affirms their position as a subject. At the end of the stories, the reader is left with one fundamental question: What does she really know about the story and the identities of the main protagonists in both texts?

Both texts use the desert of the undisclosed North African countries and the motif of sand as metaphors for subject concepts that are developed in the texts. Even if both texts have to be read as investigations in transnational politics, these investigations are not only interested in North Africa or their political agendas but also use the North African region as a mise-en-scène for discussing Western concepts of the subject. While the subject loses its frame of reference (in *Sand*), or is established as a double or copy (*Der Auftrag*), the North African desert functions as a backdrop for the texts' explorations of the Western self-understanding as an enlightened subject, as well as the supposed (pre)modern North African subject. To quote just one example from Herrndorf's *Sand*:

> Das aber war genau das Problem der Kameltreiber. Sie wollten mit dem Atom rummachen und wussten nicht, wie Zentrifuge geht. . . . Lundgren hatte schon viel Elend gesehen in dieser Welt, und er hatte irgendwann herausgefunden, was das Problem des Trikonts und seiner Bewohner war. Neben vielen anderen fanden sie Gehirntätigkeit unmännlich. Das sagte natürlich so keiner. Aber Wissenschaft stand in unscharfer Opposition zu den großen Idealen von Stolz, Ehre und Ramtamtamtam. Wissenschaft war für Weiber. . . . Und am schlimmsten die Araber. Was ihnen im Blut lag, waren Nichtstun, Intrige und Fanatismus. Aber Nachdenken war für Frauen. . . . Lundgren dachte darüber nach, und je länger er darüber nachdachte, über das, was er bei sich den Teufelskreis des arabischen Nationalcharakters nannte, desto weniger fremd erschien er ihm. Denn letztlich ging es ihm genauso. (*S*, 62–64)

> [That, however, was exactly the problem of the camel drivers. They wanted to fiddle around with the atom and didn't know how centrifuges work. . . . Lundgren had already seen too much misery in this world, and at some point he had found out what the problem of the Tricont and its inhabitants was. Besides a number of other things, they considered using their brains to be effeminate. Of course no one actually verbalized this. But science stood in blurred opposition to the great ideals of pride, honor, and hoopla. Science was something for women. . . . And the worst are the Arabs. Idleness, scheming, and fanaticism were what ran in their blood. But contemplating was for women. . . . A vicious circle. Lundgren thought about it and the more he thought about it, about that which he referred to as the vicious circle of the Arabian national character, the less foreign they appeared to him. Because in the end the same went for him.]

The quotation shows how Lundgren implicitly codes the "West" as enlightened, just as the narrator does ironically later in the text, when he states that Ludgren "mit dem Rest der Vernunft, der ihm verblieben war" (*S*, 67; with the rest of his reason, that still remained) notices that he "wusste alles" (*S*, 68; knew all), and thereby positions North Africa as (pre)modern. But it is important to emphasize that *Sand* as well as *Der Auftrag* question precisely this binary, playing with the theoretical constructions and implications embedded in this dichotomy, while simultaneously and clearly interrogating the construction of the African continent as (pre)modern and the Western nations as (post)modern or enlightened. Whereas Lundgren uses well-known stereotypes to formulate his opinion of the Tricont and nationalist terrorism to collapse the difference between "the Arabs" and himself in the last sentence of the quotation, the text itself exposes the behavior of the depicted Westerners in this unnamed country as brutal, colonizing, exploiting, and inhuman.

Its Principle Source of Revenue Was a War[11]

As Steven Vertovec shows, transnationalism from the perspective of the United States Department of Defense "means terrorists, insurgents, opposing factions in civil wars conducting operations outside their country of origin, and members of criminal groups," and these "kind of cross-border activities . . . require transnational measures and structures to combat them."[12] An argumentation like this has to be questioned, because it seems to follow a twin logic of reaction and prevention, which makes this argumentative structure itself highly problematic since transnational state-sanctioned activities and transnational terrorism are interdependent. Through an intertwining of terrorism and national, political, and economic interests, both texts demonstrate that questions of legality and of the differences between terrorist violence and state-sanctioned violence are—more than anything else—definitional ones.[13] The assumption that nations have to react on a transnational scale to confront or counteract transnational terrorism presupposes an institutionalizing of international (not transnational) law that allows transnational law enforcement activities to prevent transnational terrorism. With this differentiation I am hinting at an important point: While nations are working on establishing an international law (between countries), law enforcement is often national acting on a transnational level. This means that in this chapter, internationalism refers to acts between nations, while transnationalism focuses on national actors working together crossing national borders. But, coming back to the institutionalizing of international law, this argumentation is insofar on a structural level problematic as each setting of the law is, as Jacques Derrida points out, "a violence without a ground."[14] To follow Giorgio Agamben's argumentation, these forms of structural violence cannot be encompassed or negated by national constitutions and international legal organizations because they are enacting the law legitimizing the violence after the fact.[15]

This establishment of a new law operates within the same logic as revolutions or terrorism: In the same way that the legal constitution legalizes its violent enactment afterward (see Guantanamo or the killing of Bin Laden as examples of transnationally enacted law), terrorists anticipate through violence a legal condition that legitimizes the enacted violence afterward, as the setting of the new constitution.[16] But if I perceive both groups as utilizing similar strategies to achieve their goals (and here I return to Dürrenmatt's *Der Auftrag* and Herrndorf's *Sand* and their focus on violence as an enactment of different political interests),[17] it has to be questioned whether the common definitions of transnationalism as reference to nonstate or nongovernmental actors, and internationalism as reference to acts between nations[18] are useful when considering the political horizons that Herrndorf's and Dürrenmatt's texts delineate as they call precisely this difference into question. To formulate it differently, if the distinction between state-legalized violence and terrorist violence collapses on the structural level, does it make sense to differentiate between transnationalism as nonstate and international as between states? Or is this differentiation one that hinders far more than it helps in understanding the interweaving and reciprocity of the various forms of violence in globally operating economies as they are depicted in Dürrenmatt's novella and Herrndorf's novels?

Let's Free Ourselves from the Darkness of Enlightenment[19]

Together, the texts encompass the time between 1972 (Herrndorf's *Sand* mentions Munich as a reference point, as previously mentioned) and 1986 (Dürrenmatt's *Der Auftrag* was published in this year), and although both are situated in anonymous North African countries, they seem to allude to the Maghreb region and Morocco. Despite the fact that this region calls to mind the political situations of Algeria, Tunisia, Morocco, Libya, and Mauritania, (and with these, French and Spanish colonialism, the West Sahara conflict, and the Moroccan-American Treaty of Friendship from 1786, Operation Wooden Leg in 1985—the attack on the PLO in Tunisia by the Israeli air force—, and the war between Libya and Egypt in 1978), another much more prominent conflict also has to be considered to understand the political dimensions of the texts. The Middle East conflict is framed as a topic because of the 1972–86 date range (even if it remains unnamed in both works). Thematizing terrorism as fundamentalist, as the protagonists in Herrndorf's novel do, and international political interventions of Western nations as extremely violent and problematic, the texts set out to question the West's political agendas and the legitimization of violence.

Taking into consideration how terrorism and legal violence both have to be perceived in a similar manner, I want to draw attention to an older collection of essays from 1988 edited by Edward W. Said and Christopher Hitchens. In *Blaming the Victims*, Noam Chomsky's article "Middle East Terrorism and the American Ideological System" describes how the perception of Palestine as terrorist came into being after the foundation of the State of Israel in 1948 and how terrorists served as a form of legitimation of state-sanctioned violence. I am not as interested here in the fact that between 1972 and 1986 Palestinians were denied "representatives in eventual negotiations" with Israel and the United States, as they were "denied municipal elections or other democratic forms under Israeli military occupation."[20] I am rather more concerned with how Israeli and US politics in this time span can be understood in terms of terrorism. Chomsky polemically cites and uses a formulation by Benjamin Netanyahu, the Israeli ambassador to the United Nations between 1984 and 1988, for his own argument: "The distinguishing factor in terrorism, he [Netanyahu; T.N.] explained, is 'deliberate and systematic murder and maiming [of civilians] designed to inspire fear.'" Clearly, Chomsky argues further, "The Tunis attack [of the PLO through Israeli air force; T.N.] and other Israeli atrocities over the years fall under this definition, though most acts of international terrorism do not, including the most outrageous terrorist attacks against Israelis (Ma'alot, the Munich massacre, the coastal road atrocity of 1978 that provided the pretext for invading Lebanon, etc.)."[21]

In using a definition by an Israeli politician who justifies state-sanctioned interventions against terrorism, Chomsky challenges the clear-cut distinction between transnational terrorism and international politics espoused again and again over the past forty years.[22] Recounting a (not so slightly) different history of the Middle East conflict as it was told in the late 1980s in the press or through state officials in the Western world, he directs the gaze of the reader to the "conceptual framework"[23] that is able to exclude certain facts and issues.[24]

In the context of a discussion of transnational politics this begs the question: What makes these texts or the content of the texts German or Swiss? Do they reflect the nationality of their authors at all since Dürrenmatt was a Swiss author and Herrndorf a German one? It can be argued that this does not matter, since the focus is on the transnational subjects in the texts and not on a biographically or culturally embedded reading of the texts, but if globalization and transnationalism are "narratively-constructed at a local level,"[25] and if, at the same time (as Arjun Appadurai argues), we have to be aware that we are also dealing with problems that might manifest "themselves in intensely local forms but have contexts that are anything but local,"[26] then we have to take another look at the two texts to understand where the transnational connections lead us. The actual absent center of the stories might not be the truth or lost identity but the reference to Germany and the Holocaust. If we read both texts as discursively dealing with the political upheavals and wars in the Middle East after 1972 (*Sand*) and before 1986 (*Der Auftrag*), these political situations have to be traced back historically to the foundation of the State of Israel (after the British Mandate was voted by the UN to be replaced by an independent Arab state and an independent Jewish state), and this also means to Germany and the Holocaust. In perceiving Germany and the Holocaust as absent centers of the narrations, I am reframing the stories themselves, and I am also reframing the perception of texts. In doing so, I return to the beginning of the chapter where I argued that the definition of the texts as crime novels is somehow deceptive.

I will now take a closer look at how the texts displace their themes and negate an essentially stable knowledge production and frame knowledge within a Foucauldian power structure that is equally postmodern, fragmented, and positional. Through this, I want to investigate what else is conveyed by the political discourses of both texts. Or to phrase it differently: How do we consider the discourse of transnational state-sanctioned violence and terrorism alongside a questioning of the Western subject constructions? Margaret Scanlan argues in an article on Dürrenmatt's *Der Auftrag*, that fragmentation "of identity in the novel's unstable world leads to a longing for order that asserts itself in totalitarian politics, fundamentalist religion, and documentary realism, all disciplines in Foucault's sense, that depend on observation."[27] I follow Scanlan's "observation" to a certain degree, as the fragmentation of perception and observation is clearly demonstrated throughout *Der Auftrag*. At the beginning of the novella F. wishes "ein Gesamtportät herzustellen, jenes unseres Planeten nämlich, indem sie dies durch ein Zusammenfügen zufälliger Szenen zu einem Ganzen zu erzielen hoffte" (*A*, 10; the still vague idea of creating a total portrait, namely a portrayal of our planet, by combining random scenes into a whole). Over the course of the story, however, she comes to understand that her desire to create a portrait of the planet based on accidental observed scenes, photographed and joined together as a huge objective image of the outer world, is doomed to fail because even if she compiles the photos, perceptions of the world are still fragmented. Reality is, as she recognizes, "inszeniert" (*A*, 123; staged). An opposite position is represented by the (war-)photographer Polyphem, who believes that "ein Spiel werde inszeniert, die Wirklichkeit könne nicht inszeniert, sondern nur sichtbar gemacht werden" (*A*, 123; only plays could be staged, not reality, which could only be made visible). These two positions mark the definitional differences surrounding the depiction of reality (in *Der Auftrag* this includes the reality of war and terrorism as well as of the individual subject). Polyphem's desire to construct a portrait of F. and his belief in the objectivity of observation through the camera lens—"reine Beobachtung" (*A*, 111; pure observation)—mirrors F.'s earlier goal of an all-encompassing portrait of the planet. But as the novella demonstrates, in order to gain an understanding and insights into a person, a situation, or the planet, a process of constructing a portrait out of single, fragmented moments that are only able to tell one version of a story is taking place (in the case of *Der Auftrag*, that Tina von Lambert was killed and not Jytte Sörensen).

In my opinion, these two positions highlight the basic bias involved in observation. While observation, especially in state discourses like the NSA debate, has recently been conceptualized as a neutral form of information gathering that aims for maximum knowledge in order to control any given situation, both texts demonstrate that observation is on the one hand always embedded in power structures and on the other hand, never complete (and in this sense obsolete, since only fragmentary images can be constructed). But surprisingly it can be argued that both works depict a strengthening of different forms of fundamentalisms and totalitarianisms as a reaction toward such contrary concepts or situations as a totalizing claim of surveillance or observation, a definition of the world through the Western (enlightened) subject, or an instability of the former political order of the world. At the same time, they fundamentally question the narration as a narration and perception within Foucault's concept of power.

Returning to my previous observation that both texts seem to use North Africa as a mise-en-scène for Western subject constructions and their storylines as a mise-en-scène for theoretical discourses, I want to argue these usages can also be read—even if both novels not only thematize but also scrutinize the conflict and wars in Middle East as a consequence of transnational politics that harken back to 1933 and are enacted violently time and time again—as an occupation with forms of apartheid that are inherent in globalizing theoretical discourses. I refer here to Appadurai, whose work describes the evolution of a "double apartheid":

> The academy (especially in the United States) has found in globalization an object around which to conduct its special internal quarrels about such issues as representation, recognition, the "end" of history, the specters of capital (and of comparison), and a host of others. These debates, which still set the standard of value for the global professoriate, nevertheless have an increasingly parochial quality. Thus the first form of apartheid is the growing divorce between these debates and those that characterize vernacular discourses about

the global, worldwide, that are typically concerned with how to plausibly protect cultural autonomy and economic survival in some local, national, or regional sphere in the era of "reform" and "openness." The second form of apartheid is that the poor and their advocates find themselves as far from the anxieties of their own national discourses about globalization as they do from the intricacies of the debates in global fora and policy discourses surrounding trade, labor, environment, disease, and warfare.[28]

If the goal is to interpret the novels as depicting the "colonizing" aspects of Western politics and theories, then I argue that subject constructions as well as political interventions of Western nations in the Middle East, or the definition of what a terrorist act is and who is allowed to buy (nuclear) weapons, are framed by positions of power. Clearly marked as Western in the texts, the definitional powers colonize—not only on the political but also on the theoretical level—the enlightened, the postmodern, the (pre)modern subject, terrorism, and state-sanctioned violence. Reading the novels in this manner also means that they can be read as simultaneously dealing with transnational issues, while problematizing the investment into surveillance by various countries as a new form of colonialism. In other words, through bringing such different topics as the instability of identity and transnational political conflicts together, both texts move the reader beyond a simple perception of what global or transnational politics might be or how to perceive transnational terrorist threats. In interweaving both topics and presenting them in the form of a crime text, they fundamentally discuss knowledge productions as Western concepts that remain intimately linked to the enlightened subject, thus portraying these concepts as colonizing. As the author named Spasski in *Sand* says, "Befreien wir uns aus dem Dünkel der Aufklärung! Licht gehört nicht in jede Finsternis." (*S*, 61; Free ourselves from the arrogance of the Enlightenment! Light does not belong in every darkness.)

Notes

[1] *Epigraph:* Wolfgang Herrndorf, *Sand* (Berlin: Rowohlt, 2011), 23. All translations of Wolfgang Herrndorf's texts by Vanessa Plumly. Further references to this volume appear in the text with the abbreviation *S*.

[2] Friedrich Dürrenmatt, *Der Auftrag oder Vom Beobachten des Beobachters der Beobachter: Novelle in vierundzwanzig Sätze* (Zürich: Diogenes, 1988), 5. Friedrich Dürrenmatt, *The Assignment: Or, on the Observing of the Observer of the Observers,* translated by Joel Agee (Chicago: Chicago University Press, 2008). All translations from the English-language version. Further references to this volume appear in the text with the abbreviation *A*.

260   ♦   Tanja Nusser

³ Wolfgang Herrndorf, "Rückblende, Teil 1: Das Krankenhaus," in *Blog: Arbeit und Struktur*, accessed April 2, 2015, http://www.wolfgang-herrndorf. de/2010/09/rtl/.

⁴ In his blog, Herrndorf reflects this kind of cover blurb:

> Und es geht doch nichts über einen Lektor, der die Nöte seines Autors versteht: "wenn du willst, schreib ich dir noch einen fastpaced unputdownable high octane international male action spy thriller with flat characters and exploding helicopters and a chick with a gun klappentext."
>
> ein grausames massaker.
> ein mann ohne gedächtnis.
> eine erfindung, die die welt bedroht.
>
> [And nothing can be said about a editor, who understands the needs of his author, "if you want, I'll write a fast-paced unputdownable high octane international male action spy thriller with flat characters and exploding helicopters and a chick with a gun cover text."
>
> a savage massacre.
> a man without a memory.
> an invention that threatens the world.]

From Wolfgang Herrndorf, "Neunzehn," September 2, 2011, in *Blog: Arbeit und Struktur*, accessed May 4, 2015, http://www.wolfgang-herrndorf.de/2011/08/ neunzehn/.

⁵ Industrialized nations or late capitalist societies, Ulrich Beck argues, are confronted with changes that they themselves generate as they become "modern" but which they cannot integrate. One of these is the multiplication of actors and the diffusion of power, to the extent that industrial production and reproduction operate on a global level and work across national borders. This means, according to Ulrich Beck, that we are facing not an end of politics but an "*escape* from the categories of the national state, and even from the schema defining what is 'political' and 'non-political' action." Ulrich Beck, *What is Globalization?*, transl. Patrick Camiller (Cambridge: Polity Press, 2000), 1. Original: *Was ist Globalisierung?* (Frankfurt am Main: Suhrkamp, 1997). It can be observed, Beck argues, that the "sapping [of] the foundations of national economics and national states" through globally operating economies is "answered with a re-nationalization" (2–3). Globalization, then, describes "the processes through which sovereign national states are crisscrossed and undermined by transnational actors with varying prospects of power, orientations, identities and networks" (11).

⁶ As Arianna Dagnino aptly puts it, "Transnationalism is generally related to the study of the processes and the effects of transnational migrations on subjectivity, social identity formation and the creation of new 'transnational social spaces' rather than expressing a cultural attitude and a philosophical approach towards what Peter Burke calls the 'new global cultural order.'" Arianna Dagnino, "Transcultural Writers and Transcultural Literature in the Age of Global Modernity," *Transnational Literature* 4, no. 2 (2012): 50–101.

[7] "So sind es jetzt transnationale Bedrohungen substaatlicher Täter und Netzwerke, die die gesamte staatliche Welt herausfordern. . . . Mit den Schreckensbildern von New York haben sich auf einen Schlag Terrorgruppen als neue globale Akteure in Konkurrenz zu Staaten, Wirtschaft und Zivilgesellschaft etabliert." (Now these are actors and networks on the sub-state level that defy the whole public / state world. . . . With the horrendous images of New York terror groups established themselves at a single blow as new global actors in competition to states, economy and the civil society). Ulrich Beck, *Das Schweigen der Wörter: Über den Terror und Krieg* (Frankfurt am Main: Suhrkamp, 2002), 26.

[8] A "nihilistische Wüste" (nihilistic desert), as Wolfgang Herrndorf puts it in his blog entry "Fünfzehn." Wolfgang Herrndorf, "Fünfzehn," May 17, 2011, in *Blog: Arbeit und Struktur*, accessed April 2, 2015, http://www.wolfgang-herrndorf.de/2011/04/fuenfzehn/.

[9] See for example the review of *Sand* in *Die Zeit*: "Die Settings sind Ian-Fleming-mäßig exotisch und die Figuren rätselhaft wie bei John le Carré. Es ist ein Spionagethriller alter Schule." Andrea Hünniger, "Die Wüste ist ein sinnloser Ort," *Zeit Online*, November 22, 2011, accessed January 31, 2015, http://www.zeit. de/2011/47/L-B-Herrndorf. Friedmar Apel, professor of comparative literature at the University of Bielefeld, subtitles his review in the *Frankfurter Allgemeine Zeitung*: "Im vergangenen Jahr begeisterte er mit der Ausreißergeschichte 'Tschick.' Jetzt legt Wolfgang Herrndorf einen literarischen Thriller vor: den grandiosen Wüstenroman 'Sand.'" Friedmar Apel, "Wo Schmuggler, Hippies, Künstler und Agenten auftanken," *Frankfurter Allgemeine Zeitung*, November 11, 2011, http://www.faz.net/aktuell/feuilleton/buecher/rezensionen/belletristik/wolfgang-herrndorf-sand-wo-schmuggler-hippies-kuenstler-und-agenten-auftanken-11525376.html. "Herrndorf geht auch in die Wüste. Schreibt einen Thriller mit jeder Menge Krawumm, Zisch und Peng. Ein 'large loose baggy monster,' wie Henry James die eigenen mäandernden Romane nannte." Jan Küveler, "Sahara ist Folter: Buchpreis für Herrndorfs *Sand*," *Die Welt*, March 15, 2012, accessed January 31, 2015. http://www.welt.de/kultur/literarischewelt/article13924669/Sahara-ist-Folter-Buchpreis-fuer-Herrndorfs-Sand.html.

[10] This is an allusion to *X-Files*: "The truth is out there."

[11] "Die Haupteinmahme sei ein Krieg," Friedrich Dürrenmatt, *Der Auftrag oder Vom Beobachten des Beobachters der Beobachter*, 97.

[12] Steven Vertovec, *Transnationalism* (London: Routledge, 2009), 5.

[13] See, for example, Ulrich Schneckener, *Transnationaler Terrorismus: Charakter und Hintergründe des neuen Terrorismus* (Frankfurt am Main: Suhrkamp, 2006); Louise Richardson, *What Terrorists Want: Understanding the Enemy, Containing the Threat* (New York: Random House, 2006); Noam Chomsky, *The Culture of Terrorism* (Montreal: Black Rose, 1988); Edward Said, "The Essential Terrorist," in *Blaming the Victims: Spurious Scholarship and the Palestinian Question*, ed. Edward Said and Christopher Hitchens (London: Verso, 1988), 148–58.

[14] Jacques Derrida, "Force De Loi: Le 'Fondement Mystique De L'Autorité' / Force of Law: The 'Mystical Foundation of Authority'" *Cardozo Law Review* 11, no. 5–6 (1990): 943.

[15] See especially the second chapter in Giorgio Agamben, *State of Exception*, transl. Kevin Attell (Chicago: Chicago University Press, 2005).

[16] See, for example, Peter Weibel, "Theorien der Gewalt" in *Zur Vorstellung des Terrors: Die RAF-Ausstellung* 2, ed. Klaus Biesenbach (Göttingen: Steidl, 2005), 53.

[17] The different political interests are, for example, violently enacted in *Sand* as direct bodily violence in the case of Carl Gross being tortured by the agents of the unspecified Western country, the political threat of the nuclear bomb, and the corrupt police system in the unnamed North African country. In *Der Auftrag*, the surveillance system itself is portrayed as structural violence, the North African state indiscriminately tortures its subjects, and the Western Nations use the country as battleground to sell more weapons.

[18] See, for example, Steven Vertovec and Alejandro Portes, "Introduction: The Debates and Significance of Immigrant Transnationalism," *Global Network* 1, no.3 (2001): 181–93.

[19] "Befreien wir uns aus dem Dünkel der Aufklärung!" Wolfgang Herrndorf, *Sand*, 61.

[20] Noam Chomsky, "Middle East Terrorism and the American Ideological System," in *Blaming the Victims: Spurious Scholarship and the Palestinian Question*, ed. Edward W. Said and Christopher Hitchens (London: Verso, 2001), 97.

[21] Noam Chomsky. *The Culture of Terrorism* (Montreal: Black Rose, 1988), 101.

[22] Take, for example, a book like *Inside Terrorist Organizations*, whose contributors never question the definition of terrorism in and of itself. While an article by Bonnie Cordes sets out to focus on "terrorist motivations, mindset or indeed, on terrorist's self-perception" in order to "uncover the rationale, motivations, and mechanisms for denial," the author is not looking at the role of the state to comprehend and understand its motivations. This is all the more surprising because she acknowledges a "war of labels . . . between authorities and the terrorist challengers to win the sympathies of the public." Bonnie Cordes, "When Terrorists Do the Talking: Reflections on Terrorist Literature," in *Inside Terrorist Organizations*, ed. David C. Rapoport (London: Frank Cass, 2001). I would assume that a "war of labels" has to be investigated by not following certain assumptions (this is terrorism, and it tries to justify itself in such and such ways) but rather in questioning how terrorism is defined and by whom, which strategies are employed (why and by whom, and what the interests in naming are), and how a legal system and the constitution (for example) are defined.

[23] Chomsky, *Culture of Terrorism*, 118.

[24] For the conceptual framework of war, see also (even though she is writing about photography) Judith Butler, *Frames of War: When Is Life Grievable?* (London: Verso, 2009). "And although restricting how or what we see is not exactly the same as dictating a storyline, it is a way of interpreting in advance what will and will not be included in the field of perception" (66). "We do not have to be supplied with a caption or a narrative in order to understand that a political background is explicitly formulated and renewed through and by the frame, that the frame functions not only as a boundary to the image but as structuring the image

itself. If the image in turn structures how we register reality, then it is bound up with the interpretive scene in which we operate" (71).

[25] Stuart Taberner, "Introduction: German literature in the Age of Globalisation," in *German Literature in the Age of Globalisation*, ed. Stuart Taberner (Birmingham, AL: University of Birmingham University Press, 2004), 6.

[26] Arjun Appadurai, "Grassroots Globalization and the Research Imagination," in *Globalization*, ed. Arjun Appadurai (Durham, NC: Duke University Press, 2001), 6.

[27] Margaret Scanlan, "Terror as Usual in Friedrich Dürrenmatt's *The Assignment*," *Modern Language Quarterly* 52, no.1 (1991): 8. See Jennifer E. Michaels, "Through the Camera's Eye: An Analysis of Dürrenmatt's Der Auftrag," *The International Fiction Review* 15, no. 2 (1988), 41–147, for a discussion of the fragmentation of the world, in which "even people have lost their sense of wholeness, of identity" (146).

[28] Appadurai, "Grassroots Globalization," 3.

Appendix: Interview with Ilija Trojanow

Elisabeth Herrmann and Carrie Smith-Prei

IN OCTOBER 2013, the editors of this volume invited writer Ilija Trojanow to participate in a seminar on "Transnationalism" for the Thirty-Seventh Annual Conference of the German Studies Association in Denver, Colorado. Denied permission to enter the United States, however, Trojanow was prevented from boarding his plane in Brazil. He participated in the seminar via Skype, and the planned performance based on his novel *EisTau* (Melting Ice, 2012) for the GSA luncheon was transformed into a discussion on the subject of surveillance in a digital age. The following interview does not explicitly engage with this event, though it remains as backdrop to the conversation.

EDITORS: You are considered a transnational author and someone who is an expert and practitioner of transnationalism. From your perspective and experience, how would you describe or define "transnationalism," as a life experience, a mode of living and with regard to literature? That is, what is "transnational literature" for you?

TROJANOW: Well, it's difficult for me to answer because until the day I received your invitation, I've never used that word myself, and I've never positioned myself within this semantic framework. So this was a bit new to me. The reason I didn't do it is that "nationality" doesn't seem to figure in my kind of biographical conditioning. Right from the beginning, when we fled Bulgaria, there was always a very diverse context, starting with the refugee camps, where you have a multitude of different refugees, growing up in Kenya where you have a multilingual setting (I grew up speaking four languages) and many people from international or multinational backgrounds. So it was more of an education in cosmopolitanism, looking back on it, than in transnationalism. The only time I actually thought of myself in regards to any kind of national identity was when my father insisted that we apply for German citizenship. It was one of the weirdest conversations I've ever had because in those days there was no test. You just had to fill out a form and one of the questions was "What is your hobby?" and I wrote down "literature." The bureaucrat who was screening me looked up from his form and said, "Ah, literature! So, so. Tell me something about the German author Lenz." "I will gladly do so," I said, "but please clarify: Do you mean Siegfried, Hermann, or Jakob Michael Reinhold Lenz?" The guy, a little bit in awe, mumbled something, signed the document, and I was out of the door within a few minutes.

EDITORS: So, you passed the exam!

TROJANOW: The fastest naturalization interview in the history of the German republic. But that was the only time I've ever actually considered what it means to become the citizen of a new state, a new nation, and thus I reflected upon it for a few minutes. But otherwise it hasn't played a role. And I'm actually not sure whether some of the things you discussed were forced into a framework of the transnationalism discourse. Because many of them could be discussed under different headlines.

EDITORS: Would you actually prefer the term *cosmopolitanism*?

TROJANOW: I would, because *cosmopolitanism* to me includes also an ideal. That there is a kind of visionary aspect or element to it, while *transnationalism* has a very formal ring. The nation itself is a constructed social entity, and to me the state and nation are repressive instruments. I don't think that the term gives me a breathing space as an author. It seems to me that the term is maybe more suitable for economical, political discourse, and it doesn't seem to have any relevance to what I'm trying to achieve as an author. The one term that is close to my heart, because I have written a whole book about it, is *confluence*. For me *confluence* would be a far more precise term.

EDITORS: It is interesting that for you *transnationalism* is more of a formal or political term, when we're often talking of transnationalism primarily in literary terms. In your essayistic work, you've often referred to an eighteenth-century cosmopolitan tradition, to stay on the topic of cosmopolitanism, and especially Lessing's "Weltbürgertum heute: Rede zu einer kosmopolitschen Kultur." Where do you see cosmopolitanism as well as confluence interacting in literature today if *transnationalism* maybe isn't the term that you and other authors would think of? Where or how does cosmopolitanism, or confluence, find its way into formal elements or content-based elements in literature?

TROJANOW: Well, I would like to begin by pointing out that one of the limitations of our perception of history, looking back from the perspective of a global citizen today, is that we tend to assume that globalization is a modern or even postmodern phenomenon, while it seems to me that when we go back, both confluence and cosmopolitanism were defining features of human cultural development right from the beginning. Quite a number of authors seem to assume that there is a kind of new quality which didn't exist previously, that distinct transnational interaction is something that we now have to adapt to, that it poses new challenges to individuals and society. I think that is just historically wrong. But in regard to today's literature: I think there are actually two diverging developments. One is that there is a certain cosmopolitanism but only within the English language literature. So for those who write in English there is truly a sense of the global, because basically there are authors from all over the world writing in English. I am a member of a jury at the moment which is looking for a talented young author who has as the only defining quality, besides being very talented, that he or she has to write in English. The five jury members come from all over the world, ranging from Singapore to New Zealand and from South Africa to Canada—basically the jury spans the whole globe. So within the English language, we have a defining and very influential cosmopolitan reality. In regards to smaller languages, I actually think that there is a lessening of cosmopolitan exchange. It is extremely difficult for an author who writes in a small language today to be translated or even if translated, to be heard. While we like to assume that we live in more cosmopolitan times, as far as the reception of literature is concerned, we have to critically assess whether this is true. Even within certain countries you have this diverging development. If you take India, there is a certain English language literary elite that has been very successful on the world market, but you have very good literature, very rich literature, in Indian languages that basically doesn't travel beyond the borders of a particular language. Since you mentioned Lessing, when you look at the giants of the Classic period, it would be interesting to compare them with a world-educated citizen of today. Is there anyone in today's Germany who is equally cosmopolitan in his erudition and education, like Goethe was, for example? I doubt it.

Finally, because of the Eurocentrism or North American-centrism, you actually find these kind of Renaissance cosmopolites more in non-European, non-North American countries. You'll actually find Indians or Brazilians, just two examples from my personal world, who have such a broad outreach and outlook, which covers both European and North American literature as well as their own literature and other literatures of the developing world. But that is very rare in the centers of the north.

EDITORS: Would you say, then, that transnational literature refers more to literature written in English and cosmopolitan literature could be written in any language? Would you connect this with the term of *world literature*? That is, how does Goethe's idea of world literature, translated literature, traveling, exchange, or dialogue between different national literatures (though we would avoid *national literatures* by using the term *world literature*) connect here?

TROJANOW: It's actually a very interesting question because it implies a positive answer. It sounds enticing to have different terms for a globalization of the English language literature and a kind of impact between other literatures. To give a personal example, an author I know very well both in her works and her person is Juli Zeh. When we make fun of one another, I am the world citizen and she's the German, even West German, bourgeois, local girl— that's the established role-play that we have. She would always say, I know nothing of the world, I write very German-centered books. But it is evident that there are forms of cosmopolitanism or transnationalism in her work, which brings me to the question whether it is actually possible to have a nontransnational literature today, unless it's something which is extremely artificial. The safe thing to say would be that transnational awareness is the norm in today's literature. And nearly all the authors I know, even those that are not terribly interested in international affairs, can be discussed within this framework.

EDITORS: Since you are talking about groups of authors and the question of whether there might be a dominant, transnational sensitivity, how do alliances form between authors through questions of national and transnational import, such as politics in literature, literary engagement, and public engagement? What is literary engagement and what does it mean in this context?

TROJANOW: My understanding of cosmopolitanism led me to the belief that it would be preferable to write books together with authors from other cultures and other continents. I wrote a book together with the Zimbabwean author Chenjerai Hove, and I wrote a book together with the Indian author Ranjit Hoskote. The reason was not only friendship and practicality. I felt that if I wanted to achieve some kind of multiperspective, diverse, rich tapestry of voices, the most challenging thing to do in process and production would be to overcome the individuality of writing and start this dialogue on the level of cooperation with another author. Juli Zeh is the third partner, and the book which recently came out (short stories on Bulgaria)—there again you have a different approach because I'm cooperating with German photographer Christian Muhrbeck, whose viewpoint and perspective on Bulgaria causes a different demand: to put it bluntly, his is dominated by fascination, mine is clearly dominated by pain and disappointment.

EDITORS: Can this literary cooperation between authors from different national backgrounds be considered a transnational dialogue? And coming back to our earlier question: How are alliances formed through literature in order to engage in and discuss political matters publically?

TROJANOW: Absolutely, if you regard the creative tension between the fascination of the foreign and familiarity with one's own as one of the aesthetic preconditions. Also, if you reference the multilingual aspects of the research and discourse that went into these books. Alliances are formed through conversations, meetings, facilitated by festivals and other public events, less so by literature itself.

EDITORS: Within literature, is there such a thing as group identity? Have terms such as *minority, migrant* or *diaspora writers* established a cooperative identity among authors of different national and transnational backgrounds that does not only have a political connotation but helps to establish transnational political engagement—that is, do authors work together across borders in social or political mobilization?

TROJANOW: Regarding the way group identities in literatures are structured: It would be interesting to look at the great changes within the group of authors who are now called amongst some scholars and literary critics the "Chamisso-Autoren." In the beginning they had a very strong sense of being a group that needed to stick together and fight for acknowledgement, for respect, for a place within German literature, whether it was Franco Biondi, Aras Ören Rafik Shami etc. They knew each other, they were together in certain clubs, they organized group readings. They were successful and things started to change. The question of being acknowledged and respected as a non-German author writing in German was no longer an issue and because of the success, there is actually now less sense of a common ground. I mean there is individual respect. Let's take someone like Terézia Mora: she respects my writing and I respect hers, but it would be impossible to say that we have any kind of group identity, and the same holds true for say, Feridun Zaimoglu. Each one of us is basically engaged in his own individual cosmopolitan project, and only in the very broadest of abstract terms would it be possible to define a common ground. There has been a breaking apart of any kind of solidarity, any kind of group identity of migrant authors.

EDITORS: Within scholarly approaches to literature we also observe this kind of shift, historical shift, and paradigmatic change that has taken place. Would we have had this interview and discussion about transnationalism maybe four or five years ago, we would have talked about hybrid literature, migrant literature, and minority literatures. Now we have a different understanding of transnational literature. We no longer have a special sense of nonminority, group identity anymore. Maybe we don't need it anymore? On the other hand you were talking about this cultural exchange together with other authors and bringing in a multiperspective, a dialogue, a world's dialogue maybe, between different authors from different cultures and using different languages. Do we still need the split between minority and nonminority literatures in German language literature? On the other hand something new is emerging, namely what we might call "world literature," the actual way of thinking in terms of "world literature" that can communicate between different cultures in different languages at the same time. Would you agree with this?

TROJANOW: If I had to define my own novel *Der Weltensammler* on the basis of this, I would prefer to define it as "world literature," not as a quality statement but in order to describe what it tries to achieve, and that is to portray a world that goes way beyond the German language, although the instrument or the paint is the German language. And that would probably be a very typical definition of world literature. Another good definition for world literature or cosmopolitan literature would be a literature that doesn't hide the cosmopolitan erudition of the author. So the author draws from a vast and diverse set of influences. A book that was very important to me and probably one of the first books that does that was by the Cuban author José Lezama Lima, called *Paradiso*. I went to visit his library, and he had books ranging from Chinese art to Indian cuisine, to Aztec law, a vast global interest in nearly everything. Now this novel is set in Havana and all the characters are Cubans, but he reaches out and compares, be it in his reflections or even his idioms, and he is not afraid to bring in his vast world literature erudition. That would be the kind of literature that I'm also striving for. It might be local in its setting, and the theme might be very concrete, but the scope of the author would truly be global. I doubt many authors in Germany would see it this way.

What I'm trying to achieve, and this I say without any judgment, is that other places, such as India, not only inform my writing but actually change it.

The cosmopolitan approach would be to allow these other influences to coauthor the text. I think it would actually be impossible for someone who does not know India to give a statement [as to] whether the voices between Indian main characters are successful or not. I think that's an interesting discussion but because of my ambition, the only way you could make a qualified judgment would be if you knew Indian culture and religion.

EDITORS: This remark brings our discussion about transnationalism, cosmopolitanism, and world literature to a round figure: Transnationalism as lived experience and practice together with a cosmopolitan education and erudition is what enables an author to write literature that reaches beyond the horizon of the language in which a text is written and invites other cultures and languages not only to enrich but to coauthor the text.

Thank you very much for the conversation.

Contributors

HESTER BAER is associate professor of German and film studies at the University of Maryland, College Park. She is the author of *Dismantling the Dream Factory: Gender, German Cinema, and the Postwar Quest for a New Film Language* (2009), the editor of a special issue of *Studies in Twentieth & Twenty-First Century Literature* on "Contemporary Women's Writing and the Return of Feminism in Germany" (2011), and the coeditor of *German Women's Writing in the Twenty-First Century* (2015). She has published articles on German film, literature, and feminism in *Discourse, German Quarterly*, and *German Studies Review*, among others.

ANKE S. BIENDARRA is associate professor of German and a core faculty member in European studies at the University of California, Irvine. Research interests: literature and culture of the twentieth and twenty-first century, particularly GDR literature, and literature of unification, globalization, transnationalism, popular culture, and Europeanization. She has published widely on aspects of identity, gender, and *Engagement*, on effects of globalization in literature and film, and on pop literature. Recent publications: *Germans Going Global: Contemporary Literature and Globalization* (2012) and *Visions of Europe. Interdisciplinary Contributions to Contemporary Cultural Debates* (coedited with Gail Hart; 2014).

CLAUDIA BREGER is professor of Germanic studies, and affiliated faculty in cinema and media studies and gender studies at Indiana University, Bloomington. Her research focuses on twentieth- and twenty-first-century culture, with an emphasis on literary, media and cultural theory, as well as the intersections of gender, sexuality, and race. Recent book publications include *An Aesthetics of Narrative Performance: Transnational Film, Literature and Theater in Contemporary Germany* (2012; *Theory and Interpretation of Narrative Series*) and the small volume *'Nach dem Sex'? Sexualwissenschaft und Affect Studies, Hirschfeld-Lectures* (2014).

KATHARINA GERSTENBERGER is professor of German and chair of languages and literature at the University of Utah. She is the author of *Truth to Tell: German Women's Autobiographies and Turn-of-the-Century Culture* (2000) and *Writing the New Berlin: The German Capital in Post-Wall Literature* (2008). She coedited *German Literature in a New Century*

(2008) and *After the Berlin Wall: Germany and Beyond* (2011). She has published numerous articles on topics of twentieth- and twenty-first-century German literary culture. From 2007 to 2010 she was coeditor of *Women in German Yearbook*. She is a member of the Transatlantic Research Network in Environmental Humanities.

ELISABETH HERRMANN is associate professor of German at Stockholm University. She moved to Sweden after having spent eight years at the University of Alberta as visiting associate professor of German and Scandinavian literatures and cultures. Her research focuses on collective identities, processes of cultural interactions and transfer, as well as transnational, regional, and world literature. Recent publications include the volumes *Entwicklungen in der deutschschprachigen Gegenwartsliteratur und Medien nach 1989* (2013) with Carsten Gansel and *Embracing the Other: Conceptualizations, Representations and Social Practices of [In]Tolerance in German Culture and Literature from the 18th to the 21st Century, Special Theme Issue of Seminar, A Journal of Germanic Studies,* Volume XLVIII, Number 3 (2012), coedited with Florentine Strzelczyk. Her current research is devoted to the project of *Reconceptualizing World Literature for the Twenty-First Century*.

CHRISTINA KRAENZLE is associate professor and codirector of the Canadian Centre for German and European Studies at York University, Toronto, Canada. Her research focuses on modern German-language cultural studies, with an emphasis on issues of transnational cultural production, migration, travel, globalization, and memory. Her publications include the coedited volume *Mapping Channels Between Ganges and Rhein: German-Indian Cross-Cultural Relations* (with Jörg Esleben and Sukanya Kulkarni) as well as articles in *The German Quarterly, German Life and Letters, Transit: A Journal of Travel, Migration and Multiculturalism in the German-Speaking World* and the volume *Searching for Sebald: Photography after W. G. Sebald*.

MARIA MAYR is assistant professor of German at Memorial University of Newfoundland, Canada. Her research analyzes contemporary German-language literature written by nonethnic German authors. Currently, she analyses transnational European memory discourses in German-language literature by authors from Eastern Europe. She has published on authors such as Emine Sevgi Özdamar, Yoko Tawada, Doron Rabinowich, Nicol Ljubić, and Marica Bodrožić. Her most recent publications include "B. as in Balkan: Terézia Mora's Post-Yugoslav Berlin Republic" (*German Life and Letters,* 2014) and "'Überwältigende Vergangenheit': Questioning European Identity in Contemporary German-language Literature about the Former Yugoslavia" (ed. J. Preece, *Re-Forming the Nation in Literature and Film*, 2013).

TANJA NUSSER is DAAD visiting associate professor at the University of Cincinnati. Her research focuses on German literature, culture, and media since the nineteenth century, gender studies, the history of sciences, disability studies, as well as postcolonial and animal studies. Her most recent books are *Von und zu anderen Ufern: Ulrike Ottingers filmische Reiseerzählungen* (2002) and *»wie sonst das Zeugen Mode war«: Reproduktionstechnologien in Literatur und Film* (2011), and she has coedited *Catastrophe and Catharsis: Narratives of Disaster and Redemption in German Culture and Beyond* (forthcoming 2015); *Engineering Life: Narrationen vom Menschen in Biomedizin, Kultur und Literatur* (2008); *Askese: Geschlecht und Geschichte der Selbstdisziplinierung* (2005); and *Rasterfahndungen: Darstellungstechniken—Normierungsverfahren—Wahrnehmungskonstitution* (2003).

LARS RICHTER is a PhD candidate in German languages and literatures at the University of Alberta, Canada. He studied German and English at Freie Universität in Berlin and completed his MA in germanic languages and literatures at Washington University in St. Louis. He has coauthored (with Carrie Smith-Prei) an article on Juli Zeh's *Spieltrieb* and has presented on this author at major German studies conferences. His dissertation, tentatively entitled *Echoes and Oscillations: Modes of Realistic Writing and the Re-Politicization of Fiction*, focuses on the work of Juli Zeh.

CARRIE SMITH-PREI is associate professor of German studies at the University of Alberta. She is the author of *Revolting Families: Toxic Intimacy, Private Politics, and Literary Realism in the German Sixties* (University of Toronto Press, 2013), is coeditor of *Bloom and Bust: Urban Landscapes in the East since German Reunification* (Berghahn Books, 2014), and has published research on a variety of topics related to post-1960 German culture and contemporary feminism. She holds a major grant from the Social Sciences and Humanities Research Council of Canada for research on pop-feminism and digital culture (with Maria Stehle), is cofounder of *Imaginations: Journal of Cross-Cultural Image Studies*, and is coeditor of *Women in German Yearbook* (2014–17).

FAYE STEWART is assistant professor of German at Georgia State University, where she is affiliated with the Institute for Women's, Gender and Sexuality Studies and the Center for Human Rights and Democracy. Her teaching and research interests are twentieth- and twenty-first-century German literature and film, gender and sexuality studies, and transnationalism, justice, and human rights. She is the author of *German Feminist Queer Crime Fiction: Politics, Justice and Desire* (2014) in addition to various essays on mystery fiction. Her current research areas include Muslim belonging in Germany, contemporary queer cinema, and depictions of capital punishment.

Stuart Taberner is professor of contemporary German literature, culture, and society at the University of Leeds since 2005, and is a research associate in the Department of Afrikaans and Dutch; German and French at the University of the Free State, South Africa. His research deals with contemporary German literature, particularly in relation to transnationalism, cosmopolitanism, representations of the Holocaust, Jewish-German writing, ageing in fiction, and national identity. In 2013, he published *Aging and Old-Age Style in Günter Grass, Ruth Klüger, Christa Wolf, and Martin Walser*, and he has edited a number of volumes on contemporary German fiction. Recently, he has become interested in German-language and South African writing in relation to nation, trauma, and cosmopolitan memory, and is engaged on a three-year major research project on this topic, funded by the Leverhulme Trust.

Ilija Trojanow is a writer, journalist, and publisher. He was born in Bulgaria in 1965. In 1971 his parents fled with him to Germany, where they received political asylum. Half a year later, the family moved to Kenya, where his father worked as an engineer. He lived in Nairobi from 1972 to 1984, apart from a three-year period in Germany. He studied law and ethnology in Munich. In 1989, he founded the Marino Publishing House, which specialized in African literature. His first novel, *It's a Big World and Salvation Lurks Everywhere*, dealing with a Balkan family's experience of exile in an Italian home for asylum seekers, was published in 1996 to considerable acclaim. It was made into an internationally successful film in 2009. In 1998, Trojanow moved to Bombay for five years. In 2001, he undertook a three-month-long journey on foot through Tanzania, in the footsteps of the explorer Sir Richard Francis Burton. *Along the Ganges* is based on a trip along the Ganges from its source up to the mouth. In 2006, he published the historical novel *The Collector of Worlds*, a multiperspective view of the nineteenth century, which won the Fiction Award at the Leipzig Book Fair and the Berlin Literary Award, received rave reviews, became a national and international bestseller, and has been translated into twenty-five languages. In 2011, he published *EisTau*, and in 2015 his fourth novel, *Macht und Widerstand* appeared. He lives in Vienna.

Index